Sir David Lindsay

Poetical Works

With memoir, notes and glossary. Vol. 3

Sir David Lindsay

Poetical Works
With memoir, notes and glossary. Vol. 3

ISBN/EAN: 9783337093150

Printed in Europe, USA, Canada, Australia, Japan

Cover: Foto ©Thomas Meinert / pixelio.de

More available books at **www.hansebooks.com**

THE POETICAL WORKS

OF

SIR DAVID LYNDSAY

WITH MEMOIR, NOTES AND GLOSSARY

BY DAVID LAING, LL.D

IN THREE VOLUMES.—VOL. III

EDINBURGH: WILLIAM PATERSON

MDCCCLXXIX.

TABLE OF CONTENTS.

ANE DIALOG BETUIX

EXPERIENCE AND ANE COURTEOUR.

ANE DIALOG

BETUIX EXPERIENCE AND ANE COURTEOUR:

THE SECUND BUKE.

IN THE FIRST, THE BEILDYNG OF BABILONE BE NEMROD; AND QUHOW KYNG NYNUS BEGAN THE FIRST MONARCHIE; AND OF THARE IDOLATRYE; AND QUHOW SEMIRAMIS GOVERNIT THE IMPYRE, EFTER HIR HUSBANDE KYNG NYNUS.

COURTEOUR.

FATHER, I pray yow to me tell
The first infortune that befell,
Immediatlye efter the Flude;
And quho did first sched saikles blude?
And quho Idolatrye began?

EXPERIENCE.

Quod he, I sall do as I can:
Efter the Flude I fynde no storye
Worthy to putt in memorye,
Tyll Nemrod began to ryng Gene. x.
Above the Peple as ane Kyng,
Quhilk wes the principall man of one,
That beildar was of Babilone.

COURTEOUR.

That story, Maister, wald I knaw,
Quod I, geve ye the suthe wald schaw,
Quhy and for quhat occasioun
Thay beildit sic ane strang dungeoun.

EXPERIENCE.

Than said to me Experience,
I sall declare, with deligence,
Those questiounis, at thy command.
Bot first, Sone, thow mon understand
Of Nemrod the Genealogie,
His strenth, curage, and quantitie;
Quhowbeit Moyses, in his first Buke,
That story lychtlye did ouer luke:
Of hym no more he doith declare,
Except he was ane strang huntare.
Bot utheris Clerkis curious,
As Orose doith, and Josephus,
Discryvis Nemrod at more lenth,
Boith of his stature and his strenth.
This Nemrod was the fourt persoun
Frome Noye be lyne discendyng doun:
Noye generit Cham, Cham generit Chus,
And Chus, Nemrod: the suthe bene thus.

This Nemrod grew ane man of mycht;
That tyme in erth wes none so wycht:
He wes ane gyand stout and strang;
Perforce wyld beistis he doun thrang.

The peple of that hole Regioun
Come under his dominioun;
No man thare wes, in all that land,
His stalwartnes that durst ganestand.
No marvell wes thocht he wes wycht,
Ten cubitis large he wes of hycht,
Proportionat, in lenth and breid,
Afferand to his hycht, we reid.
He grew so gret and glorious,
So prydefull and presumptuous,
That he come inobedient
To the gret God Omnipotent.
This Nemrod was the principall man
That first Idolatrye began.
Than gart he all the peple call
To his presens, boith gret and small,
And, in that gret conventioun,
Did propone his intentioun. Gene. xi.
My Freindis, said he, I mak it knawin
The gret vengeance that God hes schawin,
In tyme of our fore father Noye,
Quhen he did all the Warld distroye,
And dround thame in ane furious flude:
Quharefor I thynk we sulde conclude
Quhow we maye make one strang defence
Aganis sick watteris violence,
For to resyste his furious ire,
Contrare boith to flude and fyre.
Lat us go spye sum plesand feilde,
Quhare one strang biggyng we may beilde,
One Citie, with ane strang dungeoun,

That none ingine may ding it doun ;
So heych, so thyke, so large, and lang,
That God tyll us sall do no wrang ;
It sall surmonte the Planetis sevin,
That we frome God may wyn the hevin.
Those peple, with one ferme intent,
All tyll his counsell did consent,
And did espy one plesand place
Hard on the flude of Euphratace.
The peple thare did thame repair,
In to the plane feilde of Synear,
Quhilk now of Caldie beryth the name,
Quhilk did lang tyme flureis in fame.

Thare gret Fortres than did thay founde,
And kaiste tyll thay gat souer grounde :
All fell to warke, boith man and chylde,
Sum holkit clay, sum brynt the tylde.
Nembroth, that curious campioun,
Devysar wes of that dungeoun.
No thyng thay sparit thare laubouris,
Lyke besy beis upone the flouris,
Or emottis travelling in to June :
Sum under wrocht, and sum abone :
With strong ingenious masonrye,
Upwarte thare werk did fortifye.
With brynt tylde, stonis large and wycht,
That Towre thay rasit to sic hycht
Abufe the airis regioun,
And junit of so strong fassioun,
With syment maid of pyk and tar,

Thay usit none uther mortar,
Thocht fyre or watter it assalit,
Contrare that dungeoun nocht avalit.
The land aboute wes fair and plane;
And it rose lyke one heych montane.
Those fuliche peple did intende
That to the Hevin it sulde ascende.
So gret one strenth wes nevir sene,
In to the warld, with mennis eine.
The wallis of that wark thay maid
Two and fyftye faldome braid.
One faldome than, as sum men sayis,
Mycht bene two faldome in our dayis:
One man wes than, of more stature
Nor two be now: thareof be sure.

Josephus haldis opinioun,
Sayand the heycht of this dungeoun
Of large pasis of measure bene
Fyve thousande, aucht score and fourtene.
Be this raknyng, it is full rycht
Fyve mylis and ane half in hycht:
Ane thousande pais tak for ane myle,
And thow sall fynd it neir that style.
This towre, in compass round aboute,
Wer mylis ten, withouttin doute:
Aboute the cietie of stagis
Foure houndreth and four score, I wys;
And, be this nommer, in compas,
Aboute three score of mylis it was:
And, as Orosius reportis,
Thare wes fyve score of brasin portis.

The translatour of Orosius
In tyll his Cronicle wryttis thus:
That, quhen the Sonne is at the hycht,
Att none quhen it doith schyne most brycht,
The schaddow of that hydduous strenth
Sax myle and more it is of lenth.
Thus maye ye juge, in to your thocht,
Gyfe Babilone be heych, or nocht.

QUHOW GOD MAID THE DYVERSITIE OF LANGUAGIS, AND MAID IMPEDIMENT TO THE BEILDARIS OF BABILONE.

EXPERIENCE.

THAN the gret God Omnipotent,
To quhom al thingis bene present;
That wer, and is, and evir salbe,
Ar present tyll his Majestie;
The hid secretis of mannis hart
From his presens may not depart;
He, seand the ambitioun,
And the prydefull presumptioun,
Quhow thir proude peple did pretende
Up throuch the hevinnis tyll ascende,
Quhilk wes gret folye tyll devyse
Sick one presumptuous interpryse:
For, quhen thay wer moste delygent,
God maid thame sick impediment,
Thay wer constranit, with hartis sore,

Frome thyne depart, and beild no more.
Sick languagis on thame he laid,
That none wyste quhat ane uthir said:
Quhare wes bot ane language affore,
God send thame languagis three score.
  Affore that tyme all spak Ebrew;
Than sum began for to speik Grew,
Sum Dutche, sum language Sarazyne,
And sum began to speik Latyne.
The Maister men gan to go wylde:
Cryand for treis, thay brocht thame tylde:
Sum said, Bryng mortar heir atonis;
Than brocht thay to thame stokis and stonis.
And Nembroth, thare gret campioun,
Ran rageand lyke one wylde lyoun,
Manassyng thame with wordis rude:
Bot nevir one worde thay understude.
Affore thay fand hym gude and kynde;
Bot than thay thocht hym by his mynde,
Quhen he so furiouslie did flyte.
Than turnit his pryde in to dispyte,
So dirk eclipsit wes his glore,
Quhen thay wald wyrk for him no more.
  Beholde quhow God wes so gratious
To thame, quhilk wer so outragious:
He nother braik thare leggis nor armis,
Nor yit did thame none uther harmis,
Except of toungis divysioun.
And, for fynall conclusioun,
Constranit thay wer for tyll depart,
Ilke cumpanye in one syndrie arte:

Sum past in to the Orient,
And sum in to the Occident,
Sum South, sum North, as thay thocht best,
And so thare poleysie left wast.
Bot quhow that cietie wes reparit
Heir efter it salbe declarit.

OF THE FIRST INVENTIOUN OF YDOLATRIE; QUHOW NEMBROTH COMPELD THE PEPLE TYLL ADORE THE FYRE IN CALDEA.

COURTEOUR.

Now, Schir, said I, schaw me the man
Quhilk first Ydolatrie began.

EXPERIENCE.

That sall I do, with all my hart,
My Sonne, said he, or we depart.
Quhen Nembroth saw his purpose failit,
And his gret laubour nocht availit,
In maner of contemptioun
Departit furth of that regioun,
And, as Orosius doith rehers,
He past in to the land of Pers,
And mony one yeir did thare remane,
And syne to Babylone come agane,
And fand huge peple of Caldie
Remanand in that gret cietie,
That wer glaid of his returnyng,

And did obey hym as thare kyng.
Nembroth, his name for tyll avance,
Amang tham maid new ordinance,
Sayand, I think ye ar nocht wyce,
That to none God makis sacrifyce.
Than, to fulfyll his fals desyre,
He gart be maid ane flammand fyre,
And maid it of sic breid and hycht,
He gart it byrn boith day and nycht.
Than all the peple of that land
Adorit the fyre, at his command,
Prosternit on thare kneis and facis,
Beseikand thare new God of gracis.
To gyf thame more occasioun,
He maid thame gret perswasioun:
This God, said he, is moist of mycht,
Schawand his bemys on the nycht:
Quhen Sonne and Mone ar baith obscure,
His hewinlie brychtnes doith indure:
Quhen mennis memberis sufferit calde,
Fyre warmyth thame, evin as thay walde.
Than cryit the Peple, at his desyre,
Thare is no God except the Fyre.
Or thare was ony imagerie,
Began this first Idolatrie.
At that tyme thare wes none usage
To carve, nor for to paynt Image.
Than maid he proclamatioun,
Quho maid nocht adoratioun
To that new God, without remede
In to that fyre sulde suffer dede.

I fynd no man, in to that lande,
His tyrannie that durste ganestande,
Bot Habraham, and Aram his brother,
That disobeyit, I fynd none uther;
Quhilk dwelland war in that countre,
With thare Father, callit Tharie.
Thir brether Nembroth did repreve;
Sayand tyll hym, Lord, with your leve,
This fyre is bot ane Element,
Praye ye to God Omnipotent,
Quhilk maid the Hevinnis be his mycht,
Sonne, Mone, and Sterris, to gyf lycht:
He maid the fyschis in the Seis,
The Erth, with beistis, herbis, and treis:
And, last of all, for to conclude,
He maid Man, to his similitude:
To that gret God gyfe pryse and glore,
Quhose ring induris evermore.
  Than Nembroth, in his furious ire,
Thir brether boith keste in the fyre:
Habraham be God he wes preservit,
Bot Aram in the fyre he stervit.
Quhen Thara harde his sonne wes dede,
He did depart out of that stede,
With Habraham, Nachor, and thare wyffis,
As the Scripture at lynthe discryffis,
And left the land of Caldea,
And past to Mesopotamia,
And dwelt in Tharan all his dayis,
And deit thare, as the story sayis.
The lyfe of Habraham, I suppose,

No thyng langith tyll our purpose:
In to the Bibyll thou may reid
His verteous lyfe in worde and deid.
Now to thee I have schawin the man
That firste Idolatrie began.

OF THE GREIT MISERIE AND SKAYTHIS THAT CUMMIS OF WEIRIS, AND QUHOW KING NYNUS BEGAN THE FIRST WEIRIS, AND STRAIK THE FIRST BATTELL.

COURTEOUR.

FATHER, I pray you, with my hart,
Declair to me, or we depart,
Quho first began thir mortall weiris,
Quhilk everilk faithfull hart effeiris,
And everie polesye doun thrawis,
Express agane the Lordis lawis;
Sen Christe, our Kyng omnipotent,
Left peace in tyll his Testament.
Quhow doith proceid this creueltie
Aganis Justice and Equitie?
In lande quhare ony weiris bene,
Gret miserie thare may be sene:
All thyng on erth that God hes wrocht
Weir doith distroye, and puttis at nocht:
Cieteis, with mony strang dungeoun,
Ar brynte, and to the erth doung doun;
Virginis and matronis ar deflorit;

Templis that rychelie bene decorit
Ar brynt, and all thare Preistis spulyeit;
Pure orphelenis under feit ar fulyeit,
Mony auld men maid childerles,
And mony childer fatherles;
Of famous Sculis the doctryne,
Boith natural science and divyne,
And everilk vertew, trampit doun
No reverence done to relegioun;
Strenthis distroyit alluterlie;
Fair ladyis forcit schamefullie,
Young wedowis spulyeit of thare spousis,
Pure laborars houndit frome thare housis.
Thare dar no merchand tak on hand
To travel nother be sea nor land,
For boucheouris, quhilk dois thame confounde:
Sum murdrist bene, and sum are drounde:
Craftis men of curious ingyne
Alluterlie put to rewyne:
The bestiall reft, the commounis slane,
The land but lauboring doith remane.
Of pollesye the perfyte warkis,
Beildingis, gardyngis, and plesand parkis,
Alluterlie distroyit bene:
Gret graingis brynt thare may be sene:
Ryches bene turnit to povertie,
Plentie in tyll penuritie.
Deith, hounger, darth, it is weill kende,
Of weir this is the fatell ende:
Justice turnit in tyrrannye,
All plesour in adversitye.

The weir alluterlie doun thrawis
Boith the civill and cannoun lawis:
Weir generit murthour and myschief,
Sore lamentyng without releif.
Weir doith distroye realmes and kyngis;
Gret princis weir to presoun bryngis;
Weir scheddis mekle saikles blude.
Sen I can saye of weir no gude,
Declare to me, Schir, gyf ye can,
Quho first this miserie began.

HEIR FOLLOWITH ANE SCHORTE DISCRIPTIOUN OF THE FOUR MONARCHEIS: AND QUHOW KYNG NYNUS BEGAN THE FIRST MONARCHIE.

EXPERIENCE.

Of Weiris, said he, the gret outtrage
Began into the secunde aige,
Be creuell, prydefull, covetous kyngis,
Revaris, but rycht, of utheris ryngis.
Quhowbeit Cayan, afore the Flude,
Wes first schedder of saikles blude,
Nynus was first and principall man
Quhilk wrangus conquessing began,
And was the man, withouttin faill,
In erth that straik the first bataill.
And first inventit imagerye,
Quhare throw came gret Idolatrye.

We most knaw, or we forther wend,
Of quhome king Nynus did discend.
Nynus, gyf I can rycht defyne,
He was frome Noye the fyft, be lyne:
Noye generit Cham, Cham generit Chus,
And Chus, Nembroth, Nembroth, Belus,
And Belus, Nynus, but lesing.
Of Assyria the secund king,
And beildar of that gret Citie,
The quhilk was callit Nynevie,
And wes the first and principall man
Quhilk the First Monarchie began.

COURTEOUR.

Father, said I, declaire to me
Quhat signifyis one Monarchie.

EXPERIENCE.

The suith, said he, Sonne, gyf thou knew,
Monarchie bene one terme of Grew:
As, quhen one Province principall
Had hole power imperiall,
During thare dominationis,
Abufe all Kyngis, and Nationis,
One Monarchie, that men doith call;
Of quhome I fynd Four principall
Quhilk heth rong sen the Warld began.

COURTEOUR.

Than said I, Father, gyf ye can,
Quhilk Four bene thay, schaw me, I pray yow.

EXPERIENCE.

My Sone, said he, that sall I say yow :
First rang the Kings of Assyrianis ;
Secundlye, rang the Persianis ;
The Greikis, thridlye, with swerd and fyre
Perfors obtenit the Thrid impyre ;
The Fourte Monarchie, as I heir,
The Romanis bruikit mony one yeir.

Latt us first speik of Nynus King,
Quhow he began his conquessing.
The auld Greik historiciane
Diodorus he wryttis plane
At rycht gret lenth of Nynus king,
Of his impyre, and conquessing ;
And of Semiramis, his wyfe,
That tyme the lustyest on lyfe.
It wer too lang to putt in wryte
Quhilk Diodore had done indyte ;
Bot I sall schaw, as I suppose,
Quhilk maist belangith thy purpose.
Quhen Nembroth, Prince of Babylone,
Oute of this wrechit warld wes gone,
And his sonne, Belus, deid alswa,
The first Kyng of Assyria,
This Nynus, quhilk wes secunde Kyng,
Tryumphandlie began tyll ryng,
And wes nocht satifyit nor content
Of his awin Regione, nor his rent :
Thynkand his glory for tyll avance

By his gret peple and puissance,
Throuch pryde, covatyce, and vaine glore,
Did hym prepare to conques more,
And gatherit furth ane gret armie
Contrare Babilone, and Caldie,
Quhareof he had ardent desyre
Tyll june that land tyll his Impyre,
Quhowbeit he had thareto no rycht:
Bot, by his tyranny and mycht,
Withouttin feir of God or man,
His conquessing thus he began.
  His peple beand in arraye,
To Caldia tuke the reddy waye;
Quhen that the Babilonianis,
Togither with the Caldianis,
Hard tell Kyng Nynus wes cummand,
Maid proclamationis throuch the land,
That ilka man, efter thare degrie,
Sulde cum, and saif thair awin countrie.
Quhowbeit thay had no use of weir,
Thay past fordwart withouttin feir,
And pat thame selfis in gude order,
To meit kyng Nynus on the border.
In that tyme, ye sall understande,
Thare wes no harnes in the land,
For tyll defende nor tyll invaid,
Quharethrow more slauchter thare wes maid:
Thay faucht, throw strenth of thare bodeis,
With gaddis of irne, with stonis, and treis.
With sound of horne, and hyddeous cry,
Thay ruschit togither rycht rudely,

With hardy hart and strenth of handis,
Tyll thousandis deid lay on the landis.
Quhare men in battell naikit bene,
Gret slauchter sone, thare may be sene.
Thay faucht so lang and creuellie,
And with uncertane victorie,
No man mycht juge, that stude on far,
Quho gat the better nor the war:
Bot, quhen it did approche the nycht,
The Caldianis thay tuke the flycht.
Than the Kyng and his cumpanye
Wer rycht glaid of that victorye,
Because he wan the first battell
That strykken wes in erth, but faill;
And peceably of that regioun
Did tak the hole dominioun.
Than wes he king of Caldia,
Alsweill as of Assyria.
As for the king of Arabie,
In his conquest, maid hym supplie.
Of this yit wes he nocht content,
Bot to the realme of Mede he went,
Quhare Farnus, king of that cuntrie,
Did meit hym, with one gret armie.
Bot king Nynus the battell wan,
Quhare slane were mony nobyll man;
And to that Kyng wald gyf no grace,
Bot planelie in one publict place,
With his sevin sonnis and his ladye,
Creuellie did thame crucifie.
Of that tryumphe he did rejoise;

Syne fordwart to the feilde he gois:
Than conquest he Armenia,
Perse, Egypt, and Pamphilia,
Capadoce, Leid, and Mauritane,
Caspia, Phrigia, and Hyrcane;
All Affrica and Asia,
Except gret Ynde and Bactria,
Quhilk he did conques efterwart,
As ye sall heir, or we depart.
Now wald I, or we further wend,
That his Ydolatrye wer kend;
Syne, efter that, withoute sudjorne,
Tyll our purpose we sall returne.

QUHOW KING NYNUS INVENTIT THE FIRST IDOLATRIE OF IMAGIS.

Nynus one Image he gart mak
For King Belus his fatheris saik,
Moist lyke his father of figoure,
Of quantitie, and portratoure:
Of fyne golde wes that figoure maid;
Ane crafty croun apone his haid,
With precious stonis, in toknyng
His father Belus wes ane Kyng.
In Babilone he ane tempyll maid,
Of crafty work, boith heych and braid,
Quharein that image gloriouslie
Wes thronit up tryumphandlie.
That Nynus gaif ane strait command

Tyll all the peple of that land,
Alsweill in tyll Assyria
As in Synear and Caldia,
Under his dominatioun,
Thay suld make adoratioun,
Apone thare kneis, to that figour,
Under the pane of forfaltour.
Thare wes no Lorde, in all that land,
His summonding that durst ganestand:
Than young and auld, boith gret and small,
Tyll that Image thay prayit, all,
And cheangit his name, as I heir tell,
Frome Belus to thare greit god Bell.
In that tempyll he did devyse
Preistis, for tyll mak sacrifyse.
Be consuetude than come one law,
None uther God that thay wald knaw;
And als, he gaif to that Image
Of Sanctuarie the privilege;
For, quhatsumever transgressour,
Ane homicede, or oppressour,
Seand that Image in the face,
Of thare gylt gat the Kyngis grace.

COURTEOUR.

Declare to me, sweit Schir, said I,
Wes thare no more Idolatry,
Efter that this fals idole Bell
Wes thronit up, as ye me tell?

EXPERIENCE.

My Sonne, said he, incontinent,

The novellis throuch the warld thay went,
Quhow king Nynus, as I haif said,
One curious Image he had maid,
To the quhilk all his natioun
Maid devote adoratioun.
Than everye cuntrie tuke consait,
Thay wald king Nynus contrafait:
Quhen ony famous man wes deid,
Sett up one Image in his steid,
Quhilk thay did honour frome the splene,
As it Immortall God had bene.
Imagis sum maid, for the nonis,
Of fyne gold, sum of stockis and stonis,
Of sylver sum, and evyr bone,
With divers namis tyll every one:
For sum thay callit Saturnus,
Sum Jupiter, sum Neptunus;
And sum thay callit Cupido,
Thare god of lufe, and sum Pluto:
Thay callit sum Mercurius,
And sum the wyndie Eolus;
Sum Mars, maid lyke ane man of weir,
Inarmit weill with sword and speir;
Sum Bacchus, and sum Appollo,
Of namis, thay had ane houndreth mo.
  And quhen one Lady of gret fame
Wes dede, for tyll exalt hir name,
One Image of hir portratour
Wald set upe in one oratour,
The quhilk thay callit thare goddess:
As Venus, Juno, and Palles,

Sum Cleo, sum Proserpina,
Sum Ceres, Vesta, and Diana;
And sum the greit goddess Minarve
With curious collouris thay wald carve.
Amang the Poetis thow may see
Of fals Goddis the genalogee.
So thir abhominationis
Did spred ouerthort all nationis,
Except gude Habraham, as we reid,
Quhilk honourit God in word and deid;
For Habraham had his beginnyng
In to the tyme of Nynus king.
Nynus began with tyrranie,
And Habraham with humylitie:
Nynus began the first Impyre;
Habraham of weir had no desyre:
Nynus began Idolatrye,
Habraham, in spreit and veritye,
He prayit to the Lorde allone,
Fals imagery be wald have none.
Of hym discendit, I heir tell,
The twelf gret Trybis of Israell.
Those peple maid adoratioun,
With humyll supplicatioun,
Tyll hym quhilk wes of kyngis King,
That hewin and erth maid of no thyng:
Dede Imagis thay held at nocht,
That wer with mennis handis wrocht,
Bot the Almychtie God of lyve.

My Sonne, now haif I done discryve
Thir questionis, at thy command,

The quhilkis thow did at me demand.

COURTEOUR.

Quhat wes the cause, Schir, mak me sure,
Idolatrye did so lang indure
Out throuch the warld so generalie,
And with the Gentilis, specialie?

EXPERIENCE.

Quod he, Sum causis principall
I fynd in my memoriall.
First, wes throuch princis commandiment,
Quhilk did Idolatrie invent:
Syne, singulaire proffeit of the preistis,
Payntours, goldsmythis, maisonis, wrychtis:
Those men of craft full curiouslie
Maid imagis so pleasandlie,
And sauld thame for ane sumptuous pryce,
So, be thare crafty merchandyce,
Thay wer maid ryche abone mesure.
As for the Preistis, I thee assure,
Large proffeit gat, ouerthort all landis,
Throuch sacrifyce and offerandis,
And be thair fayned sanctitude,
Abusit mony one man of gude;
As, in the tyme of Daniell,
Daniell xiii. The preistis of this idoll Bell.
Quhen Nabuchodonosor king
In Babilone royallie did ring,
Those priestis the kyng gart understand,
That Image, maid be mennis hand,

He wes one glorious God of lyfe
And had sic ane prerogatyfe,
That, by his gret power devyne,
Wald eait beif, muttone, breid, and wyne:
And so the King gart, every daye,
Affore Bell, on his aulter laye,
Fourty fresche wedderris, fatt and fyne,
And sax gret rowbourris of wycht wyne,
Twelf gret loavis of bowtit floure,
Quhilk wes all eaitin in one houre,
Nocht be that Image, deif and dum,
Bot be the preistis all and sum,
As in the Bibill thow may ken,
Quhose nummer wer thre score and ten:
Thay and thare wyfis, everilk day,
Eait all that on the aulter lay.
Than Daniell, in conclusioun,
Schew the King thare abusioun,
And of thare subtlety maid hym sure,
Quhow onderneth the tempyll flure,
Throuch ane passage thay cam, be nycht,
And eait that meit with candell lycht.
The Kyng, quhen he the mater knew,
Those preistis, with all thare wyffis, he slew:
Thus subtellie the Kyng was sylit,
And all the peple wer begylit.
My Sonne, said he, now may thow ken
Quhow, by the Preistis and craftismen,
And by thare craftines and cure,
Idolatrye did so lang indure.
Behauld quhow Johne Boccatious

Hes wryttin workis wonderous
Of Gentilis superstitioun,
And of thare gret abusioun,
As in his gret Buke thow may see,
Of fals Goddis the Geneologie,
Of Demogorgon, in speciall,
Fore-grandschir tyll the Goddis all,
Honourit amang Archadience,
And of the fals Philistience,
With thare gret devilische god Dagone,
With utheris idollis mony one.
  Bot I abhor the treuth to tell
Of the Princis of Israell,
Chosin be God Omnipotent,
Quhow thay brak his commandiment:
iii. Reg. xi. Kyng Salomone, as the Scripture sayis,
He doitit in his latter dayis;
His wanton wyffis to compleis,
He curit nocht God tyll displeis,
And did committ idolatrye,
Wyrschipyng carvit imagerye,
As Moloch, god of Ammonitis,
And Chamos, god of Moabitis,
Astroth, god of Sydonianis.
So, for his inobediens
And fowle abhominatioun,
Wer puneist his successioun:
His sonne Roboam, I heir tell,
Tynt the Ten Trybis of Israell,
For his Fatheris idolatrye;
As in the Scripture thow may see.

OF IMAGEIS USIT AMANG CRISTIN MEN.

COURTEOUR.

FATHER, yit ane thyng wald I speir.
Behald, in every kirk, and queir,
Throch Christindome, in burgh and land,
Imageis maid with mennis hand,
To quhome bene gyffin divers names:
Sum Peter, and Paull, sum Jhone, and James;
Sanct Peter, carvit with his keyis;
Sanct Mychaell, with his wyngis and weyis;
Sanct Katherine, with hir swerd and quheill;
Ane hynde set up besyde Sanct Geill,
It war too lang for tyll discryve
Sanct Francis, with his woundis fyve;
Sanct Tredwall als, thare may be sene,
Quhilk on ane prik heth boith hir eine;
Sanct Paull, weill payntit with ane sworde,
As he wald feycht at the first worde;
Sanct Apolline on altare standis,
With all hir teithe in tyll hir handis;
Sanct Roche, weill seisit, men may se,
Ane byill new brokin on his thye;
Sanct Eloye he doith staitly stand,
Ane new hors schoo in tyll his hand;
Sanct Ringane, of ane rottin stoke;
Sanct Duthow, boird out of ane bloke;
Sanct Androw, with his croce in hand;
Sanct George, upone ane hors rydand;
Sanct Anthone, sett up with ane sow;

Sanct Bryde, weill carvit with ane kow;
With coistlye collouris fyne and fair,
Ane thousand mo I mycht declair,
As Sanct Cosma, and Damiane,
The sowtars Sanct Crispiniane:
All thir on altare staitly standis,
Preistis cryand, for thare offerandis,
To quhome, we Commounis, on our kneis,
Doith wyrschip all thir Imagereis;
In kirk, in queir, and in the closter,
Prayand to thame our Pater Noster;
In pylgramage frome town to toun,
With offerand, and with orisoun,
To thame aye babland on our beidis,
That thay wald keip us in our neidis.
Quhat differis this, declare to me,
From the Gentilis Idolatrye?

EXPERIENCE.

Gyff that be trew that thow reportis,
It goith rycht neir thir samyn sortis:
Bot we, be counsall of Clergye,
Hes lycence to mak Imagerye,
Quhilk of unlernit bene the buikis;
For, quhen lawit folk upone thame luikis,
It bryngith to rememberance
Of Sanctis lyvis the circumstance;
Quhow, the faith for to fortifye,
Thay sufferit pane rycht pacientlye;
Seand the Image of the Rude,
Men suld remember on the blude

Quhilk Christ, in tyll his passioun,
Did sched for our salvatioun;
Or, quhen thow seis ane protrature
Of blyssit Marie, Virgen pure,
One bony Babe upone hir kné,
Than, in thy mynde, remember thé
The wordis quhilk the Propheit said,
Quhow sche suld be boith mother and maid.
Bot quho that sittis doun on thare kneis,
Prayand tyll ony imagereis,
With orisoun, or offerand,
Kneland with cap in to thare hand,
No difference bene, I say to thé,
Frome the Gentilis idolatrye.
Rycht so, of divers Nationis
I reid abominationis,
Quhow Grekis maid thare devotioun haill
To Mars, to saif thame in battaill;
Tyll Jupiter sum tuke thare voyage,
To saif thame frome the stormys rage;
Sum prayit to Venus frome the splene,
That thay thair luffis mycht obtene;
And sum to Juno, for ryches,
Thare pylgramage thay wald addres.
So doith our commoun populare,
Quhilk war too lang for tyll declare
Thare superstitious pylgramageis
To mony divers Imageis;
Sum to Sanct Roche, with deligence,
To saif thame frome the pestilence;
For thare teith, to Sanct Apolleine;

To Sanct Tredwell, to mend thare eine :
Sum makis offrande to Sanct Eloye,
That he thare hors may weill convoye :
Thay ryn, quhen thay haif jowellis tynte,
To seik Sanct Syith, or ever thay stynte ;
And be Sanct Germane, to get remeid
For maladeis in to thare heid ;
Thay bryng mad men, on fuit and horsse,
And byndis thame to Sanct Mongose crosse :
To Sanct Barbara thay cry full faste,
To saif thame frome the thonder blaste :
For gude novellis, as I heir tell,
Sum takis thare gait to Gabriell ;
Sum wyffis Sanct Margaret doith exhort
In to thare byrth thame to support :
To Sanct Anthony, to saif the sow ;
To Sanct Bryde, to keip calf and kow :
To Sanct Bastien thay ryn and ryde,
That frome the schote he saif thare syde ;
And sum, in hope to get thare haill,
Rynnis to the auld rude of Kerraill.
Quhowbeit thir simpyll peple rude
Think thare intentioun be bot gude,
Wo be to Preistis, I say for me,
Quhilk suld schaw thame the veritie.
Prelatis, quhilk hes of thame the cure,
Sall mak answeir thareof, be sure,
On the gret day of Jugement,
Quhen no tyme beis for to repent,
Quhare manyfest Idolatrye
Sall puneist be perpetuallye.

HEIR FOLLOWIS ANE EXCLAMATIOUN AGANIS IDOLATRYE.

EXPERIENCE.

IMPRUDENT Peple, ignorant and blynd,
By quhat reasone, law, or authoritie,
Or quhat autentyck scripture, can ye fynd
Leifsum for tyll commyt Idolatrie?
Quhilk bene to bow your body, or your kne,
With devote humyll adoratioun,
Tyll ony idoll maid of stone or tre,
Geveand thame offerand, or oblatioun.

Quhy did ye gyf the honour, laude, and glore,
Pertenyng God, quhilk maid all thyng of nocht,
Quhilk wes, and is, and sall be evirmore,
Tyll imagis by mennis handis wrocht?
Of follysche folke, quhy haif ye succour socht
Of thame quhilk can nocht help yow in distres?
Yit reasonably revolve, into your thocht,
In stok nor stone can be none holynes.

In the desert, the peple of Israell,
Moyses remanyng in the Mont Synaye,
Thay maid one moltin calf of fyne mettell, Exodi. xxxii.
Quhilk thay did honour as thare God verraye:
Bot, quhen Moyses descendit, I heir saye,
And did consydder thare Idolatrye,

Of that peple thre thousand gart he slaye,
As the Scripture, at lenth, doith testifye.

Daniell xiiii. Because the holye propheit Daniell
In Babilone Idolatrie reprevit,
And wald nocht worschip thare fals idoll Bell,
The hole peple at hym wer so aggrevit,
To that effect that he suld be myschevit,
Delyverand hym tyll rampand lyonis sevin :
Bot, of that dangerous den, he wes relevit
Throuch myrakle of the gret God of Hevin.

Dan. iii. Behald quhow Nabuchodonosor king
In to the vaill of Duran did prepare
One Image of fyne gold, one mervallous thing,
Thre score of cubyts heych, and sax in square,
As more cleirlye the Scripture doith declare,
To quhome all peple, by proclamatioun,
With bodeis bowit, and on thare kneis bare,
Rycht humelye maid adoratioun.

Ane gret wounder, that day, wes sene also,
Quhow Nabuchodonosor, in his ire,
Tuke Sydrach, Misach, and Abednago,
Quhilkis wald nocht bow thare kné, at his desyre,
Tyll that Idoll, gart kast thame in the fyre,
For to be brynt, or he sterit of that steid :
Quhen he belevit thay wer brynt, bone and lyre,
Wes nocht consumit one small hair of thair heid.

The Angell of the Lord wes with thame sene,
In that hait furneis passing upe and doun,

In tyll ane rosye garth, as thay had bene,
None spott of fyre distenyng cote nor goun,
Of victorie thay did obtene the croun;
And wer, to thame that maid adoratioun
To that idoll, or bowit thare body doun,
One wytnessing of thare dampnatioun.

Quhat wes the cause, at me thow may demande,
That Salomone usit none imagerye
In his triumphand Tempyll for tyll stande,
Of Abraham, Isaac, Jacobe, nor Jesse,
Nor of Moyses thare savegarde throuch the see,
Nor Josue, thare valyeant campioun:
Because God did command the contrarye
That thay sulde use sic superstitioun.

Behald quhow the gret God Omnipotent, Exod. xx
To preserve Israell frome Idolatrye, Deut. v.
Derectit thame one strait commandiment,
Thay suld nocht mak none carvit imagrye,
Nother of gold, of sylver, stone, nor tre,
Nor gyf worschip tyll ony similytude
Beand in hevin, in erth, nor in the see,
Bot onelye tyll his Soverane Celsitude.

The Propheit David planely did repreve Baru. vi.
Idolatrye, to thare confusioun
In gravit stok or stone that did beleve,
Declaryng thame thare gret abusioun;
Speakand, in maner of dirysioun,
Quhow dede idolis, be mennis handis wrocht,

Quham thay honourit with humyll orisioun,
Wer in the markat daylie sauld and bocht.

The Devyllis, seand the evyll conditioun
Of the Gentylis, and thare unfaithfulnes,
For tyll agment thare superstitioun,
In those idolis thay maid thare entres,
And in thame spak, as storyis doith expres:
Than men belevit of thame to gett releif,
Askand thame help in all thare besynes;
Bot finallye, that turnit to thare mischeif.

Traist weill, in thame is none Divinitie,
Quhen reik and rowst thare fair colour doith faid:
Thocht thay have feit, one fute thay can not flee,
Quhowbeit the tempyll byrn abone thair heid:
In thame is nother freindschip nor remeid.
In sic fyguris quhat favour can ye fynd?
With mouth, and eris, and eine, thocht thay be maid,
All men may se thay are dum, deif, and blynd.

Quhowbeit thay fal doun flatlyngis on the flure,
Thay haif none strenth thare self to rais agane:
Thocht rattonis ouir thame ryn, thay tak no cure:
Quhowbeit thai breik thare neck, thay feill no pane.
Quhy sulde men psalmes to thame sing or sane?
Sen growand treis that yeirly berith frute
Ar more to pryse, I mak it to thé plane,
Nor cuttit stockis wanting boith crope and rute.

Of Edinburgh the gret idolatrye
And manifest abominatioun,

On thare feist day, all creature may se:
Thay beir ane auld stock Image throuch the toun,
With talbrone, troumpet, schalme, and clarioun,
Quhilk hes bene usit mony one yeir bigone;
With preistis and freris in to processioun,
Siclyke as Bell wes borne throuch Babilone.

Aschame ye nocht, ye seculare prestis and freris,
Tyll so gret superstitioun to consent?
Idolateris ye have bene mony yeris,
Expresse agane the Lordis commandement:
Quharefor, brether, I counsall yow, repent:
Gyff no honour to carvit stock nor stone;
Geve laude and glore to God Omnipotent
Allanerlie, as wyselie wryttis Jhone.

Fy on yow, Freris! that usis for to preche,
And dois assist to sic idolatrye,
Quhy do ye nocht the ignorant peple teche
Quhow ane dede image, carvit of one tre,
As it were holy sulde nocht honourit be,
Nor borne on Burges backis up and doun?
Bot ye schaw planely your ipocrasie,
Quhen ye passe formest in processioun.

Fy on yow, fosteraris of idolatrye!
That tyll ane dede stock dois sic reverence,
In presens of the peple, publykelie!
Feir ye nocht God, to commit sic offence?
I counsall yow, do yit your diligence
To gar suppresse sic gret abusioun.

Do ye nocht so, I dreid your recompence
Salbe nocht ellis but clene confusioun.

Had Sanct Frances bene borne out throuch the toun,
Or Sanct Dominick, thocht ye had nocht refusit
With thame tyll haif past in processioun,
In tyll that cais sum wald haif yow excusit.
Now men may see quhow that ye have abusit
That nobyll Town, throuch your ipocrasye:
Those peple trowis that thay may rycht weill use it,
Quhen ye pas with thame in to cumpanye.

Sum of yow hes bene quyet counsallouris
Provocand princis to sched saikles blude,
Quhilk nevir did your prudent predecessouris:
Bot ye lyke furious Phariceis, denude
Of charitie, quhilk rent Christ on the rude:
For Christis floke, without malyce or ire,
Convertit fragyll faltouris, I conclude,
Be Goddis worde, withouttin sweird or fyre.

Reid ye nocht quhow that Christ hes gyffin command,
Math. xviii. Gyff thy brother doith oucht thé tyll offend;
Than secretlye correct hym, hand for hand,
In freindly maner, or thow forther wend:
Gyff he wyll nocht heir thé, than mak it kend
Tyll one, or two, be trew narratioun:
Gyf he, for thame, wyll nocht his mys amend,
Declare hym to the congregatioun:

And, gyf he yit remanith obstinat,
And to the holy Kirk incounsolable,

Than lyke ane Turke hald hym excomminicat,
And with all faithfull folk abhominabyll;
Banysing hym, that he be no more able
To dwell amang the faithfull cumpanye:
Quhen he repentis, be nocht unmerciable,
Bot hym ressave agane rycht tenderlye.

Bot our dum Doctoris of Divinitie,
And ye of the last fonde religioun,
Of pure transgressouris ye have no petie,
Bot cryis to put thame to confusioun:
As cryit the Jowis, for the effusioun
Of Christis blude, in to thare byrnand ire,
Crucifige, so ye, with one unioun,
Cryis, Fy! gar cast that faltour in the fyre.

Unmercifull memberis of the Antichrist, Roma. xvi.
Extolland your humane traditione Ephe. v.
Contrar the Institutione of Christ,
Effeir ye nocht Divyne punytione?
Thocht sum of yow be gude of conditione,
Reddy for to ressave new recent wyne;
I speik to yow auld boisis of perditione,
Returne in tyme, or ye ryn to rewyne;

As ran the perverst Prophetis of Baall, iii. Reg. xviii.
Quhilkis did consent to the idolatrye
Of wickit Achab, king of Israell,
Quhose nòmmer wer four hundreth and fyftie,
Quhilkis honourit that Idoll opinlye:
Bot, quhen Elias did preve thare abusioun,

He gart the peple sla thame creuellye ;
So at one hour came thare confusioun.

I pray yow, prent in your remembrance
Quhow the reid Freris, for thare Idolatrye,
In Scotland, Ingland, Spane, Italy, and France,
Upone one day wer puneissit pietuouslye ;
Behald quhow your awin brother, now laitlye,
In Ducheland, Ingland, Denmark, and Norowaye,
Ar trampit doun, with thare ipocrasye,
And, as the snaw, ar meltit clene awaye.

I marvell that our Byschoppis thynkis no schame
To gyf yow freris sic preheminens,
Tyll use thare office, to thare gret diffame,
Precheing for thame in opin audiens :
Bot, mycht a Byschope eik tyll his awin expens,
For ilk Sermone, ten Ducatis in his hand,
He wald, or he did want that recompens,
Go preche hym self, boith in to burgh and land.

I traist to se gude reformatione
Frome tyme we gett ane faithfull prudent King
Quhilk knawis the treuth and his vocatione :
All Publicanis, I traist, he wyll doun thring,
And wyll nocht suffer in his realme to ring
Corruppit Scrybis nor fals Pharisiens,
Agane the treuth quhilk plainlye doith maling :
Tyll that kyng cum, we mon tak paciens !

Now Fairweill, Freindis ! because I can nocht flyte :
Quhowbeit I culde ye mon hald me excusit,

Thocht I agane Idolatrye indyte,
Or thame dispyte that wyl nocht yit refuse it.
I pray to God that it be no more usit
Amang the rewlaris of this Regioun,
That commoun peple be no more abusit,
Bot gyf Hym glore that bair the creuell croun;

Quhilk techeit us, be his Devine Scripture,
Tyll rycht prayer the perfyte reddy way;
As wrytith Matthew, in his sext chepture,
In quhat maner and to quhome we suld pray
One schort compendious orisone, everilk day,
Most proffitabyll for boith body and saull;
The quhilk is nocht derectit, I heir say,
To Jhone nor James, to Peter nor to Paull,

Nor none uther of the Apostlis twelf,
Nor to no Sanct, nor Angell in the Hevin,
Bot onely tyll our Father, God hym self;
Quhilk orisioune it doith contene, full evin,
Most proffitabyll for us, petitionis sevin;
Quhilk we lawid folk the Pater Noster call.
Thocht we say Psalmis nyne, ten, or alevin,
Of all prayer this bene the principall;

Be reasoun of the makkar quhilk it maid,
Quhilk wes the Sonne of God, our Salviour;
Be reasoun, als, to quhome it suld be said,
Tyll the Father of Hevin, our Creatour,
Quhilk dwellis nocht in tempyll nor in tour.
He cleirlye seis our thocht, wyll, and intent:

Quhat nedith us at utheris seik succour,
Quhen in all place his power bene present?

Ye princis of the preistis, that suld preche,
Quhy suffer ye so gret abusioun?
Quhy do ye nocht the sempyll peple teche
Quhow and to quhome to dresse thare orisoun?
Quhy thole ye thame to ryn frome toun to toun,
In pylgramage, tyll ony imagereis,
Hopand to gett thare sum saluatioun,
Prayand to thame devotlye on thare kneis?

This wes the prettike of sum pylgramage:
Quhen fillokis, in to Fyfe, began to fon,
With Joke and Thom than tuke thay thare vayage
In Angusse, tyll the feild chappel of Dron:
Than Kyttoke thare, als cadye as ane con,
Without regarde other to syn or schame,
Gaiff Lowrie leif at layser to loupe on:
Far better had bene tyll haif biddin at hame.

I have sene pass one mervellous multytude,
Yong men and wemen, flyngand on thare feit,
Under the forme of feynit sanctytude,
For tyll adore one image in Loreit.
Mony came with thare marrowis for to meit,
Committand thare fowll fornicatioun:
Sum kyst the claggit taill of the Armeit:
Quhy thole ye this abominatioun?

Of Fornicatioun and Idolatrye
Apperandlye ye tak bot lytill cure,

Seand the marvellous infelicitye
Quhilk heth so lang done in this land indure,
In your defalt quhilk heth the charge and cure.
This bene of treuth, my Lordis, with your leve,
Sic pylgramage heth maid mony one hure,
Quhilk, gyf I plesit, planelye I mycht preve.

Quhy mak ye nocht the Scripture manifest
To pure peple, twyching Idolatrye?
In your precheing quhy haif ye nocht exprest
Quhow mony kyngis of Israell creuellye
Wer puneissit, be God, so rigorouslye?
As Jeroboam, and mony mo, but doute,
For wyrschippyng of carvit Imagerye,
War frome thare realmes rudlye rutit oute. iii Reg. xiii.

Quhy thole ye, under your dominioun,
Ane craftye preist, or fenyeit fals armeit,
Abufe the peple of this regioun,
Onely for thare perticular profeit,
And, speciallye, that Heremeit of Lawreit?
He pat the comoun peple in beleve
That blynd gat seycht, and crukit gat thare feit,
The quhilk that palyard no way can appreve.

Ye maryit men, that hes trym wantoun wyffis,
And lustie dochteris of young tender aige,
Quhose honestie ye suld lufe as your lyffis,
Permyt thame nocht to passe in pylgramage,
To seik support at ony stok Image:
For I have wyttin gud wemen passe fra hame,

Quhilk hes bene trappit with sic lustis rage,
Hes done returne boith with gret syn and schame.

Gett up ! thow slepist all too lang, O Lord ;
And mak one haistie reformatioun
On thame quhilk doith tramp doun thy gratious Worde,
And hes ane deidly indignatioun
At thame quhilk makith trew narratioun
Of thy Gospell, schawing the Verytie.
O Lord ! I mak thé supplicatioun,
Supporte our Faith, our Hope, and Charytie.

HEIR FOLLOWIS QUHOW KYNG NYNUS BEILDIT THE GRET CITIE OF NYNIVE´; AND QUHOW HE VINCUSTE ZOROASTES, THE KYNG OF BACTRIA.

[EXPERIENCE.]

THIS Nynus, of Assyria king,
Quhen he had maid his conquessing,
To beild one Citie he hym drest,
Chosing the place quhare he thocht best,
Quhare he had first dominioun,
In Assyria, his awin regioun.
Gene. x Thocht Assur, as the Scriptur says,
Quhilk come affore Kyng Nynus dayis,
And foundit that famous Citie,
The quhilk was callit Nynivé.

Bot, as rehersis Diodore,
Nynus that Citie did decore
So mervellous tryumphantlye
As ye sall heir immedeatlye,
Upone the flude of Euphrates,
Quhilk to behald gret wounder wes.
One hundreth and fyftye stageis
That Citie wes of lenth, I wys:
The wallis, one hundredth fute of heycht,
No wounder was, thocht thay wer wycht:
Sick breid, abufe the wallis thare was,
Thré cartis mycht sydlinglis on thame pas:
Four hundreth stageis and four score
In circuit, but myn or more.
Of towris, aboute those wallis, I wene,
Ane thousand and fyve hundreth bene,
Of heycht two hundreth fute and more,
As wryttis famous Diodore.
The scripture makis mentioun,
Quhen God send Jonas to that toun, Jona. iii.
To schaw thame of his puneisment,
Out throuch the Citie quhen he went,
Thre dayis jornay tyll hym it wes:
The Bybill sayis it wes no les.
My Sonne, now haif I schawin to thé
Of the beildyng of Nynivé:
For the agmentyng of his fame,
Nynus gart call it efter his name.
Quhen he that gret Citie had endit,
To conques more yit he intendit,
And did depart from Nynivé,

And rasit up one gret armie
Of the most stalwarte men and stoute
Of all his Regionis round aboute :
In gret ordour tuke thare jornay
Towarte the realme of Bactria.
Of wycht fute-men, I understande,
He had sevintene hundreth thousande,
Without hors-men and weirlyke cairtis,
Quhome he ordourit in sindry partis ;
Quhilk tyll discryve I am nocht abyll,
Quhose nummer bene so untrowabyll.
  Zoroastes, that nobyll kyng,
Quhilk Bactria had in governyng,
That prudent Prince, as I heir tell,
Did in Astronomye precell,
And fand the Art of Magica,
With naturall science mony ma ;
Seand king Nynus on the feilde,
Fordwart he cam, with speir and scheilde,
Foure hundreth thousand men he wes,
In his Armie thare wes no les ;
And mett king Nynus, on the bordoure,
Rycht vailyantlie, and in gude ordoure,
On the vangarde of his Armie.
On thame he ruscheit rycht rudelie,
And of thame slew, as I heir saye,
One hundreth thousand men, that day :
The reste that chaipit war unslane
To Nynus gret oiste fled agane.
  Of that king Nynus wes so noyit,
He restit nevir tyll he distroyit

All hoill that Regioun, upe and doun,
And frome the King did reif the croun,
And maid the realme of Bactria
Subjectit tyll Assyria.
And in that samyn land, I wys,
He tuk to wyfe Semiramis;
Quha, as myne Author dois discryve,
Was, than, the lustiest on lyve.
That beand done, without sudgeorne,
Tyll Nynivé he did returne,
With gret tryumphe of victorie.
As myne Author dois specifie,
Boith Occident and Orient
War all tyll hym obedient.
It wald abhore thé tyll heir red
The saikles blude that he did sched.
Quhen he had roung, as thow may heir,
The space of thre and fourtye yeir,
Beand in his excelland glore,
The dolent deith did hym devore,
In quhat sorte, I am nocht certane:
Sum Author sayis that he wes slane,
And left, tyll bruke his heretage,
Ane lytill Babe of tender aige:
Young Nynus wes the chyldis name,
Quhilk efter fluryste in gret fame.
Sum sayis that, be his Wyffis treasoun,
Kyng Nynus deit in presoun;
As I sall schaw, or I hyne fair,
Quhow Diodore hath done declair.

HEIR FOLLOWIS SUM OF THE WOUNDERFULL DEDIS OF THE LUSTIE QUENE SEMIRAMIS.

[EXPERIENCE.]

NYNUS luiffit so ardentlye
Semiramis, his fair ladye.
Thare wes no thyng scho wald command
Bot al obeyit wes fra hand.
Scho, seand hym so amorous,
Scho grew proude and presumptuous,
And at the King scho did desyre
Fyve dayis to governe his Impyre;
And he, of his benevolence,
Did grant hir that preheminence,
With sceptour, crown, and rob royall,
And hole power Imperiall,
Tyll fyve dayis wer come and gone,
That scho, as King, sulde ring allone.
Than all the Princis of the land
Duryng that tyme maid hir ane band:
With bankat royall myrrellie
Scho treatit thame tryumphantlie.
So, the first day, the peple all
Came tyll hir servyce, bound and thrall;
Bot, or the secunde day wes gone,
Scho tuke sic glore to ryng allone,
Be one decreit, maid thame amang,
The King scho patt in presone strang.
I reid weill of his presoning,

Bot nocht of his delyvering:
Quhow evir, it wes in tyll his flowris
He did of deith suffer the schowris,
And mycht nocht lenth his lyfe one houre,
Thocht he wes the first conqueroure:
Quhose conquessing, for to conclude,
Wes nocht bot gret schedding of blude.
Now have ye hard of Nynus king,
Quhow he began, and his ending;
Quhowbeid myne author, Diodore,
Of hym haith wryttin mekle more.
Princis, for wrangous conquessing,
Doith mak, oft tymes, ane evyll ending:
Thocht he had lang prosperitie,
He endit with miseritie.

OF KYNG NYNUS SEPULTURE.

[EXPERIENCE.]

THE Quene a sepultur scho maid,
Quhar sche King Nynus body laid,
Of curius crafty wark, and wycht,
The quhilk had stagis nine, of hycht,
And ten stagis of breid it wes:
Diodore saith it wes no les.
For aucht stagis one myle thow tak,
And thairefter thy nummer mak;
So, be this compt, it wes, full rycht,
One myle and als one stage of hycht.

Except the Towre of Babilone,
So heych one wark I reid of none.
Semiramis, this lustye Quene,
Consyddring quhat dainger bene
To haif one King of tender aige,
Quhilk mycht nocht use no vassalage,
Scho tuke one curagious consait,
Thinkand that scho wald mak debait,
Geve ony maid rebellioun
Contrar hir Sonne, or his regioun,
Quhome sche did foster tenderly,
And kepit hym full quyetly.
Scho laid apart hir awin cleithyng,
And tuke the rayment of ane king:
Quhen scho wes in tyll armour dycht,
Mycht no man knaw hir be one knycht.
Scho valyeantlye went to the weir,
And to gyf battell tuke na feir,
Dantyng all realmes rounde aboute,
That all the warld of hir had doute;
More fortunat, in hir conquessing,
Nor wes hir husband, Nynus King.
Babilone scho did fortyfie,
Templis and towris, tryumphandlie,
So plesandlye did thame prepair,
Quhilk in the erth had no compair.
Quhowbeid Nemrod, of quhome I spake,
The hydduous dungeoun he gart make,
And of the Cietie the fundiment,
To quhome God maid impediment:
Quhare Nemrod left, thare scho began,

And pat to wark mony one man
Of all the Realmes round aboute,
Of most ingyne scho socht thame oute.
Scho had, wyrkand with tre and stonis,
Twelf hundreth thousand men at onis;
Go reid the buke of Diodore,
And thow sall fynd the nummer more.
On everilk syde of Euphrates
That nobyll Cietie beildit wes;
And so that ryver of renown
Ran throuch the mydpart of the town.
Ouerthort that flude scho bryggis maid
Of marvellous strenth, boith lang and braid:
Thay wer fyve stagis large of lenth,
On everilk bryg scho maid ane strenth.
The circuit, as I said affore,
Foure hundreth stagis and foure score;
The wallis hycht, quho wald discryve,
Thre hundreth fute, thre score and fyve.
Sax cairtis mycht pas, rycht easalie,
Abufe the wallis of that Cietie,
Sydlingis, without impediment.
Consydder, be your jugement,
Geve those wallis wer hie, or nocht,
And also curiouslye wer wrocht,
As Diodore hes done defyne,
Quhilk doith transcend my rude ingyne.
Of Babilone the magnificens;
To quhome ye wald gyf no credens,
Geve I at lenth wald put in wryte,
Quhilk Diodore hes done indyte.

Compare of cieties fynd I none
Tyll Nynivé and Babilone.
Frome Nynivé, in Assyria,
Tyll Babilone, in Caldia,
By bryggis plesandlye ye may pas
Upone the flude of Euphratas.
Amang the fludis of Paradyce
This Euphratas maye beir the pryce.
All warkis quhilkis the Quene began
Transcendit the ingyne of man.
The proud Quene Pantasilia,
The Princes of Amasona,
With hir ladyis tryumphandlye,
At Troye quhilk faucht so vailyeantlye,
Nor yit the fair Madin of France,
Danter of Inglis ordinance,
To Semiramis, in hir dayis,
Wer no compare, as bukis sayis;
Except tryumphand Julyus,
Strong Hanniball, or Pompeyus,
Or Alexander the Conqueroure,
I fynd no gretter werioure.
  Wald I rehers, as wryttis Clerkis,
His wounderfull and vailyeand werkis,
It wer to me one gret laubour,
And teddious to the auditour:
Quhat scho did in Ethopia,
And in the lande of Medea;
Beildand citeis, castellis, and towris,
Parkis, and gardyngis of plesouris,
For the exaltyng of hir name,

And immortall to mak hir fame.
Of Jarcicus the heych montanis
Scho gart ryve down and mak thame planis:
Gret Orontes, that montane wycht,
Twenty and fyve stagis of hycht,
Tyll hir Palyce to draw ane louche,
By fors of men scho raif it throche.
  Had scho kepit hir chastitie,
Scho mycht have bene one A per se.
Quhen scho had ordorit hir impyre,
Of Venus wark scho tuke desyre;
One secreit mansioun scho gart mak,
Quhare scho maist plesandlye mycht tak
Young gentyll men, for hir plesour;
The quhilk scho usit abufe mesour:
One man allone mycht nocht be abyll
To stanche hir luste insaciabyll:
Quhen scho wes satifyit of one,
Scho gart ane uther cum anone;
The lustiest of all the land
Cum quyetlye, at hir command:
Quhen thay, at lenth, had lyin hir by,
Scho slew thame all, rycht creuelly.
Quhen hir Sone come tyll aige perfyte,
Of hym scho tuke so gret delyte,
Scho causit hym with hir to lye,
Amang the rest, rycht quyetlye.
Sum sayis, throuch sensuall lustis rage,
Scho band hym into mariage,
And held hym under tutorye,
To uphald hir auctoritye.

QUHOW THE QUENE SEMIRAMIS, WITH ONE GRET ARMIE, PAST TO YNDE, AND FAUCHT WITH THE KYNG STAUROBATES, AND OF HIR MISERABYLL END.

EXPERIENCE.

QUHEN scho had lang tyme levit in rest,
To conques more scho hir addrest;
Because of divers scho hard tell
Quhow that the Ynde Orientell
Preceid in gret commoditeis,
As bestiall, cornis, and fructfull treis,
Al kynde of spyce delicious,
Gold, sylver, stonis precious;
And quhow that plentuous land did beir
Corne, frute, and wyne twyse in the yeir;
With oliphantis innumerabyll,
In battell wounder terrabyll.
Scho, herand this, and mekle more,
Belevand tyll agment hir glore,
Gart mak strait Proclamationis
In all and syndrie Nationis,
Schawand quhow it wes hir desyre,
All Princis under hir impyre,
In Egypt, and Arabia,
In Perce, and Mede, and Caldia,
In Grece, in Caspia, and Hyrcane,
In Capadoce, Leid, and Maritane,

In Arminie, and Phrigia,
In Pamphilie, and Assyria,
That ilke Land, efter thare degré,
Sulde bryng tyll hir ane gret armie,
In all the gudlye haist thay may,
And meit hir in tyll Bactria;
Declaryng thame that hir intent
Was tyll pas to the Orient,
And mak weir on the king of Ynde.
Frome tyme thay knew quhat wes hir mynde,
Than, be thare selfis, ilke regioun
Come fordwart, with thare garnisoun,
Tryumphantlye, in gude array,
Tyll Bactria tuke the reddy way,
And maid thare mostouris to the Quene.
Bot sic ane sycht wes never sene,
In battell ray so mony one man
At onis, sen God the warld began.
Bot Spanye, France, Scotland, Ingland,
Ducheland, Denmark, nor yit Yrland
War nocht inhabit in those dayis,
Nor lang efter, myne Author sayis.
  Ethesias he dois specifie
The noumber of the great Armie,
Sayand, thare come, at hir command,
Fute men threttye hundreth thousand,
Of hors men, mountit galyeardlye,
Fyve hundreth thousand, veralye,
One hundreth thousand cameilis wycht,
On everilk cameill raid ane knycht,
Preparit tyll passe in to all partis.

Thare wes ane hundreth thousand cairtis:
Two thousand boittis with hir scho careis,
On hors, cameilis, and dromodareis,
Bryggis for to mak scho did conclude
Ouerthort Yndus, that furious flude,
Quhilk bene of Ynde the utmoist bordoure;
On the quhilk flude, with rycht gude ordoure,
Of hir bairgis scho bryggis maid,
Quhareon hir gret oiste saifly raid.

COURTEOUR.

Father, I wald men understude
Quhow sic ane marvellous multytude
Mycht be att onis brocht to the feild,
Reddy to feycht with speir and scheild.
Sum men wyll juge this be ane fabyll,
The mater bene so untrowabyll.

EXPERIENCE.

It may weill be, my Sonne, said he,
As, be exempyll, we may se
Quhow David, king of Israell,
His peple gart nummer and tell
Be Joab, his cheif capitane,
As Holy Scripture schawis plane:
Of feychtand men, in to that land,
He fand threttyne hundreth thousand.
Sen David, in that small countre,
Mycht have rasit sic ane armie,
To this lady it wes na wounder,
The quhilk had greter realmes ane hunder

Nor Davidis lytill regioun,
Thocht scho had mony a legioun
Of men mo nor I tauld affore:
Tharefor, my Sonne, marvell no more.
  Staurobates, the king of Ynde,
Gretlie perturbit in his mynd,
Heryng of sic ane multytude,
To mak defens he did conclude,
And send one message to the Quene,
Prayand hir Majestie serene
That scho wald, of hir speciall grace,
Gyf hym licence to leif in peace;
Failand of that, thocht he suld dee,
That he suld gar hir fecht or flee;
And tyll his god ane vowe he maid,
Gyf no peace mycht of hir be had,
And gyf he wan the victorye,
That he the Quene suld crucifye.
At this bostyng the Quene maid bourdis,
Sayand, it sall nocht be, no wourdis
Sall gar me passe frome my purpose,
Bot mychtie straikis, as I suppose.
The messingeir schew to the Kyng
Of hir presumptuous answeryng,
Than Staurobates, wyse and wycht,
Come fordwart, lyke ane nobyll knycht,
With mony one thousand speir and scheild,
Arrayit royallie on the feild;
Thynkand he wald his land defend,
Or in the battell mak ane end.
  The Quene, apone the uther syde,

Full of presumptioun and of pryde,
Hir banaris plesandly displayit,
With hardy hart and uneffrayit.
Apone Indus, that famous flude,
Thay met, quhare sched wes mekle blude.
In bote, in balingar, and bargis,
The twa Armyis on utheris chargis.
Semiramis the battaill wan,
Quhare drownit and slane wer mony one man,
So that the walter of the flude
Ran reid, myxit with mannis blude.
The King of Ynde, with all his mycht,
Frome Yndus flude he tuke the flycht:
Tyll his cheif cietie he reteirit,
Quhare in his presens thare appeirit
In battell raye ane new armye,
Of rycht invincibyll chevalrye,
With elephantis ane hydduous nummer,
Quhilk efterwart maid mekle cummer.
Semiramis and hir cumpanye,
In the mene tyme, full creuellie
Distroyit the bordouris of that land,
Tuke presonaris mo than ten thousand.
Sche tuke one couragious consait,
Gret elephantis to contrafait:
Sche had ten thousand oxin hydis,
Weill sewit togydder, bak and sydis,
With mouth, and nois, teith, eris, and eine,
Quyke elephantis as thay had bene,
Rycht weill stuft full of stray and hay,
Quhareof the Yndianis tuke affray.

Apone cameilis and dromodareis
Those fals figouris with hir scho careis.
Sere Yndianis, quhen thay saw that sycht,
Afferitlye thay tuke the flycht;
For sic one sycht wes never sene,
Gyff naturall beistis thay had bene.
The Kyng hym self wes rycht affeirit,
Tyll he the veritie had speirit,
And knew, be his exploratouris,
Thay wer bot fenyeit fals figouris.
Than, manfullye, lyke men of weir,
Fordwart thay came withouttin feir;
Rycht so Semiramis the Quene,
Quhilk for one man wes aye fyftene.
Thir two armeis full creuellye
Thay ruscheit togydder so rudlie,
With hyddous cry and trumpettis sound,
Tyll thousandis dede laye on the ground.
Semiramis had sic one nummer,
Tyll order thame it was gret cummer.
Than the gret elephantis of Ynde,
Rycht strang and hardy of thare kynde,
Fordwart thay came, and wald nocht ceis,
Tyll throuch the myddis of the preis
Of the gret oist thay rudlye ruscheit,
That men and horsse tyll erth thay duscheit.
Those fenyeit beistis, withouttin spreit,
Wer fruschit and fulyeit under feit.
The king of Ynde, with curage kene,
Met with Semiramis the quene,
He rydand on ane eliphand:

Bot scho with hym faucht hand for hand,
And gaif the King so gret assaye
That he wes nevir in sic affraye.
To stryke at hym scho tuke no feir,
So weill scho usit wes in weir.
His straikis scho had bot lytill comptit,
Wer nocht the King wes so weill mountit.
Athir at uther straik so faste
Tyll thay wer tyrit at the laste.
The King he thocht himself eschamit
With one woman to be diffamit,
And wes determit nocht to flee,
Thocht in that battell he suld dee.
As man the quhilk disparit bene,
He rudely ran upon the Quene,
And through the arme gaif hir ane wound
Quhilk tyll hir hart gaif sic one stound
That sche constrainit wes to fle.
Than all the rest of hir armie,
Quhen thay persavit that scho wes gone,
Tyll Yndus flude thay fled, ilke one.
The Quene ouerthort the flude sche raid
On bryggis quhilkis wer of botis maid;
With hir, one sobir cumpanye,
Quhilk with hir fled affraytlie.
The Yndianis followit on the chace:
Than on the bryggis come sic one praice
Of fleand folkis, quhilk wes gret wounder,
So that the bargis krake in schonder.
Sum sank, sum doun the revar ran:
Than drownit thare mony one nobyll man;

Quhilk wer gret piete tyll deplore,
As wryttis famous Diodore;
And, fynallie, for to conclude,
Wes never sched so mekle blude
At one tyme sen the Warld began,
Nor slane so mony one saikles man;
And all throw the occasioun
And the prydefull perswasioun
Of this ambitious wyckit Quene:
Sic one wes nevir hard nor sene.
  Staurobates, the kyng of Ynde,
Gretlye rejoysit, in his mynde,
Of this tryumphe and victorye:
Semiramis, with hart full sorye,
Seand sa mony tane and slane,
Tyll hir countré returnit agane,
Lamentand fortunis variance
Quhilk brocht hir to so gret myschance,
Affore quhilk wes so fortunat,
And than of confort desolat.
  Hir Sonne, one man of perfectioun,
Consyderand his subjectioun,
His lybertie he did desyre,
That he mycht governe his impyre:
Seand his Mother vicious,
And, with that, so ambitious,
As myne Author doith specifye,
He slew his Mother creuellye:
Quhat uther cause, or intentioun,
I fynd no speciall mentioun:
Sum sayis, to be at libertie;

Sum sayis, for hir adulterie;
None uther cause I can defyne,
Except punissioun devyne.
  Of this fair Lady coragious
Behald the endyng dolorous;
Quhilk wes bot twenty yeir of aige,
Quhen sche began hir vassalage,
And rang triumphandlye, but weir,
The space of two and fourtye yeir:
Quhen scho was slane, scho wes thre score,
With yeris two, scho wes no more;
As Diodore wryttis in his buke,
His Cronikle quho lyste to luke.

  Of this Lady I mak ane end,
Thynkand no way I can commend
Wemen for tyll be too manlye,
Nor men for tyll be womanlye:
For quhy it bene the Lordis mynde
All creature tyll use thare kynde;
Men for tyll have preheminens,
And wemen under obediens;
Thocht all wemen inclynit be
Tyll have the soveranitie,
As this lady, quhilk wald nocht rest
Tyll scho hir husband had suppresst,
Tyll that intent that scho mycht ryng,
Allone to haif the governyng.
  Ladyis no way I can commend
Presumptuouslye quhilk doith pretend
Tyll use the office of ane Kyng.

Or Realmes tak in governyng,
Quhowbeit thay vailyeant be and wycht,
Going in battell lyke one knycht,
As did proude Pantasilia,
The Princes of Amasona,
In mennis habyte, aganis reassoun :
Siclyke I think derisioun,
One prince to be effaminate,
Of knychtlye corage desolate,
Neglectand his auctoritie,
Throuch beistlie sensualitie,
Accompanyit, boith day and nychtis,
With wemen, more than vailyeant knychtis;
Sic kyngis I discommend at all,
Exempyll of Sardanapall.

COURTEOUR.

Father, said I, schaw me quhow lang
The su̇ccessioun of Nynus rang.

EXPERIENCE.

That sall I do, with diligens,
My Sonne, said he, or I go hens.
Sen I haif schawin, at thy desyre,
Quhat man began the First Impyre,
Now wald I it wer to thee kend
Of that Impyre the fatell end.

QUHOW KING SARDANAPALUS, FOR HIS VITIOUS LIFE, MAID ANE MISERABILL END.

[EXPERIENCE.]

BETUIX this Conquerour Nynus
And sensuall Sardanapalus
I can nocht fynd no speciall storye
Worthy to put in memorye,
Except quhilk I haif done discryfe
Of Semirame, king Nynus wyfe :
Bot I can fynde no gude at all
To wrytt of kyng Sardanapall,
Quhilk wes the saxt and threttye kyng
Be lyne from Nynus discendyng.
At lenth his lyfe for to declare
I thynk it is nocht necessare ;
Because that mony cunnyng clerkis
Hes hym discryvit in thare werkis :
Quhow he wes last of Assyrians
Quhilk had the hole preemynens,
That tyme of the First Monarchie,
In Cronicles, as thow may se,
The last and the most vitious kyng
Quhilk in that Monarchie did ryng.
That Prince wes so effeminate,
With sensuall luste intoxicate,
He did abhor the cumpanye
Of his most nobyll chevalrye :
That he mycht have the more delyte

Tyll use his beistlye appetyte,
Conversit with wemen nycht and daye,
And clothit hym in thare arraye,
So that na man that hym had sene
Could juge ane man that he had bene:
So, in huredome and harlotrye
Did keip hym self so quyetlye,
The Princis of Assyrience
Of hym thay could get no presence.
Thus levit he contynualye,
Agane nature inordinatlye.
Quhen to the Persis and the Medis
Reportit wer his vitious dedis,
With the rewlaris of Babilone,
Thay did conclude, all in tyll one,
Thay wald nocht suffer for tyll ryng
Abufe thame sic ane vitious kyng:
Bot Arbaces, ane Duke of Mede,
He darflye tuke on hand that dede.
Bot first he come to Nynivé,
To see the kyngis Majestie,
And tyll one of the kyngis gaird
He gaif one secreit ryche rewaird,
Tyll put hym in ane quyet place,
Quhare he mycht se the Kyngis grace,
And be onsene with ony wycht.
Bot he saw nother king nor knycht
In tyll his maisteris cumpanye,
Except Wemen, allanerlye:
And as ane woman he was cled,
With wemen counsalit and led;

And schamefullye he wes syttand,
With spindle and with rock spinnand.
Quhen Arbaces that sycht had sene,
His corage raisit from the splene,
And thocht it small difficultie
For tyll depryve his Majestie.
  Than raisit he the Persianis,
With Medis and Babilonianis:
Inarmit weill with speir and scheildis,
Tryumphantlye thay tuke the feildis.
  The Kyng raisit Assyrianis,
Togither with the Caldianis,
And thame resystit as he mycht;
Bot, fynallie, he tuke the flycht,
To saif hym self, in Nynivé.
Than seigit thay that gret Cietie,
Contynuallie, two yeir and more,
As wryttis famous Diodore;
Tyll that the flude of Euphrates
Arose with sic one furiousnes,
Quhare throuch ane gret part of the Toun
By violence was doungin doun.
Than, quhen the Kyng saw no remeid
Bot to be takin, or to be deid,
As man disparit full of yre,
Gart mak ane furious flammand fyre,
And tuke his gold and jowellis all,
With sceptur, croun, and robe royall,
With all his tender servitouris
That of his corps had gretest curis,
Togydder with his lustye Quenis,

And all his wantoun concubenis,
And in that fyre he did thame cast,
Syne lappe hym self in, at the last,
Quhare all wer brynt in poulder small.
Thus endit Kyng Sardanapall
Withouttin ony repentence,
As may be sene be this sentence,
Heir followyng, quhilk he did indyte
Affore his deith in gret dispyte:
Quhilk is ane rycht ungodly thing,
As ye may se be his dyting.—

EPITAPHIUM SARDANAPALI.

Cum te mortalem noris, præsentibus exple
Delitiis animum, post mortem nulla voluptas.
Et Venere, et cœnis, et plumis Sardanapali.

Now haif I schawin, with deligence,
The Monarchie of Assyrience,
The quhilk at Kyng Nynus began,
And endit at this myscheant man,
And did indure, withouttin weir,
Ane thowsand, twa hundreth, and fourty yeir,
As dois indyte Eusebius:
Reid hym, and thow sall fynd it thus.

HEIR ENDIS THE SECUND PART.

ANE DIALOG

BETUIX EXPERIENCE AND ANE COURTEOUR.

THE THRID BUKE.

AND IN THE FIRST, MAKAND NARRATIONE OF THE MISERABILL DISTRUCTIOUN OF THE FYVE CIETIES CALLIT SODOME, GOMORRE, SEBOIM, SEGORE, AND ADAMA, ETC.

COURTEOUR.

FATHER, I pray yow, to me tell
Quhat notabyll thyngis that befell
Duryng the ryng of Assyriens,
Quhilk had so lang prehemynens;
I mene of uther Nationis
Under thare dominationis.

EXPERIENCE.

That may be done in termys schorte,
Said he, as storyis doith reporte:
Induryng this First Monarchie
Become that wofull miserie
Of Sodome, Gomorre, and thare regione,
Gen xix. As Scripture makis mentione;
Quhose peple wer so sensuall
In fylthie synnis unnaturall,

The quhilk in to my vulgar veirs
My toung abhorris to reheirs:
Lyke brutall beistis, by thare myndis,
Unnaturally abusit thare kyndis
By fylthie stynkand lychorie,
And most abhominabyll sodomie.
As holy Scripture doith discryve,
In that countrie wer Cieteis fyve,
Quhilk wer Sodome, and Gomorra,
Seboim, Segore, and Adama:
Amang thame all funde wes thare none
Undefylit, bot Lott allone.
Holy Abraham dwelt neir hand by,
Quhilk prayit for Lott effectuously:
For God maid hym advertysment,
That he wald mak sic punyschement.
To Lott two Angellis God did sende,
Hym frome that furye tyll defende.
Quhen the peple of that regioun
Saw the Angellis cum tò toun,
Transformit in to fair young men,
Thay purposit thame for to ken,
And abuse thame unnaturallye
With thare foule stynkand sodomye.
Of that gude Lott wes wounder woo,
And offerit thame his douchteris twoo,
Thame at thare plesour for tyll use:
Bot thay his douchteris did refuse.
And than the Angellis, be thare mycht,
Those men depryvit of thare sycht;
And so, perfors, leit thame allone.

To Lottis lugyng quhen thay wer gone,
Thay hym commandit haistelie
For tyll depart of that Cietie.
That foule unnaturall lychorie
A vengeance to the Hevin did crye;
The quhilk did mufe God tyll sic yre,
That frome the Hevin brintstone and fyre,
With awfull thoundryng, ranit doun,
And did consume that hole regioun.
Of all that land chapit no mo
Except Lott and his douchteris two:
His wyfe wes turnit in a stone,
So wyfeless wes he left allone,
For scho wes inobedient,
And kepit no commandement.
Quhen the Angell gif thame command
Sone tyll depart out of that land,
He monyste thame, under gret pane,
Never to luke bakwart agane.
Quhen Lottis wyfe hard the thoundring
Of flammand fyre and lychtnyng,
The ugly cryis lamentabyll
Of peple most espoventabyll,
For none of thame had fors to flee,
Scho yarnit that sorrowfull sycht to see;
And, as scho turnit hir, anone
Scho wes transformit in a stone;
Quhare scho remanis tyll this daye,
Of hir I have no more to saye.
To schaw at leynth I am nocht abyll
That pietuous proces lamentabyll,

Quhow cieteis, castellis, tounis, and towris,
Villagis, bastailyeis, and bowris,
Thay wer all into poulder drevin;
Forrestis be the ruttis uprevin;
Thare Kyng, thare Quene, and peple all,
Yong and auld, brynt in poulder small:
No creature wes left in lyfe,
Foulis, beistis, man, nor wyfe;
The erth, the corne, herb, frute and tre,
The babbis upone the noryse kne,
Rycht suddantlye, in one instant,
Unwerly come thare jugement;
As it come in the tyme of Noye,
Quhen God did all the warld distroye;
For that self syn of sodomye,
And most abhominabyll bewgrye:
That vyce at lenth for tyll declare
I thynk it is nocht necessare.
  Quhen all wes brynt, flesche, blud, and bonis,
Hyllis, valais, stokis, and stonis,
The cuntre sank, for to conclude,
Quhare now standith ane uglye flude,
The quhilk is callit the Dede See,
Nixt to the cuntre of Judee,
Quhose stynkand strandis, blak as tar,
The flewre of it men felith on far.
In tyll Orosius thow may reid
Of that countre the lenth and breid;
Of lenth, fyftye mylis and two,
And fourtene myle in breid also.
  Lott of his Wyfe wes so agast

That he tyll a wyld montane past:
Of cumpanye he had no mo
Except his lustye douchteris two;
And, be thare provocatioun,
As Moyses makith narratioun,
Allone in to that montane wylde,
His douchteris boith he gat with chylde.
For thay belevit, in thare thocht,
That all the warld wes gone to nocht,
As it become of that Natioun;
Thynkand that generatioun
Wald faill, withoute thay craftellye
Gar thare Father with thame to lye:
And so thay fand ane craftye wyle,
Quhow thay thare Father mycht begyle,
And causit hym to drynk wycht wyne,
Quhilk men to lychorye doith inclyne.
Quhen he wes full, and fallin on sleip,
His douchteris quyetlye did creip
In tyll his bed, full secreitlye,
Provokand hym with thame to lye:
And knew nocht quhow he wes begylde,
Tyll boith his douchteris wer with chylde:
And bure two sonnis, in certane,
Thay beand in that wyld montane,
Of quhome two Nationis did proceid,
As in the Scripture thow may reid;
In the quhilk Scripture thow may se
At lenth this wofull miserie.
  This miserie become, but weir,
Frome Noyis flude thre hundreth yeir,

Togidder with four score and alevin,
As comptit Carione, full evin
And efter Noyis deith, I ges,
Ane and fourtye yeir thare wes;
Quhen Abraham was of aige, I wene,
Foure score of yeris and nyntene;
Quhen this foule syn of sodomye
Was puneisit so regorouslye.
Gret God preserve us, in our tyme,
That we commit nocht sic ane cryme.
  Teddious it wer for me to tell,
This Monarchie duryng, quhat befell,
And wounderis that in erth wer wrocht,
Quhilk to thy purpose langith nocht:
As quhow the peple of Israell — Exod. i
Did lang tyme in to Egypt dwell;
And of thare gret puneisioun,
Throuch Pharois persecutioun;
And quhow Moyses did thame convoye
Throuch the Reid Sey, with mekle joye, — Exod. xiiii.
Quhare kyng Pharo, rycht misarably,
Wes drownit with all his huge army;
And quhow that peple wanderand wes
Fourtye yeris in wyldernes:
Moyses, that tyme, as I heir saye, — Exod. xx.
Ressavit the Law on Mont Sinay;
That tyme, Josue throuch Jordan — Josue. iii.
Led those peple to Canaan;
Quhare Saule, David, and Salamone,
With Hebrew kyngis mony one,
Did rychelye ryng in that countre,

Induryng this First Monarchie.
The Sege of Thebes, miserabyll,
Quhare blude wes sched incomparabyll
Of nobyll men, in to those dayis,
With utheris terribyll affrayis ;
As quhow the Grekis wrocht vengeance
Apone the nobyll Troyiance,
Because that Pareis did convoye,
Perfors, fair Helena to Troye,
Quhilk wes king Menelaus wyfe,
Quhare mony one thousand lost thare lyfe.
  That tyme, the valyeant Hercules
Out throuch the warld did hym addres,
Quhare he did mony ane douchtye deid,
As in his storye thow may reid ;
And quhow, throuch Dyonere, his wyfe,
That campione did lose his lyfe :
In flammand fyre full furiouslye
The deith he sufferit creuellye.
  That tyme Remus and Romulus
Did found that Cietie most famous
Of Rome, standing in Italie,
As in thare storye thow may se.
Wald thow reid Titus Levius,
Thow suld fynd warkis wounderus ;
Quhose douchtye deidis ar weill kende,
And salbe to the warldis ende ;
Thocht thay began with creueltie,
And endit with miseritie :
As bene the maner, to conclude,
Of all scheddaris of saikles blude.

In Grece the ornat Poetry,
Medecene, Musike, Astronomy,
Duryng this First Monarchie began;
Be Homerus, that famous man,
Togydder with Hesiodus,
As divers Auctouris schawis us:
It wer to lang to put in ryme
The bukis quhilk thay wret in thare tyme.
Thir wer the actis principall,
That Monarchye duryng, quhilk befell.
As for gude Abraham and his seid, Gene. xvii.
In to the Bibyll thow may reid
Quhow, in this tyme, as I heir tell
Began the Kyngdome Spirituall,
As I have schawin to thee affore;
Quharefor I speik of thame no more.

ANE SCHORT DISCRIPTIOUN OF THE SECUND, THRID, AND FERD MONARCHIE.

COURTEOUR.

FATHER, said I, quhilk wes the man
That the nyxt Monarchye began?

EXPERIENCE.

Cyrus, said he, the Kyng of Pers,
As Cronicles hes done rehers,
Prudent, and full of pollicye,
Began the secunde Monarchye:

For he wes the most godly kyng
That ever in Pers or Mede did ryng;
For he, of his benygnitie,
II Para. xxxvi. Delyverit frome captyvitie
The hole peple of Israell,
In to the tyme of Daniell,
The quhilkis had bene presoneris,
In Babilone, sevin score of yeris:
Tharefor God, of his grace benyng,
Gaif hym ane divyne knawleging.
Duryng his tyme as I heir tell,
He usit counsall of Daniell.
Carione at lenth doith specific
Of his marvellous natyvitie,
And of his vertuous upbrynging,
And quhow he vincuste Cresus king,
With mony uther valyeant deid;
As in to Carione thow may reid,
Quhose successioun did indure
Tyll the tent Kyng, thareof be sure.
  Bot, efter his gret conquessyng,
Rycht miserabyll wes his endyng.
As Herodotus doith discryfe.
In Scythia he lost his lyfe,
Quhare the undantit Scythianis,
Vincuste those nobyll Persianis:
And, efter that Cyrus was dede,
Quene Tomyre hakkit off his hede,
Quhilk wes the Quene of Scythianis,
In the dispyte of Persianis:
Scho kest his heid, for to conclude,

In tyll ane vessell full of blude,
And said thir wourdis, creuellye :
Drynk, now, thy fyll, gyf thow be drye ;
For thow did aye blude schedding thryste,
Now drynk at laser, gyf thow lyste.
Efter that, Cyrus successioun
Of all the warld had possesioun,
Tyll Alexander, with sweird and fyre,
Obtenit perfors, the Thrid Impyre,
Quhilk wes the king of Macedone :
With valyeant Grekis mony one,
In battell fell and furious,
Vincuste the mychtie Darius,
Quhilk wes the tent and the laste kyng
Quhilk did efter king Cyrus ryng.
As for this potent Empriour,
Alexander the Conquerour,
Geve thow at lenth wald reid his ryng,
And of his creuell conquessyng,
In Inglis toung, in his gret Buke,
At lenth his Lyfe thare thow may luke ;
Quhow Alexander, that potent Kyng,
Wes twelf yeris in his conquessyng ;
And quhow, for all his gret conquest,
He levit bot ane yeir in rest,
Quhen be his servand secretlye
He poysonit wes, full pietuouslye.
Lucane doith Alexander compair
Tyll thounder, or fyreflaucht in the air,
One creuell planeit, a mortall weird
Doun thryngand peple with his sweird.

Ganges, that moste famous flude,
He myxit with the Indianis blude;
And Euphrates, with the blude of Pers:
Quhose creueltie for to rehers,
And saikles blude quhilk he did sched,
War rycht abhominabyll to be red.
Efter his schort prosperitie,
He deit with gret miseritie.
It wer too lang for to dissyd it.
Quhow all his realmes wer devydit.
  Aye quhill that Cesar Julyus,
Quhen he had vincust Pompeyus,
Wes chosin Empriour and Kyng,
Abufe the Romanis for tyll ryng,
That potent Prince wes the first man
Quhilk the Ferd Monarchie began;
And had the hole dominioun
Of everilk land and regioun:
Quhose successouris did ryng, but weir,
Ouer the warld, mony one hundreth yeir,
Bot gentyll Julyus, allace!
Rang Empriour bot lytill space,
Quhilk I thynk pietye tyll deplore:
In fyve moneth and lytill more,
By fals exhorbitant treasoun,
That prudent Prince wes trampit doun
And murdrest, in his counsall hous,
By creuell Brutus and Cassius.
  Efter that Julyus wes slane,
Did ryng the gret Octaviane,
Of Emprlouris one of the best:

Duryng his tyme wes peace and rest
Ouer all the warld, in ilk regioun,
As storyis makith mentioun.
And als I mak it to thee plane,
Duryng the tyme of Octaviane,
The Sonne of God, our Lord Jesew,
Tuke mankynd of the Virgine trew,
And wes that tyme, in Bethelem borne,
To saif mankynde, quhilk wes forlorne; Math. ii.
As Scripture makith narratioun
Of his blyst Incarnatioun.
Now haif I tald thee as I can,
Quhow the Foure Monarchyis began.
Bot, in thy mynd, thow may consydder
Quhow warldly power bene bot slydder;
For all thir gret Impyris ar gone:
Thow seis thair is no Prince allone
Quhilk hes the hole dominioun,
This tyme, of every Regioun.

COURTEOUR.

Father, quhat reasone had those Kyngis
Rewarris to be of utheris Ryngis,
But ony rycht or juste querrell,
Quhairthrouch that thay mycht mak battell,
And commoun pepyll to doun thryng?
To this, said I, mak answeryng.

EXPERIENCE.

My Sonne, said he, that sall be done
As I best can, and that rycht sone.

Thir Monarcheis, I understand,
Preordinat wer by the command
Of God, the Plasmatour of all,
Dani. vii. For to doun thryng and to mak thrall
Undantit peple vitious,
And als for to be gratious
To thame quhilk vertuous wer and gude:
As Daniell heth done conclude,
At lenth, in tyll his Propheseis,
Quhow thare suld be Foure Monarcheis.
His secund chepture thow maye see:
Quhow, efter the First Monarchie,
Quhen Nabuchodonosor kyng
Ane ymage sawe, in his slepyng,
With austeir luke, boyth heych and breid;
And of fyne pure gold wes his heid,
His breist and armes of sylver brycht,
His wambe of copper, hard and wycht,
His loynis and lymmis of irne rycht strong,
His feit of clay, irne mixt among.
Frome a montane thare come allone,
But hand of man, a mekle stone,
Quhilk on that figouris feit did fall,
And dang all doun in poulder small.
Of quhose interpretatioun
Doctouris doith mak narratioun:
The hede of gold did signifye,
First, of Assyrianis Monarchye;
The sylver breist thay did apply
To Persianis, quhilk rang Secundly;
The wambe of copper or of brasse,

Thridly, to Greikis comparit was ;
His loynis and lymmis of irne and steill,
Clerkis hes thame comparit weill
To Romanis, throuch thare diligence
To have the Feird preemynence
Abufe all uther Natioun.
Be this interpretatioun,
The myxit feit with irne and clay
Did signifye this letter day,
Quhen that the warld sulde be devydit,
As efterwart salbe disydit,
To Christ is signifyit the stone,
Quhose Monarchie sall never be gone ;
For under his dominioun
All Princis sall be trampit doun.
Quhen that gret Kyng Omnipotent
Cumis to his Generall Jugement,
His Monarchie, than, salbe knawin,
As efter sall be to thee schawin.
  And als the Scripture sall thee tell
Quhow, in the aucht of Daniell,
He saw, in to his visioun,
Be ane plane expositioun,
Quhow that the Grekis sulde wyrk vengeance
Upone the Medis and Persience ;
Comparand Grekis tyll ane goate
With ane horne, feirs, furious, and hote,
Quhilk slew the ram with hornis two,
Comparit tyll Pers, and Mede also.
And so, be Daniellis prophesyis,
All thir gret mychtie Monarchyis,

The quhilkis all uther realmes supprysit,
Be the gret God thay wer devysit:
As He of Tytus the Romane,
Sonne and air to Vespasiane,
Maid hym ane furious instrument,
To put the Jowis to gret torment;
Quhilk I purpose, or I hyne fair,
Schortlie that processe to declair.

OF THE MOST MISERABILL AND MOST TERRABILL DISTRUCTIOUN OF JERUSALEM.

COURTEOUR.

FATHER, said I, declare to me
Induryng this Ferd Monarchie
The maist infortune that befell.

EXPERIENCE.

My Sonne, said he, that sall I tell.
The moist and manyfest misarie
Became apon the gret cietie
Baru. vi. Jerusalem, quhen it wes supprest,
As storyis makis manifest.
Bot, as the Scripture doith devyse,
Jerusalem wes distroyit twyse;
First, for the gret idolatrye
Quhilk thay commyttit in Jowrye:
The honour aucht to God allone
Thay gaif figuris of stoke and stone.
Affore Christis Incarnatioun

Come this first desolatioun,
Fyve hundreth yeris, four score, and ten,
In Cronicles as thow may ken:
Quhow Nabuchodonosor kyng
That famous citie did doun thryng;
Thare Kyng, with peple mony one,
Brocht thame, all bound, to Babilone,
Quhare thay remanit presoneris
The space of thre score and ten yeris:
And that first desolatioun
Wes callit the Transmigratioun.
Wes no man left, in all thare landis,
Bot purellis lauborand with thare handis,
Tyll mychtie Cyrus, king of Pers,
As Daniell heth done rehers,
Wes movit, be God, for tyll restore
The Jowis quhare that thay wer afore.
  Geve I neglect, I wer to blame,
The last Sege of Jerusalem,
Quhose rewyne wes most miserabyll,
And for to tell rycht terrabyll;
Wes never, in erth, citie nor toun,
Gatt sic extreme distructioun:
The townis of Tyre, Thebes, nor Troye,
Thay sufferit never half sic noye:
The Emprioure Vespasiane
He did devyse that Sege certane.
  Thare wes the Prophesie compleit Luc. xix. xxi.
Quhilk Christ spake on mont Olyveit. Mark. xiii.
Quhen he Jerusalem beheld,
The teiris frome his eine disteld:

Seand, be Divyne prescience,
The gret distructioun and vengence
Quhilk wes to cum on that cietie,
His hart wes persit with pietie,
Sayand, Jerusalem, and thow knew
The gret rewyne, sore wald thow rew;
For no thyng I can to thé schaw,
The veritie thow wyll nocht knaw,
Nor hes in consydderatioun
Thy holy visitatioun;
Thy peple wyll no way consydder.
Mathew xxiii. Quham gadderit I wald haif togidder,
As errand scheip bene with thare hirdis;
Or as the hen gadderis hir byrdis
Under hir wyngis, tenderlye,
Quhilk thay refusit dispitfullye:
Quharefor sall cum that dulefull day,
That no remedy mak thow may;
Thy dungeounis sall be dung in schounder,
So that the warld sall on thé wounder;
Thy Tempyll, now most tryumphand,
Mathew xxiv. Sall be tred doun amang the sand.
And, as he said, so it befell,
As heir efter I sall thé tell.

COURTEOUR.

Schaw me, said I, with circumstance,
The speciall cause of that myschance.

EXPERIENCE.

Quod he, As Scripture doith conclude,

For scheddyng of the saikles blude
Of Prophetis, quhilkis God to thame send,
And, als, because that thay myskend
Jesu, the Sonne of God Soverane,
Quhen he amang thame did remane.
For all the myraklis that he schew,
Maliciouslye thay hym mysknew;
Thocht, be his gret power divyne,
The walter cleir he turnit in wyne, Jhon. ii.
And, be that self power and mycht,
To the blynde borne he gaif the sycht,
And gaif the crukit men thair feit,
And maid the lippir haill compleit;
He hailit all, and raisit the dede; Jhon. xi.
Yit held thay hym at mortall fede. Math. x.
Because he schew the veritie,
Thay did conclude that he sulde dé.
  The Byschoppis, princis of the preistis,
They grew so boldin, in thare breistis; Math. xvii.
The Scrybis, the Doctouris of the law,
Of God nor man quhilkis stude none aw
On Christ Jesu to wyrk vengeance;
Rycht so, the fals Pharesiance,
Ane sect of fenyeit religioun,
Devysit his confusioun,
And send thare servandis, at the last,
And with strang cordis thay band hym fast, Jho. xix.
Syne scurgit hym, boith bak and syde,
That none for blude mycht se his hyde:
Thare wes nocht left ane penny breid
Unwoundit, frome his feit tyll heid.

In maner of derisioun,
Thay plett for hym ane creuell croun
Of prunyeand thornis, scharpe and lang,
Quhilk on his hevinlye heid thay thrang;
Syne gart hym, for the gretter lack,
Beir his awin gallous on his back,
Tyll the vyle place of Calvarie,
Quhare mony ane thousand man mycht se.
That Innocent thay tuke, perforce,
And platt hym bakwart to the Croce;
Throuch feit and handis greit nalis thay thryst.
Tyll blude aboundantlye out bryst:
Without grunschyng, clamor, or crye,
That pane he sufferit patientlye.
And, for agmentyng of his grefis,
Thay hangit hym betuix two thefis;
Quhare men mycht se the bludy strandis
Quhilkis sprang furth of his feit and handis:
Frome thornis thristit on his heid,
Ran doun the bulryng stremis reid:
In the presens of mony one man,
That blude royall on roches ran.
Schortly to say, that hevinlye Kyng
In extreme dolour thare did hyng,
Tyll he said, *Consummatum est*,
With a loud crye, he gaif the gaist.
Quhen he was dede, thay tuke one dart,
And peirst that Prence outthrouch the hart,
Fra quham thare ran walter and blude.
The eirth than trymblit, to conclude;
Phebus did hyde his beymes brycht,

That throuch the warld thare wes no lycht;
The gret vaill of the tempyll rave;
The dede men rais out of thare grave,
And in the Citie did appeir,
As in the Scripture thow may heir,
  Than Joseph, of Abarimathie,
Did bury him rycht honestlie:
Bot yit he rose, full gloriouslye, Jhon xx.
On the third day, tryumphandlye.
With his Disciplis, in certane,
Fourtye dayis he did remane;
Efter that, to the Hevin ascendit. Actis i.
Thir Jowis no thyng thare lyfe amendit,
Nor gaif no credens tyll his sawis,
As at more lenth the storye schawis,
Bot cruellye thay did oppres
All men that Christis name did profes,
And persecutit mony one:
Thay presonit boith Peter and Johne; Actis v.
And Stewin thay stonit to the dede; Actis vii.
Frome James the less thay straik the hede.
This wes the cause, in conclusioun,
Of thare creuell confusioun.
  The prudent Jow, Josephus, sayis
That he wes present in those dayis;
And, in his buke, makith mentioun,
Quhow, efter Christis Ascensioun
The space of twa and fourty yeris,
Began those creuell mortall weris,
The secund yeir of Vespasiane,
Quhare mony takin wer and slane.

Josephus planely doith conclude,
Wes never sene sic one multytude,
Affore that tyme, in to the toun,
Quhilk come for thare confusioun.
Thare gret infortune so befell,
That all the Princis of Israell
Convenit agane the tyme of Pace,
Bot tyll returne thay had no grace.
The bald Romanis, with thare chiftane,
Tytus, the sonne of Vespasiane,
Thare army ouer Judea spread:
Than all men to the cietie fled,
Belevand thare to get releif;
Bot all that turnit to thare myschief.
  The Romanis lappit thame about,
That be no waye thay mycht wyn out.
Sax moneth did that Sege indure,
Quhare loste wer mony one creature,
Quhilkis thare in misary did remane,
Tyll thay wer takin, all, or slane.
Duryng the tyme of this assailye,
Thare meit, and drynk, and all did failye;
For thare wes sic ane multytude,
That thousandis deit for falt of fude.
Necessitie gart thame eit, perforsse,
Dog, catt, and rattone, asse, and horsse.
Ryche men behuffit tyll eate thare gold,
Syne deit of hunger mony fold.
Sic hunger wes without remeid
The quick behuffit tyll eate the deid:
The fylth of closettis mony eit;

To lenth thare lyfe thay thocht it sweit.
The famous ladyis of the toun,
For falt of fude, thay fell in swoun:
Quhen thay mycht gett none uther meit,
Thay slew thare propir bairnis to eit;
Bot all for nocht, dispytfullye,
Thare awin sowldiouris, full gredelye,
Reft thame that flesche most miserabyll;
And thay, with murnyng lamentabyll,
For extreme hunger, zald the spreit.
Thare wes the Prophesie compleit, Luc. xxiiii.
As Christ affore made narratioun,
The day of his grym Passioun.
Quhen that the ladyis for hym murnit,
Full pietuouslye he to thame turnit,
And said, Douchteris, murne nocht for me;
Murne on your awin posteritie:
Within schort tyme sall cum the day
That men of this Cietie sall say,
Quhen thay ar trappit in the snair,
Blyst be the wambe that never bair;
The barren paupis, than thay sall blys:
That dulefull day ye sall nocht mys.
This Prophesie it come to pas,
That day, with mony lowde Allas!
Sic sorrowfull lamentatioun
Wes never hard in that natioun.
Seand those lustye ladyis sweit
Deand for hunger in the streit,
Thare husbandis, nor thare chyldring,
Mycht geve to thame na comforting,

Nor yit releif thame of thir harmis,
Bot atheris deand in utheris armis.
Efter this wofull indigence,
Amang thame rose sic pestilence,
Quharein thair deit mony hounder,
Quhilk tyll declare it wer gret wounder.
 And, for fynall conclusioun,
Those weirlyke wallis thay dang doun.
Prince Tytus, with his chevalrye,
With sound of trompe, triumphandlye
He enterrit in that gret Cietie.
Bot tyll declare I thynk pietie
The panefull clamour horribyll.
Of woundit folk most miserabyll.
Thare wes nocht ellis bot tak and slay;
For thare mycht no man wyn away.
The strandis of blude ran throuch the streitis
Of dede folk trampit under fetis;
Auld wedowis in the preis wer smorit;
Young virginis, schamefully deflorit;
The gret Tempyll of Salamone,
With mony a curious carvit stone,
With perfyte pynnakles on hycht,
Quhilkis wer rycht bewtyfull and wycht,
Quhare in ryche jowellis did abound,
Thay ruscheit rudlye to the ground,
And sett, in tyll thare furious yre,
Sancta Sanctorum in to fyre;
And, with extreme confusioun,
All thare gret dungeounis thay dang doun.
 Thare bursin wer the boldin breistis

Of byschoppis, princis of the preistis :
Thare takin wes the gret vengeance
On fals scrybis and pharisience.
All thare payntit ipocrasie,
That tyme, mycht mak thame no supplie.
That day thay dulefullye repentit
That to the deith of Christe consentit :
Thocht it wes our salvatioun,
It wes to thare dampnatioun.
The vengeance of the blude saikles,
Frome Abell tyll Zacharies, Math. xxiii.
That day apon Jerusalem fell.
Bot teddious it wer to tell
The gret extreme confusioun,
And of blude sic effusioun :
Wes never slane so mony ane man,
At one tyme, sen the warld began.
The Jowis, that day, gat thare desyre,
Quhilk thay did aske, in to thare yre,
As bene in Scripture specifyit,
The day quhen Christe wes crucifyit.
Quhen Ponce Pylat, the president, Math. xxvii.
Said to thame, I am innocent
Of the just blude of Christ Jesus,
Thay cryit, His blude lycht upon us,
And on our generatioun :
Thay gat thare supplicatioun :
That day, with mony cairfull cry,
Thare blude was sched aboundantly.
  Josephus wryttith, in his buke,
His Cronicle quho lyste to luke,

Duryng that creuell sege, certane,
Wer alewin hundreth thowsand slane;
Of presonaris, weill tauld and sene,
Foure score of thousandis, and sevintene.
Out of the land thay did expell
All the peple of Israell,
And, for thare gret ingratytude,
Thay leif yit under servytude.
Thare is no Jow, in no countre,
Quhilk hes one fute of propertie,
Nor never had, withouttin weir,
Sen this day fyftene hundreth yeir,
Nor never sall, I to thé schaw,
Tyll that thay turne to Christis law.
  Sum sayis that Jowis mony fald
Wer thretty for ane penny sald;
As Judas sauld the Kyng of Glore
For thretty pennyis, and no more.
  Efter that mony wer myschevit,
Quhen novellis past quhow lang thay levit
Apone thare gold, withouttin doute
Thay slyt thare bellyis, to sers it oute.
The rest in Egypt thay did sende,
Presonaris to thare lyvis ende.
Tytus tuke in his cumpanye
Gret nummer of the most worthye,
With him to Rome, he led thame bound,
Syne creuelly did thame confound:
His victory for tyll decore,
And for agmentyng of his glore,
Gart put thame in to publict placis,

Quhare all folk mycht behald thare facis;
Syne with wyld lyonis creuellye
He gart devore thame dulefullye.
This hie, tryumphand, mychtie Toun
At Pasche wes put to confusioun,
Because that in the tyme of Pace
Thay crucifyit the Kyng of Grace.
Sum hes this mater done indyte
More ornatly than I can wryte;
Quharefor I speik of it no more:
Onely to God be laude and glore.

OF THE MISERABILL END OF CERTANE TYRANE PRINCIS; AND SPECIALLYE THE BEGYNNARIS OF THE FOURE MONARCHEIS.

EXPERIENCE.

Now have I done declare, at thy desyris,
As thow demandit, in to termys schort,
And quhow began the principall Impyris,
As Cronicle and Scripture dois report:
Quhairfor, my Sone, I hartly thee exhort,
Perfytlie prent in thy remembrance
Of this inconstante warld the variance.

The Princis of thir Foure gret Monarcheis,
In thare most hiest pompe Imperiallis,
Traistyng to be moist sure sett in thare seis,
The fraudful warld gaif to thame mortall fallis,
For thare rewarde, bot dyrk memoriallis:

Thocht ouir the warld thay had preheminence,
Of it thay gat none uther recompence.

For, siclyke as the snaw doith melt in May,
  Throuch the reflex of Phebus bemys brycht,
Thir gret Impyris rycht so ar went away:
  Gone bene thare glore, thair power, and thare mycht,
  Because thay wer revaris withouttin rycht,
And blude scheddaris full creuell, to conclude:
Rycht creuellye, tharefor, wes sched thare blude.

Behald quhow God, aye sen the warld began,
  Hes maid of Tyrrane Kyngis instrumentis
To scurge peple, and to keill mony one man,
  Quhilkis to his law wer inobedientis:
  Quhen thay had done perfurneis his ententis,
In dantyng wrangus peple schamefullye,
He sufferit thame be scurgit creuellye;

Evin as the scule maister doith mak ane wand,
  To dant and dyng scollaris of rude ingyne,
The quhilkis wyll nocht study at his command:
  He scurgis thame, and only to that fyne,
  That thay suld to his trew counsall inclyne;
Quhen thay obey, and meisit bene his yre,
He takis the wand and castis in to the fyre.

God of kyng Pharo maid one instrument,
  Quhilk wes the gret kyng of Egyptience,
His awin peculiar peple to torment:

That beand done, he wrocht on hym vengence, Exo. vii.
And leit hym fall throuch inobedience;
And, fynallie, he, with his gret armye,
In the Reid Sey thame drownit dulefullye. Exo. xiiii.

Rycht so, of Nabuchodonosor kyng,
God maid of hym ane furious instrument,
Jerusalem and the Jowis to doun thryng,
Quhen thay to God wer inobedient; Dan. iiii.
Syne reft hym frome his ryches and his rent,
And hym transformit in ane beist brutell,
Sevin yeris and more, as wryttis Daniell.

Alexander, throuch prydefull tyrranye,
In yeris twelf did mak his gret conquest,
Aye scheddand saikles blude full creuellye;
Tyll he wes Kyng of kyngis, he tuke no rest:
In all the warld quhen he wes full possest,
In Babilone thronit tryumphantlye,
Throuch poysoun strang, deceisit dulefullye.

Duke Hanniball, the strang Cartagiane,
The danter of the Romanis pompe and glorye,
Be his power wer mony one thousand slane,
As may be red at lenth in tyll his storye.
At Cannas, quhare he wan the victorye,
On Romanis handis that dede lay on the ground,
Three heipit buschellis wer of ryngis found.

In to that mortall battell, I heir sane,
Of the Romanis moste worthy weriouris,

By presonaris, wer fourty thousand slane;
  Of quhom thare wes thretty wyse Senatouris,
  And twentye Lordis, the quhilkis had bene Pretouris,
That deit in to defence of thare countre,
And for tyll hald thare lande at lybertie.

Quhat rewarde gatt this creuell campioun,
  Quhen he had slane so gret one multytude,
And quhen the glasse of his glorye wes roun?
  Ane schamefull deith, and, schortlye to conclude,
  This bene reward of all scheddaris of blude;
For he gat sic extreme confusioun,
He slew hymself in drynking strang poysoun.

Behald the twa moste famous campionis,
  That is to say, Julyus and Pompey,
Quhilkis did conquesse all erthly Regionis,
  Alsweill maine land as Ylis in the sey,
  And to the toun of Rome gart thame obey:
For Pompeyus subdewit the Orient;
And Julyus Cesar, all the Occident.

Bot fynaly, thir two did stryve for stait,
  Quharethrow three hundreth thowsand men were slane;
Bot Pompeyus, efter that gret debait,
  He murdreist wes, the storye tellis plane.
  Than Julyus wes prince and soverane,
Abufe the hole warld Empriour and Kyng;
Bot, in to rest, schorte tyme indurit his ryng:

For, within fyve moneth and lytill more,
Amyd his Lordis in the counsall hous,
He murdreist wes, quhat nedeth proces more?
As I have said, be Brute and Cassius.
Geve thow wald knaw thare dethis dolorous,
Thow most lenth go reid the Romane storye,
Quhilk hes this mater put in memorye.

Gone is the Goldin warld of Asserianis,
Of quhome kyng Nynus wes first and principall;
Gone is the Sylver warld of Persianis;
The Copper warld of Grekis now is thrall;
The warld of Irne, quhilk wes the last of all,
Comparit to the Romanis in thare glore,
Ar gone, rycht so, I heir of thame no more.

Now is the warld of irne myxit with clay,
As Daniell at lenth hes done indyte:
The gret Impyris ar meltit clene away;
Now is the warld of dolour and dispyte.
I sé nocht ellis bot troubyll infinyte:
Quharefor, my Sonne, I mak it to thé kend,
This Warld, I wait, is drawand to ane end.

Tokynnis of darth, hunger, and pestilence,
With creuell weris, boith be sey and land,
Realme aganis realme with mortall violence,
Quhilk signifyis the last day evin at hand:
Quharefor, my Sonne, be in thy faith constand,
Rasyng thy heart to God, and cry for grace,
And mend thy lyfe, quhill thow hes tyme and space

HEIR FOLLOWIS THE FYRST SPIRITUALL AND PAPALL MONARCHIE.

COURTEOUR.

FATHER, Is thare no Prynce ringand,
Quhilk hes the Warld now at command;
As had the Kyngis of Asserianis,
The Persis, Grekis, or the Romanis?
Quho hes now, most dominioun
Of everilk land and regioun?

EXPERIENCE.

Thare is no Prince, my Sonne, said he,
That hes the principall Monarchie
Abufe the warld universall,
With hole power Imperiall,
As Alexander, or Darius,
Or as had Cesar Julyus:
For Orient and Occident
To thame wer all obedient.
Nochtwithstandyng, I find one kyng
Quhilk in tyll Europe doith ryng,
That is, the potent Pope of Rome,
Impyrand ouir all Christindome,
To quhome no Prince may be compare,
As Canon Lawis can declare.
All Princis of the Occident
Ar tyll his Grace obedient;
For he hes hole power compleit

Boith of the body and the spreit,
Quhilk never had no Prince affore,
Except the mychtie Kyng of Glore:
To Christe he is gret Lewtennand,
In holy Peteris saitt syttand:
So he is of all kyngis Kyng
Quhilkis in to Europe now doith ryng.
  And, as the Romane Emprìouris,
Havyng the Warld under thare curis,
Had princis, knychtis, and campiounis,
Rewlaris in tyll all Regiounis,
Uphaldyng thare auctoritie,
Usyng justice and policie;
Rycht so, this potent Pope of Rome,
The soverane kyng of Christindome,
He hes, in tyll ilk countré,
His Princis of gret gravytie;
In sum countreis, his Cardinallis,
In thare moste precious apparallis;
Archbyschoppis, byschoppis, thow may se,
Defendyng his auctoritie,
With uther potent patriarkis;
Collegis full of cunnyng clerkis;
Abbottis and priouris, as ye ken,
Misrewlaris of religious men;
Officiallis, with thare procuratouris,
Quhose langsum law spoilyeis the puris;
Archidenis and denis of dignitie;
Gret doctouris of divynitie;
Thare chantouris, and thare sacristanis,
Thare tresouraris, and thare subdenis;

Legionis of preistis seculeris,
Personis, vicairis, monkis, and freris,
Of divers Ordouris mony one,
Quhilk langsum wer for tyll expone,
In syndrie habitis, as ye ken,
Different frome uther Christin men;
Fair ladyis of religioun
Proffessit, in every regioun;
Fals heremitis, fassionit lyke the freris;
Proude parische clerkis, and pardoneris,
Thare gryntaris, and thare chamberlanis,
With thare temporall courtissianis,
Thus, all the warld, be land and sey,
His Sanctitude thay do obey:
Nocht onely his Spirituall kyngdome,
Bot the gret Empriour of Rome,
And Kyngis of everilk regioun,
That day quhen thay resave thare crown,
Thay mak aith of fidelytie
Tyll defende his auctorytie:
Moreovir, with humyll reverence,
Thay mak tyll hym obedience,
Be thare selfis, or ambassadouris,
Or utheris ornate oratouris.
Quho doith ganestand his Majestie,
His lawis, or his lybertie,
Or haldis ony opinioun
Contrar his gret dominioun,
Outher be way of deid or wordis,
Ar put to deith, be fyre or swordis:
Sanct Peter stylit wes *Sanctus;*

Bot he is callit *Sanctissimus*:
His style at lenth gyf thow wald knaw,
Thow moste go luke the Canon Law,
Boith in the Sext and Clementene:
His staitly style thare may be sene:
Thare sall thow fynd, reid gyf thow can,
Quhow he is nother God nor man.

COURTEOUR.

Quhat is he than, be your jugement?
Quod I, me thynk hym different,
Far from our Soverane, Lord Jesus,
And tyll his kynd contrarious:
For Christ wes God and naturall man. Jhon I.
Gyf he be nother, quhat is he than?

EXPERIENCE.

The Canon Law, my Sonne, said he,
That questioun wyll declare to thé.
It doith transcend my rude ingyne
His Sanctitude for tyll defyne,
Or to schaw the auctoritie
Pertenyng to his Majestie.
So gret one Prince quhare sall thow fynd,
That spiritually may lowse and bynd;
Nor be quhame synnis ar forgyffin,
Be thay with his disciplis schrevin?
Quhame ever he byndis by his mycht,
Thay boundin ar in Goddis sycht:
Quhame ever he lousis in erth heir doun,
Ar lousit be God in his regioun.

Als he is Prince of Purgatorie,
Delyvering saulis frome paine to glorie:
Of that dirke dungeoun, but doute,
Quham evir he plesis he takis thame oute.
Oure secreit synnis, every yeir,
We mon schaw to sum preist or freir,
And tak thare absolutioun,
Or ellis we gett no remissioun;
So, be this way, thay cleirly ken
The secretis of all seculare men;
Thare secretis we knaw nocht at all:
Thus ar we to thame bound and thrall.
Quhat evir thare ministeris commandis
Most be obeyit, without demandis.
Quharefor, my Sonne, I say to thé,
This is ane marvellous Monarchie,
Quhilk hes power Imperiall
Boith of the body and the saull.

COURTEOUR.

Father, quod I, declare to me
Quhow did begyn this Monarchie.

EXPERIENCE.

Quod he, Christ Jesus, God and Man,
That Impyre gratiouslye began,
Nocht be the fyre, nor be the swourde,
Bot be the vertew of his wourde;
Ephes. i. And left, in tyll his Testament,
Luc. ix. Mony ane devote document,
With his successouris to be usit,

Thocht mony of thame be now abusit.
For Peter and Paull, with all the rest
Of thare brethrin, maid manifest
The law of God, with trew intent,
Precheing the Auld and New Testament.
Thay led thare lyfe in povertie,
Devotioun, and humilytie,
As did thare maister, Christ Jesus;
And war nocht half so glorious
As thare successouris now in Rome,
Impyrand ouer all Christindome.
  Efter the deth of Peter and Paull,
And Christis trew disciplis all,
Thare successouris, within few yeris,
As at more lenth thare storye beris,
Full craftelye clam to the heycht,
Frome Spirituall lyfe to Temporall mycht.

COURTEOUR.

  Father, or we passe forthermore,
Quhen did begyn thare Temporall glore?

EXPERIENCE.

  Sonne, said he, thow sall understand,
Or ever ane Pape gat ony land,
Twa and thretty gude Papis in Rome
Ressavit the Crown of martyrdome,
Bot nocht the thrinfald diadame;
To weir thré crownis thay thocht gret schame:
Tyll Sylvester the Confessoure
Frome Constantene the Emprioure
Ressavit the Realme of Italie,

Rycht so, of Rome the gret cietie.
That wes the rute of thare ryches:
Then sprang the well of welthynes.
Quhen that the Pape wes maid ane kyng,
All Princis bowit at his biddyng:
This act wes done, withouttin weir,
Frome Christis deith thre hundreth yeir.
  Than Lady Sensualitie
Tuke lugeing in that gret Cietie,
Quhare scho sensyne hes done remane,
As thare awin lady Soverane.
Than Kyngis, in tyll all Nationis,
Maid Preistis gret fundationis:
Thay thocht gret mereit and honour
To contrafait the Empriour;
As did David, of Scotland kyng,
The quhilk did founde, duryng his ryng,
Fyftene Abbayis, with temporall landis,
Withouttin teindis and offerandis;
Be quhose holy simplicitie
He left the Crown in povertie.
  Now haif I, schawin thee as I can,
Quhow thare Temporall impyre began,
Ascendying up, aye gre by gre,
Abufe the Empriouris Majestie.
So, quhen thay gat amang thare handis
Of Italie all the Empriouris landis,
Efter that, in ilke countrie
Sprang up thare temporalitie,
With so gret ryches and sic rent,
That thay gan to be negligent
In makyng ministratioun

To Christis trew Congregatioun,
And tuke no more paine in thare precheing,
And far les travell in thare techeing;
Changeing thare Spiritualitie
In Temporall sensualitie.

COURTEOUR.

Father, thynk ye that thay ar sure
That thare Impyre sall lang indure?

EXPERIENCE.

Apperandlye it may be kende,
Quod he, thare glore sall have ane ende:
I mene, thare Temporall Monarchie
Sall turne in tyll humylitie.
Throuch Goddis worde, without debait,
Thay sall turne to thare first estait:
As Daniellis prophesie apperis,
Thareto sall nocht be mony yeris.
Quhowbeit Christis faith sall never faill,
Bot more and more it sall prevaill;
Thocht Christis trew Congregatioun
Suffer gret trybulatioun.

COURTEOUR.

Father, said I, be quhat reasoun
Thynk ye thare Impyre may cum doun?

EXPERIENCE.

Consydderyng thare preheminence,
Quod he, for inobedience;

Abusyng the commandiment
Math. xxv. Quhilk Christ left in his Testament;
Usyng thare awin traditioun
More than his institutioun:
For Christ, in his last conventioun,
The day of his Ascensioun,
Math. xxviii. Tyll his Disciplis gaif command,
Jhone xv. That thay suld passe in every land,
Acts i. To teche and preche, with trew intent,
His law and his commandiment:
None uther office he to thame gaif:
He did nocht bid thame seik nor craif
Cors presentis, nor offerandis,
Nor gett Lordschipis of temporall landis.
  Bot now it may be hard and sene,
Baith with thyne eiris and thyne eine,
Quhow Prelatis now, in every land,
Takis lytill cure of Christis command,
Nouther in to thare deidis nor sawis;
Neglectyng thare awin Canon Lawis,
Usying thame selfis contrarious,
For the maist part, to Christ Jesus.
Math. iiii. Christ thocht no schame to be ane precheour,
And tyll all peple of trewth ane techeour.
Ane Pope, Byschope, or Cardinall,
To teche nor preche wyll nocht be thrall:
Thay send furth Freris, to preche for thame,
Quhilk garris the peple now abhor thame.
  Christ wald nocht be ane Temporall kyng,
Jhon vi. Rychely into no realme to ryng,
Bot fled Temporall auctoritie,

As in the Scripture thow may se.
All men may knaw quhow Popis ryngis,
In dignitie abufe all kyngis,
Als weill in Temporalitie
As in to Spiritualitie.
Thow may se, be experience,
The Popis princely preheminence.
  In Cronicles geve thow lyst to luke,
Quhow Carion wryttis, in his buke,
Ane notabyll narratioun :
The yeir of oure Salvatioun
Ellewin hundreth and sax and fyftie,
Pope Alexander, presumptuouslie,
Quhilk wes the thrid Pope of that name,
To Frederike Empriour did diffame
In Veneis, that tryumphand town ;
That nobyll Empriour gart ly down
Apone his wambe, with schame and lake,
Syne treid his feit apone his bake,
In toknyng of obedience.
Thare he schew his preheminence,
And causit his Clergy for to syng
Thir wourdis efter following :

Super Aspidem et Basiliscum ambulabis,
Et conculcabis Leonem et Draconem.—(*That is,*)
Thow sal gang upon the eddar and the coketrice, Psal. xci.
And thow sal tred down the lyoun and the dragoun.

Than said this humyll Empriour,
I do to Peter this honour !
The Pope answerit, with wordis wroith,
Thow sall me honour, and Peter boith !

Christ, for to schaw his humyll spreit,
Did wasche his pure Disciplis feit:
The Popis holynes, I wys,
Wyll suffer Kyngis his feit to kys.
Luc. ix. Birdis had thare nestis, and toddis thare den;
Bot Christ Jesus, saiffer of men,
In erth had nocht ane penny breid
Quhare on he mycht repose his heid.
Quhowbeit, the Popis excellence
Hes castellis of magnifycence;
Abbottis, Byschoppis, and Cardinallis
Hes plesand palyces royallis:
Lyke Paradyse ar those prelattis places,
Wantyng no plesoure of fair faces.
Acts iiii. Jhone, Androw, James, Peter, nor Paull
Had few housis amang thame all:
Frome tyme thay knew the veritie
Thay did contempne all propertie,
And wer rycht hartfully content
Of meit, drynk, and abuilyement.
Jhon xix. To saif Mankynde, that wes forlorne,
Christ bure ane creuell crown of thorne;
The Pope, thre crownis, for the nonis,
Of gold, poulderit with pretious stonis.
Of gold and sylver, I am sure,
Christ Jesus tuke bot lytill cure,
And left nocht, quhen he yald the spreit,
To by hym self ane wynding scheit.
Bot his successoure, gude Pope Johne,
Quhen he deceisit in Avinione,
He left behynd hym one treassoure

Of gold and sylver, by mesoure,
Be one juste computatioun,
Weill fyve and twentye myllioun,
As dois indyte Palmerius :
Reid hym, and thow sall fynd it thus.
  Christis Disciplis wer weill knawin
Throuch vertew, quhilk wes be thame schawin,
In speciall fervent charitie,
Gret pacience, and humylitie :
The Popis floke, in all regiounis,
Ar knawin best be thare clyppit crounis.
  Christ he did honour matrimonie
In to the Cane of Galalie,
Quhare he, be his power Divyne,
Did turne the walter in to wyne ;
And, als, cheisit sum maryit men
To be his servandis, as ye ken :
And Peter, duryng all his lyfe,
He thocht no syn to haif ane wyfe.
Ye sall nocht fynd, in no passage,
Quhare Christ forbiddith mariage ;
Bot leifsum tyll ilk man to marye,
Quhilk wantis the gyft of chaistytie.
  The Pope hes maid the contrar lawis
In his kyngdome, as all men knawis :
None of his Preistis dar marye wyfis,
Under no less paine nor thare lyfis.
Thocht thay haif concubynis fyftene,
In to that cace, thay ar ouersene.
Quhat chaistytie thay keip in Rome
Is weill kend ouer all Christindome.

Math. xvii. Christ did schaw his obedience
On to the Empriouris excellence,
And causit Peter for to pay
Trybute to Cesar for thame tway.
Paull biddis us be obedient
To Kyngis, as the most excellent.
The contrar did Pope Celistene,
Quhen that his sanctytude serene
Did crown Henry the Empriour:
I thynk he did hym small honour;
For with his feit he did hym crown,
Syne with his fute the crown dang doun,
Sayand, I haif auctoritie
Men tyll exalt to dignitie,
And to mak Empriouris and Kyngis,
And syne depryve thame of thare ryngis.
Peter, be my opinioun,
Did never use sic dominioun.
Apperandlye, be my jugement,
That Pope red never the New Testament:
Gyf he had lernit at that lore,
He had refusit sic vaine glore,
As Barnabas, Peter, and Paull,
And rycht so, Christis disciplis all.
The Capitane Cornelius,
Acts x. Quhen Sanct Peter come tyll his hous,
Tyll worschyp hym, fell at his feit;
Bot Sanct Peter, with humyll spreit,
Did rais hym up, with diligence,
And did refuse sic reverence.
Rycht so, Sanct Johne the Evangelist

The Angellis feit he wald haif kist; Apoca. xix. and xxii.
Bot he refusit sic honoure,
Sayand, I am bot servitoure,
Rycht so, thy fallow and thy brother:
Gyff glore to God, and to none uther.
  Alykewyis Barnabas and Paull
Sic honour did refuse at all: Acts xiv.
In Listra, quhare thay wroucht gret workis,
The preist of Jupiter, with his clerkis,
And all the peple, with thare avyse,
Wald haif maid to thame sacrifyse;
Of quhilk thay wer so discontent,
That thay thare clothyng raif and rent;
And Paull amang thame rudely ran,
Sayand, I am ane mortall man:
Gyf glore to God, of kyngis Kyng,
That maid hevin, erth, and every thyng.
Sen Peter and Paull vaine glore refusit,
With Popis quhy sulde sic glore be usit?
  Peter, Andro, Johne, James, and Paull,
And Christis trew disciplis all,
Be Goddis worde thare faith defendit;
To byrne and skald thay never pretendit.
The Pope defendis his traditioun
Be flammand fyre, without remissioun:
Quhowbeit men breik the law Divyne,
Thay ar nocht put to so gret pyne,
For huredome, nor idolatrye,
For incest, nor adulterye;
Or quhen young virginnis ar deflorit,
For sic thyng men ar nocht abhorit.

Bot quho that eitis flesche in to Lent
Ar terriblye put to torment;
And gyf ane preist happinnis to marye,
Thay do hym baneis, cursse, and warye,
Thocht it be nocht aganis the law
Of God, as men may cleirlie knaw:
Betuix thir two quhat difference bene,
Be faithfull folke it may be sene.
Sic antitheses mony mo
I mycht declare, quhilkis I lat go,
And may nocht tary to compyle
Of ilk Ordour the staitlye style.
The seilye Nun wyll thynk gret schame,
Without scho callit be Madame;
The pure Preist thynkis he gettis no rycht,
Be he nocht stylit lyke ane knycht,
And callit Schir, affore his name,
As Schir Thomas, and Schir Wilyame.
All monkrye, ye may heir and se,
Ar callit Denis, for dignitie:
Quhowbeit his mother mylk the kow,
He mon be callit Dene Androw,
Dene Peter, Dene Paull, and Dene Robart.
With Christ, thay tak ane painfull part,
With dowbyll clethyng frome the cald,
Eitand and drynkand quhen thay wald;
With curious countryng in the queir:
God wait, gyf thay by Hevin full deir,
My lorde Abbot, rycht venerabyll,
Ay marschellit upmoste at the tabyll;
My lord Byschope, moste reverent,

Sett abufe Erlis in Parliament;
And Cardinalis, duryng thare ryngis,
Fallowis to Princis and to Kyngis;
The Pope exaltit, in honour,
Abufe the potent Empriour.
  The proude Persone, I thynk trewlye,
He leidis his lyfe rycht lustelye;
For quhy? he hes none uther pyne
Bot tak his teind, and spend it syne:
Bot he is oblyste, be resoun,
To preche untyll his perrochioun:
Thoucht thay want precheing sevintene yeir,
He wyll nocht want ane boll of beir.
Sum Personis hes at thare command
The wantoun wencheis of the land;
Als thay have gret prerogatyffis,
That may depart ay with thare wyffis,
Without divorce or summondyng,
Syne tak ane uther but weddyng:
Sum man wald thynk ane lustye lyfe,
Ay quhen he lyst to chenge his wyfe,
And tak ane uther of more bewtie:
Bot Secularis wantis that lybertie,
The quhilk ar bound in mariage;
Bot thay, lyke rammis in to thair rage,
Unpissilit rynnis amang the yowis,
So lang as Nature in thame growis.
  And als the Vicar, as I trow,
He wyll nocht faill to tak ane kow,
And umaist claith, thoucht babis thame ban,
Frome ane pure selye housband man;

Quhen that he lyis for tyll de,
Haiffeing small bairnis two or thre,
And hes thre ky, withouttin mo,
The vicare moste have one of tho,
With the gray cloke, that happis the bed,
Howbeit that he be purelye cled:
And gyf the wyfe dé on the morne,
Thocht all the babis suld be forlorne,
The uther kow he cleikis awaye,
With hir pure coit of roploch graye.
And gyf, within tway dayis or thre,
The eldest child hapnis to de,
Of the thrid kow he wylbe sure.
Quhen he hes all than under his cure,
And father and mother boith ar dede,
Beg mon the babis, without remede:
Thay hauld the corps at the kirk style,
And thare it moste remane ane quhyle,
Tyll thay gett sufficient souertie
For thare Kirk rycht and dewitie.
Than cummis the landis lord perfors,
And cleiks tyll hym ane herield hors.
Pure laubourars wald that law wer doun,
Quhilk never was fundit be resoun:
I hard thame say, onder confessioun,
That Law is brother tyll Oppressioun.

My Sonne, I have schawin, as I can,
Quhow this Fyft Monarchie began;
Quhose gret Impyre for to report
At lenth, the tyme bene all too schort.

HEIR FOLLOWIS ANE DESCRIPTIOUN OF THE COURT OF ROME.

COURTEOUR.

Father, said I, quhat rewll keip thay in Rome,
  Quhilk hes the Spirituall dominatioun
And Monarchie abufe all Christindome?
  Schaw me, I mak yow supplicatioun.

EXPERIENCE.

  My Sonne, wald I mak trew narratioun,
Said he, to Peter and Paull thocht thay succeid,
I thynk thay preve nocht that in to thare deid:

For Peter, Androw, and Johne war fyschearis fyne,
  Of men and wemen, to the Christin faith;
Bot thay haif spred thare net, with huik and lyne,
  On rentis ryche, on gold, and uther graith:
  Sic fyscheing to neglect thay wylbe laith;
For quhy? thay haif fyscheit in, ouerthort the strandis,
Ane gret part trewlye of all temporall landis:

With that, the tent part of all gude movabyll,
  For the uphaldyng of thare digniteis:
So bene thare fyscheing wounder profitabyll
  On the dry land als weill as on the seis.
  Thare herywalter thay spread in all countreis.

And, with thare hois nett, daylie drawis to Rome
The most fyne gold that is in Christindome.

I dar weill say, within this fyftie yeir,
  Rome hes ressett, furth of this Regioun,
For Bullis and Benefyce, quhilk thay by full deir,
  Quhilk mycht ful weil haif payit a kingis ransoun.
  Bot, war I worthye for to weir ane crown,
Preistis suld no more our substance so consume,
Sendyng yeirlye, so gret ryches to Rome.

In to thare tramalt nett thay fangit ane fysche,
  More nor ane quhaill worthye of memorye,
Of quhome thay have had mony dayntay dysche,
  Be quhome thay ar exaltit to gret glorye ;
  That marvelous monstour callit Purgatorye.
Howbeit tyll us it is nocht amyable,
It hes to thame bene veray profytable.

Lat thay that fructfull fysche eschaip thare nett,
  Be quhome thay haif so gret commoditeis,
Ane more fatt fysche I traist thay sall nocht gett,
  Thocht thay wald sers ouerthort the occiane seis.
  Adew the daylie dolorous Derigeis !
Selye pure preists may syng with hart full sorye,
Want thay that painefull palyce, Purgatorye.

Fairweill, monkyre, with chanoun, nun, and freir !
  Allace ! thay wylbe lychtleit in all landis :
Cowlis wyll no more be kend in kirk nor queir,
  Lat thay that fructfull fysche eschaip thare handis.
  I counsall thame to bynd hym fast in bandis :

For Peter, Androw, nor Johne culde never gett
So profytable ane fysche in to thare nett.

Thare merchandyce, in tyll all Nationis,
  As prentit lede, thare walx, and perchement,
Thare pardonis, and thare dispensationis,
  Thay do exceid sum temporall princis rent:
  In sic trafyke thay ar nocht neglygent.
Of benefyce thay mak gude merchandyce,
Throuch symonie, quhilk thay hald lytill vyce.

Christ did command Peter to feid his scheip;
  And so he did feid thame full tenderlye: Jhon xxi.
Of that command thay take bot lytill keip;
  Bot Christis scheip thay spulye petuouslye;
  And with the woll thay cleith thame curiouslye:
Lyk gormand wolfis, thay tak of thame thare fude,
Thai eit thair flesche, and drynkis boith mylk and blude.

For that office thay serve bot lytill hyir:
  I thynk sic Pastouris ar nocht for to pryse,
Quhilk can nocht gyde thare scheip about the myir,
  Thay ar so besye in thare merchandyse.
  Thocht Peter wes porter of Paradyse, Mat. xvi.
That plesand passage craftelye thay close:
Throuch thame rycht few gettis entres, I suppose.

Christ Jesus said, as Matthew did report,
  Wo be to Scribes and to Pharisience, Mat. xxiiii
The quhilkis did close of Paradyse the port.

Of thame we haif the same experience:
To enter thare thay mak small diligence,
Thay tak sic cure in temporall besynes;
Rycht so, frome us thay stop the plane entres.

Those spiritual keis quhilkis Christ to Peter gaif,
Thare colour cleir with reik and rowst ar fadit;
Unoccupyit thay hald thame in thare neif:
Of that office thay serve to be degradit,
With Goddis worde without that thay remeid it,
Oppinyng the port quhilk lang tyme hes bene closit,
That we may enter, with thame, and be rejoisit.

Contrar tyll Christis institutioun,
Jhon x. To thame that deis in habit of ane freir,
Rome hes thame grantit full remissioun,
To pass tyll hevin straucht way, withouttin weir,
Quhilk bene in Scotland usit mony ane yeir.
Be thare sic vertew in ane Freris hude,
I thynk in vane Christ Jesus sched his blude.

Wald God the Pope, quhilk hes preheminence,
With advyse of his Counsall Generall,
That thay wald do thare detfull deligence,
That Christis law mycht keipit be ouir all,
And trewlye preicheit baith to gret and small,
And geve to thame Spirituall auctoritie
Quhilk culde perfytlie schaw the veritie!

Quho can not preche, a Preist sulde not be namit,
As may be previt be the Law Divyne;

And, be the Canon law, thay ar defamit
That takis Priestheid bot onely to that fyne :
Tyll all vertew thare hartis thay suld inclyne,
In speciall, to preche with trew intentis.
And minister the neidfull Sacramentis.

As for thare Monkis, thair Chanounis, and thare Freris,
And lustye Ladyis of Religioun,
I knaw nocht quhat to thare office efferis ;
Bot men may se thare gret abusioun.
Thay ar nocht lyke, in to conclusioun,
Nother in to thare wordis nor thare warkis,
To the Apostolis, Prophetis, nor Patriarkis.

Geve presentlye thare Prelatis can nocht preche,
Than latt ilke Byschope haif ane Suffragane,
Or successour, quhilk can the peple teche,
On thare expensis yeirlye to remane,
To cause the peple frome thare vyce refrane :
And, quhen ane Prelate hapnith to deceace,
Than put ane perfyte precheour in his pleace.

Do thay nocht so, on thame sall ly the charge,
Geveand unhable men auctoritie ;
As quho wald mak ane steirman tyll ane barge
Of ane blynd borne, quhilk can no dainger se.
Geve that schyp drown, forsuth, I say for me,
Quho gaif that steirman sic commissioun
Suld of the schip mak restitutioun.

The humane Lawis that ar contrarious
And nocht conformyng to the Law divyne,
Thay suld expell, and hald thame odious,
Quhen thay persave thame cum to no gude fyne,
Inventit bot be sensuall menis ingyne,
As that law quhilk forbiddis mariage,
Causyng young Clerkis byrne in lustys rage.

Rom. vii. Difficill is chaistitie tyll observe,
But speciall grace, laubore, and abstinence,
In tyll our flesche aye ryngith, tyll we sterve,
That first Originall syn, concupiscence,
Quhilk we, throuch Adamis inobedience,
Hes done incur, and sall indure for ever,
Quhill that our saull and body Deith dissever.

Tharefor God maid of mariage the band,
Gen. ii. In Paradyse, as Scripture doith recorde:
In Galelie, rycht so, I understand,
Jhon ii. Wes mariage honourit be Christ our Lorde
Auld Law and New thareto thay do concorde.
I thynk for me, better that thay had sleipit,
Nor tyll have maid ane law and never keip it.

Mat. i. Tuke nocht Christ Jesu his Humanitie
Of ane Virgene in marriage contractit,
Luc. i. And of hir flesche cled his Divynitie?
Quhy haif thay done that blysfull band dejectit,
In thare kyngdome? wald God it wer correctit;
That young prelattis mycht mary lustye wyffis,
And nocht in sensuall luste to leid thare lyffis.

Did nocht Christ cheis of honest maryit men,
Alsweill as thay that kepit chaistitie,
For to be his disciplis as ye ken?
As in the Scripture cleirlye thay may se,
Thay keipit, styll, thare wyffis, with honestie;
As Peter, and his spousit bretherin, all,
Observit chaistitie matrymoniall.

Bot now apperis the prophesie of Paull, 1 Tim. iiii.
Quhow sum suld ryis, in to the latter aige,
That frome the trew faithe sulde depart and fall,
And sulde forbid the band of mariage;
Als thow sall fynd, into that sam passage,
Thay sulde command frome meitis tyll abstene,
Quhilk God creat his pepyll to sustene.

Bot, sen the Pope, our Spirituall prince and kyng,
He dois ouersie sic vyces manifest,
And in his kyngdome sufferith for to ryng
The men be quhome the veritie bene supprest,
I excuse nocht hym self more than the rest.
Allace! how suld we membris be weill usit,
Quhen so our spirituall heidis bene abusit?

The famous ancient doctor Aviceane,
Savis, quhen evyll rewme descendis frome the heid
In to the membris, generith mekle pane,
Without thare be maid, haistelye, remeid.
Quhen that cald humour dounwart dois proceid,
In senownis it causis Arthetica,
Rycht so, in to the handis, crampe Chiragra.

Of maladeis it generis mony mo
  Bot gyf men gett sum soverane preserve,
As in the theis Siatica Passio,
  And in the breist, sumtyme the strang Caterve,
  Quhilk causis men rycht haistellye to sterve,
And Podagra, difficill for to cure,
In mennis feit, quhilk lang tyme dois indure.

So, to this moste tryumphant Court of Rome
  This simylitude fuill weill I may compare,
Quhilk hes bene heirschyp of all Christindome,
  And to the warld ane evyll examplare,
  That umquhyle was lod sterre and lumynare,
And the moste sapient sors of sanctytude,
Bot now, allace! bair of beatytude.

Apoc. xviii. Thare Kyngdome may be callit Babilone,
  Quhilk umquhyle was ane brycht Hierusalem,
As planelye menis the Apostill Johne.
  Thare moste famous Citie hes tynt the fame;
  Inhabitaris thareof, thare nobyll name;
For quhy? thay haif of Sanctis habitacle
To Symon Magus maid ane tabernacle.

And horribyll vaill of everilk kynd of vyce,
  Ane laithlye loch of stynkand lychorye,
Ane curssit cove, corrupt with covatyce,
  Bordourit aboute with pryde and symonye,
  Sum sayis, ane systerne full of sodomye,
Quhose vyce in speciall gyf I wald declair,
It wer aneuch for tyll perturbe the air.

Of treuth the hoill Christian Religioun
Throuch thame are scandalizat and offendit.
It can nocht faill bot thare abusioun
Affore the Throne of God it is ascendit:
I dreid, but doute, without that thay amend it, Luc. xiii.
The plaiges of Johnis Revelatioun Apoc. xviii
Sall fall upone thare generatioun.

O Lord! quhilk hes the hartis of everilk kyng
In to thy hand, I mak thee supplication,
Convert that Court, that, of thair grace benyng,
Thay wald mak generall reformatioun
Amang thame selfis, in everilk Natioun
That thay may be ane holy exemplair
Tyll us, thy pure lawid commoun populair,

Hungrit, allace! for falt of Spirituall fude,
Because from us bene hid the veritie.
O Prince! quhilk sched for us thy precious blude,
Kendle in us the fyre of Charitie,
And saif us frome Eterne miseritie,
Now lauboryng in to thy Kirk Militant,
That we may, all, cum to thy Kirk Tryumphant.

FINIS.

HEIR ENDIS THE THRID PART.

ANE DIALOG

BETUIX EXPERIENCE AND ANE COURTEOUR.

THE FOURT BUKE.

MAKAND MENTIOUN OF THE DEITH: AND OF THE ANTICHRIST: AND GENERALL JUGEMENT: AND OF CERTANE PLESOURIS OF GLORYFEIT BODYIS: AND QUHOW EVERY CREATURE DESYRIS TO SEE THE LAST DAY: WITH ANE EXHORTATIOUN, BE EXPERIENCE TO THE COURTEOUR.

COURTEOUR.

PRUDENT Father Experience,
Sen ye, of your benevolence,
Hes causit me for to consydder
Quhow warldlye pompe and glore bene slydder,
By divers storyis miserabyll,
Quhilkis to reheirs bene lamentabyll;
Yitt, or we passe furth of this vaill,
I pray yow geve me your counsaill,
Quhat I sall do, in tyme cumyng,
To wyn the glore evirlesting.

EXPERIENCE.

My Sonne, said he, sett thy intent
To keip the Lordis commandiment,

And preis thee nocht to clym ouer hie
To no warldlie auctoritie.
Quho in the warld doith moste rejose,
Ar farrest aye frome thare purpose.
Wald thou leve warldlye vaniteis,
And thynk on foure extremeteis
Quhilkis are to cum, and that schortlye,
Thou wald never syn wylfullye.
Prent thir four in thy memorye:
The Deith, the Hell, and Hevinnis Glorye,
And extreme Jugement Generall,
Quhare thow man rander compt of all;
Thow sall nocht faill to be content
Of quyet lyffe and sobir rent;
Considdryng no man can be sure
In erth one hour for tyll indure;
So all warldly prosperitie
Is myxit with gret miseritie.
  Wer thow Empriour of Asia,
Kyng of Europe and Affrica,
Gret dominator of the Sey,
And thocht the Hevinnis did thee obey,
All fyschis sowmyng in the strand,
All beist and fowle at thy command,
Concludyng, thow wer Kyng of all
Under the hevin Imperiall;
In that most heych authoritie
Thow suld fynd leist tranquilitie.
Exempyll of kyng Salamone, II. Par. ix.
More prosperous lyfe had nevir none;
Sic ryches, with so gret plesoure,

Eccle. ii. Had never Kyng nor Emprioure,
With moste profunde intelligence,
And superexcelland sapience.
His plesand habitatiounis
Precellit all utheris Natiounis;
Gardyngis and parkis for hartis and hyndis,
Stankis with fysche of divers kyndis;
Moste profunde maisteris of musike,
That in the warld wes none thame like;
Sic tresour of gold and pretious stonis
In erth had nevir no kyng att onis:
iii. Re. xi. He had sevin hundreth lustye quenis,
And thre hundreth fair concubenis;
In erth thare wes no thyng plesand
Eccl. i. Contrarious tyll his command:
Yitt all this gret prosperitie
He thoucht in vaine and vanitie,
And mycht nevir fynd repose compleit,
Without afflixioun of the spreit.

COURTEOUR.

Father, quod I, it marvellis me,
He, haveand sic prosperitie,
With so gret ryches by mesoure,
Nor he had infynite plesoure.

EXPERIENCE.

My Sonne, the suth gyf thow wald knaw,
The veritie I sall thee schaw.
Thare is no warldly thyng, at all,
May satyfie ane mannis saull;

For it is so insaciabyll,
That Heuin and Erth may nocht be abyll
One saull allone to mak content,
Tyll it se God Omnipotent:
Wes never none, nor never salbe,
Saciate, that sycht tyll that he se.
Quharefor, my Sonne, sett nocht thy cure
In Erth, quhare no thyng may be sure, Mat. vi.
Except the Deith allanerlye, Luc. xii.
Quhilk followis man continuallye.
Tharefor, my Sonne, remember thee
Within schorte tyme that thow mon de,
Nocht knawing quhen, quhow, in quhat place,
Bot as plesit the Kyng of Grace.

OF THE DEITH.

Of Miserie moste miserable
Is Deith, and most abhominable,
That dreidful dragone, with his dartis
Aye reddy for to peirs the hartis
Of everilk creature on lyve,
Contrar quhose strenth may no man stryve.
 Of dolent Deith this sore sentence
Wes gyffin throw inobedience
Of our parentis, allace tharefor!
As I have done declare affore,
Quhow thay and thare posteritie
Wer, all, condampnit for to dee.
Quhowbeit the flesche to deith be thrall,

God hes the saull maid immortall,
And so, of his benignytie,
Hes myxit his Justice with mercie.
Tharefor, call to remembrance
Of this fals warld the variance,
Quhow we, lyke pylgramis, evin and morrow,
Ay travellyng throw this vaill of sorrow;
Sum tyme in vaine prosperitie,
Sum tyme in gret miseritie,
Sum tyme in blys, sum tyme in baill,
Sum tyme rycht seik, and sum tyme haill,
Sum tyme full ryche, and sum tyme pure.
Quharefor, my Sonne, tak lytill cure
Nother of gret prosperitie,
Nor yitt of gret miseritie;
Bot plesand lyfe and hard myschance,
Ponder thame boith in one ballance;
Considdryng none auctoritie,
Ryches, wysedome, nor dignitie,
Empyre of realmes, bewtie, nor strenth,
May nocht one day our lyvis lenth.
Sen we are sure that we moste dé,
Fairweill all vaine felycitie!
  Gretlye it doith perturbe my mynde,
Of dolent Deith the divers kynd.
Thoucht Deith tyll every man resortis,
Yitt strykith he in syndrie sortis;
Sum be hait feveris violence;
Sum be contagious pestilence;
Sum be justice execution,
Bene put to deith without remissioun;

Sum hangit ; sum doith lose thare heidis ;
Sum brynt ; sum soddin in to leiddis ;
And sum, for thare unleifsum actis,
Ar rent and revin apone the ractis ;
Sum ar dissolvit by poysoun ;
Sum on the nycht ar murdreist doun ;
Sum fallis in to frynasie ;
Sum deis in hydropesie,
And utheris strange infirmiteis,
Quharein mony ane thousand deis,
Quhilk humane Nature dois abhor,
As in the gutt, gravell, and gor ;
Sum, in the flux, and fevir quartane,
Bot ay, the houre of deith uncertane.
Sum ar dissolvit suddantlye,
Be cattarve, or be poplesye ;
Sum doith distroy thame self also,
As Hanniball and wyse Cato ;
Be thounder Deith sum doith consume,
As he did the thrid kyng of Rome,
Callit Tullius Hostilius,
As wryttis gret Valerius ;
For he and his househald attonis
Wer brynt be thounder, flesche and bonis.
Sum deith be extreme excesse
Of joy, as Valerie doith expresse ;
Sum be extreme malancholye
Wyll de, but uther maladye.
In Chronicles thow may weill ken,
Quhow mony hundreth thousand men
Ar slane, sen first the warld began,

In battell; and quhow mony one man
Apone the see doith lose thare lyvis,
Quhen schyppis upone roches ryvis.
Thocht sum dé naturally, throuch aige,
Far mo deis raiffand in one raige.
Happy is he the quhilk hes space
Att his last hour to cry for grace.
Quhowbeit deith be abhominabyll,
I thynk it suld be comfortabyll
Tyll all thame of the faithfull nummer;
For thay depart frome cair and cummer,
Frome trubyll, travell, sturt, and stryfe,
Tyll joy and evirlestand lyfe.
  Polidorus Virgilius
To that effect he wryttis thus:
In Trace, quhen ony chylde be borne,
Thare kyn and freindis cumis thame beforne,
With dolent lamentatioun,
For the gret trybulatioun,
Calamitye, cummer, and cure,
That thay in erth ar to indure;
Bot, at thare deith and burying,
Thay mak gret joy and bankettyng,
That thay have past from miserie
To rest and grett felycitie.
  Sen Deith bene fynall conclusioun,
Quhat valis warldly provisioun,
Quham wysedome may nocht contramand,
Nor strenth that stoure may nocht ganestand
Ten thousand myleone of treasoure
May nocht prolong thy lyfe one houre;

Efter quhose dolent departyng,
Thy spreit sall passe, but tarying,
Straucht way tyll joye inestimabyll,
Or to strang pane intollerabyll:
Thy vyle corruptit carioun
Sall turne in putrefactioun,
And so remane, in pulder small,
On to the Jugement Generall.

ANE SCHORT DISCRIPTIOUN OF THE ANTICHRIST.

COURTEOUR.

Quod I, Father, I heir men say
That thair sall ryse, affore that day
Quhilk ye call Generall Jugement,
One wickit man, from Sathan sent,
And contrar to the law of Christ,
Callit the creuell Antichrist.
And sum sayis, that myschevous man
Discende sall of the trybe of Dan.
And sulde be borne in Babilone,
The quhilk dissave sall mony one.
Infydelis sall, of every art,
With that fals Propheit tak one part:
And quhow that Enoch and Elias
Sall preche contrar that fals Messias;
Bot fynally, his fals doctryne
And he sall be put to rewyne,
Bot nother be the fyre nor swourd,
Bot be the vertew of Christis wourd:

And, gyf this be of verytie,
The suith, I pray yow, schaw to me.

EXPERIENCE.

My Sonne, said he, as wryttis Johne,
Thare sall nocht be one man allone,
Havyng that name in speciall;
Bot Antichristis in generall
Hes bene, and now ar, mony one:
And, rycht so, in the tyme of Johne
1 Jhon ii. Wer Antichristis, as hym self sayis;
And presentlye, now in thir dayis,
Ar rycht mony, withouttin dout,
Wer thare fals lawis weill soucht out.
Quha wes one greter Antichrist,
And more contraryous to Christ,
Nor the fals Propheit Machomeit,
Quhilk his curste lawis maid so sweit?
In Turkye yit thay ar observit,
Quhare throuch the hell he hes deservit.
All Turkis, Sarazenis, and Jowis,
2 Jhon i. That in the Sonne of God nocht trowis
Ar Antichristis, I thee declare,
Because to Christ thay ar contrare.
Dan. viii. Daniell sayis, in his Propheseis,
That, efter the gret Monarcheis,
Sall ryse ane marvellous potent Kyng,
Quhilk with ane schameles face sall ryng,
Mychtie and wyse in dirk speikyngis,
And prospir in all plesand thyngis:
Throuch his falsheid and craftynes,

He sall flow in to welthynes;
The godlye pepyll he sall noye
By creuell deith, and thame distroye;
The Kyng of Kyngis he sall ganestand,
Syne be distroyit withouttin hand.
  Paull sayis, Affore the Lordis cumyng, 2 Thes. ii
That thare salbe one departyng,
And that man of iniquitye
Tyll all men he sall opened be,
Quhilk sall sitt in the Holy sait,
Contrary God to mak debait:
Bot that Sonne of perditioun
Salbe put to confusioun
Be power of the Haly Spreit,
Quhen he his tyme hes done compleit.
  Beleve nocht that, in tyme cumyng,
One gretar Antichriste to ryng
Nor thare hes bene, and presentlye
Ar now, as Clerkis can espye.
Tharefor, my wyll is, that thow knaw,
Quhat ever thay be that makis one law,
Thocht thay be callit Christin men,
By naturall reassoun thow may ken,
Be thay never of so gret valour,
Pape, Cardinall, Kyng, or Empriour,
Extolland thare traditionis
Abufe Christis institutionis,
Makand lawis contrar to Christe.
He is ane verray Antichriste;
And quho doith fortifye or defend
Sic law, I mak it to thé kend,

Be it Pape, Empriour, Kyng, or Quene,
Gret sorrow sall be on thame sene,
Att Christis extreme Jugement,
Without that thay in tyme repent.

HEIR FOLLOWIS A SCHORT REMEMBRANCE OF THE MOST TERRABYLL DAY OF THE EXTREME JUGEMENT.

COURTEOUR.

FATHER, said I, with your lycence,
Sen ye haith sic Experience,
Yitt one thyng at yow wald I speir:
Quhen sall that dreidfull day appeir
Quhilk ye call Jugement Generall?
Quhat thyngis affore that day sall fall?
Quhare sall appeir that dreidfull Juge?
Or quhow may faltouris gett refuge?

EXPERIENCE.

Quod he, As to thy first questioun,
I can mak no solutioun:
Quharefor, perturbe nocht thyne intent
To knaw day, hour, nor moment:
To God allone the day bene knawin,
Quhilk never was to none Angell schawin.
Howbeit, be divers conjectouris,
And principall expositouris

Of Daniell and his Prophecie,
And be the sentence of Elie,
Quhilkis hes declarit, as thay can,
How lang it is sen the Warld began,
And for to schaw hes done thare cure,
How lang thay traist it sall indure,
And als, how mony ages bene,
As in thare warkis may be sene.
  Bot, tyll declare thir questionis,
Thare bene divers opinionis.
Sum wryttaris hes the Warld devidit
In sex ageis; as bene desidit
In to *Fasciculus Temporum*,
And *Cronica Cronicorum*;
Bot, be the sentence of Elie,
The Warld devydit is in thre;
As cunnyng Maister Carioun
Hes maid plane expositioun,
How Elie sayis, withouttin weir,
The Warld sall stand sax thousand yeir,
Of quhome I follow the sentence,
And lattis the uther Bukis go hence.
From the Creatioun of Adam
Two thousand yeir tyll Abraham;
Frome Abraham, be this narratioun,
To Christis Incarnatioun,
Rycht so, hes bene two thousand yeris;
And, be thir Propheceis, apperis
Frome Christ, as thay mak tyll us kend,
Two thousand tyll the Warldis end,
Of quhilkis ar by gone, sickirlye,

Fyve thousand, fyve hundreth, thre and fyftie;
And so remanis to cum, but weir,
Four hundreth, with sevin and fourtye yeir:
And than the Lorde Omnipotent
Suld cum tyll his gret Jugement.

Mat. xxiiii. Christ sayis, the tyme salbe maid schort,
As Matthew planelye doith report,
That, for the warldis iniquitie,
The letter tyme sall schortnit be,
For plesour of the chosin nummer,
That thay may passe from care and cummer.
So, be this compt, it may be kend,
The Warld is drawand neir ane end:
For legionis ar cum, but doute,
Of Antichristis, wer thay soucht out;
And mony toknis dois appeir,
As efter, schortlye, thow sall heir,
Quhow that Sanct Jherome doith indyte,
That he hes red, in Hebrew wryte,
Of fyftene signis in speciall,
Affore that Jugement Generall.
Off sum of thame I tak no cure,
Quhilk I fynd nocht in the Scripture:
One part of thame thocht I declare,
First wyll I to the Scripture fare.

Mat. xiii. Christ sayis, Affore that day be done,
Thare sallbe signis in Sonne and Mone:
Mat. xxiiii. The Sonne sall hyde his beymes brycht,
So that the Mone sall gyf no lycht;
Sterris, be mennis jugement,
Sall fall furth of the firmament.

Of this signis, or we forther gone,
Sum morall sence we wyll expone,
As cunnyng Clerkis hes declarit,
And hes the Sonne and Mone comparit,
The Sonne, to the stait Spirituall,
The Mone, to princis Temporall,
Rycht so the sterris thay do compare
To the lawd common populare.
The Mone and sterris hes no lycht
But the reflex of Phebus brycht:
So, quhen the Sonne of lycht is dyrk,
The Mone and sterris man be myrk.
Rycht so, quhen pastouris spirituallis,
Popis, Byschoppis, and Cardinallis,
In thare begynning schew gret lycht.
The Temporall stait wes rewlit rycht.
Bot, now, allace! it is nocht so:
Those schynand lampis bene ago,
Thare radious beymes ar turnit in reik:
For now in erth no thyng thay seik,
Except ryches and dignitie,
Followyng thare sensualitie.
Mony prelatis ar now ryngand,
The quhilkis no more dois understand
Quhat doith pertene to thare offyce,
Nor thow can kendyll fyre with yce.
Wo to Papis, I say for me,
Quhilk sufferis sic enormitie,
That ignorant warldly creaturis
Suld in the kirk haif ony curis!
No marvell thocht the peple slyde,

Quhen thay have blynd men to thare gyde!
For ane Prelat that can nocht preche,
Nor Goddis law to the peple teche,
Esay. lvi. Esaye compareth hym, in his wark,
Tyll ane dum dog that can nocht bark;
And Christ hym callis, in his greif,
Jhon x. Moste lyke ane murdrer, or ane theif.
The cunnyng doctour Augustyne
Wolfis and devyllis doith thame defyne.
The Canon Lawe doith hym defame
That of ane Prelat beris the name,
And wyll nocht preche the Divyne lawis,
As the Decreis planelye schawis.
Bot those that hes auctoritie
To provyde spirituall dignytie
Mycht, geve thay plesit to tak pane,
Gar thame lycht all thare lampis agane:
Bot ever, allace! that is nocht done,
So dirknit bene boith Sonne and Mone.
War Kyngis lyvis weill declarit,
The quhilkis ar to the Mone comparit,
Men mycht consydder thare estate
Frome charitie degenerate.
I thynk thay sulde thynk mekle schame
Of Christ for to take thare surname,
Syne leif nocht lyke to Christianis,
Bot more lyke Turkis and to Paganis.
Turke contrar Turke makis lytill weir;
Bot Christiane princis takis no feir,
Quhilkis suld aggre as brother to brother,
But now ilk ane dyngis doun ane uther.

I knaw no ressonabyll cause quharefore
Except pryde, covatyce, and vaine glore
The Empriour movis his ordinance
Contrar the potent Kyng of France;
And France, rycht so, with gret regour,
Contrar his freinde the Empriour;
And rycht swa, France agane Ingland;
Ingland alsso, aganis Scotland;
And als the Scottis, with all thare myeht,
Doith feycht, for tyll defend thare rycht:
Betuix thir realmes of Albione,
Quhare battellis hes bene mony one,
Can be maid none affinitie,
Nor yit, no consanguinitie;
Nor, be no waye, thay can consydder
That thay may have lang peace togydder,
I dreid that weir makis none endyng,
Tyll thay be boith onder ane kyng.
Thocht Christ, the Soverane Kyng of Grace,
Left, in his Testament, lufe and peace,
Our Kyngis frome weir wyll nocht refrane,
Tyll thare be mony ane thousand slane,
Gret heirschipis maid be see and land,
As all the Warld may understand.

COURTEOUR.

Father, I thynk that temporall kyngis
May feycht, for tyll defend thare ryngis;
For I haif sene the Spirituall Stait
Mak weir, thare rychtis tyll debait.

I saw Pape Julius manfullye
Passe to the feild tryumphantlye,
With ane rycht aufull ordinance,
Contrar Lowis, the kyng of France;
And, for to do hym more dispyte,
He did his Regioun interdyte.

EXPERIENCE.

My Sonne, said he, as I suppose,
That langith weill tyll our purpose;
How Sonne and Mone ar boith denude
Of lycht, as Clerkis dois conclude,
Comparyng thame, as ye hard tell,
To Spirituall Stait and Temporell,
And Commoun peple, half disparit,
Quhilk to the Sterris bene comparit.
Lawid peple followis ay thare heidis;
And speciallye, in to thare deidis,
The moste part of Religioun
Bene turnit in abusioun.
Quhat dois availl religious weidis,
Quhen thay ar contrar in thare deidis?
Quhat holynes is thare within
Ane wolf cled in ane wedderis skin?
So, be thir toknis, dois appeir,
The day of Jugement drawis neir.
Now latt us leif this morall sens,
Proceidyng tyll our purpose hens,
And of this mater speik no more,
Begynning quhare we left affore.
Mat. xxiiii. The Scripture sayis, efter thir signis

Salbe sene mony marvellous thyngis :
Than sall ryse trybulationis — Mat. xiii.
In erth, and gret mutationis, — Luc. xxi.
Als weill heir under, as above,
Quhen vertewis of the hevin sall move.
Sic creuell weir salbe, or than,
Wes never sene sen the Warld began,
The quhilk sall cause gret indigence,
As darth, hunger, and pestilence.
The horribyll soundis of the sey
The peple sal perturbe and fley.
Jerome sayis, it sall ryse on heycht
Abone montanis, to mennis sycht ;
Bot it sall nocht spred ouer the land,
Bot, lyke ane wall, evin straycht upstand,
Syne sattell doun agane so law
That no man sall the walter knaw.
Gret quhalis sall rummeis, rowte and rair,
Quhose sound redound sall in the air ;
All fysche and monstouris marvellous
Sall cry, with soundis odious,
That men sall wydder on the erd,
And wepyng, wary sall thare weird,
With lowde allace and welaway !
That ever thay baid to se that day ;
And, speciallye, those that dwelland be
Apone the costis of the see.
Rycht so, as Sanct Jerome concludis,
Sall be sene ferleis in the fludis :
The sey, with movyng marvellous,
Sall byrn with flammis furious.

Rycht so, sall byrn fontane and flude;
All herb and tre sall sweit lyk blude;
Fowlis sall fall furth of the air;
Wylde beistis to the plane repair,
And, in thare maner, mak gret mone.
Gowland with mony gryslye grone.
Ezeck. xxxvii. The bodeis of dede creaturis
Appeir sall on thare sepulturis:
Than sall boith men, wemen, and bairnis
Cum creipand furth of howe cavernis,
Quhare thay, for dreid, wer hyd affore,
With seych, and sob, and hartis sore;
Wandryng about as thay war wode,
Affamysit for falt of fude.
None may mak utheris confortyng,
Bot dule for dule, and lamentyng.
Quhat may thay do bot weip and wounder,
Quhen thay se roches schaik in schounder,
Throw trimlyng of the erth and quakyng?
Of sorrow, than, salbe no slakyng.
Quho that bene levand, in those dayis
May tell of terrabyll affrayis:
Thare ryches, rentis, nor tressour,
That tyme, sall do thame small plesour.
Bot, quhen sic wonderis dois appeir,
Men may be sure the day drawis neir,
Dan. xiii. That juste men pas sall to the glore,
Injuste, to pane for ever more.

COURTEOUR.

Father, said I, we daylie reid
One Artikle, in to our Creid,

Sayand, that Christ Omnipotent,
In to that generall Jugement,
Sall juge boith dede and quick also.
Quharefore, declare me, or ye go,
Geve thare sall ony man, or wyve,
That day be foundin upon lyve.

EXPERIENCE.

Quod he, As to that questione,
I sall mak sone solutione.
The Scripture planelye doith expone, Mat. xxiiii.
Quhen all tokynnis bene cum and gone,
Yitt mony one hundreth thousand
That samyn day salbe levand:
Quhowbeit, thare sall no creature
Nother of day nor hour be sure;
For Christ sall cum so suddantlye,
That no man sall the tyme espye;
As it wes in the tyme of Noye,
Quhen God did all the warld distroye.
Sum on the feild salbe lauborand;
Sum in the templis mariand;
Sum afore jugis makand pley;
And sum men sailand on the sey.
Those that bene on the feild going
Sall nocht returne to thare luging.
Quho bene apone his hous above
Sall haif no laser to remove.
Two salbe in the myll grindyng,
Quhilkis sall be taking, but warnyng;
The ane, tyll everlestyng glore,

The uther, loste for ever more.
Two salbe lying in one bed ;
The one, to plesour salbe led,
The uther, salbe left allone,
Gretand with mony gryslie grone.
And so, my Sonne, thow may weill trow,
The warld salbe as it is now,
The peple usyng thare besynes,
As Holy Scripture doith expres.
Sen no man knawis the hour, nor day,
The Scripture biddis us walk and pray,
And for our Syn be penitent,
As Christ wald cum incontinent.

THE MANER QUHOW CHRIST SALL CUM TO HIS JUGEMENT.

EXPERIENCE.

Quhen all takinnis bene brocht tyll end,
Than sall the Sone of God discend :
As fyreflaucht haistely glansyng.
Discend sall the most Hevinly Kyng,
As Phebus, in the Orient,
Lychtnis in haist the Occident,
So plesandlye he sall appeir
Amang the hevinlye cluddis cleir,
With gret power and majestie,
Above the countrie of Judee,
As Clerkis doith concludyng, haill,
Direct above the lustye vaill

Of Josaphat and Mont Olyveit : Actis i.
All prophesie thare salbe compleit.
The Angellis of the Ordoris Nyne Mat. xxv.
Inviron sall that throne Divyne
With hevinlye consolatioun,
Makand hym ministratioun.
In his presens thare salbe borne
The signis of cros, and croun of thorne,
Pillar, nalis, scurgis, and speir,
With everilk thyng that did hym deir,
The tyme of his grym Passioun ;
And, for our consolatioun,
Appeir sall, in his handis and feit,
And in his syde, the prent compleit
Of his fyve woundis precious,
Schynand lyke rubeis radious,
Tyll reprobatt confusioun ;
And, for fynall conclusioun,
He, sittand in his tribunall,
With gret power Imperiall.
There sall ane Angell blawe a blast 1 Cor. xv.
Quhilk sall mak all the Warld agast, Mat. xxiiii.
With hyddeous voce, and vehement
Ryse, Dede folk, cum to Jugement !
With that, all reassonabyll creature
That ever was formit be Nature
Sall suddantlye start up attonis,
Conjunit with saull, flesche, blude, and bonis.
That terribyll trumpet; I heir tell,
Beis hard in Hevin, in Erth, and Hell :
Those that wer drownit in the sey Apoc. xx.

That boustious blast thay sall obey ;
Quhare ever the body buryit wase,
All salbe fundyng in that plase.
Mar. xiii. Angellis sall passe in the four airtis
Of Erth, and bryng thame frome all partis,
And, with one instant diligence,
Present thame to his Excellence.
Sanct Jerome thoucht continuallye
On this Jugement, so ardentlye,
He said, quhidder I eit, or drynk,
Or walk, or sleip, forsuth me thynk
That terrabyll trumpat, lyke ane bell,
So quiklye in my eir doith knell,
As instantlye it wer present,
Ryse, Dede folk, cum to Jugement!
Geve Sanct Jerome tuke sic ane fray,
Allace! quhat sall we synnaris say?
All those quhilk funding bene on lyve
Salbe immortall maid belyve ;
1 Pet. iiii. And, in the twynkling of one Ee,
1 Cori. xv. With fyre thay sall translatit be,
And never for to dee agane,
As Divyne Scripture schawis plane,
Als reddy, boith for pane and glore,
As thay quhilk deit lang tyme affore.
The Scripture sayis, thay sall appeir
In aige of thre and thretty yeir,
Quhidder thay deit young or auld,
Quhose gret nummer may nocht be tauld.
That day sall nocht be myst one man
Quhilk borne wes sen the warld began.

The Angellis sall thame separait, Math. xxvi.
As hird the scheip doith frome the gait ;
And those quhilk bene of Beliallis band
Trymling apone the erth sall stand,
On the left hand of that Gret Juge,
But esperance to get refuge.
  Bot those quhilk bene predestinate 1 Thes. iiii.
Sall frome the erth be elevate;
And that moste happy cumpanye
Sall ordourit be tryumphantlye,
At the rycht hand of Christe, our Kyng,
Heych in the air, with loude lovyng.
  Full gloriouslye thare sall compeir,
More brycht than Phebus in his speir,
The Virgene Marie, quene of quenis,
With mony ane thousand brycht Virgenis.
The Fatheris of the Auld Testament,
Quhilk wer to God obedient.
Father Adam sall thame convoye,
With Abell, Seth, Enoch, and Noye ;
Abraham, with his faithfull warkis,
With all the prudent Patriarkis;
Johne the Baptiste thare sall compeir,
The principall and last messyngeir,
Quhilk come bot half ane yeir affore
The cumyng of that Kyng of Glore ;
Moyses, Esayas, honorabyll,
With all trew Prophetis venerabyll ;
David, with all the faithfull Kyngis
Quhilk verteouslye did rewle thare ryngis ;
The nobyll cheiftane Josue,

With gentyll Judas Machabé,
With mony one nobyll campioun,
Quhilk, in thare tyme, with gret renoun,
Manfullye, tyll thare lyvis ende,
The Law of God thay did defende.
  With Eve, that day, salbe present
The Ladyis of the Auld Testament:
Delbora, Adamis douchter deir,
With the four lusty ladyis cleir
Quhilk kepit wer in the Ark with Noye.
Sara and Cithara, with joye,
The quhilkis to Abraham wyffis bene;
With gude Rebecka, thare salbe sene
The prudent wyffis of Israell,
Gude Lya, and the fair Rachell;
With Judeth, Hester, and Susanna,
And the rycht sapient Quene Saba.
  Thare sall compeir Peter and Paull,
With Christis trew disciplis all,
Lawrence and Stevin, with thare blyst band
Of Martyris, mo than ten thousand;
Gregore, Ambrose, and Augustyne,
With confessouris, ane tryumphand tryne;
With Sanct Francis, and Dominick,
Sanct Bernard, and Sanct Benedick;
With small nummer of Monkis, and Freiris,
Of Carmeletis, and Cordeleiris,
That, for the lufe of Christ onlye,
Renuncit the warld unfenyeitlye.
  With Elizabeth and Anna,
All gude wyffis sall compeir that day;

The blyst and holy Magdelane,
That day, affore hir Soverane,
Rycht plesandlye scho sall present
All synnaris that wer penitent,
Quhilk of thare gylt heir askit grace:
In Hevin, with hir, sall have ane place.
But wo beis to that bailfull band
Quhilk sall stand lawe at his left hand!
Wo, than, to Kyngis and Empryouris
Quhilkis wer unrychteous conquerouris;
For thare glore and perticular gude,
Gart sched so mekle saikles blude!
But sceptour, crown, and robe royall,
That day thay sall mak compt of all,
And, for thare creuell tyrrannye,
Sall punyste be perpetuallye.

Ye Lordis and Barronis, more and les,
That your pure tennantis dois oppres,
Be gret gyrsome, and dowbyll maill,
More than your landis bene availl,
With sore exhorbitant cariage,
With Merchetis of thare mariage,
Tormentit boith in peace and weir,
With burdyngis more than thay may beir;
Be thay haif payit to yow thare maill,
And, to the Preist, thare teindis haill,
And, quhen the land agane is sawin,
Quhat restis behynd I wald wer knawin!
I traist thay and thare pure househauld
May tell of hunger and of cauld.

Without ye haif of thame pieté,
I dreid ye sall gett no mercie,
That day, quhen Christ Omnipotent
Cumis tyll his Generall Jugement.
  Wo beis to publict oppressouris,
To tyrrannis, and to transgressouris,
To murderaris, and commoun theifis,
Quhilk never did mend thare gret mischeifis!
Fornicatouris, and ockararis,
Commoun publict adulteraris,
All pertinat wylfull heretykis,
All fals dissaitfull scismatykis,
All salbe present in that place,
With mony lamentabyll Allace!
  The cursit Cayn, that never wes gude,
With all scheddaris of saikles blude;
Nemrod, fundar of Babilone,
With fals ydolateris mony one;
Nynus, the kyng of Asseriay,
With gret dule sall compeir that day,
Quhilk first inventit ymagery,
Quharethrouch come gret ydolatry:
For makyng of the image, Bell,
That day his hyre salbe in hell.
  The gret oppressour, kyng Pharo,
The tyrrane Empriour Nero,
Sall with thame cursit Kyng Herode bryng,
With mony uther cairfull kyng.
The crouell kyng Antiochus,
With the moste furious Olofernus,
Gret oppressouris of Israell,

That day thare hyre salbe in Hell.
With Judas sall compeir ane clan
Of fals tratouris to God and man.
Thare sall compeir, of everilk land,
With Ponce Pylat, one bailfull band
Of Temporall and of Spirituall statis;
Fals jugis, with thare advocatis.
Thare sall our Senyeouris of the Sessioun
Of all thare faltis mak cleir confessioun.
Thare salbe sene the fraudfull failyeis
Of Schireffis, Provestis, and of Bailyeis;
Officiallis, with thare Constry clerkis,
Sall mak compt of thare wrangous werkis;
Thay, and thare perverst Procuratouris,
Oppressouris boith of ryche and puris,
Throw delatouris full of dissait,
Quhilk mony one gart beg thare meit.
Gret dule, that day, to Jugis bene,
That cumis nocht with thare conscience clene:
That day sall pas be Peremptouris,
Without cawteill or dillatoris;
No Duplicandum, nor Triplicandum,
But schortlye pas to Sentenciandum,
Without continuatiounis,
Or ony appellatiounis:
That sentence sall nocht be retraitit,
Nor with no man of Law debaitit.
  Ye Lauboraris be sey and landis,
Perfyte craftismen, and ryche merchandis,
Leif your dissait and crafty wylis,
Quhilk syllie simpyll folk begylis;

Mak recompence heir, as ye may,
Remembryng on this dreidfull day.

With Machomeit sall compeir, but doute,
Of Antichristis one hydduous route:
Byschope Annas, and Cayphas,
With hym in cumpany sall pas;
With Scrybis and fals Pharisianis,
Quhilk wrocht on Christ gret violencis;
With mony one Turk and Sarracene,
With gret sorrow thare salbe sene:
Papis, for thare traditionis
Contrar Christis institutionis,
With mony one cowle and clyppit crown,
Quhilk Christis lawis strampit down,
And wald nocht suffer for to preche
The veritie, nor the peple teche,
Bot Lawit men pat to gret torment,
Quhilk usit Christis Testament.
All Kyngis and Quenis thare salbe kend,
The quhilk sic lawis did defend.
In that Court sall cum mony one
Of the blak byik of Babilone.
The innocent blude, that day, sall crye
Ane loude vengeance, full pietuouslye,
On those creuell bludy bowchouris,
Martyris of prophetis and prechouris,
Sum with the fyre, sum with the sworde,
Quhilk planely precheit Goddis worde;
That day thay sall rewardit be,
Conforme to thare iniquitie.

The Sodomitis and Gomoreance,
On quhome God wrocht so gret vengeance,
With Chore, Dathan, and Abyrone,
With thare assistance, mony one,
The holy Scripture wyll thee tell,
Quhow thay sank all doun to the hell.
With Symon Magus sall resort
Of proude Preistis ane schamefull sort.
That samyn day thare salbe sene
Mony one creuell cairfull Quene:
Quene Semirame, kyng Nynus wyfe,
Ane tygir full of sturt and stryfe,
Togydder with Quene Jezabell,
Quhilk wes boith covetous and creuell;
The fals dissaitfull Dalyla;
The creuell Quene Clytemnestra,
The quhilk did murdreis, on the nycht
Agamemnon, boith wyse and wycht,
The quhilk wes hir awin soverane lorde,
As Grekis storyis dois recorde.
With creuell Quenis mony one,
Quhilk langsum wer for tyll expone.

Ye wantoun Ladyis, and Burges wyvis,
That now for sydest taillis stryvis,
Flappand the fylth amang your feit,
Rasyng the duste in to the streit,
That day, for all your pomp and pryde,
Your tailis sall nocht your hyppis hyde:
Thir vaniteis ye sall repent,
Without that ye be penitent.

With Phitonissa, I heir tell,
Quhilk rasit the Spreit of Samuell,
That day, with hir, thare sall resorte
Of rank wytcheis one sorrowfull sorte,
Brocht frome all partis, mony one myle,
Frome Savoy, Atholl, and Argyle,
And frome the Ryndes of Galloway,
With mony wofull wallaway!

Ye Brether of Religioun,
In tyme leif your abusioun,
With quhilk ye haif the warld abusit,
Or ye, that day, salbe refusit.
I speik to yow all, generallye,
Nocht till one Ordoure speciallye.
That day, all creature sall ken
Geve ye war sanctis, or warldly men,
Or gyf ye tuk the skapellarye,
That ye mycht leif more plesandlye,
And gett ane gude grosse portioun,
Or for godlye devotioun;
That day, your faynit sanctytudis
Sail nocht be knawin be your hudis:
Your superstitious ceremoneis,
Participand tyll ydolatreis,
Corde, cuttit schone, nor clippit hede,
That day sall stande yow in no stede:
For cowlis blak, gray, nor begaird,
Ye sall, that day, get no rewaird.
Your polit payntit flatterye,
Your dissimulat ypocrasye,

That day thay sall be cleirlye knawin,
Quhen ye sall scheir as ye have sawin.
Tharefore, in tyme be penitent,
Or ellis that day ye wylbe schent.
  I pray yow hartlie, as I may,
Remember on that dreidfull day,
Ye Abbot, Pryour, and Pryores:
Consydder quhat ye did profes,
And quhow that your promotioun
Wes no thyng for devotioun;
Bot tyll obtene the Abbacye,
Ye maid your vow of Chaistitye,
Of Povertie, and Obedience:
Tharefor, remord your conscience,
Quhow thir thre vowis bene observit,
And quhat rewarde ye have deservit.
Quharefore, repent, quhill ye have space;
Sen God is lyberall of his grace.

COURTEOUR.

  Father, quod I, declare to me
Quhare sall our Prelatis ordourit be,
Quhilk now bene in the warld levand;
With quhome sall cum that Spirituall band?

EXPERIENCE.

  Quod he, As Sanct Barnard discryvis,
Without that thay amend thare lyvis,
And leve thair wantoun vicious warkis,
Nocht with Prophetis nor Patriarkis,
Nocht with Martyris nor Confessouris,

The quhilkis to Christ wer trew prechouris:
Thare predecessouris, Peter and Paull,
That day wyll thame mysken, at all;
So sall they nocht, I say for me,
With the Apostillis ordourit be.
I traist thay sall dwell on the bordour
Of Hell, quhare thare salbe non ordour.
Endlang the flude of Phlegetone,
Or on the brayis of Acherone;
Cryand on Charon, I conclude,
To ferrie thame ouer that furious flude,
Tyll eternall confusioun,
Without thay leif thare abusioun.
I traist those Prelatis, more and les,
Sall mak cleir compt of thare ryches,
That dreidfull day, with hartis sore,
And quhat service thay did tharefore.
The princely pomp nor apparell
Of Pope, Byschope, nor Cardinall,
Thare Royall rentis, nor dignitie,
That day sall nocht regardit be.
Thare sall no tailis, as I heir say,
Of Byschoppis be borne up that day.
Cum thay nocht with thare conscience clene,
On thame gret sorrow salbe sene,
Without that thay thare lyfe amend
In tyme: And so I mak ane end.

HEIR FOLLOWIS THE MANER QUHOW CHRIST SALL GIVE HIS SENTENCE.

EXPERIENCE.

QUHEN all thir Congregatiounis
Beis brocht furth frome al natiounis,
Quhilk wilbe without lang process,
Thocht I haif maid sum lang degress;
For, in the twinkling of one E,
All mankynd sall presentit be
Affore that Kyngis Excellence, Math. xxv.
Than schortlye sall he geve sentence;
First sayand to that blysfull band,
Quhilk beis ordourit at his rycht hand,
Cum, with my Fatheris benysoun,
And ressave your possessioun,
Quhilk bene for yow preordinat,
Affore the Warld wes first creat.
Quhen I wes hungry, ye me fed;
Quhen I was naikit, ye me cled;
Oftymes ye gave me herberye,
And gaif me drynk, quhen I was drye,
And vesyit me with myndis meik,
Quhen I wes presonar and seik:
In all sic trybulatioun,
Ye gaif me consolatioun.
Than sall thay say, O potent Kyng,
Quhen saw we thé desyre sic thyng?

We never saw thyne excellence
Subdewit to sic indigence.
Yes, sall he say, I yow assure,
Quhen ever ye did ressave the pure,
And, for my saik, maid thame supplie,
That gyft, but doute, ye gaif to me:
Tharefor sall now begyn your glore,
Quhilk sall indure for ever more.
  Than sall he luke on his left hand,
And say unto that bailfull band,
Pas, with my maledictioun,
Tyll eternall afflictioun,
In cumpany with feindis fell,
In everlestyng fyre of Hell:
Quhen I stude, naikit, at your yett,
Houngry, thristy, cauld, and wett,
Rycht febyll, seik, and lyke to dé,
I never gat of yow supplie;
And, quhen I lay in presoun strang,
For yow I mycht haif lying full lang,
Without your consolatioun,
Or ony supportatioun.
  Trymbling for dreid, than sall thay say,
With mony hydduous harmisay,
Allace! gude Lorde, quhen saw we thee
Subject to sic necessitie?
Quhen saw we thee cum to our dure,
Houngry, thristy, naikit, pure?
Quhen saw we thee in presoun ly,
Or thee refusit herbery?
  Than sall that most precelland Kyng

Tyll those wretchis mak answeryng,
That tyme quhen ye refusit the puris
Quhilkis neidfull cryit at your duris,
And of your superfluitie
For my saik maid thame no supplie,
Refusand thame, ye me refusit,
With wrecheitness so ye wer abusit:
Tharefor ye sall have, to your hyre,
The everlestyng byrning fyre,
But grace, but peace, or confortyng.
Than sall thay cry, full sore weipyng,
That we were maid, allace! gude Lorde!
Allace! is thare non misericorde?
But thus, withouttin hope of grace,
Tyne presens of thy plesand face?
Allace for us! it had bene gude,
We had bene smorit in our cude.
  Than, with one rair, the erth sall ryve,
And swallow thame, boith man and wyve;
Than sall those creaturis forlorne
Warie the hour that thay wer borne,
With mony yamer, yowt, and yell,
Frome tyme thay feill the flammis fell
Apone thare tender bodeis byte;
Quhose torment salbe infinyte:
The erth sall close, and frome thare sycht
Sall takin be all kynde of lycht.
Thare salbe gowlyng and gretyng,
But hope of ony confortyng:
In that inestimabyll pane
Eternallye thay sall remane,

Byrnand in furious flammys rede,
Ever deand, but never be dede;
That the small minute of one hour
To thame salbe so gret dolour,
Thay sall thynk thay haif done remane
Ane thousand yeir in to that pane.
Allace! I trimbyll tyll heir tell
The terribyll tormentyng of Hell.
That panefull pytt quho can deplore,
Quhilk mon indure for ever more?
  Than sall those glorifyit creaturis,
With myrth and infinyte plesouris,
Convoyit with joy angelicall,
Passe to the Hevin imperiall.
With Christ Jesu, our Soverane Kyng,
In glore eternallye to ryng,
Of man quhilk passis the ingyne
The thousand part for tyll defyne
Allanerlie of the leist plesoure
Preordinat for ane creature.
  Than sall ane fyre, as Clerkis sane,
2 Pet. iii. Mak all the hyllis and valeyis plane.
Frome Erth, up to the Hevin impyre,
All beis renewit by that fyre,
Purgeyng all thyng materiall
Under the Hevin imperiall:
Boith erth and water, fyre and air,
Salbe more perfyte maid, and fair,
The quhilkis affore had myxit bene,
Sall than be purifyit and maid clene.
The Erth lyke christall salbe cleir;

And everilk Planeit in his speir
Sall rest, withouttin more moveyng.
Boith Sterny Hevin and Christellyng,
The first and hiest Hevin movabyll,
Sall stand, but turnyng, firme and stabyll.
The Sonne in to the Orient
Sall stand, and in the Occident
Rest sall the Mone, and be more cleir
Nor now bene Phebus in his speir.
And, als, that lantern of the Hevin
Sall gyf more lycht, be greis sevin,
Nor it gave sen the Warld began.
The Hevin renewit salbe than;
Rycht so the Erth, with sic devyse,
Compair tyll hevinlye Paradyse.

So Hevin and Erth salbe all one,
As menith the Apostill Johne. Apo. xx.
The gret Sey sall no more appeir,
Bot lyke the christall pure and cleir,
Passing imaginatioun
Of man to mak narratioun, 1 Cor. ii.
Of glore, quhilk God haith done prepair
Tyll every one that cummis thare,
The quhilk with eiris, nor with eine
Of man, may nocht be hard nor sene.
With hart it is unthynkabyll,
And with toungis inpronunciabyll;
Quhose plesouris salbe so perfyte,
Haveyng in God so gret delyte,
The space now of one thousand yeir, 2 Pet. iii.

That tyme sall nocht one hour appeir;
Quhilk can nocht comprehendit be,
Tyll we that plesand sycht shall se.
  Quhen Paull wes revyst, in the spreit,
2 Cor. xii. Tyll the thrid Hevin, of glore repleit,
He sayith, the secretis quhilk he saw
Thay wer nocht leifsum for to schaw
To no man on the erth leveand:
Quharefor, preis nocht tyll understand,
Quhowbeit thareto thow haif desyre,
The secretis of the Hevin impyre.
The more men lukis on Phebus brycht,
The more febyll salbe thare sycht:
Rycht so, latt no man sett thare cure
To sers the heych Divyne nature:
The more men studye, I suppose,
Salbe the more frome thare purpose.
To knaw quhareto sulde men intend,
Quhilk Angellis can nocht comprehend?
Bot, efter this gret Jugement,
All thyng tyll us salbe patent.
  Latt us, with Paull our mynde addres,
He, beand full of hevinlynes,
Full humilye he techeit us,
Nocht for to be too curious
Quhowbeit men be of gret ingyne
To seik the heych secretis divyne,
Rom. xi. Quhose jugementis ar unsercheabyll,
And strange wayis investigabyll,
That is to say, past out fynding,
Of quhome no man may fynd endyng.

It sufficith us for tyll implore
Greit God, to bryng us to that glore!

OF CERTANE PLESOURIS OF THE GLORIFYEIT BODEIS.

EXPERIENCE.

SEN thare is none, in erth, may comprehend
The Hevinlye glore and plesouris infinyte,
Quhairfor, my Sone, I pray thee not pretend
Ouer far to seik that maner of delyte
Quhilk passit naturall reasoun to indyte,
That God, affore that He the Warld creat,
Preparit to thame quhilk ar predestinat.

All mortall men salbe maid immortall,
That is to say, never to dé agane,
Impassabyll, and so celestiall
That fyre nor swerd may do to thame no pane;
Nor hete, nor cald, nor frost, nor wynd, nor rane,
Thocht sic thyng wer, may do to thame no deir.
Those creaturis, rycht so, salbe als cleir

As flammand Phebus in his mansioun:
Considder than, gyf thare salbe gret lycht,
Quhen every one in to that regioun
Sall schyne lyke to the Sonne, and be als brycht;
Lat us, with Paull, desyre to sé that sycht:
To be dissolvit Paull had a gret desyre,
With Christ to be in tyll the Hevin impyre. Phil. i.

And, more attour, as Clerkis can discryve,
Thare marvellous myrthis beis incomparabyll:
Amang the rest, in all thare wyttis fyve
Thay sall have sensuall plesouris delectabyll.
The hevinlye sound, quhilk salbe innarrabyll,
In thare eris continuallye sall ryng.
And, als, the sycht of Christ Jesus, our Kyng,

In his tryumphant throne Imperiall,
With his Mother, the Virgene Quene of quenis,
Thare salbe sene: the Court Celestiall,
Apostolis, Martyris, Confessoris, and Virgenis,
Brychtar than Phebus in his speir that schynis.
The Patriarkis, and Prophetis venerabyll,
Thare salbe sene, with glore inestimabyll.

And with thare Spirituall Eis, salbe sene
That sycht quhilk bene most superexcelland,
God, as he is and evermore hes bene.
Continuallye that sycht contempland,
Augustyne sayis, he had lever tak on hand
To be in Hell, he seying the essence
Of God, nor be in Hevin but his presence.

Quho seis God in his divynitie,
He seis, in hym, all uther plesand thyngis,
The quhilk with toung can nocht pronuncit be.
Quhat plesour bene to se that Kyng of Kyngis!
The gretest pane the dampnit folk doun thryngis,
And, to the Devyllis, the most punytioun,
It is of God to want fruitioun.

And mairattour, thay sall feill sic ane smell
Surmountyng far the fleure of erthly flouris,
And, in thare mouth, ane taist, as I heir tell,
Of sweit and supernaturall sapouris;
Als thay sall se the hevinlye brycht colowris
Schynyng amang those creaturis divyne,
Quhilk tyll discryve transcendith mannis ingyne.

And als, thay sall haif sic agilitie,
In one instant to passe, for thare plesour,
Ten thousand mylis in twynkling of one E:
So thare joyis salbe without mesour.
Thay sall rejoyis to sé the gret dolour
Of dampnit folk in hell, and thare torment;
Because of God it is the juste jugement.

Subtellytie thay sall have marvellouslye:
Supponyng that thare wer ane wall of bras,
One glorifeit body may rycht haistellye
Out throw that wall, without impediment, pas,
Siclyke as doith the sonne beime throw the glas;
As Christ tyll his Disciplis did appeir, John xx.
All entres clois, and none of thame did steir.

Quhowbeit, in Hevin, thocht everilk creature
Have nocht alyke felicitie, nor glore,
Yitt everilk one sall haif so gret plesure, I Cor. xv.
And so content, thay sall desyre no more:
To have more joye thay sall no way implore;
Bot thay salbe all satysfeit and content,
Lyke to this rude exempyll subsequent.

Tak ane crowat, one pynt stope, and one quart,
One galloun pitchair, one punsioun, and one tun,
Of wyne, or balme ; gyf everilk one thare part,
And fyll thame full, tyll that thay be ouir run:
The lytill crowat, in comparisoun,
Salbe so full, that it may hald no more
Of sic misouris, thocht thare be twenty score.

In to the tun, or in the punsioun,
So all those vesschellis, in one qualitie,
May hald no more, without thay be ouir run ;
Yitt haif thay nocht alyke in quantitie :
So, be this rude exempyll, thow may se,
Thocht everilk one be nocht alyke in glore,
Ar satysfeit so that thay desyre no more.

Thocht presentlye, be Goddis proviance,
Beistis, fowlis, and fyschis in the seis,
Ar necessar, now, for mannis sustenance,
With cornis, herbis, flowris, and fructfull treis,
Than sall thare be non sic commoditeis :
The Erth sall beir no plant, nor beist brutall,
Bot, as the Hevinnis, brycht lyke burall.

Suppone sum be on erth, walkand heir doun,
Or heycht abone, quhare ever thay pleis to go,
Of God thay have, ay, cleir fruitioun,
Boith Est, or West, up, doun, or to or fro.
Clerkis declaris plesouris mony mo,
Quhilk dois transcend al mortal mennis ingyne
The thousand part of those plesouris divyne.

In to the Hevin thay sall perfytlie knaw
Thare tender freindis, thare father, and thare mother,
Thare predecessouris quhilkis thay never saw,
Thair spousis, bairnis, syster, and thare brother;
And everilk one sall have sic lufe tyll uther,
Of utheris glore and joy thay sall rejoyse,
As of thare awin, as Clerkis doith suppose.

Than salbe sene that brycht Jerusalame Apoc. xxi.
Quhilk Johne saw, in his Revelatione.
We mortall men, allace! ar far to blame, Esa. i., xvi.
That wyll nocht haif consideratione,
And one continuall contemplatione,
With hote desyre to cum on to that glore,
Quhilk plesour sall indure for ever more.

O Lorde, our God and Kyng Omnipotent,
Quhilk knew, or thow the hevin and erth creat, Rom. viii.
Quho wald to thee be inobedient,
And so disarve for to be reprobat,
Thow knew the noumer of predestinat,
Quhome thow did call, and hes thame justifeit,
And sall, in Hevin, with thee be glorifeit.

Grant us to be, Lorde! of that chosin sort
Quhome, of thy mercy superexcellent,
Did purifie, as Scripture doith report,
With the blude of that holy Innocent,
Jesu, quhilk maid hym self obedient
On to the deth, and stervit on the Rude:
Latt us, O Lord! be purgit with that blude.

All creature that ever God creat,
Rom. viii. As wryttis Paull, thay wys to se that day
Quhen the childryng of God, predestinat,
Sall do appeir in thare new fresche array;
Quhen corruptioun beis clengit clene away,
1 Cor. xv. And changeit beis thare mortall qualitie
In the gret glore of immortalitie.

And, moreattour, all dede thyngis corporall,
Onder the concave of the Hevin impyre,
That now to laubour subject ar, and thrall,
Sone, mone, and sterris, erth, walter, air, and fyre,
In one maneir thay have ane hote desyre,
Wissing that day, that thay may be at rest,
As Erasmus exponis manifest.

We sé the gret Globe of the Firmament
Continuallie in moveyng marvellous;
The sevin Planetis, contrary thare intent,
Ar reft about, with course contrarious;
The wynd, and see, with stormys furious,
The trublit air, with frostis, snaw, and rane,
Unto that day thay travell ever in pane.

And all the Angellis of the Ordouris Nyne,
Haveand compassioun of our misereis,
Thay wys efter that day, and to that fyne,
To sé us freed frome our infirmiteis,
And clengit frome thir gret calamiteis
And trublous lyfe, quhilk never sall have end
On to that day, I mak it to thee kend.

ANE EXHORTATIOUN

GYFFIN BE FATHER EXPERIENCE, UNTO HIS SONNE THE COURTEOUR.

EXPERIENCE.

MY Sonne, now mark weil in thy memory,
Of this fals Warld the trublous transitory,
Quhose dreidfull dayis drawis neir ane end.
Tharfor, call God to be thy adjutory;
And every day, my Sonne, *Memento Mori;*
And watt not quhen, nor quhare that thow sal wend.
Heir to remaine I pray thee nocht pretend;
And, sen thow knawis the tyme is verray schort,
In Christis blude sett all thy hole comfort.

Be nocht too myche solyst in temporall thyngis;
Sen thow persavis Pape, Empriour, nor Kyngis Math. vi.
In to the erth haith no place permanent,
Thow seis that Deith thame dulefully doun thryngis,
And reivis thame from thare rent, ryches, and ringis,
Tharefor, on Christ confirme thyne hole intent;
And of thy callyng be rycht weill content.
Than God, that fedis the fowlis of the air,
All neidfull thyng for thee he sall prepair.

Consydder, in thy contemplatioun,
Ay, sen the warldis first creatioun,
Job xiii. Mankynd hes tholit this misery mortall,
Ay tormentit with trybulatioun,
With dolour, dreid, and desolatioun.
Gentiles, and chosin peple of Israell,
To this unhap, all subject ar, and thrall;
Quhilk misery, but doute, sall ever indure,
Tyll the last day: my Sonne, thareof be sure.

That day, as I have maid narratioun,
Salbe the day of consolatioun
Tyll all the childryng of the chosin noumer:
Thare endit beis thare desolatioun.
And als, I mak thee supplycatioun,
In erthlye materis tak thee no more cummer.
Dreid nocht to dee; for Deith is bot ane slummer:
Leve ane just lyfe, and with ane joyous hart,
And of thy guddis tak pleasandlye thy part.

Of our talkeing now latt us mak ane end.
Behald quhow Phebus dounwart dois discend,
Towart his palyce in the Occident.
Dame Synthea, I se, scho dois pretend
In tyll hir wattry regioun tyll ascend,
With vissage paill, up frome the Orient.
The dew now donkis the rosis redolent:
The mareguildis, that all day wer rejosit
Of Phebus heit, now craftelly ar closit.

The blysfull byrdis bownis to the treis,
And ceissis of thare hevinlye armoneis :
The cornecraik in the crofte, I heir hir cry;
The bak, the howlat, febyll of thare eis,
For thair pastyme, now in the evenyng fleis;
The nychtyngaill, with myrthfull melody,
Hir naturall notis persith throw the sky,
Tyll Synthea, makand hir observance,
Quhilk on the nycht dois tak hir dalyance.

I se Pole Artike in the North appeir,
And Venus rysing, with hir bemis cleir :
Quharefor, my SONNE, I hald it tyme to go.

COURTEOUR.

Wald God, said I, ye did remane all yeir,
That I mycht of your hevinlye lessonis leir :
Of your departyng I am wounder wo.

EXPERIENCE.

Tak pacience, said he ; it mone be so :
Perchance, I sall returne with deligence.—
Thus I departit frome EXPERIENCE :

And sped me home, with heart sychyng full sore,
And enterit in my quyet Oritore.
I tuke paper, and thare began to wryt
This Miserie, as ye have hard afore.
All gentyll Redaris hertlye I implore
For tyll excuse my rurall rude indyte,
Thoucht Phareseis wyll have at me dispyte,

Quhilkis wald not that thare craftynes wer kend:
Latt God be Juge! And so I mak ane end.

FINIS.

QUOD LYNDESAY.

1552.

NOTES AND VARIOUS READINGS.

ANE DIALOG BETUIX EXPERIENCE AND ANE COURTEOUR.—Vol. II. page 223.

"This historical work, as it is the largest, is certainly the last of the labours of Lyndsay. How long he was compiling *the Monarchie* it is impossible to tell, as he has left nothing which can enable us to judge of the quickness of his composition, or of the time that this poetical history required. He has, however, given us a chronological calculation, in his fourth book, which clearly evinces that the work was finished at the end of 1553. In his *Epistle Nuncupatorie*, the author tells his *lytil quair* to

> Ga first till James, our prince and protectour,
> And his brother our spiritual governour.

But James, Earl of Arran and Duke of Chatelherault, relinquished the regency of Scotland to the Queen-mother, on the 10th of April 1554, so that the work must have been finished before this great event took place by a formal act. The first edition of this elaborate work is said in the titlepage to have been 'Imprintit at the command and expensis off Doctor Machabæus. In Capmanhouin. Quod Lyndsay, 1552.' This titlepage is universally acknowledged to have been feigned, for the purpose of deception. The author, we see, avowed himself, but the printer skulked behind a deceptious titlepage. Such was the shoal on which the printer was afraid to wreck his all. Yet is it apparent that this Dialogue of Lyndsay was not printed either at Copenhagen, or London, or at Rouen: but at St Andrews, by Jhone Skott. The *Dialogue* was again printed in the edition of 1558. It was included as well in the edition of 1568, as in all the subsequent editions, Scottish, English, and Irish. The Copmanhoun edition of the *Monarchie*, thus printed by Skott, at St Andrews, within the short distance of eight miles from Lyndsay's residence at the Mount, may be regarded as a faithful copy of what the author wrote, except the *spelling* of some words in the English mode, which was so natural to Skott, an English printer, who had been transplanted from London to St Andrews by Archbishop Hamilton."

Mr CHALMERS, in another part of his edition, resumes the subject, and says:

"LYNDSAY, who seems to have exhausted all his merriment in the *Historie of Squyer Meldrum*, sat down to write his *Dialog of the miserabill Estait of this Warld*, in the vain hope of benefiting mankind by his labours. Musing on the misery which he saw daily increase on earth, notwithstanding his efforts of twenty years, he tried to divert himself and to instruct others by a Dialogue between Experience and a Courtier, on the instability of states, and the sad changes of sublunary things. He had lived to see much of that instability within his own country, and he was in the frequent habit of giving vent to his feelings in order to make others feel. He had obviously before him two books, which prompted his purpose, supplied him with thoughts, furnished him with facts, and taught him manner: Gower's *Confessio Amantis*, he had always before him, and Lydgate's *Fall of Princes* showed him where to find examples of 'the chaunge of worldly variance,' and how 'his style to dresse,' and how 'ditties of mournyng and complayning do not partayne unto *Caliope*.' With those works before his eyes, and a recollection of Chaucer in his mind, 'lamenting Lyndsay' seems to have meditated many years on this *Dialogue* of the *World's Miserie*. It was put down, perhaps, and taken up, at many intervals of several years. It was undoubtedly ended in 1553, whenever it may have been begun. A manuscript of this poem, in the Lambeth

Library [No. 332], states it to have been begun on the 11th of June 1556, as the elaborate historian of English Poetry has remarked. Yet the meaning is, that *the transcript* was begun on that day, according to a common practice in that age, of transcribing what was already printed, owing to the fewness of copies, and the abundance of transcribers. Warton regards *The Dreme* and *The Monarchie* as the principal of Lyndsay's performances. In the Prologue to the *Dreme*, the critic sees in Lyndsay strong talents for high description and rich imagery. In his prologue to the *Monarchie* our poet has, perhaps, outdone himself in a grand display of the higher qualities of his art; in elegant metaphors, artful fictions, mythological retrospections, and picturesque recitals. Nor ought we to be surprised at this exhibition of poetic talent, when we recollect that, after rejecting the *mischeant muses, beforetime used in poetrie*, he beseeched the great God himself to be his *heavenlie muse.* Yet, at this elevation, Lyndsay seems not to have delighted to remain for any length of continuance, out of his natural port of level thinking, and colloquial writing. After that prefatory effort, our poet cries out,

> I lose my tyme, allace! for to rehers
> Sik unfrutefull and vane discriptioun;
> Or wryte into my rural raggit vers,
> Mater, without edificatioun.

"After his brilliant prologue of seven-line stanzas, consisting of ten-syllable verse, he proceeds to his historical poem, which, like other *universal histories* at the revival of learning, begins with the creation of the world, and ends with the day of judgment. This poem is said by Warton to contain much learning, but when we advert to his facilities, from preceding writers in prose and rhyme, he can only be allowed to have made a great display, without much exertion of original thought, or literary retrospect. This

Dialogue between Experience and a Courtier is the largest of Lyndsay's labours. This mode of conducting a narrative, by means of an imaginary mystagogue, was adopted from Boetius, says the learned historian of English Poetry. Our *Maker* now enters a park which was decorated well by dame Nature, where he saw the sun rise, and heard the birds sing, like other poets, who seem all to have taken their pleasure in such inspired inclosures, and where he was joined by Experience. They now ran over the story of the world together, making such remarks as occasion offered, or the purpose required. This history is written merely on the plan of the *old romances*, with a religious cast. At length Experience left the poet, and the dialogue ended as the evening approached.

When Phœbus downwart dois descend
Toward his palice in the occident.

"This instructive but tedious *Dialog* was at length finished, and was sent to the press, at the supposed expense of Dr Maccabæus, who certainly died at Copenhagen in 1557, as we learn from the *Annales* Biörnonis. After much of this work had been printed, Mr Heber had the goodness to put into my hand an edition of this *Dialog*, which has the year 1552 at the conclusion, and which he yet supposes to be a different edition from that of Mr Hill, beforementioned, and from an edition in the Bodleyan library, that is the same as Mr Hill's. Mr Heber's copy is the same as the edition which Herbert had before him, and which was the only one that he had ever seen.—Typ. An. vol. iii. p. 1484. By collation with the edition in the Bodleyan, Mr Heber had satisfied himself that his copy is certainly different. And, indeed, there cannot be a doubt about the fact; for the first edition was said to have been printed at the expensis of Doctor *M*achabæus; whereas this third edition calls the doctor *N*achabeus. But there is an instructive insertion in the title-page of this third edition, which is very decisive, and which is as follows:—'Attouir thare is bukis imprentit in France, of twa sortis, the quhilkis ar verray fals as it is knawin, and wantis mekle that this buke hes, for this is juste and trew, and nane bot this buke. Be war with thame for thay wyll dissave yow.' The *twa sortis of bukis* which are herein said to have been *imprentit* in *France*, are obviously the two Jascuy editions in 1558, the one in 4to and the other in 12mo. This intimation shows that Mr Heber's copy must have been printed certainly, after the year 1558; and I think, probably, in 1559, from the alertness of the printer, though he has deceptiously put the year 1552, at the conclusion of the whole. We have here, also, an additional proof, that the first edition of this *Dialog* was printed by John Scott at St Andrews, for, this third edition is printed with the same types and characters as the first; to say nothing of the deception and struggle that we may perceive throughout the whole transaction. Whatever there may be in all this, there can be no doubt, whatever any of the title-pages may say, that Lyndsay finished this *Dialog* in the year 1553."—CHALMERS.

The peculiarities of these early editions of Lyndsay's Dialog will be fully described in the Bibliographical Notices in the Appendix to this volume. The present text is taken from the earliest edition by John Scot, in 1554, with occasional corrections in orthography from the later impressions by Charteris. The year 1552 at the conclusion of the poem, p. 169, may stand for 1552-3, that is before the 25th of March 1553, but this date evidently refers not to the printing, but to the completion of the Dialog. Scot retains the same date of 1552, in his second edition, which could not have been printed till 1559.

ANE DIALOG, &c.—Page 225.

The Latin motto or quotation which occurs on the title page of the two early editions of the Dialog, printed by John Scot, was transferred to this place by Charteris, in 1568. In the Vulgate, the words are :—*Michi autem absit gloriari nisi in cruce Domini nostri Jesu Christi.* (Galat. vi. 14.)

THE EPISTIL TO THE REDAR.—So in the editions by Scot and Jascuy, 1554-1559. In the edition by Charteris 1568, and subsequent impressions, including that of Chalmers, the title is changed to :—THE EPISTILL NUNCUPATORIE OF SCHIR DAVID LYNDSAY OF THE MONT, KNICHT, ON HIS DIALOG OF THE MISERABILL ESTAIT OF THE WARLD.

"The Epistill *Nuncupatorie* of Lyndsay may be considered as somewhat analogous to the *L'Envoy* of the antient English Poetry: Yet, was this *Epistill* always printed, till the present edition, *before* The Monarchie, though certainly with no propriety, or usefulness. It was long the fashion of the antient poets of our island to dismiss their *quairs*, with discommendations: This practice continued, from the days of Lydgate to the period of Spenser, who sent out his *Shepheardes Calender*, in the same spirit of affected disregard :—

> Goe, little booke! thyselfe present,
> As childe, whose parent is unkent.

"The *Epistill* of Lyndsay is very curious for the historical notices which it contains; and which are among the most singular in the Scotish Annals: It also pourtrays the sad state of his own mind, after it had dwelt so thoughtfully for years on the *Miserabill Estait of the Warld.* This *Epistill* was certainly written while the Regent Arran still governed Scotland, and during the year 1553."—CHALMERS.

The Epistill was no doubt written by Lyndsay after he had finished the Dialog, and Chalmers has so placed it, at the end, with the above note. I think it preferable, however, to allow it still to retain its original position. It was the practise indeed, of both English and French poets, to place the l'Envoy at the end; but here it more appropriately serves, like the Preface of a book, as a kind of introduction. Nor is there any authority to suppose the Author himself, in this title to the Epistill, used the word Nuncupatorie. No doubt it was employed by English writers in the sense to declare publickly, from the Lat. *Nuncupatio*, a pronouncing of words in a solemn manner; or to sum up, by the Author, when dismissing his book. But it is also to be found used for the dedication of a book. In this sense it occurs in the Praefatio by the elder Pliny of his Historia Naturalis, addressed to the Emperor Titus Vespasian, "Sed hæc ego mihi nunc Patrocinia ademi Nuncupatione," &c. (And by this Dedication I have deprived myself of the benefit of challenge.)

Chalmers omits to notice that the Epistill is not given by Purfoote in any of his three English editions of Lyndsay, 1566, 1575, and 1581.

Line 1.—*Thow lytill Quair*. *Quair* is applied to Book: thus we have "The Kingis Quair," "The Quair of Jealousy," and Mr Halliwell quotes from MS. Rawlinson, C. 86.

Thow litell Quyar, how durst thow shew thy face,
Sith thow art rude, &c. (*v.* Quaire).

Line 12.—*Our Quene*. Mary Stuart succeeded to the throne on the death of her father, King James the V., 14th December 1542. She was then an infant of only six days old. Unfortunately for herself and her country, she was sent for her education to France, setting out from Dunbarton in April 1548; and she remained in that country not only till her marriage with the Dauphin 24th of April 1558, but until her return to Scotland, as a youthful widow, 20th of August 1561.

Line 13.—*Scho dwellith.* Changed in 1568 and later editions to *scho dwellis.*

Line 26.—*James our Prince and Protectour.* James, Earl of Arran, afterwards Duke of Chattelherault in France, during the Queen's minority, as next heir to the crown, failing her issue, was chosen Regent or Governor 20th of December 1542. After a period of eleven years, having been constrained to resign this high office, the Queen Dowager, Mary of Guise, was proclaimed Regent of Scotland, on the 12th of April 1554. (*See* Knox's History, vol. i., p. 242, note.)

Line 27.—*And his Brother, our Spiritual Governour*
And Prince of Preistis in this Natioun.

John Hamilton, Abbot of Paisley, was the natural brother of the Governor. He arrived from France on the 18th of April 1543, and after Cardinal Beaton's death in 1546, he was promoted to the See of St Andrews; which entitled him to be called "the Prince of Preistis."

Line 30.—*Under thare feit.* This address or profession of submission, *Be thay content, etc.*, sounds very strange coming from one like Lyndsay, who, by taking refuge in the Castle of St Andrews, when besieged by the said Governor, after the Cardinal's murder in 1547, seemed to have cast in his lot with Knox and the early Reformers.

Line 44.—*Inventit be mennis traditioun.* The edit. 1592, and others, insert the word *lewd* (ignorant, vulgar) before *mennis.*

Line 91.—*Thair esperance.* "Their hope; as in Shakespeare, though the word is not now in use:—

Yet, there is a credence in my heart,
An *esperance*, so obstinately strong."—CHALMERS.

It is in fact the French word *Espérance*, hope, expectation.

Line 94.—*The Realme of France, etc.* "The meaning, I presume is, if they repent and trust in God, they need not be obliged to France, for any *ordinance*. The allusion here is to the campaigns of 1548 and 1549, when the French auxiliaries fought the battles of Scotland against England."—CHALMERS.

Line 136—*Like aurient peirles:* "So in the earlier editions; *aurient* in the later ones was changed to *orient*, the East, as used by English poets. "Like orient perlis, on the twistes (twigs) hung." Lyndsay preceded Shakespeare in the use of the elegant figure of the *orient pearls*:

> The liquid drops of tears that you have shed,
> Shall come again, transform'd to *orient pearls*.

And Milton thus:—

> the crisped brooks
> Rolling on *orient pearl*."—CHALMERS.

Line 149.—*Quhen he did declyne*
Towart his Occident Palyce Vespertine.

The words are nearly synonymous with lines 6299, 6300, at the conclusion of his Dialog:—

> Behald how Phebus downwart dois descend
> Towart his Palyce in the Occident.

Vespertine is from the Latin *Vespertinus*, of, or in the evening, as in Cicero, "tum Vespertinis temporibus tum Matutinis." These words have a reference to the motion of the planet Saturn, where Cicero says,—"In quo cursu multa mirabiliter efficiens, tum antecedendo, tum retardando, *tum Vespertinis temporibus* delitescendo, tum Matutinis rursum se aperiendo," &c.—(De Natura Deorum, Lib. ii., 20.) But Horace uses *vespertina regio*, for the Western part of the Earth:—

Hic mutat merces surgente a sole, ad eum quo
Vespertina tepet regio. (Sat. i. iv. 29.)

Line 153—*But Synthea.* The later editions and more correctly have *Cynthia*, a classical name given to the Moon, "the horned Night's Queen."

Lines 160 to 166—This stanza is omitted in the smaller edition by Jascuy 1558, a blank space being left to show that some lines were wanting. In the copies I have seen of the larger edition of that date, it occurs in the usual form.

Line 165—*The Pole Artick, Ursis, and Sterris all,*
Quhilk situat are in the Septentrional,
Till errand schyppis quhilkis ar the souer gyde.

That is, the Polar Star, the Ursis (or Bear), and other Northern Constellations, were reckoned in early times, the only sure guide to seamen. The edit. 1582 and later copies, have, in place of the *souer* (sure) *gyde*, the words *quhilkis ar without all gyde.*

Line 185—*Neptune that day and Eoll held thame coye*, or still. In other words, says Chalmers, "the Waves and Winds were quiet." *Eoll* in the later editions is changed to *Eolus*, the god of the Winds.

Line 235—*Malmontrye* for *Mammontry*, idolatry, in the earlier editions, was altered in 1582, and other copies to *Mahumetrie*, a reading adopted by Chalmers, without any reference to the older name.

In "the Gude and Godly Ballates" (p. 63, edit. 1868) is a Carol or Song against Idolatrie, one verse of which explains this word.

Quha dois adorne Idolatrie,
Is contrair the Haly writ;
For stock and stone is *Mammontrie*,
Quhilk men may carue or quhite.

Line 237—*Raveand Rhamnusia, Goddes of dispyte.* This name was given by the Latin Poets to the goddess Nemesis of the Greeks. In Greek Mythology, Nemesis was the deity having the care of revenging the crimes which human justice left unpunished. But the Latin poets used the name Rhamnusia, from Rhamnus a town of Athia, where a temple was dedicated to the goddess, in which there was a statue carved of one stone, ten cubits high.

Line 278—*That Longeous did grave in tyll his syde*, referring to the words in John xix. 33, 34. "But when they came to Jesus, . . . one of the soldiers with a spear pierced his side, and forthwith came there out blood and water." Chalmers, following the later editions 1582, &c., in which, according to tradition, the soldier is called Longinus.

In the Pseudo-Gospel of Nicodemus, we read "Accipiens autem Longinus miles lanceam, aperuit latus ejus, et continuo exivit sanguis et aqua."—Jo. Alb. Fabricius, (Codex Apocryphus Novi Testamenti, vol. i., p. 259), in a long note on these words adds "Sic, et in Martyrologio Romano (xv. Martii) aliisque plurimis vocatur iste perfossor, cujus nomen reticet Johannes, xix. 34. . . . . Alias Latinorum fabulas de Longino isto vide sis apud Martinum Polonum lib. 3, Chron. p. 113. Græcis quibusdam non hic lateris Christi percussor λογχοφορος sed Centurio, Matth. xxvii. 54, vocatur nomine Longini," &c. See also his Paralipomena on the same passage, p. 472. The Bollandists (Acta Sanctorum, xv. Martii., tom. ii., pp. 374-400) under that date have recorded at great length all that could be discovered respecting the two persons of the name, Longinus the soldier, and Longinus the Centurion, and of their companions in Cappadocia.

Line 301.—*Quhose beird wes weill thre quarter lang.* "Whose beard was full three quarters of an ell long."—Chalmers.

Line 455.—Chalmers points out that the editions 1597, and 1634 read, *Ar all inclynit.*

Line 487.—*But fenzeying.* "Without feigning, dissimulation."—CHALMERS.

Line 489.—*But as thou wald wer done to thee.* Lyndsay at line 662, repeats the same precept. "So Gawin Douglas, more tersely :—

Do to ilk wicht, as done to thou wald be."—CHALMERS.

Line 529.—*That storye thare.* Charteris in 1568, and in his later editions, reads *That historie thare;* but in edit. 1597 it is, *That historie thow sal not mis.*

Line 538.—*Gentyll Redar.* "This apology for writing in the maternal language, was also made by Chaucer and Lydgate, by Gawyn Douglas, and Wedderburn, the author of the Complaynt of Scotland, 1549."—CHALMERS.

Lyndsay not only urges on Prelates the propriety of allowing the people to pray and read the Scriptures in a language they could understand, as necessary for salvation, but likewise, that for the benefit of the Commonwealth, the Laws of the kingdom should be made accessible in the vulgar tongue.

Various changes in this respect took place in the course of time, in the proceedings of civil as well as ecclesiastical courts, registration of deeds, &c., by adopting the common vernacular language. One instance may be noticed. In the Register of Burgesses admitted in Edinburgh, commencing at the end of the fifteenth century, on the 15th of March 1560-61, it was ordered, "That all Actis, &c., in this Book be written and extracted in oure awin maternall toung."

Lines 550, 551.—*Directit* and *lackit*, in the old copies,

deractit and *lactit.* Lyndsay never hesitated in altering a word to suit the rhyme; and in line 580, in place of *Romanes* he has *Romance.*

Line 563.—*Wryt in Latyne or in Grew.*

Line 575.—*Wrait nocht in Caldye language nor in Grew.* *Grew,* frequently used for Greek: In Gawyn Douglas we have—

> Like as in Latine, bene Grew termes sum.

And so, adds Chalmers, *Gru* for Greek, in R. of Brunne's translation of Bishop Grosethed's Castle of Love.

Line 635.—*I thynk sic pattryng is not worth twa prenis* Pattryng, *pratling,* in edit. 1597; *pattering* means recitin rapidly: To patter, to make a noise, like the quick step of many feet; as in Dryden, 'Pattring hail comes pouring on the main.'—*Twa prenis,* two pins."—CHALMERS.

Line 820.—*Possedit.* So Chalmers says, in the first four editions; *possessit,* in the edit. 1597: *possedit* was the word in use; as in G. Douglas,

> Than lat us stryve, that realme to possede.

Line 865.—*Quhen God the Plasmatour of all. Plasmatour,* Maker, Creator; as in Gawin Douglas, speaking of God, *Hie Plasmatour of thyngis universal.* The word is from the Greek Πλάσμα, workmanship, Πλάσσω, to form, to make.

Line 985.—*And maid thame breikis of levis grene,*
That thair secretis suld nocht be sene.

In the English reprints of Lyndsay *breikis* is changed to *breeches;* and this word occurs in all the editions of the Geneva translation of the Bible: In the first edit. "Printed at Geneva by Rouland Hall, 1560," in Gen. iii. 7, we have, "And they sewed fig-tree leaves together, and made themselves *breeches*," with this marginal gloss:—" *Ebr.* Thinges girde about them to hide their privities."—We frequently hear of a copy of *the Breeches Bible*, as something of wonderful rarity and value, upon the supposition that the phrase was peculiar to one edition. The Genevan version in which it occurs was so often reprinted between the year 1560 and 1615, or even down to 1640, that it would be no easy matter to reckon them. A late English collector (Mr Lea Wilson) in his Catalogue of Bibles enumerates not less than forty editions in his own possession, by John or Christopher Barker, including six different impressions, all of them professing to be "Printed at London, by John Barker," in 1599, 4to. Bassandyne's Bible at Edinburgh in 1576, and Hart's in 1610, have *breeches* as in the Genevan and English copies. In Coverdale's earlier version, 1537, &c., the word employed is *apurns*, being only a variety of spelling *aprons*, in our present authorized translation.

Line 1239.—*I thynk great schame to put in wryte,*
All that Paul Orose doith indyte.

"*Evin as Paul Orose dois indyte*, is the reading of the edit. 1597. Orosius lived at the beginning of the fifth century; his history was translated into Anglo-Saxon by the great Alfred, and translated into English by the Hon. Daines Barington, and published by him, in 1773."—CHALMERS.

A brief notice of Orosius is given under line 3481.—" The Anglo-Saxon Version from the Historian Orosius, by Ælfred the Great. Together with an English translation from the Anglo-Saxon," &c. Lond. 1773, 8vo. This is chiefly valuable for the language, as it is by no means a literal version. Among the many passages omitted is the one to which Lyndsay alludes; it forms chap. v. of Book I. in the best edition of "Pauli Orosii Adversus Paganos Historiarum Libri Septem," recensuit etc., Sig. Havercampus. Lugd.

Batav. 1767, 4to. The title of the chapter sufficiently indicates its purport. "Pentapolim regionem ob nefanda libidinis scelera coelo tactam et exustam fuisse." Orosius gives the name Pentapolis to that district on the confines of Arabia, where the five cities of the Plain were situated, namely: Sodoma, Gomorra, Adama, Seboim, and Segor.

At the beginning of his Third book, Lyndsay again adverts to the destruction of these cities, adopting their names as given by Orosius: see Note on lines 3309 and 3481.

Line 1355.—*The Barne is till us borne.* This in the edit. 1597, as Chalmers points out, *is to be borne*, referring to the words of Isaiah, ix. 4, predicting the birth of our Saviour.

Line 1377.—*Ane richt Cubeit.* "Lyndsay seems not to have had a distinct notion of the *cubit.* In the Scripture the *cubit* is of two different lengths: the one, according to Dr. Arbuthnot, is equal to 1 foot 9 inches $\frac{888}{1000}$ of an inch English measure, being the fourth part of a fathom. The other cubit is equal to $1\frac{824}{1000}$ foot. The cubit, which was in use among the ancients, was taken from the ordinary extent of a man's arm, between the elbow and the tip of the hand. The Jewish cubit was equal to 1·8245 English feet, or 21·894 inches. See the table in Calmet's Dict. iii. p. 571."—CHALMERS.

Line 1594.—*It langis nocht:* It belongs not: so G. Douglas—"All dantyis langand till ane kingis feist."—CHALMERS.

Line 1628—*Nemrod, that beildar was of Babylon*, (or the Tower of Babel.) Lyndsay chiefly follows Orosius, who has confounded this Tower with the great city of Babylon erected at a later period. According to some old writers, including St Jerome, this Tower still formed the centre of the city, round which structure the temple of Belus was built." See note to line 2087.

Line 1644.—*Orosius and Josephus.* Neither of these historians furnish any minute particulars regarding Nimrod or Nembroth. The latter speaks of him as "a bold man, and of great strength of hand," and says, he excited his people to a contempt of God, asserting that it depended on their own courage to procure happiness. (Antiq. Lib i. cap. iv.) Orosius, (Lib. ii. cap. vi.,) mentions him as the founder of Babylon. "Namque Babyloniam a Nimrod gigante fundatam."

Line 1682.—*They buildit ane strang dungeon.* Dungeon is evidently from the French *Donjon*, a strong tower in the middle of a castle or fort, as explained by Cotgrave. Chaucer uses it for the tower or place where prisoners were kept.—"*Dungeon*, the principal tower or keep of a castle. Prisoners were kept in the lower story, and hence the modern term applied to a close place of confinement."—HALLIWELL.

Line 1736.—*Fyve mylis and ane half.* "*Sax* in edit. 1552 and 1558: *Fyve* in edit. 1568, 1574, &c., must be the true reading: For, he mentions before, 5 thousand, 8 score and 14 large paces: There are only 1056 geometrical paces in a mile: So, this number would only make 4 miles, 7 furlongs, and nearly 8 poles."—CHALMERS.

Line 1741.—*About the cietie, of stagis.* Here and elsewhere (see note to line 2854) *staigis* occurs in the earliest editions. Chalmers adopts *of staidis;* and adds this note, "The Jewish *stadium* or furlong, was equal to 125 geometrical paces, or 667½ English feet."

Line 1908.—*Under feit or fulyeit.* "*Fulzeit* properly

means defiled; but the *sense* is here, as in other instances, sacrificed to the *sound:* a rhyme was wanted for *spulzeit* or robbed; and *fulzeit* was used in the meaning of *trampled.*" —CHALMERS.

Line 1967.— . . . . . *that greit Citie*
The quhilk was callit Ninivie.

The founder of Nineveh, the capital of the Assyrian, the greatest empire in the world, is here assigned to Ninus; while Nimrod is called the founder of Babylon; Nimrod being the third, and Ninus the fifth in descent from Noah.

Lines 1628, 1960, and 2087.

Line 1974.—*Monarchie bene one terme of Grew.* Both old English and Scottish writers use *Grew* for *Greek.* See note to line 563. The original word, monarchy, is from the Greek Μοναρχια, kingdom, empire; as in Shakespeare, the government of a single person: from μόνος single, and ἀρχὴ government.

Line 1979.—*Ane Monarchie that men doth call*
Of quhome I find Four principall
Quhilk hes rung sen the Warld began.

Lyndsay in his account of the Four great Monarchies has not sufficiently distinguished the Babylonian or Chaldean from the Assyrian, which he reckons as the First; the Next, was the Medo-Persian; the Third, the Macedonian or Grecian; and the Fourth, the Roman, which according to the Prophet Daniel's interpretation of Nebuchadnezzar's dream, should bruise every other kingdom to pieces; but which itself should afterwards be divided into ten lesser kingdoms.

Line 1980.—The five great ancient Monarchies were Chaldæa, Assyria, Babylonia, Media, and Persia. Of these empires, established from the remotest times in the valley of Tigris and Euphrates, a late writer says, it may be considered doubtful whether the banks of the Euphrates or the Nile was the earliest seat of civilization and royal power. (Philip Smith's Ancient History, vol. i., p. 188.) The four Monarchies, according to Lyndsay, were Assyria, Persia, Greece and Rome.

Lines 2000, 2065, 2087, 2719, 2736, 2810, 2897, 2917, 2922, 3190, 3215, 3231, 3346.

These references to Diodorus Siculus, afford sufficient proof that Lyndsay had studied this old historian with great care. He was, as his name indicates, a native of Sicily; and flourished during the times of Julius and Augustus Cæsar. His "Historical Library," a kind of universal history, written in Greek, extended to forty books, in which he incorporated extracts from many older authors, whose works have perished.

A portion of the existing fifteen books of the original was first published at Basel, in 1539. It is not likely that Lyndsay knew much if anything of Greek, but the work was accessible in a printed form to the Scottish poet in the Latin version by Poggio Bracciolini the Florentine. See note to line 3029.

Line 2056.—*But faill.* "Without doubt: But, the Battle of Thembria, which was fought 548 years before the birth of Christ, is the first victory that skill and discipline obtained over numbers and valour."—CHALMERS.

Line 2087.—*Nynus ane image he gart mak,*
For King Belus his father's saik;
,, 2111.—*And changit his name, as I heir tell,*
From Belus to thair great god Bell.

Bel, it is scarcely necessary to add, became the national

god of the Babylonians. The ancient city and tower of Babel are supposed to have occupied the site of the celebrated Babylon, the capital of the ancient kingdom of Babylonia, or Chaldæa, founded by Semiramis or by Belus, and enlarged and completed with its hundred gates of brass and lofty towers, by Nebuchadnezzar. Herodotus, in his First Book, describes the great extent and grandeur of the city, with its palaces, hanging gardens, walls, and fortifications, covering several times as large a space as London.

In the minute account given by Diodorus Siculus of the building of Babylon by Semiramis, it is said, that having provided architects, artists, and all things necessary for the work, she brought two millions of men from different parts of the empire to carry on this great undertaking. He more than once quotes Ctesias as his authority. For instance, "The height of the walls was such as exceeded all men's belief that heard of it, as Ctesias relates," &c. Poggio's Latin version differs in some respects, and his words may be given as the source of Lyndsay's statements.

"Semiramis magni mulier animi cupiens virum rerum gloria excellere urbem in Babylonia condidit: accersitis undique opificibus atque architectis cæterisque quæ ad tantam rem pertinebant paratis: Addidit ad id opus perficiundum ex omni regio hominum milia terdecies centena: Urbs ab utroque latere Eufratis, ut medius interfluat, ædificata: cujus moenia ambitu stadia trecenta et sexaginta complectebantur frequentibus turribus ac magnis. Erat tanta operum magnificentia ut in muri latitudine sex equorum currus una prodire possent. Altitudo incredibilis audientibus; ut ETHESIAS Gnidius ait." Sig. e. b.

Line 2137.—*From the splene.* Lyndsay and the other poets of his time (says Chalmers) frequently use the *splene* for the *heart.* On other occasions he has, "His courage raise up from the *splene.*" Again—

Some prayit to Venus *from the splene*
That they their luffis mycht obtene.

Dunbar, in his *Thistle and the Rose*, says—

A lark sang *fro the splene.*

Lines 2247.—*Johne Boccatius. . in his gret Buke,*
Of fals Goddis the Genealogie.

This work of the celebrated Boccaccio, "De Genealogia Deorum," was written in Latin, and first printed in the year 1472. He calls Dæmogorgon the father of the Terrestrial Deities, and of all things; his companions being Eternity and Chaos. He was, as his name imports, the Genius of the Earth. Of his various children, the first-born was Litigium or Discord; the second, the god Pan; the Three Fates were his daughters.

The English poets have not overlooked this formidable infernal deity. Thus Spenser, Faerie Queene (I. 5. 22.,)

———— That great house of Gods cælestiall,
Which wast begot in Dæmogorgon's hall,
And saw'st the secrets of the world unmade.

And again, of "the Three Fatall Sisters house." (IV. 2. 47.)

Downe in the bottome of the deepe Abysse,
Where Demogorgon in dull darknesse pent,
Farre from the view of God's and heaven's bliss,
The hideous Chaos keepes, their dreadfull dwelling is.

Milton, likewise, in Paradise Lost, (II., 959)

———— When strait behold the Throne
Of Chaos, and his dark Pavilion spread
Wide on the wasteful Deep; with him Enthron'd
Sat sable-vested Night, eldest of things,
The consort of his Reign; and by them stood
Orcus and Ades, and the dreaded name
Of Demogorgon.

Line 2280.—*Behald, in every kirk, and queir*
Throch Christendome, in high and low,
Imageis maid with mennis hand
To quhome bene gyffin divers names.

On these lines CHALMERS says, "Lyndsay here justifies, by his enumeration of saints, the remark of Warton, that our old poets are never more happy than when they get into a catalogue of persons and things." In separate notes he gives explanations of the characteristic symbols attributed to the several saints, mentioned in the lines that follow, on which it would be unnecessary to enlarge.

Line 2508.—*On thair feist day . . .*
Thay beir ane auld stock image throuch the Toun.

"The *auld stock image*, which is here reprobated by Lyndsay, was the image of St. Giles, the patron saint of Edinburgh; and which was yearly, on the first of September, carried through the town in grand procession. The last procession was, probably, in the year 1558, five years after this reprobation, when the procession was interrupted by the populace.—*Maitland's Hist. of Edinburgh*, p. 15; and Knox gives a rapturous (?) account of this, in his History. Lyndsay, however, forgets the armbone of St. Giles, that was discovered in foreign parts by Preston of Gorton, during the reign of James II., and bequeathed to the city, for which the magistrates granted to his heirs the privilege of carrying *this armbone*, in all processions." (*Arnot's Hist. Edin.*, p. 267.)—CHALMERS.

Respecting the fate of this wooden image or figure of St Giles, and the tumult that took place at the annual procession of the priests through the streets of Edinburgh on the Saint's day, the 1st of September 1558, of which Knox has given a graphic description not unworthy of Sir David Lyndsay: see Knox's Works, vol. i., pp. 259, 558, and the preface to the Bannatyne Club volume, "Registrum Cartarum Ecclesiæ Sancti Ægidii de Edinburgh," &c. 1859, 4to.

Line 2579.—*Auld boises.* Chalmers explains this phrase as meaning "hollow blocks, blockheads." It is rather applicable to drunkards, as in Knox (Works, vol. i., p. 99), when he speaks of a "Dean of Restalrig, and certane old *boses* with him" (apparently meaning worthless or drunken companions); from *boss*, a small cask for holding wine.

Line 2656.—*The feild chappel of Dron, in Angus.* "In Angus, within the parish of Auchterhouse, there is the village of *Dron*-law, and near a mile northward from it there is a hamlet named Eastfield. Here was probably *the field chapel of Dron*, which is so emphatically mentioned by our poetical reformer. The Statistical Account is silent. This is the only place named *Dron* in Angus. There is, indeed, the parish of *Dron* in Perth; but Lyndsay knew what he meant to reprobate."—CHALMERS.

This chapel, which belonged to the abbey of Coupar-Angus, was in Perthshire, being situated on the high ground above the village of Dron, in the parish of Longforgan. It was erected in 1164 by Malcolm IV. for a community of Cistercian monks. Some parts of the ruined walls still exist. It may have been a place of resort for pilgrims on account of the fountain which still sends forth the purest and most limpid water, near the site of the chapel. (New Statistical Account: Perthshire, p. 408.)

Lines 2664, 2689. *Lareit, Lawreit.* The chapel of Loretto, near Musselburgh. See note, vol. ii. p. 319.

"The chapel of *Loreit*, near Musselburgh; a great place of pilgrimage, where there lived a hermit, who pretended to work miracles, which roused the indignation of Lyndsay. To this shrine James V. made a pilgrimage from Stirling in

1536, in order to procure a propitious passage to France in search of a wife. In 1543 the Earl of Hertford, during his destructive voyage to the Forth, destroyed, with other objects of greater consequence, 'The chapel of the Lady of Lauret.'" (*Merlin's Life*, 1641, p. 313.)—CHALMERS.

Line 2854.—*The quhilk had stagis nine of hycht,*
And ten stagis of breid it wes . .
For aucht stagis ane myle thow tak,
And thairefter thy nummer mak.

In these lines, and also 2905, 2908, 2958 *Stage*, *Staigis*, is the reading of the earlier editions—changed by Henry Charteris and subsequent printers, including the edition of Chalmers, to *staid*, *staidis*. *Staid* is derived from the Lat. *stadium*, and Fr. *stade*, a furlong. *Stage* usually means the story or flat as well as the steps of a house. Both words however are nearly synonymous.

Line 2911.—*Sax cairtis mycht pas rycht easilie*
Abufe the wallis of that Cietie.

The prophet Jeremiah, in predicting the desolations of that great city, says (ch. L. 1), "The word that the Lord spake against Babylon, and against the land of the Chaldeans by Jeremiah the prophet. Declare ye among the nations, and publish, and set up a standard, publish and conceal not: say, BABYLON IS TAKEN, BEL IS CONFOUNDED, Merodach is broken in pieces, her idols are confounded, her images are broken in pieces." (ch. LI. 44, 58), "And I will punish BEL IN BABYLON. . . . Thus saith the Lord of hosts, *The broad walls* of Babylon shall be utterly broken, and her high gates shall be burned with fire," &c.

Line 2937.—*The fair Maydin of France,*
Danter of Inglis ordinance.

The fair maiden of France, the daunter of Englishmen,

was the celebrated Joan of Arc, who, instigated by supposed visions, assumed, at the age of 27, the character of one inspired to deliver her country from the usurpations of the English. This was in the year 1425, and having especially distinguished herself at the siege of Orleans—hence her name, the Maid of Orleans. Her final condemnation to the stake, having been burned alive in the market-place of Rouen, reflects undying disgrace on the English monarch and his saintly advisers.

Line 3029.—*Ethesias he dois specifie*
The noumber of the great Armie,
Sayand, &c.

Such is the reading in all the editions of Lyndsay. Not finding the name of Ethesias in any work among the writers of antiquity, it occurred to me whether by mistaking the letter C for E the reference might not have been to the Greek historian Ctesias. Upon examination this conjecture proved to be well founded.

Ctesias (Κτησιας ὁ Κνίδιος) a native of Cnidos, was a Greek physician and historian, who flourished in Caria, one of the maritime provinces of Asia Minor, in the fourth century before the Christian era. He was taken prisoner and carried to Persia, where he became chief physician to Artaxerxes Mnenon. After spending seventeeen years in that country, he returned to Greece, and died at Macedon. Having obtained access to the royal archives, he compiled, among other works, a history of Persia, in twenty-three books. But only portions have been preserved in the extracts which are given by Photius, Diodorus Siculus, Plutarch, and other ancient authors.

In a collected form, one edition has the title, "Ctesiae Cnidii quae supersunt. Nunc primum seorsum emendatius, atque auctius edita: cum Interpretatione Latina, et Annotationibus, etc. adjecit Albertus Lion." Gottingæ, 1823, 8vo.

The numerous passages which are in this volume collected and arranged under the two divisions "Persica," and "Indica," prove the high character attached to his writings in early times.

The first five books of "the famous Diodore" were translated into Latin by the eminent scholar Poggio Bracciolini, who died in 1459. His translation was first printed in 1472, again in 1476, as well as at Basel in 1530.

It was from these extracts given by Diodorus, as they appear in Poggio's translation, that the Scottish poet had any knowledge of this ancient writer, and here he found the name Ethesias. One or two short extracts will sufficiently prove this.

In mentioning the incredible number of men collected by Semiramis, after two years preparation, for the invasion of Persia, we read:

"His biennio confectis tertio copias omnis in Bactris coegit. Fuit millitum numerus, ut ETHESIAS tradit, terdecies centena millium: Æquitum millia quingenta: Currus ad millia centum; erant totidem numero Homines supra camelos, cum gladiis cubitorum quattuor: Naves divisae ad duo millia," etc. (Venetiis, 1476, folio, sign. e. iiij.) That is three times ten hundred thousand men, five hundred thousand horsemen, one hundred thousand chariots, and the same number of men mounted upon camels, with swords four cubits long. The vessels that might be taken asunder were two thousand, &c.

Again Diodorus, referring to the mode of interment of the Ethiopians, says—"Quemadmodum scribit Erodotus: quod Gnidius Ethesias improbat."

In noticing the death of Semiramis, he adds,—"Vixit annos quemadmodum ETHESIAS Gnidius scripsit duos et sexaginta: cum quadraginta duobus regnasset." It would be superfluous to quote other passages in which the name of Ethesias, in place of Ctesias, occurs as Lyndsay's authority.

Line 3055—*How David, King of Israell*
His pepill gart nummer . . .
Of fechtand men, into that land,
He fand threttene hundreth thowsand.

Of this large number, 1,300,000—Chalmers says, the edition 1597, has interpolated *threttie* for *threttene*. A mere typographical mistake like this cannot well be called an interpolation. The passage in "Haly Scripture," where Joab was commanded to number the people of Israel, which occasioned the divine displeasure, is that related in 2 Sam. chap. xxiv. ver. 2, "For the king said to Joab, the captain of the host, which was with him, Go now through all the tribes of Israel, from Dan even to Beer-sheba, and number ye the people, that I may know the number of the people. . . . V. 8. So when they had gone through all the land, they came to Jerusalem, at the end of nine months and twenty days. V. 9. And Joab gave up the sum of the number of the people unto the King: and there were in Israel eight hundred thousand valiant men that drew the sword; and the men of Judah were five hundred thousand men."

Lines 3069, 3089, and 3199.—*Staurobates the King of Ynde.* In the original, Diodorus calls him Stabrobates—Σταβροβατες. Lyndsay, from his mode of writing the name, undoubtedly followed the Latin version of Poggio. See note to line 2000, &c. Wesseling, the editor of Diodorus and of Herodotus, says, that this Indian expedition of Semiramis and other matters related of her, were reckoned doubtful, even by the ancients. The Latin Diodorus used by Lyndsay was probably the edition printed at Basel in 1530, 4to.

Line 3309.—*In that countrie wer Cieties fyve,*
Quhilk wer Sodom and Gomora,
Seboim, Segore, and Adama.

See previous note on line 1239. Of these Cities in the Plain or Vale of Siddim, the last three are better known to Scripture readers by their names Zeboim, Zoar, and Admah. (Gen. xiv. 2, 8; x. 19; xix. 24; and Hosea xi. 8). Zoar, originally called Bala, was spared at the intercession of Lot as a place of refuge, when the fire of destruction from heaven overwhelmed Sodom and the other cities.

Line 3377.—*As dois indyte Eusebius,*
Reid and thow sall fynd it thus.

In stating that the Assyrian monarchy lasted 1240 years, between Nynus the first king, and Sardanapalus. The passage relating to the termination of the Assyrian monarchy, is as follows:—"Usque ad id tempus fuisse Regie Assyriorum historia refert, et fiunt simul anni 1197. Omnes autem anni regni Assyriorum a primo anno Nini supputantur 1240." (fol. 51.)

Eusebius Pamphilus, Bishop of Cæsaria, in Palestine, in the fourth century, was a celebrated writer on Ecclesiastical History. He received holy orders from Agapius, Bishop of Cæsaria, whom he succeeded in A.D. 315. He was much in favour with the Emperor Constantine; and died about the year 340. His *Chronicon* is little more than a set of chronological tables, with occasional brief notices. An edition enlarged by Palmerius, and probably the one which Lyndsay possessed, was the Latin version, printed at Paris, by Henry Stephenus, in 1518, under this title:—"Eusebii Cæsariensis Episcopi Chronicon: quod Hieronymus presbyter diuino eius ingenio Latinum facere curauit, et vsque in Valentem Cæsarem Romano adiecit eloquio. Ad quem et Prosper et Matthæus Palmerius, et Matthias Palmerius complura addidere. Quibus demum nonnulla ad hæc vsque tempora subsecuta: adiecta sunt.—Henricus Stephanus. (Colophon.)—Absolutum est in alma Parisiorum Academia hoc Eusebii Cæsariensis de temporibus Chronicon; cum nonnullis additionibus huic operi non parum accommodis, per Henricum Stephanum, &c. Anno ab incarnatione Domini cuncta gubernantis 1518, Octobris 30." 4to.

Line 3456.—*Bastalyeis.* "Strongholds. Several of the Border-strengths in Roxburgh and Berwickshire, were called *bastile*-houses."—CHALMERS.

In old English, "*Bastile*, a temporary wooden tower, used formerly in military and naval warfare. Sometimes the term is applied to any tower or fortification."—HALLIWELL.

Line 3477.—*The Dead Sea.* Lyndsay, in the lines that follow, quotes Orosius for its extent, as being 52 miles in length and 14 miles in breadth. The statements of early writers in such matters are seldom very exact. According to the latest and best authorities, the Dead Sea is about 39 or 40 geographical miles long from north to south, and 9 or 10 miles wide from east to west, surrounded with lofty ridges, varying on the different sides from 1500 to 2500 feet above the water.

Line 3480—*The flewre of it.* In this edit. *fleure* which also occurs at line 6550, is printed *flewre* for flavour, scent. In this sense it occurs in the Complaynt against Syde Taillis, vol. i., p. 13, line 131.

Line 3481.—*In tyll Orosius thow may reid.* The edition 1568, 1581, &c., have the name Orontius, a mistake which Chalmers has retained The editions 1554, 1558, 1559, have Orocius, but the London editions, 1566, &c., more correctly read Orosius.

Paulus Orosius, who flourished in the fifth century, in the times of the Emperors Arcadius and Honorius, was a native of Tarragonia in Spain, and was in priest's orders. At the request of St Augustine, he undertook his History, sometimes called *Hormista*, in which he exhibits a view of the most important events from the Creation of the world to his own time; his object was to justify the Christians from the reproach that Alaric, King of the Goths, owed his success in overthrowing the Roman Commonwealth, to the adoption of the Christian faith by the Romans, and also to show that great calamities had happened in every age.

Orosius is by no means accurate in his Chronology, but his work was much esteemed during the middle ages. It was first printed in the year 1472, and was often republished. The best edition is that by Havercamp, as quoted in the note to line 1239.

Line 3518.—*As comptit Carioun.* The account given by Carion "Of the Destruction of Sodome," to which Lyndsay refers, is as follows in the old English translation:—"The fourescore and nyntenth yeare of Abraham's age, hath God, for the abhominable euyll dedes, horrible and uncomly lecheryes, destroied fyue cities: Sodome and Gomorre, and the other cities lyeng therby, burnyng them with fyre from heauen. The place where the cityes were is become a great marasse, whose length and bredth conteyneth the space of certain miles: euen yet at this time, as though it were ful of pitche, doth burne with continual smoke and vapor for a token of God's indignation and vengeaunce for so greate synnes. This happened the thre hundreth and fourscore and eleventh yere after the Floude, after that Noe was deade the fourtieth and one. Of thys wyse hath God other whyles wytnessed to the worlde, that he wyll bee auenged, and judge synners."—Fol. x. Lond. 1550, 4to.

Line 3563.—*Dyonera, his wyfe.* So in the earlier writers. In the Lond. edit. 1566, Edinb. 1582, &c., it is Dianira, that is Deianira of the classical writers, who by her jealousy of Omphale was the cause of the death of Hercules.

Line 3576.—*Endit with miseritie.* "*Miseritie* for the rhyme in the edit. 1552 and 1558. The edit. 1568, 1574, and 1597, have substituted *greit miserie.*"—CHALMERS. The edit. 1582 and 1592 also read *greit miserie.*

Line 3608.—*Sevin score of yeiris.* Chalmers notices that the edit. 1597 alters this from the earlier editions to "full sevintie yeiris."

Line 3613.—*Carioun at lenth.* "John Carion's Chronicle, which, says Bayle, Carion did not write. Carion wrote a Sketch, which was enlarged and improved by Melanchthon. It was translated into English by Gwalter Lynne, and printed at London 1550. Carion was born in 1499, and died in 1538. Carion's Chronicle was the greatest of authorities among the Reformers. It was translated into many languages."—CHALMERS.

Line 3622.—*Rycht miserabill wes his ending,*
As Herodotus doith discryfe.

For the death of Cyrus, and the horrible revenge taken by Tomyris, Queen of the Scythians, see Herodotus, Book I. ch. 212-214.

Line 3652.—*In Inglis toung, in his gret Buke, &c.* That is, the old English metrical Romance of Alexander the Great, which I imagine existed at this time in a printed form, although no perfect copy is known.

Line 3659.—*Lucane doith Alexander compare tyll thounder, &c.*—In these lines, Lyndsay adopts a passage of the Latin Poet's work "De Bello Civili, vel Pharsalia," (Lib.

x. 20-52.) Cæsar having arrived in Egypt at Alexandria, he visited the tomb of the Macedonian conqueror, and Lunca takes occasion to inveigh against the cruelties and mad ambition of Alexander:—

Macetum fines, latebrasque suorum
Deseruit, victasque patri despexit Athenas:
Perque Asiæ populos fatis urgentibus actus
Humana cum strage ruit, gladiumque per omnes
Exegit gentes: ignotos miscuit amnes,
Persarum Euphraten, Indorum sanguine Gangen.
Terrarum fatale malum, *fulmenque*, *quod omnes*
Percuteret pariter *Populos*, et sidus iniquum
Gentibus.

Line 3783.—*Supprisit*, Chalmers explains, as "Oppressed, kept under," and adds, so Spenser,

Yet nathemore him suffred to arise,
But, still suppressing.

Line 3949.—*Josephus sayis.* The great Jewish historian, (Wars of the Jews, Book V.) gives a detailed account of "the second desolation" of Jerusalem, connected with the siege here mentioned. From the coming of Titus Cæsar, son of the Emperor Vespasian, to besiege the city, until it was taken, an interval elapsed (according to Whiston in his translation of Josephus) of about seven months. This was in the second year of Vespasian's reign, or A.D. 70.

Line 4097.—Lyndsay here quotes from Josephus the number of Jews who were reckoned to have been slain or taken prisoners at the destructive siege of Jerusalem. To account for the vast number of persons within the walls of the City at the time of the siege, the Jewish historian explains that, during a cessation of hostilities, Eleazar, the leader of one of the factions in Jerusalem, on the feast of unleavened bread, opened the gates of the inmost court of the temple, and admitted into it such of the people as were desirous to worship the Most High. (Josephus' Wars of the Jews, v., iii. 1.) The inhabitants from all parts of Judæa flocked to the city to avail themselves of this unwonted spiritual privilege, and were thus drawn like "sheep to the slaughter."

Line 4245.—In the earlier editions this title reads, *The Fyft Spirituall Monarchie*, &c. In the London edit., 1566, and subsequent copies, it is more correctly given. "The First Spirituall and Papall Monarchie." The author himself expressly limited his Dialog to the Four Great Monarchies: The Assyrian, the Persian, the Greek, and the Roman Empires. The Spiritual or Papal monarchy, he introduces, as it were, incidentally.

Line 4306.—*Gryntaris.* "Bailiffs. A granary, among the country people in Scotland, is called a *gryntal*-house. Cardinal Beaton had his *granitarius*, or manager of the victual, as we may learn from the Cardinal's account-book in the Advocates Library."—CHALMERS.

Line 4330.—*Ga luke the Canon Lawis,*
Boith in the Sext and Clementène.

"Such is the reading of the oldest edition. The allusion is to the works of Pomponius Sextus, the great Jurist of the third century; and to the collections of Pope Clement, which were published in 1317, after his death."—CHALMERS.

In the old editions there is no special difference, unless that the English editions 1566, &c., have *Boith in Sextus.* It is quite absurd to mention the old Roman Jurist Pomponius Sextus (who flourished in the second century, before Canon Law was in existence), of whose writings only some fragments are preserved. The collection to which Lyndsay refers is the Liber Sextus Decretalium D. Bonifacii Papæ VIII. It consists of Five books, but was called Liber Sextus, being intended as Supplementary to the collection of the Decretals of Pope Gregory IX., which is divided into Five books. These Decretals form no inconsiderable portion of the great body of the Ecclesiastical Law of the Romish Church, known as the "Corpus Juris Canonici."

The other work mentioned by Lyndsay is the "Constitutiones Clementis Papæ V. in Concilio Vienensi editæ." Several editions of these works were printed during the fifteenth century.

Line 4424—*David of Scotland, Kyng.* Bellenden in his translation of Hector Boyce's Chronicle of Scotland, B. xii., ca. 17, says "Kyng David biggit xv. Abbayis in Scotland, quhais namis ar, &c. Sundry precedent men nathing approvit the gret liberalitie of King David toward the Kirk, for he dotat the Kirk sa richely with the landis pertening to the Crown that his successouris micht not sustene thair Riall estait efter hym sa weil as thai did afore. . . . . Thairfoir the wise prince, King James the First (quhen he cum to David's sepulchre at Dunfermelyng) said, *He was ane soir Sanct for the Crown*, as he wald mene that Kyng David left the Kirk ouir riche and the Crown ouir pure. For he tuke fra the Crown (as Maister Johne Mair writtis in his Croniklcs) ix M. li. [£9000] Scots, &c. (Edinb. c. 1542, fol. C. lxxxvi.).

In the Satyre of the Thrie Estatis, line 2976, the author also refers to the fifteen Abbacies which were founded by David the First, and says—

King James the First, roy of this regioun,
Said, that he was ane sair Sanct to the Croun:
I heir men say, that he was sumthing blind
That gaif away mair nor he left behind.

The words used by John Major or Mair may be quoted.

After mentioning the foundation, and rich endowment of these Abbeys, and repeating what he calls "Jacobi Primi scomma," or taunting exclamation, "*Maneas illic, Rex pientissime, sed reipublicæ Scoticæ et Regibus inutilis,*" he adds, "Et ejusdem sententiæ sum Ego ipse; nam ultra sexies viginti millia francicorum de terris perpetuis regiis illis coenobiis impertivit; et sine multo majori pecunia illa coenobia extruere nequibat." (De Gestis Scotorum, Lib. III. fol. xlviii. Paris, 1522, 4to, p. 111. Edinb. 1740, 4to.)

Line 4490.—*Thay send furth Freris, to preche for thame,*
Quhilk garris the peple now abhor thame.

This is the reading of Scot's first edition, and also of Jascuy's in 1558. Purfoote's editions alter the last line—

Which makes the people now to abhor thame:

while in Scot's second edition (1559), and later copies, there is this emendation—

Quhilk garris the peple mok thame with schame.

Line 4504—The incident of the Emperor Frederick's submission to Pope Alexander III., in the year 1156, in St Mark's Church, Venice, is recorded by various writers besides Carion, Lyndsay's great authority for historical facts. John Foxe, in his Actes and Monuments, best known as the Book of Martyrs, in the earlier editions, gives a spirited woodcut of "Pope Alexander treading on the neck of Fredericke the Emperoure," with this account:—

"So the Emperour cumming to Venis; at Saincte Markes church, where the Bishop was, there to take his absolution was bid to knele downe at the Pope's feete. The proude Pope setting his foote upon the Emperour's necke, said the verse of the Psalme: *Super aspidem et basiliscum ambulabis et concultabis leonem et draconem.* That is, Thou shalt walke upon the adder, and the basiliske: and shalt treade downe the lion and the dragon, etc., to whom the Emperour answering againe, saide, *Non tibi, sed Petro*, that is, Not to thee, but to Peter. The Pope againe, *Et mihi, et Petro*. The Emperour fearing to geve any occasion of further quareling, helde his peace, and so was absoyled, and peace made betwene them. The conditions whereof were these: First, that he should receave Alexander for the trew Pope. Secondly, that he shulde restore agayn to the Church of Rome, all that he had taken awaye before. And thus," etc. (First edit., Lond. 1565, fol. 41.)

Line 4517.—*The wordis following*. The Latin quotation *Super aspidem*, etc., are from the Vulgate translation, Psalm xci. 15. The translation, as Chalmers notices, was first introduced into the edition 1568, by Henry Charteris.

Line 4557.—*As dois indyte Palmerius*. Palmerius in his additions to the Chronicle of Eusebius (see note to line 3377) may be quoted, in regard to the accumulated wealth of Pope John XXII., elected 7th August 1316. He died at Avignon 4th December 1334, in the 90th year of his age.

"Ioannes Pontifex ætatis suæ anno. 90. pridie nonas Decembrias [A.D. 1334,] Auinione moritur, relinquens in thesauris suis ingentem vim auri atque argenti: cujus recta computatio fuit aurearum drachmarum. 25. milia; hoc est millies. 25. milia: quod scripsisse arduum quippe videtur, nec legitur aliis temporibus Ecclesia Romana fuisse locupletior." (Paris. 1518, 4to fol. 145 *b*.)

Platina in his Lives of the Popes, as translated by Sir Paul Rycaut, says that John XXIII, "In the year 1334, just when John [XXIII] the Pope died in the ninetieth year of his age, and the nineteenth year and the fourth month of his Pontificate, and left behind him in the treasury such a mass of gold, as never any Pope did before him." (p. 310.)

Line 4591.—*Pope Celestine*. This was Pope Celestine III.

(1191-1198). According to Palmerius, after stating that his Pontifical coronation was celebrated on the 16 Kal. Maij 1192, he adds, "Postridie Henricum Romæ coronavit." (fol. 138). Platina passes over in silence the mention of this Pope's insolent treatment of the Emperor in first crowning him, and then kicking the crown from his head, to shew, as Lyndsay expresses it, his authority not only to make kings and emperors, but also to deprive them of their kingdoms.

Lines 4609, 4911.—In the small edition of Lyndsay by Jascuy, 1558, the words *come tyll his house* are, by mistake, repeated, in place of *with humyll spreit.*

Line 4666.—*The pure Preist thynkis he get no rycht,*
Be he nocht styled like ane Knight,
And callit Schir afore his name,
As Schir Thomas and Schir Wilyame.

"Such (says Chalmers) was the practice in Chaucer's time; they were called the Pope's Knights." Dr Jamieson, in his Dictionary, has a long disquisition on this term. Knight or Cnecht was an Anglo-Saxon word for servant, but usually applied to military service, and it may have been given to Priests as the Pope's servants or soldiers, perhaps in derision. Until the Reformation, Dominus or Sir was given to such of the inferior Clergy or Priests of the Church of Rome who had not studied, or at least obtained the degree of Master of Arts, in some University either at home or abroad. For instance, we always find 'Master (never Sir) Gawyn Douglas,' afterwards Bishop of Dunkeld; and 'Sir (never Master) John Knox,' the Reformer; owing to the fact that the one had taken his academical degree, the other not. In these cases Master invariably preceded the Christian name; afterwards 'Master Knox,' in a general sense, as a mark of respect, in speaking of the Reformer, was occasionally used.

Line 4966—*Eterne miseritie.* So in the earliest editions, the later ones substitute "eternall miserie." See note to line 3576.

Line 5057—*King of grace.* "The edit. 1597, with its usual licentiousness, [carelessness would have been a more suitable word], has omitted the last two verses."—CHALMERS.

Line 5141—*Polydorus Virgilius*
To that effect, he wryttis thus,
In Thrace, quhen ony child is borne, &c.

I find the passage to which Lyndsay alludes occurs in Lib. vi., cap. x. of the edition, "Polydori Vergilii de Inventoribus Rerum prior editio, tribus primis contenta libris, ab ipso Autore recognita, et locupletata &c. Parisiis, ex officina Roberti Stephani M.D.XXVIII," 4to. It is as follows:—"Quapropter Thraces hujus rei memores Natales hominum (prout in tertio hujus operis volumine diximus) flebiliter, Exequias cum hilaritate merito celebrabant," (fol. 109-110.) The previous passage referred to may also be quoted. It occurs in Lib. iii. cap. x. (fol. 53,) "Thraces defunctos per lusum et lætitiam terræ demandare, referentes quot malis liberati in omni essent felicitate, contra ædito puero, propinqui cum comploratione prosequebantur, recensentes quascunque necesse foret illi, quod vitam ingressus esset, perpeti humanas calamitates: Institutum me hercule inter tot vitæ mala sapientiæ plenum. Eorum autem Optimates simul atque combusti erant, sepeliebantur. . . . . Optimates etiam Thracum (ut diximus) comburebantur. Sed de hac re Funerea plura alibi dicemus, cum de anniversariis nostrorum Exequiis disseretur." (Lib. vi. cap. ix.)

Lines 5172.—Here and elsewhere in place of *Anti-Christ*, the editions of Jascuy and other early copies have *Ante-*

Christ. The scribe or printer of these copies not marking the essential difference in the prefix *Anti*, from the Greek, *Against*, *In opposition to*; and *Ante*, from the Latin, *Before*, *Previous to.*

Line 5277—*Into Fasciculus Temporum.* A well-known work entitled "Fasciculus Temporum, omnes antiquorum Cronicas complectens," containing a History of the World from the Creation. The author, Werner Rolewick, was a Carthusian Monk of Cologne, where the work was first printed in 1474. In 1481 it was corrected and enlarged; and previous to the year 1492, Hain, in his "Repertorium Bibliographicum," has described no less than twenty-four editions, besides later impressions, and translations into German, French, and Flemish.

Line 5278—*And Cronica Cronicorum.* "My copy of the *Chronica Chronicorum* was printed at Frankfort, 1614. As De Bure is silent, I cannot ascertain the edition which Lyndsay used."—CHALMERS.

It evidently was quite a different book to which Lyndsay refers. It might have been the *Liber Cronicarum*, a large and imposing volume filled with woodcuts, best known as The Nuremberg Chronicle, from having been printed there in 1493. There is also an abridgment, in French, of the *Fasciculus Temporum* with the title, "Cronica Cronicarum abbrege et mis par figures descentes et Rondeaulx," &c., printed at Paris 1521, and again in 1532.

Lines 5295 to 5298,

Of quhilkis ar by gone, sickirlye,
Fyve thousand, fyve hundreth, thre and fyftie;
And so remanis to cum but weir,
Four hundreth, with sevin and fourtye yeir.

Lyndsay's words, as above, in the earlier impressions, (including that of Charteris 1592,) evidently refer his calculations as dating from the Creation. The World, according to "Maister Carioun's exposition," shall continue 6000 years, of which 2000 were from the Creation of Adam to Abraham; 2000 to Christ's Incarnation; and 2000 should therefore be to the World's end. Five thousand therefore is a correct enough reading. But CHALMERS says, "By a strange blunder, every edition before that of 1597 has put *fyve*, for *ane:* The context shows, that Lyndsay was calculating the *by-gone* years; in order to ascertain the years to come: And it thus appears, that Lyndsay was writing this *Fourt buke* in 1553, though the Printer has put 1552, in the Colophon."

Whether we read *ane* or *five* it cannot be said to change the matter, except as regards the point from which the calculation of "the by-gone years" was made. Lyndsay's calculation was evidently from the date of the Creation, not from the Birth of Christ, or after the lapse of the first four thousand years.

This, however, is a passage with which subsequent printers thought they might use their own discretion in altering. In Purfoote's editions 1566, 1575, and 1581, the lines read,—

Of which are passed, so may I thriue,
A thousande fyue hundred sixty fyue:
And so remaines, as doth appeare
Foure hundred fyue and thirty yeare.

In the editions 1614, &c., we have:

Of which are bygone sickerlie,
A thousand five hundreth three and fiftie:
And so remaines to come but weere,
Foure hundreth seven and fourty yeir.

In still later editions, 1634, &c., we have this variation:

Of which are by-gone, as I weene
A thousand, sixe hundreth, ten and thirteene;
And so remaines to come, but were,
Three hundreth, threescore and eighteene yere.

Line 5417.—*I saw Pape Julius manfully*
Pass to the feild triumphantly
With ane richt awful ordinance,
Contrair Louis the King of France.

"Julius II., who took the field in person, in 1510, against Louis XII., died 21st February 1512-14: Louis died in 1515."—CHALMERS.

From these lines some writers have inferred that Lyndsay had served a campaign in Italy in 1510, but this seems not to be at all probable. See Memoirs of Lyndsay in vol. I.

Pope Julius II. was elected on the 1st November 1503, and crowned the 19th of that month. He died in February 1513.

Line 5661—*Delbora*, in later editions Debora. In 1614 Deboir. We find in Scripture, Debora, the nurse of Rebecca (Gen. xxxix. 8), and Debora, the prophetess, along with Barak as deliverers of Israel (Judges iv.), but no mention is made of a daughter of Adam, of that name.

Line 5664.—*Sara and Cithara, with joye,*
The quhilkis to Abraham's wyffis bene.

In the editions 1582, &c., Cethura: in some later copies, Keturah, or Kethura. In our present version, after the death of Sarah it is said "Then again Abraham took a wife, and her name was Keturah." (Gen. xxv. 1.) In another passage she is called "Keterah, Abraham's concubine." (1 Chron. i. 32.) It has been suggested, for reconciling these passages, that Keturah, like Hagar, might have lived with Abraham as his secondary wife, and had children by him during Sarah's life, such marriages not being prohibited by the Jewish law.

Line 5668—*Gude Lya*, or Leah, the eldest daughter of Laban, and first wife of Jacob (Gen. xxix.)

Line 5703—*Be gret gyrsome, and dowbyll maill.* In edit. 1582 so *gersome*, the same as Grassum, or the sum paid to a landlord by a tenant on entering upon the lease of a farm, with double maill or rent.

Line 5706—*With Merchetis of thare marrigs.* The *merchetis mulierum* in the Regiam Majestatem or Auld Laws of Scotland "is the fine, which, it is pretended, was paid to a superior for redeeming a young woman's virginity at the time of her marriage."—JAMIESON.

Line 5733.—*Nynus, the Kyng of Assiriah.*

In the note to line 3377, referring to the duration of the Assyrian monarchy for *fuisse Regie Assyrianus*, read *Reges.* The repentance of the Ninevites in the time of Jonah was not of long duration. The prophet Nahum "who lived about 90 years later than Jonah, foretold its destruction, which took place about 60 years thereafter, when the Medes and Babylonians rebelled together, and overturned the Assyrian empire." (See Dr Smith of Campbelton on the Prophets, edited by the Rev. Peter Hall. Lond. 1835, 12mo.

Line 5753—*Senyeours of the Sessioun.* Some of the early copies have *Cessioun*, that is, the Judges or Lords of Council and Session.

Line 5757—*Thair Constry clerkis*, that is, Clerks of the Commissary Court, *Constry* being a vulgar contraction for the sake of the metre. The author in his Satyre uses the term in its correct form.

Line 3061.—And I ran to the Consistorie, for to pleinze.

,, 3079.—We man reform thir Consistory lawis.

Line 5771—*Retraitit.* Retracted, reversed. The forensic or law terms in the previous lines require no illustration.

Line 5798.—*The blak byik of Babilone*, meaning, no

doubt, the Church of Rome, or the Spiritual Babylon. A *byik* or *byke*, a hive or nest of bees, was used in a secondary sense for an association, a collective body.

Line 5821—*Dalyda* or Dalida, as in the Vulgate translation, but better known as *Dalilah*, the mistress and betrayer of Samson. (The Book of Judges, xvi.)

Line 5822.—*Clytemnestra*, in the earlier editions *Clitamistra:* wife of Agamemnon, commander of the Greeks in the Trojan war.

Line 5830.—*Sydest Taillis stryve.* "For longest trains strive. *Syde tails*, in the days of Chaucer and Lyndsay, were considered as sinful." Again CHALMERS says—

Line 5915.—*Taillis.* "There seems to be no end to Lyndsay's indignation against tails. His own dress, as a Herald, was more gaudy and ridiculous, than any tail, either male or female, in all Scotland."

Line 5840—*Of rank wytcheis.* I don't know where Lyndsay may have found the name of the Witch of Endor; or why he should have fixed upon Atholl, Argyle, and part of Galloway, along with Savoy, as peculiarly the abodes of witches.

Line 5843—*The Ryndes of Galloway.* "Two remarkable promontories on the western extremity of that county."—CHALMERS. He explains the word *Ryn*, *rinn*, a point, a promontory; plur. *rynnis.* See also Jamieson's Dict. *Rins, Rhyns.*

The Rynnes of Galloway form a kind of peninsula, comprehending the maritime parishes, of about twenty-nine miles from north to south, in Wigtonshire, or the western part of the ancient district of Galloway. It is bounded on the west by the Irish Channel. The Mull of Galloway is the southern, and Kirkcolm, or Corswall, the northern extremity; Luce Bay being in the south-east, and Loch Ryan on the north-east of this peninsula, leaving an intervening space of about six miles, which joins it with the county.

Line 5894.—*The Skapellarye.* Scapulary, part of the habit of a friar, consisting of two narrow strips of cloth, worn over the rest of the dress, reaching almost to the feet.

Line 5901 and 5902.—*Phlegeton.* "Flagiton, in the edit. 1552 and 1558; Phlegeton in the subsequent edit. The last is the proper spelling, as it is derived from the Greek φλεγω.—According to the poets, this is a river of Hell, which rolls torrents of fire, and surrounds the prison of the damned. *The brais of Acheron.* The banks of Acheron, one of the fabulous rivers of Hell."—CHALMERS.

Line 6038—*And everilk Planeit in his speir*
Sall rest, without more moveyng, &c.
,, 6241— . . . *all dede thyngis corporall.*
,, 6244—*Sone, Mone, and Sterris, Erth, Watter, Air, and Fyre*
In ane maneir, thay have a hote desyre,
Wissing that day, that thay may be at rest:
As Erasmus exponis manifest.

In this remarkable passage, Lyndsay seems to quote an exposition of Erasmus. I have not happened upon the precise passage here quoted. In one of his notes, Erasmus uses this simile: "All natural things mourneth with us, and, like a woman drawing near the birth of her child, wisheth an end of labour and sorrow." In the Hebrew Prophets are many bold figures of speech calling the whole creation to attend when Jehovah speaks. For instance, "Hear, O Heavens! and give ear, O Earth! for the Lord hath spoken" (Isaiah i. 2.) "Be astonished, O ye Heavens, at this, and be horribly afraid" (Jer. ii. 12.) See also Micah vi., calling on man to urge his plea before the mountains, &c. Marginal references afterwards occur in Lyndsay to the words of Paul, "We know that the whole creation groaneth and travaileth in pain together until now" (Rom. viii. 22); and of Peter in the third chapter of his second epistle. By the above bold figure of speech. the author, whoever he was, concludes, that the earth having been purified by fire, at the general judgment, the heavenly bodies, or the whole stellar universe, will participate in the great change; insomuch that the sun, moon, stars, and planets, like animated beings, worn out by fatigue and labour, will rejoice in the prospect of being released from their present continuous motion, to remain fixed and immoveable, in the enjoyment of perpetual rest.

Line 6140.—*Augustyne sayis.* The reference may probably be to a passage in the Soliloquies or Meditations, a portion of his works which the Benedictine Editors place at the end, among doubtful or spurious compositions attributed to St. Augustine.

Line 6325—*And sped me home, &c.* In the next line the latter editions have Oritoir, Oritore.

The English editions vary in several words, and the concluding stanza, as a specimen of the liberty used in altering the text, may be quoted literally from that of 1566—

And hyed me home with hart right sorye :
And entred my quiet Oratorye :
I toke paper and their began to write
This misery, that ye haue hearde before.
All gentell Readers hartely I implore,
For to excuse this that I did indite ;
Thouggh Ipocrites will haue at me dispite.
Which would not their craftines were scaude.
Let God be Judge, and so I make an ende.

FINIS.

APPENDIX.

APPENDIX.

No. I.

THE PREFACE TO EARLY EDITIONS OF SIR DAVID LYNDSAY'S POEMS.

I.

THOMAS PURFOOTE. *London*, 1566.

In the editions of Lyndsay's Poems, before Purfoote's, printed for William Pickering, in 1566, there is no prefatory matter. License had been granted to a London printer in 1563-4 to publish an edition of the Dialogue, as we learn from the following entry in the Register of the Stationers' Company London—

1563-4—"Received of Rychard Seerlle, for his lycense for pryntinge of a boke intituled a Dialoge betwexte the Experyence and a Courteour of the myserable eastate of the Worlde. . . . . iiijd."

There is, however, no evidence to show that this edition by Searle was actually printed. Two years later a similar license was granted to Pyckering, but we may likewise conclude that his intended plan of publishing the work in a double form of Scots and English, had been abandoned, although Mr Payne Collier in his Extracts from these Registers seems to suppose otherwise. "Had this impression (he says) been preserved, it would have afforded a curious comparison between the dialects of the two countries."

But the license in question, it will be observed from the following extract, was *for printing*, not *for having printed* the work.

1565-6—"Received of Wylliam Pekering, for his lycense for prynting of a boke intituled Dyalogue betwene Experyence and a Courtiour, compyled by mr Davy Lynsaye, both in Englessh and Skottessh." . . . . . [no sum.]

An exact copy of the title of Purfoote's first edition is given on the opposite page. On the reverse, along with the Colophon on fol. 154, is a facsimile of a woodcut, which I imagined had been specially designed for the volume. But while this sheet was at press, having an opportunity of examining some of the typographical rarities in the University Library, Cambridge, I found my mistake. The same cut occurs on the title of a unique tract of four leaves, "THE DEMAUNDES JOYOUS. Emprynted at London in Flete Strete by me Wynkyn de Worde. In the yere of our lorde. M.CCCC. and XI." 4to.

The edition of 1566 must have proved a successful speculation, as Purfoote reprinted the volume in 1575, and again in 1581. The editions, in which Purfoote's name alone appears as the proprietor, are chiefly worthy of notice, in proof that Lyndsay's writings were not unknown in England. In these editions the Preface is the same, but no information is given from what source the text was taken.

A note of the minor Poems which were added to the Dialogue, although printed with the running title of the Fourth Part, will come in afterwards. See page 274.

¶ A Dialogue be=tweene Experience and a Courtier,

of the miserable estate of the worlde, first compiled in the Schottishe tongue, be syr Dauid Lyndsey Knight, (a man of great learning and science) nowe newly correc=ted, and

made perfit Englishe, pleasaunt and profitable for al estates but chiefly for Gent=lemen, and such as are in au=thoritie.

¶ Hereunto are anexid certaine other pithy pieces of woorkes, inuen=ted by the said Knight, as shal largely ap=peare in the ta=ble after fo=lowing.

(.:.)

Anno; 1566.

DIALOGUE BETWEEN EXPERIENCE AND THE COURTIER.

(COLOPHON on fol. 104.)

Imprinted at Lon-
don by Thomas Purfoote, and
William Pickering.
An. 1566.

An Epistle to the Reader.

PLATO the Prince of Philosophers perfectly perceiving, by proofe of experience, that we are not borne to benefite our selves alone, but likewyse our frendes, together with the common wealth and countrey wherein we have received life and living: did not onely commende this sacred saying unto letters, for profit of posteritie, but also laboured to accomplishe it with toyling travaile and great anxietie. For howe much he hath deserved, as well of straungers studious in vertue, as of his own native nation: his worthy woorkes, and devine volumes, most abundantly declare and testifie. Whose counsell, and example, divers men diversly have followed, studying rather the wealth of many than the ease and pleasure of one.

But in my judgement, they are first to be registred in the booke of fame: who by their watche and labour, leave in letters, ornatly and pleasantly penned, the state and condition of former time, wherin (as it were a glasse) what end, doings good or evill have had, we may clearely see and beholde. Therefore the Author of this booke meriteth no small praise: who being a Gentleman, borne of a woorshipfull house, had his childhod furnished with good letters, as he that was play-felowe with the Prince: and after that spent al his youth, and most of his age, in the Court, where, for his wisedome, gravitie, and learning, he was alwayes occupied in the most waightie affaires of the kingedome. And nowe, after he came unto crooked olde age, applied himselfe to write suche thinges as the Court had taught him by experience, for the behoofe and instruction of others.

But what inditeth he: the seemely sightes? the pleasure or delightes? the blisse and bravery of the Court? nothing lesse, but the misery, the chaunge, and instabilitie of the world. Why (I pray you) is that to be learned in the Court? In no place soner, for the higher a tree groweth, the more is it subject to the blast and tempest: so that if the roote be losened and shaken, most great and fearful is the fal therof, as in this worke by many reasons and examples, is made most plaine and manifest. Therefore, I will no longer deteine thee (gentle Reader) from reading so fruitful a booke, but now keepe silence, that thou maist heare himselfe speake thereof.

FAREWELL.

To the bier[1] of this booke.

Reade and regarde, then gratefull gaine
 Thou shalt receive hereby,
Both to requite thy cost and paine,
 Though deare thou doe it bie.[2]
Thy Pecock pride it pulleth downe,
 Thy hart to honour bent:
It telles thee how fortune can frowne,
 And take that she had lent.
It telles thee how the lowest tree,
 The wynde doth seldome blowe:
But those that are growen upon hie,
 Doth often overthrowe.
Therefore to heaven lift up thy hart,
 This world is short and vayne;
Then from it willingly depart,
 With God in yoies[3] to reigne.

FINIS.

[1] In edit. 1575, "Byer;" in edit. 1584, "Buyer."
[2] In later edit. "buy." [3] "Yoies" for "joyes."

II.

Henry Charteris. *Edinburgh* 1568.

An accurate copy of the title-page of the first edition of Lyndsay by Charteris is given on the next leaf, followed by his Preface to the Reader, and his poetical Adhortation of all Estates, &c. These are reprinted in his subsequent impressions, 1571 to 1597. In his long Preface, Charteris has given some interesting information respecting the Author, and the representation which he himself had witnessed of Lyndsay's Play in the Greenside, Edinburgh, in the presence of the Queen Dowager.

Henry Charteris, an enterprising bookseller in Edinburgh, afterwards carried on also business as a printer. He evidently had a strong predeliction for the poetical literature of Scotland, as exemplified in the various works of this class, now of the greatest rarity, which were printed at his expense. In his Preface to the edition of Sir William Wallace 1570,[1] he refers to his own descent from the family of Charteris, of Kinfauns, near Perth. His metrical Adhortation, in his editions of Lyndsay, furnishes a proof of his own skill as a writer of verse. We could, however, have wished that he had collected and recorded any personal recollections of Lyndsay instead of saying they were known in 1568 to many of his readers. He might surely have imagined that his readers would not be confined to his own generation, more especially when issuing editions of the Poems so late as 1592 and 1597, in which the following Preface and Adhortation were retained.

Charteris was successful in business, and became one of the Magistrates of Edinburgh, holding the office of First

[1] Reprinted in the Bannatyne Miscellany, vol. iii. p. 161, from the edit. 1594 The only copy known of the 1570 impression, in the British Museum, is imperfect, wanting the preliminary leaves.

Baillie in 1589. He died 29th August 1599. His eldest son, Mr Henry Charteris, was educated for the ministry, and became one of the Regents, and succeeded Rollock as Principal of the University of Edinburgh. Having no turn for his father's business, it was carried on by his brother Robert, to whom, in consequence, the types and printing materials were specially bequeathed.

In the Bannatyne Miscellany, vol. ii., 1836, there is a series of Wills and Inventories of Stock in Trade of Scottish Booksellers and Printers from 1577 to 1687, extracted from the Records of Confirmed Testaments in the Commissariat of Edinburgh. Among these is that of Henry Charteris, or, as he is called, "Charterhouse."

In the Inventory we find that in his Buith there were seven hundred and eighty-eight Dauid Lyndesayis valued at viij^{s}. the pece—summa iij^{c} xv li.

Item, xl Squyres of Meldrum at ij^{s} the pece—summa iiij li.

These were no doubt copies of the editions 1597 and 1594.

Margaret Wallace, sometime spouse to Robert Charteris, burgess of Edinburgh, died 1st of February 1603.

In the Inventory of "the said umquhile Margaret Wallace and her said spouse," among other books in his Buith there were—Item, sex hundreth Dauid Lyndesayis Buikis at vij^{s} the pece—summa ij^{c} x li. Item, fyve hundreth Dauid Lyndesayis Playis at iiij^{s} the pece—summa j^{c} li.

The Will of Robert Charteris himself is not recorded. He was appointed King's Printer in 1603, and being sometimes designed *Mr Robert*, this shews that he had received a liberal education. His name occurs on various books, printed at Edinburgh in the years 1600 to 1610, when, probably on account of his health, he seems to have relinquished his employment as a printer.

¶ The warkis of the famous and vorthie Knicht

Schir Dauid Lyndesay of the Mont, Alias, Lyoun King of Armes. Newly correctit, and vindicate from the former errouris quhairwith thay war befoir corruptit: and augmentit with sindrie warkis quhilk was not befoir Imprentit.

(***)

¶ The contentis of the buke, and quhat warkis ar augmentit, the nixt syde sall schaw.

¶Viuet etiam poſt funera virtus.

IOB. VII.

¶Militia eſt vita hominis ſuper terram.

¶ Newlie Imprentit be IOHNE SCOT, at the expensis of Henrie Charteris: and ar to be sauld in his Buith, on the north syde of the gait, abone the Throne.

CVM PRIVILEGIO REGALI.
ANNO. DO. M. D. LXVIII.

THE CONTENTIS OF THIS BVKE FOLLOWING.

UNTO THE GODLIE AND CHRISTIANE REIDAR, HENRIE CHARTERIS, WISCHIS GRACE AND PEICE FROM JESUS CHRIST OUR SALVIOUR, WITH THE PERPETUAL ASSISTENCE OF HIS HALIE SPIRITE.

It is the commoun and accustomit maner (gentill Reidar) of all them quhilk dois prohemiate upon ony uther manis wark, cheiflie to travel about two pointis. The ane is, to declair the properteis of the Authour, nocht onlie externall, as his originall, birth, vocatioun, estait, streuth, giftis of the bodie, substance, and maner of leving: bot alswa internall: as the qualiteis, habites, and dispositiones of the mynde, his ingyne, knawlege, wisdome, giftis of the Spirit, and all uther vertewis quhilk culd justlie be knawin to have bene in him. Bot seing it is nocht monie yeiris past, sen it hes pleisit the Eternall God, to call our Authour, out of the miserabill and trubilsum calamiteis of this transitorie lyfe, untill his celestiall joy, and hevinlie habitatioun, swa that the memorie of him is bot as yit recent, and not out of the hartis of mony yit levand, to quhome his haill maner of lyfe was better knawin than unto me, I think it not greitlie neidfull to tary thee thairon, bot will remit thee to lerne it at thir mouthis. The uther is, to declair his maner of wryting, the utilitie of his warkis, and quhat frute, profite, and commoditie may ensew and follow to the diligent reidar and revolvar of the samin. Nouther in this is it greitly neidfull to me to travell, seing the samin may be maist esilie and perfytelie knawin be his awin pen. For besydis the pleasand and delectabill versis, besydis the craftie and ingenious poeticall inventiounis, besydis the frutefull and commodious Historyis, baith humane and divine: baith recent and ancient: besydis the hailsum and notabill counsellis and admonitionis to Princis, to Prelatis, and to all estatis, quhat vice or iniquitie rang in his dayis, quhilk he did not rebuke? not onlie of the spiritual bot alswa of the temporal estait? quhat verteous or commendabill fact, hes he not praisit, and desyrit to be had in the dew honour, and honorabill estimatioun. Bot gif we sall consider and wey the tyme, quhen he did wryte the maist pairt of thir warkis, being ane tyme of sa greit and blind ignorance, of manifest and horribill abhominationis and abuses: it is to be mervellit how he durst sa planelie invey aganis the wycis of all men: bot cheiflie of the Spirituall Estait, being sa bludie, and cruell boucheouris. He never ceissit baith in his grave and merie materis, in ernist and in bourdis: in wryting, and in wordis to challenge and carp them. It cummis to my memorie ane prettie trik, quhilk sumtyme I have hard reportit of him. The Kingis grace, James the Fyft, beand on ane certane tyme accompanyit with ane greit nowmer of his Nobillis, and ane greit menye of Bischoppis, Abbottis and Prelatis standing about, he quickly and prettilie inventit ane prettie trik to teine thame. He cummis to the King, and efter greit dewgard and salutationis, he makis him, as thocht he war to requyre sum wechtie thing of the Kingis grace. The King persavand, demandis quhat he wald have? He answeris: Schir, I have servit your Grace lang, and lukis to be rewardit as utheris ar. And now your maister tailyeour at the pleasure of God is departit, quhairfoir I wald desyre of your Grace, to bestow this lytil benefice upon me, as ane part of reward for my lang service, to mak me your maister tailyeour. The King belevand in deid his tailyeour to be departit, sayis to him, Quhairto wald thow be my tailyeour? thow can nouther schaip nor sew! He answeris, Schir, that makis na mater; for ye have gevin Bischoprikis and benefices to mony standing heir about yow: and yit can thay nouther teiche, nor preiche. And quhy may I not than asweill be your tailyeour, thocht I can nouther schaip nor sew: seing teiching and preiching is na les requisite to thair vocatioun, than schaiping and sewing is to ane tailyeouris. The King incontinent persavit his consait, and leuch merilie thairat: bot the Bischoppis at sic bourding leuch never ane quhit. Na les ernist and vehement was he aganis thame, in his fairsis and publict playis, quhairin he was verray craftie and excellent. Sic ane spring he gaif thame in the Play, playit besyde Edinburgh, in presence of the Quene Regent, and ane greit part of the Nobilitie, with ane exceding greit nowmer of pepill, lestand fra. ix. houris afoir none till. vj. houris at evin, quhair amangis mony baith grave materis, and merie trikkis he brocht in ane Bischop, ane Persone, ane Freir, and ane Nun, deckit up in thair papisticall ornamentis, and maner of rayment. And thairefter brocht in King Correctioun, quha reformand sindrie deformiteis in his Realme, passit to the tryall of his Clergie. And findand thame to be altogidder idiotis, unworthie of ony function ecclesiasticall, decernit thame to be degradit of thair dignities, and spulzeit of thair officis: quhilk beand executit, and thay denudit of thair upmaist garmentis, thay war fund bot verray fulis, hypocrites, flatteraris, and nouchtie persones. Quhairby he signifyit to the pepill, that howsaever thay war estemit of the warld, thay had na thing quhairin thay micht justlie glorie to be pastouris of Christis Kirk, and feidaris of his flock, bot onlie thair outward ornamentis, and triumphant tytillis. Bot beand inwardlie considerit, thay wald be fund bot verray hyrelingis, enemeis to Christ, and devoraris of his flock. This Play did enter with sic greif in thair hartis, that thay studyit be all menis to be avengit thairof. Thay convenit thair Provinciall Counsellis, thay consultit how thay suld best sustene thair kingdom inclynand to ruyne, quhilk laitlie had gotton sa publict ane wound: thay zeid about to have his haill warkis condempnit, for hereticall, and cessit not in Kirk and markit, publictlie and privelie, to rage and rayll aganis him, as ane Heretike. But to returne to our purpose. Nochtwithstanding the birnand fire borne aganis him in thair breistis, the hatrent consavit in thair hartis, thair puissance and power evin in that tyme, quhen they had the ball at thair fute, quhen nouther Prince, nor uther was abil to withstand thame, yit culd thay never get power over this sempil man, nor haif thair hartis satiat of him. Thay had thair Canoun Lawis: thay had the Municipal Lawis of the Realme, and actis of Parliament haldin be that samin King, quhame he servit, with quhome from his youth up he conversit, that no man suld ressoun or call in dout the authoritie of thair spirituall Father: that Imagis suld be honourit: that the libertie of halie Kirk (as thay namit it) suld be mantenit, and defendit. And gif ony war suspectit in ony hereticall point, aganis the commandementis of this thair Kirk, incontinent thay war cytit, thay war apprehendit, and incarcerat in strang presoun: and finallie thay war compellit outher to abjure (quhairthrow thay remanit infamit all thair dayis, nouther micht enjoy honouris, nor digniteis for thair tyme) or ellis thay behovit maist cruellie suffer the fyre.

How cummis it than, that this our Author being sa plane aganis thame, and as it war professit enemie to thame, culd eschaip thair snairis, quhen utheris in doing les hes cruellie perischit? Sum will think because his wryting was commounlie mixit with mowis, and collourit with craftie consaitis (as Chaucer and utheris had done befoir) the mater was the mair mitigate. Bot this can not satisfie: for na mowis in sic materis culd mitigate thair bludie breistis. Sum will think because he was continualie in Court, and servit the King, he was eslie oversene. Bot in my jugement, that is the greiter cause of offence: namelie to haif thair vaniteis and wickitnes publischit in Court, and sicht of Princis. Nouther culd this be saiftie to utheris. M. Patrik Hammiltoun, Abbot of Feirn, being of the blude Royall, being ane man of greit literature, and of sic lyfe, that the verray enemeis thame selfis war enforcit to commend and allow him. Yit did he nocht eschaip thair malice, bot sufferit cruell deith be fyre. Robert Forester, alswa gentilman, on the samin maner was tormentit. And howbeit thir did cruellie perische, yit in all agis, and in all nationes, it hes plesit God, of his greit mercy, to rais and steir up his Prophetis and servandis, quhame he hes michtilie preservit, to repreif the generationis present of thair unrichteousnes: to utter and oppin to the pepill the corruptioun than regnand: and as it war aganis the Devill, and the warld to testifie his treuth: to walkin thame out of thair Ignorance. He steirit up the auld and ancient Doctouris, to impugne and stranglie confute all heresyis springand and rysand. Bot thame at this present I will omit for brevitie, and will speik rather sumquhat sen corruptioun and superstitioun enterit amangis thame quhilk war rewlaris and Pastouris of the Kirk of God: sen thai begouth to leif preiching of pure Christ, and to set up thame selfis: to conqueis Realmis, provincis, and cuntreis: to subdew Princis and Potentatis, and finallie to exalt thame selfis abone all that is callit God. In quhilk dayis war mony leirnit men and godlie Bischoppis in this countrie, as Servanus, Columba, Aidanus, Finnanus, Colmannus, Levinus, Gallus, and mony ma, quha baith in this Realme, and in Ingland, did lang debell and hald out the Romische superstitionis, and ceremoneis, as is at lenth contenit in the auld Historyis of Beda, and utheris. He rasit up alswa in the dayis of Carolus Magnus, twa of our cuntrie men, baith of greit eruditioun and leirning, the ane callit Johne, surnamit Mailrosius: the uther, Claudius Clemens.

Thir twa passand out of Scotland, at command of King Achaius (as Boethius wrytis) to ye partis of France, come to Paris, and war the occasioun of the foundatioun of the Universitie of the samin and sindrie utheris, and war the first professouris of liberall sciencis in thame. Nouther ceissit thay with ane Adelbertus, ane Frencheman, and Bertramus, to inwey on the stait of the Kirk, than tendand and declynand fast to corruptioun, untill Claudius and Adelbertus war clappit in clois presoun, and Johne departit the cuntrie, and come in Ingland: quhair (as sum wrytis) at the perswasioun of certane Monkis, he was slaine, be certane his awin discipulis, impacient of his admonitiones and correctionis. Efter thir quhen the sindrie sectis of Freiris began to spring up, he raissit in France Guilielmus de S. Amore, Nigellus, Nicolaus, and Arnoldus de Villa Nova: in Italie, the Abbot Joachimus Calaber: in Germanie, Hildegardis the Prophetess with sindrie utheris, quhilk stranglie wrait aganis the superstitionis and Idilteth of the begging Freiris, and uther abusis of the Clergie. And howbeit thair admonitiones culd not be hard, nor thair wryting tane in gude part, bot utterlie rejectit and despysit, yit war thay not cummit to that furie and rage, as to bruyle and scald quha sa ever suld speik aganis thame, bot contentit thame selfis with presoun, or banischement of sic persones, as war contrarious to thame, degraiding thame of thair digniteis and offices: and excommunicating thame out of thair Kirkis. Bot quhen thair iniquiteis was cummin to maturitie, God raisit up in Ingland, Johne Wicleif, quha seand the haill Ecclesiasticall estait, to be altogidder corrupt: the word of God to be cummit to neglect and contempt: and mennis traditionis above it to be extollit: did maist ernistlie teiche, and wryte ane huge nowmer of volumis and bukis aganis thame. Than was the beist unquyetit of his resting sait, and began to rage and fret, to seik the deith and destruction of this pure man. Bot all for nocht. The

Lord did potentlie preserve him from thair snairis and girnis: and nochtwithstanding all thair furie, departit in the Lord in peice. And howbeit efter deith rancour commounlie ceissis, yit xlj. yeiris efter his deith thai tuke up his banis and brint thame. Persewand alswa with maist extremitie all that adheirit to him, or did allow his doctrine. Thay brint the Lord Cobham, Schir Roger Actoun Knicht, Williame Thorpe, Williame Tayler, Richard Howeden, Johne Cleydon. Thay banischit Elenor Cobhame: thay murderit in presoun Johne Astoun, Reginald Pecock, Bischop of Chichester, with ane infinite nowmer ma. Thair was na end in thair furie. Quhill thay war thus busie in Ingland, began Johne Hus, and Hierome of Praga, to preiche in Boheme, men of sic leirning, and lyfe, that thay war in admiratioun evin to the verray adversaris thame selfis, quhairof remanis yit sufficient testimoneis writtin be Poggius, and vtheris of the Antichristiane menze. Thay beand cytit to the counsall of Constance, come upon ane saifconduct of Sigismundus the Empriour, than king of Boheme, present at the counsall: and thair gaif ane resoun and declaration of thair faith and doctrine: fra the constant professioun quhairof, quhen thai culd nocht be disswadit: thay, contrair the saifconduct, contrair all promises, cruellie brint thame. Satisfyand the Empriour with this godlie Law, of thair awin forgeing, *Quod nulla fides sit hereticis seruanda:* Thair is na promis to be keipit to heretikes. Quhat frute this gudelie Law hes wrocht, the battell betuix the Turk, and Lowes King of Ungarie, and Boheme, and the occasioun thairof quhair the said Lowes perischit, to the greit hurt of all Christianitie, will declair: and mony uther histories alswa, quhilkis for schortnes I omit. Now our Prelates, laith to ly behind, willing to schaw thair gude service to the Halie Sait, apprehendit heir in Scotland, Paull Craw, teiching the doctrine, quhilk Wicleif and Hus had teichit, and maid ane Sacrifice of him in Sanctandrois.

And findand the sawour of this Sacrifice fragrant and smelland thay tuke the Vicar of Dolour, Freir Kelour, Symsone, Bawerage, Kennedie, Stratoun, Gourlay, and mony ma, quha because thai culd not allow thair vaine superstitiones and Idolatries, expres aganis the commandement of the Lord thair God war cuttit of be the fyre. Thay had now lernit to dispute with fyre and faggot, for our auld Bischoppis and Pastouris war decayit, quhilkis war wont to be lampis, and as it war leidsternis, to all nationis adjacent: from quhome passit furth mony lernit men to all cuntreis, to Ingland, France, Germanie, Saxone, Pruse, and uther partis, as thair Chronikillis testifyis, plantand and teichand the Christiane faith, and all godlie sciencis. Bot now dull Asynis had ascendit to thair rowmis, beand maryit with dame Propertie and riches, and fair lady Sensualitie: and swa efter the rait of uther Realmis, war becummit Idil bellyis, ignorant blokkis, and dum doggis. Nouther war thay idill in Italie: thair cruellie sufferit Thomas Rhedonensis the Carmelite. And in Florence, the godlie blak Freir, Hieronymus Savoronola.

Thus continewand thair rage in all Realmis, evin to the uttermaist of thair power, it pleisit the mercyfull God, of his greit mercy, and favourabill lufe towartis man, quhairby he wald not haif man utterlie to perische, to gif (as it war) lycht to the warld: and that be reveilling of his word and Evangel, be the mouthis of his servandis Luther, Bucer, Zuinglius, Oecolampadius, Calvine, and mony utheris: be quhome he hes discoverit thair cankerit corruptioun, and auld festur in sic sort, that na man (except he wilbe willfullie blind) may not persaif the vennome and fylth thairof. And yit hes the maist part of thir (how saever the poweris of the warld has bene contrarious to thame) departit in the Lord in quietnes. Now sum wil say, thir war preicheouris and ministeris of the word, and had bene sumtyme anoyntit schavelingis, markit with the beistis mark, and had maid defectioun from thame, quhairfoir thay persewit thame the mair scharplie and cruellie. Bot the Lord Cobhame, Robert Forester, Straitoun, wer nouther schavelingis nor preicheouris. Richard Mekinnis, ane boy of xvij. yeiris of age, brint in Londoun, was na preicheour. The lyke jugement sufferit Maistres An Askew, with mony wemen, quhilk yit war na preicheouris.

Yit forther, sum will object the equitie of the tyme, quhairin our Authour levit: that the power of the adversaries was restraynit, that thay culd not rage and rin at ryot at thair libertie, and plesour, as thay war wont. And yit ane lyttill before his deith thay brint M. George Wischart, and Adam Wallace mariner. And schortlie efter our Authoris deith, thay tuke the auld man Walter Mill, and cruellie brint him: althocht fra that fyre rais sic ane stew, quhilk struke sic sturt to thair stomokis, that they rewit it ever efter. Than hes it not bene seriousnes intermixit with jocunditie: it hes nocht bene continuall abyding nor serving in court, it hes nocht bene blude royall, nor favour of Princes: nouther teiching nor preiching: nor equitie of tyme, culd be protectioun to ony aganis sa cruell and feirs adversaries, of equall will, rage, and furie indifferentlie agains all. It is rather the provydence, the jugement, the power, and the inmensibill favour, and mercy of God towartis his sanctis and elect: quhilk upon the ane part, of his lufe towardis his chosin, to satisfie thair thrist and desyre, quhilk thay had to be dissolvit, and to be with Christ, that thai suld not be langer enforcit to behald the wickit vaniteis of this warld: Partlie of his just jugement, because the warld was not worthie of thame, for it hes lufit mirknes rather than licht, and delytit mair in leis than in the treuth. And partlie to manifest to all pepill the cruell, bludie, and insatiabil hartis of the memberis of Antichrist, the pilleris of the malignant Kirk, he did (as it wer) gif ovir into thair handis, the lyfis, the possessionis, gudis, and quhatsumever externall thing thai had, to be maid mokking stokkis, and to be disponit at thair libertie and plesour. On the uther pairt, to declair his michty providence and power, quhairby he will not suffer ane hair of the heidis of his chosin to perische, but his permissioun: and to encorage his elect, seeing that nouther gude nor evill can fall unto thame, by the will of thair Father: he hes maist michtilie manteynit thame, amangis the middis of this malignant generatioun. This jugement man we lykewise haif of our David Lyndesay: to quhome we will returne, omittand the speciall abusis of the Clergie, for eschewing of prolixitie, and tediousnes, to be socht out of his awin warkis be the diligent reidar. Now as he hes bene scharp and vigilant in marking the enormiteis of the Spiritualitie, swa hes he not bene negligent nor sleuthfull in rebuking the defaltis of the Temporalitie, and all Estatis thairof. He hes not spairit King, Court, Counsalouris, Nobilitie, nor uthers of inferiour estait. And howbeit thai war not altogidder cummit to sic corruptioun and furie, that thai micht not beir mair equallie with generall admonitionis and reprochis, than the spiritualitie. Yit als lytill amendement followit in the ane stait, as in the uther. Quhat laubouris tuke he that the landis of this cuntrie micht be set out in fewis, efter the fassioun of sindrie uther Realmes, for the incres of policie and riches? Bot quhat hes he profitit? Quhen ane pure man with his haill raice and ofspring hes laubourit out thair lyfis, on ane lytil piece of ground, and brocht it to sum point and perfectioun: than must the Lairdis brother, kinnisman, or surname haif it: and the pure man, with his wyfe, and babeis, for all thair travellis, schot out to beg thair meit. He that tuke lytill laubouris on it, man enjoy the frutes, and commoditeis of it: he man eit up the sweit and laubouris of the pure mannis browis. Thus the pure dar mak na policie, nor bigging, in cace thai big thame selfis out. Bot althocht men wink at this, and ovirluke it, yit he sitts abone that seis it, and sal Iuge it. He that heiris the sichis and complaintis of the pure oppressit, sall not for ever suffer it unpunischit. Quhat hes he alswa writtin aganis this Herald hors, devysit for mony pure mannis hurt? Bot quha hes dimittit it? Finallie, quhat oppressioun or vice hes he not repreuit? Bot thair sall suffice for exempill. And gif he had leifit in thir lait dayis, quhat had he said of the unnatural murtheris: the cruel slauchteris: the manifest reiffis: the continuall heirschippis: the plane oppressionis: the lytill regard of all persones to the commoun weilth: the mantening of derth, to the universall hurt of the pure in transporting of victuallis furth of the Realme, contrarie to the statutis thairof, for the particular weill of few, and hurt of mony: the Importing of greit quantiteis of fals cunze, sklenderlie serchit, and lychtliar punischit: The multitude of Kirkis destitute of Ministeris throw the hail cuntrie: The slaw administratioun of Justice, and fer les executioun: with all kynde of impieteis (as it wer) publictlie and frelie regnand. Yit nochttheles we luke for redres and reformatioun of all sic horribil deformiteis, at the handis of sic rewlaris, as God hes, and sall strenthin with his Spirit, lychtin with the pure word of his Evangel, endew with his feir (quhilk is the beginning of all wisdome) with sic knawlege sic jugement, and zeill, that thai sall to thair uttermaist endevour, avance and set fordwart all justice, and equitie, and suppres all vice and iniquitie: to the glorie of God: to the avancement of his word: to the edificatioun of his Kirk, and to the confort and quietnes of this trubillit and afflictit commoun weilth. Quhilk God of his greit mercie, grant that we may schortlie se. *Amen.*

I have alreddie passit the boundis of ane Preface: yit ane thing restis to admonische the (gentill Reidar) of thir warkis following. The mair part of thame hes bene sindrie tymes in sindrie places imprentit: as heir in Scotland, quhilk yit war not sa correct as neid requyrit. Thay haif bene Imprentit in Rowen, bot altogidder sa corrupt and fals, that na man can be abill to atteyne to the Authoris mynde be thame. For besydis the wrang ortographie, and fals spelling, the transpositiones of wordis, and lynis: thair is alswa sic defectiones, that sumtymes wil want twa or thrie lynis in ane sentence: sumtymes als mony abound, and be doublit. Quhairthrow the myndis of honest men ar alienatit from reiding of sa frutefull warkis: youth is abusit and corruptit: the Authour, and his warkis schamefullie blottit, and barbulzeit: the cuntrie infamit: and sic personis as laubouris for just correctioun utterlie discuragit seand thair laubourcs and travellis sa haistilie thairefter to be corruptit, at the private appetite and gredines of certane godles ignorantis: quhilk in respect of thir greit hurtis, deservis na small punischement. Thay ar lykewise laitlie Imprentit in Londoun, with lyttill better succes than the uther. For thai haif gane about to bring thame to the southerne language, alterand the vers and collouris thairof, in sic placis as thai culd admit na alteratioun: quhairfoir the native grace and first mynd of the wryter is oftentymes pervertit. And for the Ortographie, transpositiones, and defectiones, thay ar almaist commoun with the uther.

Thus seing this famous Authour and his notabill warkis to be sa velanouslie handillit, and sa miserabillie and malitiouslie mankit and alterat: we haif gane about, and takin sum travellis, to vindicate thame from thir blottis and corruptiones: and to reduce and bring thame to the native integritie and first mening of the wryter. Quhilk salbe esilie persavit in the reiding: bot maist esilie, gif ony wil confer this editioun with thame that hes precidit: quhairin quhat difference is betuix rycht and wrang wryting, betuix correct and uncorrect imprenting, salbe cleirlie sene.

Mair we haif eikit sindrie Warkis of the samin Authour, quhilkis hes not bene befoir Imprentit: to the intent, that na thing of sa Nobill ane wryter suld perische, throw negligence or sleuthfulnes of this present age, bot suld be reservit to the frute of all posteriteis following. And forther intendis (be the help of God) to use the lyke diligence in all Warkis of this wryter quhilkis sall heirefter, be ony menis, cum to our handis.

I will deteyne thee na langer (gude Reidar) from the Warkis thame selfis: bot will commit thee to the protectioun of the Almychtie our God: ernistlie desyrand thee to call upon him: that he will rais and steir up mony David Lyndesayis: that will continuallie admonische baith Prince and Pepill of thair dewtie and vocatioun quhairunto the Lord thair God hes callit thame: that will rebuke and repreif all sic defaltis as salbe fund in thame: that will commit to letteris, and wryte the honour, the gloir, the fame, and succes of vertew, and inbraceris thairof: The dishonour, the schame, the defame, and mischeif of vyce and impietie, and enhanceris thairof. To be notifyit, and maid knawin to all agis to cum: that it may be ane prik and spur to the verteous and godlie to ga fordwart in all richteousnes and equitie: that it may be ane stay and brydill to reteyne and hald bak the wickit and ungodlie from all wickitnes and iniquitie. To the intent: that God may be glorifyit: his Kirk edifyit: and this commoun weilth confortit and quietit.

ANE ADHORTATIOUN OF ALL ESTATIS,

TO THE REIDING OF THIR PRESENT WARKIS.

[By Henry Charteris, 1568.]

Sen that it is maist worthie for to be
Lamentit, of euerilk warldlie wicht:
To se the warkis of pleasand Poetrie,
To ly sa hid, and sylit from the sicht
Of those in hart, quha dois rejois aricht
In Vulgar toung for to behald and heir
Vertew and vyce disclosit, and brocht to licht,
In thair riche collouris planelie to appeir.

Thairfoir (gude Reidar) haif I travell tane,
Intil ane volume now brieflie for to bring
Of David Lyndesay, the haill warkis ilk ane,
Knicht of the Mount, Lyoun of Armis King,
Quha in our dayis now did laitlie ring,
Quhais pregnant practick, and quhais ornate style
To be commendit be me, neidis na thing:
Lat Warkis beir witnes, quhilkis he hes done compyle.

Thocht Gawine Dowglas Bischop of Dunkell
In ornate meter surmount did euerilk man:
Thocht Kennedie and Dunbar bure the bell
For the large race of Rethorik they ran.
Yit never Poeit of Scottische clan,
Sa cleirlie schaw that Monstour with his markis.
The Romane God, in quhome all gyle began,
As dois gude David Lyndesay in his Warkis.

Quhairin na stait be spairit, bot stoutlie schew thame,
How thay baith God and man had sore offendit:
With fleschehukis of flatteric he never clew thame,
Of quhat degre sa ever thay discendit,
Thair auld misdeid he prayit them ay to mend it
Empriour, nor King, Duke, Erle, Prince, nor Paip,
Gif thay to quell Christis flock yit still pretendit:
Goddis just jugementis na way suld they eschaip.

With prettie problemis, and sentences maist sage,
With plesand proverbis in his warkis all quhair,
With statlie storyis aggreing to our age,
With similitudis semelie he dois declair,
With weill waillit wordis, wyse and familiar.
Of queynt convoy, this joyous gem jocund,
Intill his bukis to speik he did nocht spair
Aganis all vyce, ay quhair it did abound.

Princes approche, cum Rewlaris in ane randoun:
Reid heir, ye Lordis of the meyner menze,
The end of hicht, your pryde lerne to abandoun.
Cum schameles schavelingis of Sathanis senze,
Rynnand in vyce, ay still with open renze,
Of proud Prelatis reid heir the suddane fall:
Quha for to stoup yit never denze,
Under the yock of him that creat all.

Cum teynefull tyrannis, trimmilling with your trayne:
Cum nouchtie Newtrallis, with your bailfull band:
Ye haif ane cloik now reddy for the rayne,
For fair wether, ane other ay at hand:
Idolateris draw near to burgh and land,
Reid her your lyfe at large, baith mair and min,
With Hypocrites ay slyding as the sand,
As humloik how of wit, and vertew thin.

Oppressouris of the pure, cum in till pairis:
Flatteraris flok fordwart, for I hard tell,
Ye had ane saw richt sicker for all sairis.
Lawieris, and Scrybis, quha hes your saulis to sell:
Craftismen, and Merchandis, gif ye do mell,
With fraud or falset, than I yow desire,
Reid in this buke, the speiche gif ye can spell,
Quhat just reward ye sall haif for your hyre.

Amang the rest, now Courteouris cum hidder,
Thocht ye be skeich, and skip abone the skyis,
Yit constantlie I pray yow to considder,
In to this scrow, quhat Lyndesay to yow cryis.
Cum all degreis. in lurdanerie quha lyis,
And fane wald se of sin the feirfull fyne:
And lerne in vertew how for to upryis
Reid heir this buke, and ye sall find it syne.

With Scripture, and with storyis naturall,
Richelie replenischit from end till end.
In till this buke, quha list to reid, thay sall
Find mony lessoun largelie to commend
The braid difference quhairin weill may be kend
Betwene verteous and vicious leving.
Lat us thairfoir our lyfe in vertew spend,
Sen vyce of mankynd is the haill mischeving.

Lat LYNDESAY now as he war zit on lyif,
Pas furth to lycht, with all his sentence hie:
Unto all men thair dewtie to descryve
Quhairin thay may ane lyvelie Image se,
Of his expressit mind in Poetrie,
Prentit, as he it publischit with his pen.
That him self speik, I think it best for me.
Gif gloir to God, quhilk gaif sic giftis to men.

FINIS.

THE

WORKES OF THE FAMOVS AND worthie Knight Sir DAVID LYNDESAY *of the Mont aliâs Lion, King of Armes.*

Newly corrected and vindicate from the former errours wherewith they were corrupted, and augmented with ſundrie workes neuer before imprinted.

IOB 7.

Militia eſt vita hominis super terram.
Viuet etiam post funera virtus.

EDINBURGH
Printed by ANDRO HART, *Anno Dom.* 1614.

THE WORKES OF *THE FAMOVS AND* worthy Knight, Sir *David Lindeſay of* the Mount, Aliàs, Lyon, *King of Armes:*

Newlie corrected and vindicate from the former errours wherewith they were corrupted: and augmented with ſundrie workes, &c.

Iob 7.

Militia eſt vita hominis ſupra terram

Vivet etiam poſt funera virtus.

EDINBVRGH printed by [*the Heires of*] Andrew Hart. 1634.

III.

ANDREW HART. *Edinburgh* 1614.

ANDREW HART, a well-known citizen of Edinburgh, likewise carried on business first as a Bookseller, and for many years also as a Printer. He may be said to have been the first in Scotland (like the Bleans' and Elzevirs' in Holland) to publish in a smaller and more commodious form than his predecessors such popular works as Lyndsay, Bruce, and Wallace, and some of the Latin classics used in schools, for instance, Virgil, Ovid, and Terence. His Testament and Inventory are printed in the Bannatyne Miscellany, vol. ii. p. 241. His brief preface to Lyndsay in 1614, as follows, is not of any importance, but it was retained in nearly all the editions of a later date. Hart died at Edinburgh in December 1621, and his "Heires" carried on his printing business for several years.

The Printer to the Reader.

IT hath pleased God in all ages, to raise up faithfull and worthy men of singular giftes and graces (especially in the time of greatest defection) to beare witnesse to his trueth, and to rebuke the world of sinne. As *Noah* to preach repentance to the corrupt world, for the space of 120 yeares before he sent that universall deluge. *Lot* in *Sodome* whose righteous soule they vexed from day to day, with their unlawfull deedes: *Moses* in *Egypt* to be a deliverer of his people, and to threaten King *Pharao* for their oppression, who chused rather to suffer adversitie with the people of God, then to enjoy the pleasures of sinnes for a season. And all his Prophets from time to time to reproove and correct the enormities, not onely of his owne people of the Jewes, but also of the adiacent Gentiles for their iniquities.

And in the time of the Gospell what a multitude of notable men of all Nations, hath he stirred up, whereof there was many holy Martyrs, who exponed their bodies to cruell torments for the testimonie to his trueth. And even here in our owne Nation, amongst many other learned and faithfull men, it pleased his Majestie (even in the time of palpable darknes) to stirre up this our Author Sir *David Lyndesay*, albeit a Courteour of his calling, and exercised about matters of estate, yet a man of such sinceritie and faithfulnesse, that he spared not aswell in his satyricall farses and playes, as in all his other workes, to enveigh most sharply, both against the enormities of the Court, and the great corruptions of the Clergie, that it is to be wondred how euer he escaped their bloodie hands, they having such power at that time and beeing so fiercely bent to shedde the blood of Gods Saints: as they practised in those daies upon the bodies of Gods deare servants, *Master Patricke Hammilton*, *Robert Forrester*, gentleman, *George Wishard*, and *Walter Milne*, with diuers others, who gaue their liues for the testimonie of Gods trueth. And yet this our Author ended his dayes in peace for all their cruell menassings.

This lets us see the wonderfull power and prouidence of the Almightie, that albeit he suffer the Wicked to execute their crueltie upon the bodies of some of his dearest Saints (as it may best serve to the glory of his owne Name, and to their singular good) yet he can and will preserve others of his owne children, that the enemies shall not have power to touch one haire of their heades, but as it pleaseth his Majestie to permit them. Leauing any further commendation of the Author, because his owne workes shall better testifie of his faithfulnesse and sinceritie, then I can expresse, I will not detaine thee good Christian Reader, any longer from perusing of the same. Praying God, that thou may read them with as sincere a minde, as he hath written the same. AMEN.

No. II.

THE TRANSLATION OF LYNDSAY'S POEMS INTO DANISH VERSE. 1591.

The title of the volume is as follows :—

"DIALOGUS, eller En Samtale, Imellom Forfarenhed, oc en Hofftienere, om Verdens elendige vœsen, oc begribis vdi fire Böger om Monarchier. Fordum screffuen paa Skotske, aff velbyrdige Herre, Herr DAUID LYNDSAY, Ridder de monte, etc. Oc nu nylige transfererit aff Skotske maal paa Latine, ved Anders Robertson födt i Aberdÿn i Skotland, oc siden aff Latine paa Danske Rÿm, ved Jacob Mattssön Kiöbenhaffn, Aar 1591. Effter Fortalen skal findis it Register, &c. Prentet i Kiöbenhaffn: 1591." 4to, black letter. Title, &c., 16 leaves, Text, fol. 1 to 210 (Colophon.) "Prentet i Kiöbenhaffn, aff Hans Stockelman. 1591."

("A Dialogue, or Conversation between Experience and a Courtier, about the miserable things of the world, and is contained in four books of the Monarchies. Formerly written in Skotske by wellborn (Master) Sir Dauid Lyndsay, Knight of the Monte, &c. And now just translated from Scotske language in Latin by Anders Robertson, born in Aberdeen in Scotland, and since from Latin into Danish Rhyme, by Jacob Mattssón. Printed in Copenhagen, 1591.)

The volume contains the Dialog, in Four books, followed by The Dreme, The Complaynt to the King, The Papyngo, The Tragedy of the Cardinal, and the Deploration of Quene Magdalene.

ANDREW ROBERTSON, the translator of Lyndsay, was a native of Aberdeen, but we are not informed under what circumstances he found himself in Denmark. In 1589 he printed some Latin verses, "Carmen Lugubre in Obitum D. Doct. Andreæ Laurentii Hafniensis Academiæ Professoris S.S.T. Primarii: qui exspiravit 3 Nov. 1589." A single leaf in folio printed at Hafnia, or Copenhagen, signed, "Lugubre hoc cecinit Carmen, Regiæ Majestatis munificentissimæ in Dania alumnus, Andreas Robertsoneus Scotus."

The arrival of King James the Sixth, in Norway and Denmark, and his marriage with the Princess Anna, presented too favourable an occasion to be neglected; and Robertson accordingly prepared a series of encomiastic verses, in the form of an *Epithalamium* on the marriage, a *Congratulatio* on the arrival of King James, a *Salutatio* to Christian the Fourth King of Denmark and Norway, along with an *Encomium* to the Queen Sophia, and a *Salutatio* to her daughter Anna, now Queen of Scotland, all comprised in a tract of eight leaves, Hafniae, 1590, 4to. The dedication to James ends with the lines,—

> Ergo Danorum residens peregrinis in oris,
> Scotorum Regem, Scotus et ipse, canam.

The Danish translation of Lyndsay is a literary curiosity, and seems to have been unknown in this country, until (now many years ago) I procured in Denmark a few copies from various collections. Dr Irving, in his History of Scottish Poetry (p. 347), has given a detailed account of the volume. But being interested to ascertain precisely the character of the translation, I lately obtained from an intelligent Danish scholar (Mr Börge Pontopiddan) a comparison of certain passages, with a literal version, from which I am enabled to give the following notice and extracts.

The volume is addressed "To the faithful, wellborn and dread Lords, and appointed councillors of the Realm: Niels Kaas of Torupgaard, the King's Majesty's Chancellor. Peder Munck de Estvadgaard, Admiral of the realm.

Jörgen Rosenkrantz of Rosenholm, Hack Ulffstand of Heckebierg: my gracious lords and special patrons. Grace and peace from the Lord God by Jesus Christ." In this it is said, "A wellborn lord, David Lyndsay, a Knight in the Kingdom of Scotland, and chamberlain of King James the Fifth, has in the olden times written some books, with delightful rhymes, in the Scottish language, which contain earnest acts, taken from old writers and histories, which are just fitting to our time and habits," &c. This dedication, in Danish, is dated Kiobenhaffn (or Copenhagen), 20th July 1591, with the name "Andreas Robertsonus Scotus, Abredonensis."

The dedication is followed by "En Fortale screffuen udaff Skotsk oc nu paa Danske." (A Preface written in Scots, and now in Danish.) With one or two omissions, this is a literal translation of the Preface by HENRY CHARTERIS (already given, see p. 229), but whose name is ignored by ANDREW ROBERTSON, who wishes Grace and Peace to the Reader. Nor is there any allusion to his coadjutor, Jacob Mattsön (Mathewson, or son of Matthew), whose name occurs on the title page: see page 249.

A few lines from the Dialog, with a literal translation, may be given as a specimen. The first extract contains lines 2501 to 2508.

Ande Bog om Monarchier.—Fol. 50. *b.*

I Edinburg Skotlands Hoffuitstad,
Paa en Höytids dag naar huer mand er glad,
Da kunde alle see stor daarlighed,
Affguderi oc verstyggelighed,
It gammelt Trœbillede i Staden bœris,
Met Sang oc atskillig spil det œris,
Met Piber oc Trummer, met Harper oc Gijer,
Trometer, Skalmeyer, Tromper oc Lirer,

Slig statz er brugit i disse Aar,
Aff Prester oc Muncke som i process gaar,
Lige som Bel bleff baaren i fordum tid,
I Babylons Stad saa stor oc vijd.

In Edinburgh, Scotland's capital,
On a day of festival, when every man is glad,
Then all might see great sinfulness,
Idolatry, and abomination :
An old wooden image about town is carried,
Honoured with song and different kinds of play (music),
With fifes and drums, with harps and guitars,
With trumpets, clarions.
The like festivals have been used in these years
By priests and monks who go in procession,
Likewise as Bel was carried of old
About the City of Babylon, so large and wide.

The next extract corresponds with lines 4242 to 4261 of the original.

Tredie Bog om Monarchier.—Fol. 86. *b.*

OM DEN FEMTE OC GEISTLICHE OC PAPISKE MONARCHIE.

Hofft.—Jeg sagde, Fader, monne icke nogen Förste vere,
Der vijt offuer Verden nu monne regere,
Som de Assyriske oc Persiske vaare,
Grekiske oc Rommerske som höy Titel baare,
Huor er nu nogen i disse tide,
Der sit Herredom vdstrecker saa vijde.

Exper.—Hand suarede ingen Förste nu findis kand,
Der har slig Herredom offuer alle hand,
Met saadan almindelig Keyserlig mact,
Som Darius oc Alexander vaare i stor act,
Eller oc som Julius Keyser haffde,
Der Oster oc Vester Land under sig lagde :

Dog kand maud nu i Europa finde,
En veldig Konge huo ret vil besinde,
Some binder offuer den gantske Christendom,
Det er den mectige Pawe i Rom,
Slœt ingen Förste kand vere hans lige,
Hans Decreter kand oss det nock som sige.

(*Marginal note.*)—Delte screff Lyndesius den tid Pawens Religion vaar alleuegue i Christendommen ved mact.

Court.—I said, Father, is there not now any prince,
Who reigns over the whole world,
As did the Assyrians and Persians,
The Grecians and Romans, who wore such high titles?
Where is any one now to be found,
Who lords it over such broad lands?
Exper.—He answered: No prince is to be found now,
Who reigns like these over all the world,
With such imperial power, as caused
Darius and Alexander to be so esteemed,
Or as had Julius Cæsar,
Who subjugated the Orient and Occident.
Still is to be found in Europe now?
A powerful king, if we will recollect,
Who holds the sway over the whole Christianity,
It is the great Pope in Rome,
No Prince with him can be compared, &c.

In the translation of "An Adhortation of all Estatis, to the reiding of thir present Warkis," by H. Charteris, Robertson has almost wholly altered the second stanza (See page 242), as follows:

En Formaning til alle Stater at de gierne læse denne nærnerendis Bog.

Saadant vaar mig den höyeste Aarsag,
At ieg ey sparede denne wmag,
At vende denne Bog met arbeyd stort
Paa Danske Rÿm som för Skotsk vaar giort,
Aff Dauid Lyndesio i Skotland,
En Ridder de monte oc velbyrdig mand,
Som ey lang tid siden vaar ved mact,
Hos mange Danske folck i stor act,
Hans forstandighed i denne Scrifft vdnisis
Oc er ey fornöden aff mig at prisis
Thi Gierningen roser sin Mester sel,
Naar den er giort enten ilde eller vel.

Translation from the poetical Preface.

This was to me the most stirring cause,
Why I did not spare myself the labour
With great work this book to alter
Into Danish rhymes, which was before composed in Scots,
By David Lyndesay in Scotland,
A knight de Monte and a wellborn man,
Who was not long ago in great power,
By many Danes highly esteemed.
His prudence in this writing is shewn,
And does not need to be praised by me,
For the work praiseth its maker (master) itself,
When it is done either ill or well.

That the process of rendering Lyndesay's Poems into Danish verse is correctly stated on the title page, need not be doubted. We are not indeed to understand that Robertson had prepared a formal Latin translation—and curious enough he makes no mention of any translation into Latin in his Preface, nor any reference to his coadjutor. Nevertheless we may conclude, that without the assistance of a native Danish scholar, he never could have completed his task. In his dedication he tells us that he had translated it from Scottish into Danish, as there is contained in it much wisdom and godliness, and as it is praised by many learned and pious men. But as he was afraid that some might think it very unnecessary to translate anything from Scottish into Danish, as Denmark was well provided with good books, or that he himself was not likely as a foreigner to translate anything well, he begs leave to dedicate his book to the "Regsraader," that their name might prove a protection for him. And this he has done with the advice of some good men, thinking also that there is something in the book that the "Regsraader" may profit by; such as Exhortations to Kings and Regents, the glorious renown of those who have governed well, and the miserable fate of those who have led a bad and wicked life. Lastly, A. R. humbly thanks his Majesty (Christian IV., then a minor) who has provided for him at the University, etc.

My Danish friend adds this note:

"As A. R. in the preface is always speaking of himself as the translator of the book from Scots into Danish, I think that he has translated it himself into Latin, and that he, not being very well versed in the Danish language, has used Jacob Mattsen as a sort of assistant, who was however to reap nothing of the advantage that might be got by the translation, and is therefore not mentioned in the preface or dedication."

No. III.

NOTICES OF JOHN SCOT, PRINTER AT EDINBURGH AND ST. ANDREWS, 1539-1572.

The name of Scot is so connected with the earliest editions of Lyndsay's Poems known to have been printed in Scotland, that a brief notice of him may not be considered as out of place. There is some uncertainty regarding his early history, and Mr Chalmers (vol. i. p. 82), in describing the original edition of Lyndsay's Dialog as having been printed "at St. Andrews by Jhone Skott," says, "The Copmanhoun edition of the *Monarchie*, thus printed by Skott, at St. Andrew's, within the short distance of eight miles from Lyndsay's residence at the Mount, may be regarded as a faithful copy of what the author wrote, except the *spelling* of some words in the English mode, which was so natural to *Skott, an English printer, who had been transplanted from London to St Andrews, by Archbishop Hamilton.*"

Such a misconception originated in the conclusion drawn that Scot was the same person with John Skott, or Scott, a printer at London, whose name appears on six books dated from 1521 to 1537, while seven others are without date, as described in Dibdin's edition of Ames and Herbert's Typographical Antiquities (vol. iii. pp. 73-80). Except the similarity of name, all the rest is mere conjecture. The peculiar device and monogram of the English printer was never used by the other; while some books actually from his press without having his name are easily distinguished by the frequent repetition of a few large initial letters, and the above woodcut of Hercules and Centaur. Mr Chalmers was not aware at the time that JOHANNES SCOT IMPRESSOR, had been established as a printer in Edinburgh in 1539, if not earlier, and at least four years before John Hamilton, Abbot of Paisley, afterwards Archbishop of St. Andrews, had arrived from France, and thirteen years before the Catechism of 1552 had appeared. (See supra, p. 180.)

On the sixth of June 1539, two houses on the north side of the Cowgate, at the foot of Borthwick's Close (entering at number 186 High Street), having fallen into the King's hands by the death of David Gilliespie, baker, a bastard, a grant of one of them was made by the King to William Chepman and John Scot, Printer, jointly, the former occupying the upper part of the house, Scot the two rooms or chambers on the ground floor, and two cellars below.

No remains of Scot's early printing in Edinburgh have been preserved; and it is a mere conjecture on my part, that when the city was burned by the English in 1544, Scot may have removed his printing press to Dundee before settling at St. Andrews, where he, it is supposed, printed that curious volume "The Complaynt of Scotland," in 1548. It has, however, neither printer's name, place, nor date. Upon examining the "Annals of Printing in Scotland," by Mr Chalmers (an unpublished MS. in the Advocates Library), I find he had become aware of the above grant in 1539; and also of the Privy Council proceedings against him for some unnamed offence in 1547.

According to the Minutes of Privy Council, 5th April 1547, letters had been addressed "charging John Skrymgeour of Glastrae, Constable of Dundee, and Provost of the same, to take and apprehend JOHNE SCOTT, Prentar, and to bring him and present him within the castell of Edinburgh, and to deliver him to the Capitane thairof to be punist for his demereitis and faltis, &c. . . . The said Johne Skrymgeour compeirand, shew, how he had socht the said John Scott, but could not apprehend him," &c. (Reg. Secr. Concilii, fol. 65.) A commission like this addressed to the Provost of Dundee (who had no jurisdiction in St. Andrews) led me to suggest whether Scot might not have been settled at Dundee before removing to St. Andrews. At the same time, the Privy Council ordained the Sheriff, within their respective bounds of Forfar, Kincardine, Perth, Fyfe, "and other places thairabout, to seik for the said Johne, that he might be punished for his evill deidis."

When we attend to the dates, it is a fair inference that Scot's offence consisted in his having printed Lyndsay's poem, "The Tragedy of the Cardinal." Mr Chalmers, I find, also draws the conclusion, that it was this "and other works of a similar tendency, which had well-nigh proved fatal to Scot."

The well known volume usually called "Archbishop Hamilton's Catechisme," 1552, has not Scot's name, although certainly from his press. The colophon reads, "Prentit at Sanct Androus be command of Johne Archbischop of Sanct Androus, &c., the 29 day of August 1552." 4to. The only known work which actually has his name as printer at St. Andrews, is the rare volume by Patrick Cockburn, "In Dominicam Orationem pia Meditatio, &c.—Ex typographia Johannis Scot, in Ciuitate Sancti Andreæ 15. Calendas Octobris, 1555," sm. 8vo. On the last page, at the end of a list of Errata, his name is repeated in the colophon: "Excudebat Joannes Scott, 1555." Soon after this, he probably returned to Edinburgh.

No. IV.

A BIBLIOGRAPHICAL ACCOUNT OF THE EDITIONS OF SIR DAVID LYNDSAY'S POETICAL WORKS.

1538.

COMPLAYNT OF THE POPINJAY.

That some of Lyndsay's Poems were printed in Scotland during the reign of James the Fifth, is at least highly probable. After the appearance of the Breviarium Aberdonense from the press of Walter Chepman, 1509-1510, it is usually supposed, that during an interval of about twenty years, printing had ceased. This is a false conclusion.

The successive burnings of Edinburgh during the English invasions in 1544 and 1547, may sufficiently account for a great destruction of the floating literature of the time.

So far, however, as can be discovered, the edition of Lyndsay's Papyngo, printed at London in 1538, was the earliest of his poems submitted to the public. A facsimile of the title of this early edition is given on the next leaf; and on F 3 is this Colophon—

¶ Here endes the complaynt, & testament of the
kynge of Scottes Papingo, compyled by
Dauid Lyndesay of the mount, and
finysshed the .xiiij. day of Decem-
bre, in the yere of our lorde. 1530.

¶ Imprynted at London in Fletestrete, at
the sygne of the Sonne, by John
Byddell. The yere of our
lorde . M.D.xxxviij.

CVM PRIVILEGIO.

This edition is of great rarity. It is a small 4to in black letter, signature A to F 3 in fours, or 23 leaves. One copy in the King's Library, British Museum, marked C. 12. g 2. is bound at the end of Jascuy's 4th edition of the Dialog, &c. Another is described by Mr Payne Collier in his privately printed and valuable "Catalogue, Bibliographical and Critical, of early English Literature, forming a portion of the Library at Bridgewater House," p. 180, Lond. 1837, 4to; and is repeated in his "Bibliographical Account of Early English Literature," vol. i. p. 506. Lond. 1865, 2 vols. 8vo. Mr Hazlitt, in his Hand-book, p. 362, mentions a third copy in private hands.

Mr Collier says, "Byddell seems to have rendered it (Lyndsay's poem) more palatable to English ears by rejecting some of the pure Scotticisms in respect of orthography." A specimen of the text is given in the Notes, vol. i. p. 260. There is little doubt that this poem was first printed at Edinburgh. The following list of a few various readings may be added,—

Line 283.—Wherfore seyng thou has sik capacite.
,, 321.—Trustynge to scape that fatall destenye.
Entreate euery true baron as he were thy brother.
,, 349.—Not sparing papes, emperours, nor kynges.
,, 367.—Seyng ylk court bene vntrust and transitorye.
,, 388.—And how fonde fayned fules and flatterars.
,, 392.—Blasphematours braggars and common bardes.
,, 451.—It had ben good those barnes had bene vnborne.
,, 815.—Syluester that tyme was Pape in Rome.
,, 871.—Dame Chastete dyd steale away for schame.
,, 881.—Tyred for trauell she to the preestes past.
,, 891.—They wolde receyue no rebell out of Rome.
,, 1060.—Pew quod the gled, thou preches all in vayne.
The secular folk has of cares no cures.
I graunt quod sche.

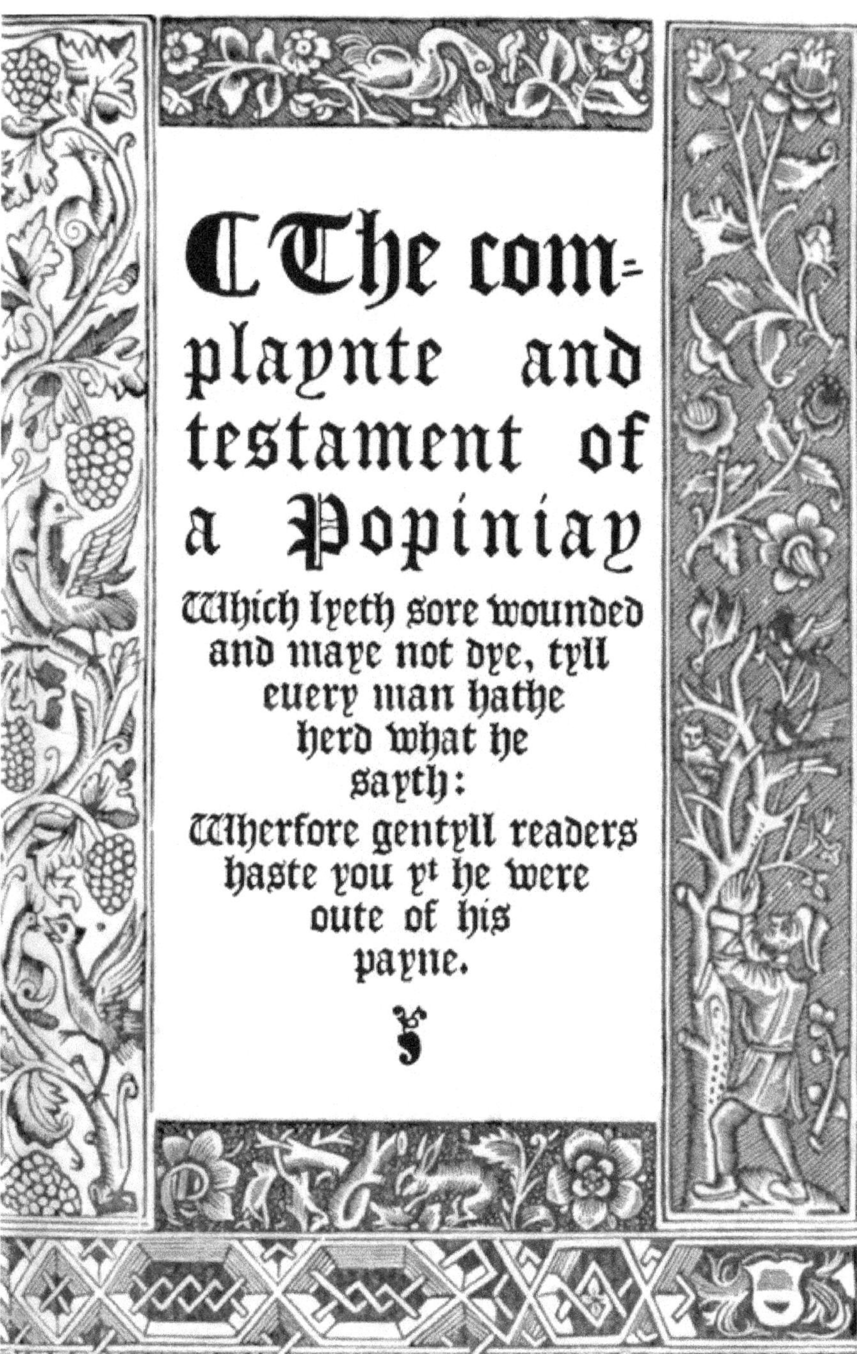

¶ The com-playnte and testament of a Popiniay

Which lyeth sore wounded and maye not dye, tyll euery man hathe herd what he sayth: Wherfore gentyll readers haste you yt he were oute of his payne.

1547.

THE TRAGEDY OF CARDINAL BEATON.

This forms only a portion of a little rare volume printed at London by John Daye, under the following title:—

"THE TRAGICAL DEATH OF DAUID BEATON, Bishoppe of sainct Andrewes in Scotland: Wherunto is ioyned the martyrdom of maister George Wyseharte gentleman, for whose sake the aforesayd bishoppe was not longe after slayne. Wherein thou maist learne what a burnynge charitie they shewed not only towardes him: but vnto al suche as come to their hãdes for the blessed Gospels sake."

There is no imprint on this title, and the colophon has no date, but it may be assigned to the end of year 1547.

(Colophon, on sig. F 6.) "Imprinted at London by John Daye, and William Seres, dwellynge in Sepulchres parish at the signe of the Resurrection, a little aboue Holbourne conduite. Cum gratia et priuilegio ad imprimendum solum."

After the title is a preface, "Robert Burrant to the reader," extending to twelve leaves, ending on B. iiij. Then comes Lyndsay's poem, which is printed in a smaller type: the title reads thus,—"Here foloweth the Tragedy of the late moste reuerende father Dauid, by the mercie of God Cardinall and Archbishoppe of sainct Andrewes. And of the whole realme of Scotland, Primate, Legate and Chaunceler. And administrator of the bishoprich of Merapois in Fraunce. And cõmendator perpetuall of the Abbay of Aberbrothoke, compiled by sir Dauid Lyndsaye of the mounte knyghte. Alias Lione, Kyng of armes. Anno. M.D. xlvi. ultimo Maij. The wordes of Dauid Beaton the Cardinall aforesaied at his death. Alas alas, slaye me not, I am a Priest!"

Lyndsay's poem ends on C vij, and on the back of the leaf begins, "The accusation of maister George Wysehart gentleman, who suffered martyrdome for the faith of Christ Jesu, at S. Andrewes in Scotland, the first day of March. &c." This account of Wishart's trial is copied by Foxe, in his Actes and Monuments, and by Knox, in his History of the Reformation. See Knox's Works vol. i., (and Notes) pp. 148, 151, 171.

The text of the edition by Daye, of the Cardinal's Tragedy, is very much Anglified. The first stanza of the Prolog, vol. i. p. 139, may be quoted as a specimen.

Not long sence, efter the houre of prime
Secretely sittyng in myne Oratorie
I toke a boke, to occupie the tyme
Where I found many Tragedy and storie
Which John Bochas had put in memory
How many a prince, conquerour and captaine
Were dolfully deposed from thair raigne.

The only copy known, appears in the Harleian Catalogue, 1743, vol. i. No. 8375. At the Duke of Roxburghe's Sale, 1813, No. 8736, it was bought by Mr Heber. At his Sale, 1836, Part ix. No. 1712, it was purchased for Mr Grenville, and passed with his collection to the British Museum. It has the press mark 954. It is a small 8vo, black letter, signature A to F 6 in eights, excepting B, which has only six. In all 44 leaves.

Dr M'Crie in the Appendix to the second edition of his Life of Knox, was the first to describe minutely this rare volume, having obtained a loan of it from Mr Heber, who deserves to be honourably remembered for his great liberality in granting access to his literary treasures.

1554.

ANE DIALOG BETUIX EXPERIENCE AND ANE COURTEOUR. Copmanhouin, no date, 4to.

The signatures run thus, the title and two leaves for A, B in 4, C to F in eights, G in 4, H to R 1, in eights, in all 116 leaves, not paged. A facsimile of the title and last page is given on the next leaf. For the sake of comparison some facsimiles of Scot's second impression immediately follow it At the end "Finis. Quod Lyndesay, 1552" has no reference to the date of printing. A circumstance that renders the first edition peculiarly interesting, is, as Mr Chalmers suggests, that it was printed under the Author's immediate inspection. That it was, at least, printed at St. Andrews, by John Scot, about 1554, and during Lyndsay's life, there can be little doubt, although recourse was had on the title to a fictitious name and place for its publication.

In regard to these fictitious names, Copmanhouin stands for Copenhagen. Dr John Machabeus was a native of Scotland, and educated at St Andrews. This celebrated divine, who was an exile from his native country on account of religion, became a minister of the Reformed Church in Denmark. He was brother-in-law of Myles Coverdale; and was one of the translators of the Bible into Danish, printed at Hafnia, (the Latin name of Copenhagen), 1550-1, folio. He died in Denmark in the year 1557. That he had no concern whatever in the publication of Lyndsay's Dialog, need scarcely be said.

A fine copy of this rare edition is in the Bodleian Library. Another perfect copy (formerly in the Heber collection), is in Mr Christie Miller's Library at Britwell; I have a third; a fourth was recently acquired for the University Library of Edinburgh (see p. 272); and a fifth used for the reprint by the English Text Society, is in private hands.

Heir followis the

Dreme, of Schir Dauid Lyndesay of the mont, Familiar Seruitour, to our Souerane Lord Kyng James the Fyft. &c.

THE EPISTIL.

Rycht Potent Prince, of hie Imperial bluide
Unto thy grace, I traist it be weill knawin
My seruyce done, unto thy Celsitude
Quhilk nedis nocht, at lenth for to be schawin
And thocht my zouthed now be neir ouer blawin
Exercit in seruyce, of thyne Excellence
Hope hes me hecht, ane gudlie recompence.

Quhen thow wes zoung, I bure þe in myne armis
Full tenderlie, tyll thow begouth to gang
And in thy bed, oft happit the full warme
With lute in hand, syne sweitlie to the sang
Sumtyme in dansing, feiralie I flang
And sumtyme playand farsis on the flure
And sumtyme on myne office, takkand cure.

D

And tak me in my letter aige
Unto my sempyll Hermytage
And spend it that my eldaris woun
As did Matussalem in his toun
Off this complaynt with mynd full meik
Thy graces answeir schir I beseik.

☞ FINIS.

Quod Lindesay to kyng.

☞ Gentyll redaris, I wyll aduertis zow that thare is of thir Bukis, Imprentit in France, The quhilkis ar verray fals. And wantis the tane half, and all wrang spelit, and left out heir ane lyne, and thair twa wordis.

¶ To Conclude thay ar all fals, and wantis mekle that this buke hes as may be sene, quha lyste tyll luke thame baith ouer, thay sall fynd my sayingis verray trew and wors nor I do say preue and se, than ze wyll geue me credence. thay ar nocht worthe ane plake.

❧ Ane Dialog betuix Experience and ane Courteour,

Off the Miserabyll Estait of the Warld, ☞ Compylit be Schir Dauid Lyndesay of ye Mont Knycht alias, Lyone Kyng of Armes.
And is Deuidit in Foure Partis.
As efter Followis. .&c.

And Imprentit at the Conmand and Expensis off Doctor,
MACHABEVS,
In Copmāhouin.

Absit Gloriari, Nisi in Cruce Domini nostri Iesu Christi.

I se Polartike, in the North appeir
And Venus rysing with hir bemes cleir
Quharefor my Sonne, I hald it tyme to go
Wald God (said I) ze did remane all zeir
That I mycht of zour heuinlye Lessonis leir
Off zour departyng, I am wounder wo
Tak pacience (said he) it mone be so
Perchance I sall returne, with deligence
Thus I departit, frome Experience.

And sped me home, with hert sychyng full sore
And enterit in my quyet Oratore
I tuke paper, and thare began to wryt
This Miserie, as ze haue hard afore
All gentyll Redaris, hertlye I Implore
For tyll excuse, my rurall rude Indyte
Thoucht Phareseis, wyll haue at me dispyte
Quhilkis wald not pat, thare craftynes wer kend
Latt God be Juge, and so I mak ane end.

FINIS.

Quod Lyndesay.

.1552.

1558.

ANE DIALOG AND OTHER POEMS. "Imprinted at the command and expenses of Maister Sammuel Jascuy, in Paris, 1558."

There are two editions, with this imprint, one in 4to, the other in small 8vo, both in black letter. We cannot say (nor it a matter of much importance) which of the two was the earliest. They may have appeared simultaneously. Both editions are of great rarity, and merit a somewhat minute description.

Each of these consists of four distinct parts. The woodcut figure on the title of the quarto edition (see facsimile) may have been meant as an imaginary portrait of the author in his official costume as Lyon King at Arms—having on a herald's short coat or tabard, with the royal arms of Scotland displayed.

I. Ane Dialog betuixt Experience and ane Courteour Off the Miserabill Estait of the Warld. Compilit be Schir Dauid Lyndesay of ye Mont, knycht *Alias* Lyone Kyng of Armis. And is Deuidit in foure partis. As efter followis. &c.

Absit Gloriari, Nisi in Cruce Domini nostri Iesu Christi.

(woodcut portrait.)

And Imprintit at the command, and expenses of
Maister Samuel Jascuy, In Paris. 1558.

The Dialog is page for page with Scot's first edition, and this leaves no doubt that it was reprinted from a copy deficient of four leaves; and in this mutilated state copies had been put into circulation. Whether it was in consequence of Scot's exclamation, when republishing the Poems in 1559, we can only conjecture, but the French printer found it necessary to cancel and reprint various leaves of signature G. in the 4to and of sign. D, in the smaller edition. The omissions which these extra leaves supplied, correspond with signs. F. 2, F. 3, F. 6, and F. 7, of Scots edit. of 1554, and contain lines 1733 to 1837 ; and 1888 to 2057.

The collation in the 4to varies from the earlier edition, namely, sign. A. to E. in fours; F. in eight; G. having twelve, by the addition of four extra leaves to supply the omissions in the text ; H. to O. in eights, the last two leaves marked O. vij, and. O viij, are apparently reprinted to replace two leaves supposed to have been cancelled ; and P to R iiij. in eights—in all 116 leaves.

At the end of The Fourt Buke (on the reverse of R. 4), we have, without any date, as follows—

Finis Quod Lyndesay.

II. Heir followis the Testa ment and Complaynt of our souuerane Lordis Papyngo, &c. (same cut and imprint as No. 1.), sign. A. to F. in fours, 22 leaves, F. 4 is blank except having the woodcut figure repeated on the reverse of the leaf. In the facsimile title, and first page, the size of the type is somewhat reduced, on account of the breadth—but the actual size of type is shewn in the lines on the reverse, printed across the page.

III. Heir followis the dreme of Shir Dauid Lindsay of the mont, Knycht &c. (same cut and imprint). Sign. A. to G. 2 in fours, 26 leaves. The last four leaves contain Lyndsay's poem, The deploratioun of the deyth of Quene Magdalene.

IV. Heir followis the Tragedie of the vmquhyle Maist Reuerend Fader Dauid, be the mercy of God, Cardinal, and Archibyschope of Sanctandrous, &c. (same cut and imprint as before). Sign. A. and B. in fours, 8 leaves. On the reverse of the last leaf is the following cut.

QVOD

LINDESAY.

Of this quarto volume, there is a copy in the British Museum, marked C. 12. g. 2. On the title is the autograph,

"Ex lib. Ro. Gray colleg. Med. Edinburg. et Lond. Socii." Another is in Trinity College Library, Cambridge. I had the use of a remarkably fine copy, in the original wooden boards, from a private collection in Scotland many years ago. In these copies the Dialog contains the extra leaves of sign. G. At a sale of Pinkerton's books, in 1811, the minor pieces, bound separately, were bought by Mr Heber; and at the sale of his library in 1834, they were purchased for the Britwell collection. A separate copy of the Cardinal's Tragedy occurred at a London sale, in 1864.

1558.

ANE DIALOG AND OTHER POEMS. *Samuel Jascuy, at Paris. Small 8vo.*

This edition, like the 4to, is also divided into four parts, on the title of each, the cut is repeated of the figure of a naked female, with long hair, holding feathers in one hand, and carrying a jar in the other, and a tablet, with the initials I. P. "And Imprentit at the command and expenses of Maister Sammuel Jascuy, In Paris, 1558." See facsimile on the third leaf after this.

I. Ane Dialog betwix Experience and ane Courteour, &c. (same title as in 4to edition. Contains signatures a i. to n. 7, in eights, or 103 leaves. In some copies part of sign. d. was reprinted with four additional leaves marked dd., as already described.

II. Heir followis the Dreme of Schir Dauid Lyndsay of the Mont Knyt, &c., same cut and imprint in the Dialog. Sign. A. B. and C. in eight, 24 leaves. The last four leaves have The deploration of the deyth of Quene Magdalene.

III. Heir followis the Tragedie of the vnqhyle Maister, &c. (Cardinal Beaton.) (Same cut and imprint.) Sign. A., 8 leaves.

¶ Heir followis the testament and complaynt of our souuerane lordis papyngo. Kyng James the Fyft.

¶ Quhilk lyis sore woundit and may nocht dee, tyll euery man haue harde quhat he sayis. Quharefore gentyll redaris, haist zow that he wer out of his pane.

¶ Compylit be the said Schir Dauid Lyndesay of the Mont, knycht Alias Lyoun, kyng of Armes.

And Imprentit at the command, and expenses of maister Sammuel Jascuy, In Paris.

1558.

Rycht potent prince, of hir Imperiall blude
Onto thy grace I traist it be weill knawin
My seruice done onto thy celsitude
Quhilk neidis nocht at lenth for to be schawin
And thocht my ȝowtheid now be neir ouerblawin
Excersit in seruice, of thyn excellence
Hope his me hecht, ane gudly recompence.

Quhen thow was ȝowng I bure the in myne arme
Full tenderlye tyll thow begowth to gang
And in thy bed oft happit the full warme
With lute in hand syne softlye to the sang
Sum tyme in dansyng ferely I flang
And sum tyme playand farsis on the flure
And sum tyme on myne office tankand cure.

And sum tyme lyke ane feind transfigurate
And sum tyme lyke the gryslie gaist of gye
In diuers formis oftymes disfigurate
And sum tyme disagysit full plesandlye
So sen thy birth I hefe continewallye
Bene occupyit and ay to yi plesoure
And sum tyme sewar copper and carboure.

Thy purs maister, and secreit thesaurare
Thy yschar ay sen thy natiuite
And of thy chalmer cheif cubiculare
Quhilk to this hour hes keipit my laute
Louing be to the blissit trinitie
That sic ane wracheit worme hes maid so habill
Till sic ane prince to be so aggrea bill.

Bot now thow art be influence naturall
Hye of ingine and richt inquisityue

Heir followis the dreme of Shir Dauid lindsay of the mont Knyt, alias Lion Kyng of armes derecket onto our souerane Lord Kyng James the Fyft.

And Imprentit at the command, and expenses of maister Samuel Jascuy, In Paris.

1 5 5 8.

Suppose I had Ingyne angelicall.
With sapience more than Salamonicall
I not quhate mater putt in memorie
The Poetis aulde in style Heroycall
In breue subtell termes rethorycall
Off euerilke mater, tragedie and storie
So ornatlie to thare heych laude and glorie
Haith done Indyte, quhose supreme sapience
Transcendith far, the dull Intelligence.

¶ Off Poetis now, in tyll our vulgare toung.
(For quhy) the bell of Rethorick bene roung
Be Chawceir, Goweir, and Lidgate laureate
Quhoo dar presume, thir Poetis tyll Impung
Quhose sweit sentence, throuch Albione bene soung
Or quho can now, the werkis cuntrafate
Off Kennedie, with termes aureate
Or of Dunbar, quhilk language had at large
As maye be sene, in tyll his goldin targe.

Sumtyme. Mersar, Rowle, Henderson, Hay, & Holād
Thoucht thay bene dede, thare Libellis bene leuande
Quhilkis to rehers, makeith redaris to reiose
Allace for one, quhilk lampe wes of this land
Off Eloquence the flowande balmy strand
And in our Inglis, rethorick the rose
As of Rubeis, the Charbunckle bene chose
And as Phebus, dois Synthia precell
So Gawane Dowglas, byschope of Dunkell.

Rycht potent prince, of hie Imperiall blude
Onto thy grace I traist it be weill knawin
My seruice done onto thy celsitude
Quhilk neidis nocht at lenth for to be schawin
And thocht my zowtheid now be neir ouerblawin
Excersit in seruice, of thyn excellence
Hope hes me hecht, ane gudlye recompence.

¶ Quhen thow was zowng I bure the in myne arme
Full tenderlye tyll thow begowth to gang
And in thy bed oft happie the full warme
With lute in hand syne softlye to the sang
Sum tyme in dansyng ferely I flang
And sum tyme playand farsis on the flure
And sum tyme on myne office takand cure.

IV. Heir followis the Testament and complaynt of our Souerane Lordis Papyngo Kyng James the Fyft (same cut and imprint.) Sign. AA, BB, and CC 5 in eights, 21 leaves.

In the two editions by Jascuy there are some slight variations in orthography, but not worth noticing.

Of the smaller edition, two fine copies (one having previously belonged to Mr Chalmers) were bought for Mr Miller of Craigentinny, at the Heber sale, and are now in Mr Christie Miller's library at Britwell. One copy has sign. d., as originally issued, the other has the extra leaves. A third copy belongs to the Cathedral Library of Peterborough. If I remember, it has the extra leaves of sign. d. I have in my own possession two imperfect copies (from the Heber and Constable collections), the one has the extra leaves, with the first title and several leaves are supplied in MS., and the other containing only the Dialog, and the Dreme, is still more defective. Singularly enough, in all these copies, one of the introductory stanzas (line 160 to 166) is left blank; while it occurs in the 4to copies.

I wish we could have ascertained who MAISTER SAMUEL JASCUY, or the person was to whose liberality or enterprise the two foreign editions of Lyndsay's Poems owed their publication. We can only surmise that he was a Protestant, and was in some way connected with Scotland. I am inclined to think the name of Jascuy to be fictitious, and the place of printing purposely concealed, in imitation of the first Copmanhouin edition; as it is indisputable that both editions were actually printed at Rouen by the successor of John Petit, in 1558. Many copies, no doubt, had reached Scotland, as John Scot, the Edinburgh printer, in the following year, refers to them as having been printed in France; while Charteris, in 1568 and other editions, expressly says of "The Complaynt unto the Kingis Grace," "*omittit in the imprentingis of Rowen and Londoun.*"

The initial letters I. P. confirm the statement that Jascuy's volumes were printed at Rouen, as the same woodcut of the female figure, in the smaller edition, had been used by Jehan Petit, who carried on printing at Rouen from 1540 to 1557, in this form—

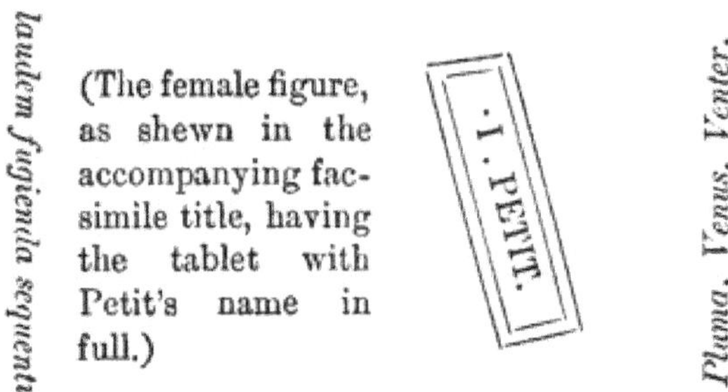

A facsimile of this cut is given in the curious work by L. C. Silvestre, "Marques Typographiques ou Recueil des Monogrammes, Chiffres," &c., Paris, 1853, and completed in 1867, 8vo. In 1558, Petit's successor, whoever he was, in the smaller edition of Lyndsay, retained the same cut, leaving only the initial letters.

Again, I find the first of the little figures at p. 266 copied from Jascuy's 4to edition, occurs with two similar figures on the title-page of a rare little poetical tract "Les Complaintes et regretz de tous Estats. Nouuellement composez sur le temps present. Par I. G. (*woodcut figures*) A Rouen, chez Iean du gort, et Iaspar de rémortier tenant leur bouticque au portail des Libraires." [1561] 8 leaves, 12mo.

In the first half of the sixteenth century there were several printers of the name of Petit (in Latin, Parvus) in Paris. Thomas Petyt, supposed by Ames to have been related to the older John Petit, at Paris, settled in London, at St Paul's Churchyard, at the sign of the Maiden's-head. In the Typographical Antiquities of Ames, Herbert, and Dibdin, various books are mentioned, printed by him between 1536 and 1554, besides others without date.

1559.

ANE DIALOG AND OTHER POEMS. Copmanhouin, no date. 4to.

I. The Dialog is a republication by John Scot of his previous edition page for page. The facsimiles of the title and other pages, by the process of photo-zincography, will serve to identify the two editions.

At the end of the Third Buke, (sign. N. 8) the printer, who had introduced the cut of Hercules and the Centaur (see p. 256) in this republication, has substituted the initials of his own name, **I. S.** On the last page (R 1.) "Finis Quod Lyndsaye. 1552." is retained. But along with the Dialog several of Lyndsay's minor Poems were now added; and the printer's allusion, both on the first title and of the last page, to the inaccurate editions printed in France, namely, the two described, which have the date 1558, serve in fixing Scot's republication to the year 1559. The minor Poems which he added, are as follows:—

II. "Heir followis the Tragedie, of the Umquhyle maist Reuered Father Dauid be the Mercy of God, Cardinall and Archbyschope of Sanctandrous, &c., Compylit be Schir Dauid Lyndesay of the Mont king of armes." This title, over the woodcut of Hercules and the Centaur, is on sign. S, eight leaves.

III. "Heir followis the Testament, and Complaynt of our Souerane Lordis Papyngo Kyng James the Fyft," &c. Under the title, a woodcut of two birds, is repeated on the last page; the sign. are A, B, and C, in eights, or 24 leaves.

IV. Heir followis the Dreme of Schir Dauid Lyndesay of the Mont, Familiar Seruitour to our Souerane Lord Kyng James the Fyft, &c., (woodcut of Hercules, &c.) It begins on sign. D. On F. v. "Heir endis the Dreme, and begynnis the

Exhortation to the Kyngis Grace;" and on F 7, "Heir begynnis the Complaynt of Schir Dauid Lindesay," ending on the last half of G 8, or 32 leaves in all.

In place of the usual colophon mentioning the place and date of printing and the printer's name, we have a notice to the Reader, crying down the foreign editions for their imperfections and inaccuracies, as utterly worthless. See the facsimile pages already given after p. 264. When Scot says these editions *were not worth ane plack*, he could scarcely have made a lower estimate, *a plack* being a small copper coin equal to the third part of an English penny. His exclamation against their want of accuracy is well enough founded, but it is easily explained, being printed by workmen ignorant of the language. As to mere typography, Scot's edition will not bear any comparison with those of Jascuy. Scot himself, in the additional poems may have adopted Jascuy's text, if so, while correcting obvious mistakes, his own carelessness is quite inexcusable. On the title he changes the name *Machabeus* to *Nachabeus*, and on the headline he frequently puts *Monarce* for *Monarchie*, *Te* for *The* &c.; and so far as omissions are concerned, he has overlooked the interesting poem, "The Deploration for the death of Queen Magdalen."

Of this volume there are fine and perfect copies in the Bodleian Library, the Lambeth Library, and the Cathedral Library at York. Gough and Heber's copy is now in the collection at Britwell House. The copy I have (not quite perfect in the Dialog) has the additional poems supplied from the volume used by the English Text Society. In the University Library, Edinburgh, the additional Poems are bound with the First edition of the Dialog.

1566.

A DIALOGUE, &c., AND OTHER WORKS. This is the first edition printed at London by Thomas Purfoote.

Heir followis the

Testament, and Complaynt of our Souerane Lordis Papyngo. Kyng James the Fyft. Quhilk lyith sore woundit, and may not dee. Tyll euery man haue hard quhat he sayis. Quharefor gentyll redaris haist ȝow that he wer out of pane.

Compylit be Schir Dauid Lyndesay of the mont Knycht, *Alias*, Lyone Kyng of Armes.

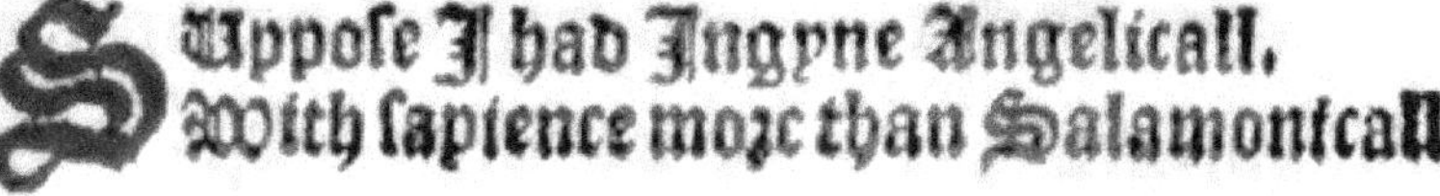

SUppose I had Ingyne Angelicall,
With sapience more than Salamonicall

I not quhat mater put in memorie
The Poetis auld, in style Heroycall
In breue subtell termes Rethorycall
Off euerilke mater, tragedie and storie
So ornatlie, to thare heych laude and glorie
Haith done Indyte, quhose supreme sapience
Transcendith far, the dull Intelligence,

¶ Off Poetis now, in tyll our vulgare toung,
(For quhy) the bell of Rethorick bene roung
Be Chawceir, Goweir, and Lidgate laureate
Quhoo dar presume, thir Poetis tyll Impung
Quhose sweit sentence, throuch Albione benē sōg
Or quho can now, the workis cuntrafait
Off Kennedie, with termes aureait
Or of Dunbar, quhilk language had at large
As maye be sene, in tyll his goldin targe.

Quintyng, Mersar, Rowle, Hederſon, hay ⁊ hol=
Thocht thay be ded, par libells bene leuād (land
Quhikis to reheirs, makeith redaris to reioſe
Allace for one, quhilk lampe wes of this land
Off Eloquence, the flowand balmy strand
And in our Inglis, rethorick the rose
As of Rubeis, the Charbunckle bene chose
And as Phebus, dois Synthia presell
So Gawane Dowglas, Byschope of Dunkell.

¶ Had quhen he wes, in to this land on lyue,

Ane Dialog betuix Experience and ane Courteour.

Off the Miserabyll Estait of the warld.
Compylit be Schir Dauid Lyndesay of the mont Knycht Alias, Lyone Kyng of Armes.
And is Deuidit in Four partis As efter Followis.
And Imprentit at the Command and Expensis of Doctor
NACHABEVS.
In Copmanhouin.

Attouir thare is bukis imprentit in France, of twa sortis the quhilkis ar verray fals as it is knawin, & wantis mekle that this Buke hes for this is Juste and trew, and nane bot this Buke.
be war with thame for thay wyll dissaue 3ow.

Absit gloriari, nisi in Cruce domini nostri Iesu Christi.

I se Polartick, in the north appeir
And Venus rysing with hir bemes cleir
Quharefor my Sonne, I hald it tyme to go
Wald God (said I) ze did remane all zeir
That I mycht of zour heuinnlye Lessonis leir
Off zour departyng, I am wounder wo
Tak pacience (said he) it mon be so
Perchance I sall returne, with delygence
Thus I departit, frome Experience

And sped me home, with hart seyching full sore
And enterit in my quyet Oratore
I tuke paper, and thare began to wryte
This Miserie, as ze haue hard afore
All gentyll Redaris, hartlye I Implore
For tyll excuse, my rurall rude Indyte
Thocht Phareseis, wyll haue at me dispyte
Quhilz wald not ẏ thare craftynes wer kend
Lat God be Juge, and so I make ane end.

FINIS.

Quod Lyndesaye.

1552.

A facsimile of the title page is given above (page 221), followed by an Epistle to the Reader. The "certain other pithy pieces," added to the Dialog, commence on fol. 105, although the running title, "The Fourth Part," is continued to the end of the volume, on fol. 164.

The contents are as follows:—

In this edition there are various woodcuts. One of these cuts, engraved in a ruder style, of two figures conversing, and copied on the reverse of the title at p. 222, I imagined had been designed for Experience and the Courteour; but see note p. 220. There are about eighteen or twenty other woodcuts (some of which are repeated two or three times) well designed and engraved—forming evidently part of a set of Bible prints, not always peculiarly applicable as illustrations of Lyndsay's Dialog. For instance, a cut of Jonah thrown overboard is introduced to illustrate Noah leaving the Ark. The average size of the cuts is 2⅝ inches by 1⅞. Some of them, indeed, are exactly copied from Beham's beautiful set of woodcuts in his work: "Biblische Historien, figürlich fürbildet, Durch den wolberümpten Sebald Behem von Nüremberg," published at Frankfurt, 1535, and again in 1536, with the monogram H. S. B. (Hans Sebald Beham). Small 8vo.

A fine copy of Purfoote's 1566 edition is in the University Library, Cambridge. Another is at Britwell, from the library of Baron Bolland. The one in the Advocates Library, from the collection of Sir M. M. Sykes, has the last two leaves reprinted; while another that belonged to Herbert and Chalmers, now in my own possession, is imperfect at both beginning and end.

1568.

THE WARKIS of the famous and worthie Knicht SCHIR DAUID LYNDESAY of the Mount &c.

Newlie Imprentit [at Edinburgh] be Iohne Scot, at the expensis of Henrie Charteris. Anno M.D.LXVIII.

In 4to. Of this rare edition, the first collected publication by Henry Charteris, the full title, and also his long Preface and the Adhortation in verse, are given at pages 227-244.

The collation is somewhat irregular: the Title, &c., marked +, A and B, in fours, the Dialog, sign. C to F in eights, G in four, H to R i. in eights. The Papyngo has a new set of signatures, A, B, C, in eights; the Dreme, &c., D, E, F in eights; G in four, and H i; then I, K and L, in eights, containing in all 198 leaves.

The head lines are in small roman capitals—

THE FIRST BUKE // OF THE MONARCHIE.
with an average of 30 lines on each page.

The copy of this edition described by Herbert, was bought at the Roxburghe sale by Mr Heber; it afterwards passed into the hands of Mr Miller of Craigentinny, and is now at Britwell. It was long supposed to be unique, but another copy has recently been discovered in the library of Lord Mostyn, at his seat in Flintshire.

1571.

¶ The warkis of the famous and vorthie Knicht

Schir Dauid Lyndesay of the Mont, Alias, Lyoun King of Armes. Newly correctit, and vindicate from the former errouris quhairwith thay war befoir corruptit: and augmentit with sindrie warkis quhilk was not befoir Imprentit.

¶ The contentis of the buke, and quhat warkis ar augmentit, the nixt syde sall schaw.

¶ Viuet etiam, &c.

¶ Imprentit at Edinburgh be Johne Scot

at the expensis of Henrie Charteris: and ar to be sauld in his Buith, on the North syde of the Gait, abone the Throne.

☞ Cum Priuilegio Regali.

ANNO DO. M.D.LXXI.

In 4to black letter. Title and prefixes eight leaves, (A and B in fours.) The Monarchy, B to R 1 in eights; the Minor Poems also in eights, except that B and G are in fours. A full page has 29 lines. This edition is a literal reprint of that of 1568—the contents on the back of the title are precisely the same, ending with *The Justing*, &c., and retaining the words after "Ane Answer to the Kingis flyting—*neuer befoir Imprentit.*"

At the end of the Epistil, in place of a circular ornament, there is substituted the woodcut of two heads, which afterwards was used on the title of Ralf Coilzear, 1572; and some of the ornaments in Scot's edition 1559, are repeated. At the end of the Dialog, on sign. R 1, we have

☞ FINIS ☜ | QVOD LYNDESAY. | 1569. |

In the 1568 edition there is no date.

The copy in the Bodleian Library, amongst Bishop Tanner's Books, No. 187, is imperfect at the end, breaking off with sign. L 3, or the first leaf of Kittie's Confessioun. Another copy, apparently the same edition (notwithstanding a difference detected by Mr Bradshaw in the woodcut at the end of the Epistil) is among Thomas Baker's books, in the Library of St. John's, Cambridge. It is marked Cc. 10. 56, and wants the title and three leaves, also sign. L at the end, in which the imprint and date may have been repeated.

1574.

THE WARKIS OF the famous and worthie Knicht SCHIR DAUID LYNDESAY of the Mont, Alias Lyoun King of Armes, &c. Newlie corrected, &c.

Imprentit at Edinburgh be Thomas
Bassandyne, dwelland at the nether Bow.
M.D.LXXIIII.
Cum Priuilegio Regis.

In 4to, signatures A in six, B to Z in eights, and Æ in five. The copy described in Herbert's Typographical Antiquities (vol. iii. p. 1497), at the sale of Mr Chalmers's Library was acquired by Mr Miller of Craigentinny, and is now at Britwell. It is the only copy known. After the title, "Ane Adhortation of all Estates," is followed by "The Epistil Nuncupatorie," but the Preface by Henry Charteris is omitted. At the end of Book Fourth of the Monarchie there is no date, simply "Finis. Quod David Lyndesay."

On the last page the imprint and date are repeated.

"Newlie correctit and imprentit at Edinburgh be Thomas Bassandine, dwelland at the Netherbow. M.D.LXXIIII.

The printer, Thomas Bassandyne, died at Edinburgh, 18th October 1577. In the inventory of his stock, printed in the Bannatyne Miscellany, vol. ii., p. 197, we find specified,

"Item, fyue hundreth and fyue Dauid Lyndesayis, unbund, price of the pece, iij s. *Summa* lxxxx li. xv s.

"Item, fyue Dauid Lyndesayis, bund, the pece iiij s. *Summa* xx s."

1575.

A DIALOGUE betweene Experience and a Courtier, of the miserable state of the Worlde. Compiled in the Scottish tung by SIR DAUID LYNDSEY Knight, a man of great learning and science: First turned and made perfect Englishe: And now the seconde time corrected and amended according to the first copie.

Imprinted at London in Paules Churchyarde, by Thomas Purfoote. Anno Domini 1575.

In 4to, A to T 4, eights. On the last page (numbered as folio 140) is the same imprint, without date. The minor poems have the same running title carried on from the end of

The fourth booke // of the Monarch.

1581.

A DIALOGUE betweene Experience and a Courtier, of the miserable state of the Worlde. Compiled in the Scottish tung, by SYR DAUID LYNDSEY Knight, &c. First turned, &c.

Imprinted at London, in Newgate Market within the New Rentes, by Thomas Purfoote. An. Dom. 1581.

A to T 4 in eights. In 4to. This is a literal reprint, page for page, of Purfoote's edition, 1575, even to the misnumbering of the folios, and repeating on the title the words, "And now the seconde [*for* third] time," &c.

In both these editions the woodcuts used by Purfoote in 1566 are wholly omitted, but there is added

"The Complaynt and publique Confession of the King's olde Hounde called Bagsche:" but it breaks off with line 120. See note in vol. i. p. 277.

In other respects, the editions are exact repetitions, although a minute collation might detect some various readings. One, for instance, may be pointed out: line 16 of the Prelog to the Popinjay in the 1566 edition, in place "Of KENNEDIE," the name of a Poet wholly unknown in England, has "Of SKELTON, with his tearmes aureate."

The copies of the two later impressions are not uncommon: in the British Museum, at Britwell, and in other libraries. The Roxburghe copy of this 1581 edition is in the Advocates Library. I have both the 1575 and 1581 editions.

1582.

THE WARKIS, &c., of SIR DAVID LYNDSAY, &c. An exact copy of the title of this edition, by Henry Charteris, is given on the opposite page.

THE VVARKIS OF the Famous and Worthie Knicht Sir David Lyndsay of the Mont, alias Lyoun King of Armes. Newlie correctit, and vindicate from the former errouris, quhairwith they war befoir corruptit: and augmentit with sindrie Warkis, quhilk was not befoir Imprentit.

The Contentis of the Buik, &c.

¶ IMPRENTIT AT EDINburgh, be Henrie Charteris.

ANNO, M.D.LXXXII.

¶ CVM PRIVILEGIO REGALI.

In 4to, Title, Preface, &c., eight leaves, sign. A (not numbered,) and B to X in eights, pp. 316 [for 318] pages 75 and 76 being repeated. A full page has 35 lines.

The table of Contents on the back of the title, include "The Complaint unto the Kingis Grace, *omittit in the Imprentingis of Rowen, and Londoun;*" also,

"Ane Answer to the Kingis Flyting, *neuer befoir Imprentit,*"—although they are actually contained in the two previous editions of 1568 and 1571, by Charteris. But in this table there is added for the first time,

"The Historie of the Squyer William Meldrum of the Benis, *neuer befoir Imprentit.*

"The Testament of the said Squyer."

The copy in the Advocates Library, purchased at the sale of Mr D. Constable's books at London, 1828, at a very extravagant price, does not contain the Squyer Meldrum, and yet was considered to be perfect. I remember the copy in its original parchment cover, and it evidently never contained anything else bound with it. At that time the volume was in the hands of a Glasgow bookseller, who priced it at ten guineas. In the table of contents a former possessor, in an old hand, having marked the pages of the various poems, has added *deest* to these two articles.

The head lines in roman capitals—

¶ THE FIRST BVIK // OF THE MONARCHIE.

with 35 lines on a page.

On the last page, instead of any imprint, there is inserted, as on the opposite page, the woodcut device used by John Ross, the printer, who died in July 1580. (Bannatyne Miscellany, vol. ii. p. 204.) In the inventory of his stock, there is no allusion to any edition of Lyndsay's works, as having issued from his press. It was not unusual for one printer to use the device as well as the types and ornaments of his predecessor.

I have been able to identify two other copies of this edition of 1582, one in the Bodleian Library, defective of the under half of the title page; the other in the Cathedral Library of Peterborough, wanting the entire title page, with the date 1568 marked in MS. In neither copy is there the slightest indication that Squyer Meldrum had ever been in the volume.

1582. (?)

THE HISTORIE OF THE SQUYER WILLIAM MELDRUM of the Bynis, and the Testament of the said Squyer.

It is somewhat uncertain when Squyer Meldrum was first printed. As just stated, although professing to be annexed to the edition of Lyndsay's Poems by Henry Charteris, 1582, it must have been printed about the same time in a separate form. This is proved by the fact, that in the inventory of the stock-in-trade of Robert Gourlay, bookseller in Edinburgh, who died 6th September 1585, six copies of "The Squyer of Meldrum, black" were valued at 12d. each, *Summa* vjs.; and seven copies of "Lyndsay (the Poems,) black," at iiijs vjd. *Summa* xxxjs vjd.[1] The latter were no doubt copies of the 1582 edition. (Bannatyne Miscellany, vol. ii., p. 214.)

1588. (?)

THE WARKIS OF THE FAMOUS AND WORTHIE Knicht Sir David Lindesay, at the command of King James the Fyft. With a print of Justice and Religion, and H. C. (Hen. Charteris,) 1588, 4to.

An edition is so described by Ames and repeated by Herbert, without stating in whose possession there was a copy. In the sale catalogue of Mr Heber's Library, 1834, Part IV. No. 1388, we find "Lyndesay's (Sir David) Poetical Works, black letter, russia. Edinburgh be Henrie Charteris, 1588." 4to. This copy, (it is added,) wants the title and part of the last leaf, and four leaves after K ij, otherwise it is perfect. It was bought for Mr Miller of Craigentinny, and is now at Britwell. But no edition printed in 1588 is known to exist. The copy in question, (rebound perhaps half a century before) no doubt has that date on the back; but having compared the book with the editions printed by Charteris in 1582, 1592, and 1597, it is clearly the edition of 1597, wanting, besides the Title, the Preface, &c., eight leaves.

1592.

THE VVARKIS OF THE FAMOUS AND VVORthie Knicht, Sir Dauid Lyndsay of the Mont, alias Lioun King of Armes. Newlie correctit, &c.; and augmentit with sindry warkis, quhilk was not befoir imprentit.

The Contentis of the Buik, and quhat Warkis ar augmentit, the nixt side sall schaw.

Imprentit at Edinburgh, be Henrie Charteris.

Anno, M.D.LXXXXII.

Cum Priuilegio Regali.

In 4to, black letter, contains sign. A to X in eights, numbered (not reckoning sign. A) pp. 318. It is a reprint, page for page, from the edition 1582. A full page has 35 lines. The head lines are in roman capitals—

THE FIRST BVIK // OF THE MONARCHIE.

In the Advocate's Library, and another copy in private hands. The table of contents is quite the same as that of 1582, including:

"17. The Hystorie of the Squyer William Meldrum of the Bynnis, neuer befoir imprentit.

"18. The Testament of the said Squyer."

Both the title and colophon at the end, (p. 318,) have the date distinctly, Anno Dom. M.D.LXXXXII., but no Squyer Meldrum of that date is known.

1594.

THE HISTORIE OF

ANE NOBIL AND WAILZE-
and Squyer, William Meldrum, vmquhyle
Laird of Cleiſche and Bynnis. Compylit be Sir Dauid
Lyndesay of the Mont, alias, **Ly-
oun, King of Armes.**

¶ H ¶ ¶ C ¶

THE

(☞) Teſtament of the ſaid WILLIAME MELDRVM

Squyer. Compylit al-
ſwa be Sir Dauid
Lyndeſay, &c.

(*,*) (*,*)
(*,*)

Cicero Philip. 14.
Proprium ſapientis eſt, grata eorum virtutem memo-
ria proſequi, qui pro Patria vitam profunderunt.
Ovid. 2. Faſt.
Et memorem famam, qui bene geſſiit habet.

Imprentit at Edinburgh
be HENRIE CHARTERIS.
ANNO M.D.XCIIII.
Cum Priuilegio Regali.

In 4to black letter, A to D iiij, in eights, or 28 leaves.

In the copy in the British Museum there is written at the foot of the title, "Tho. Arrowsmyth, seruant to Henry Bowes, Esquire. Empt. in Edenbr. Marche ij° 1597. pr^{t}. xxx d. Scottish." In the Advocates Library copy, and the one in private hands, it is bound with the 1592 edition of the Works.

1597.

THE

Warkis of the

famous & worthie
Knicht Sir Dauid Lindſay of the
Mont, alias Lyoun King of Armes.
Newlie correctit and vindicate from the former errouris, quhairwith they war befoir corruptit: and augmentit with ſindrie Warkis, quhilk was not befoir Imprentit.

Imprentit at Edinburgh be Henrie Charteris. 1597.

Cum Priuilegio Regali.

In 4to black letter, not paged, signature A to X in eights. A full page has 35 lines. The headlines

The Thrid Buik // of the Monarchie.

The contents are the same as in the previous editions by Charteris, and the above title is within a small border of metal ornaments. It also professes to include Squyer Meldrum, "*neuer befoir imprentit;*" but it is not contained in the copy bought at the Chalmers sale, which is now in the library, Britwell House. On the last page is the woodcut of two female figures, with the initials H. C., as given in vol. ii. p. 289. Of this edition, I was able to identify a copy in the Cathedral Library at Durham, wanting the title, &c. (the text beginning on sign. B.), and also Squyer Meldrum.

HENRY CHARTERIS died 29th August 1599. In his stock there were 788 David Lyndesayis, at 8s. the pece, unbound, *summa* £315. Also 40 Squyeres of Meldrum, at 2s., *summa* £4. (Bannatyne Miscellany, vol. ii., p. 224.)

1602.

ANE SATYRE OF THE THRIE ESTAITS, in commendation of Vertew, and vituperation of Vyce. Maid be Sir Dauid Lindesay &c.
At Edinburgh, printed be Robert Charteris, 1602. 4to.

In 4to, title, one leaf. There is no prefatory matter, the text beginning on sign. B to V in fours, or pp. 155, roman letter.

In the facsimile of the title given in vol. ii. page 289, the word "and" has been omitted in line 5. There are copies in the Bodleian Library, and at Britwell, (the two described as above); also in the Advocates Library; the Cathedral Library, Lincoln (wanting the title, &c.) A fine copy was bought at the Roxburghe sale by Mr Heber, and resold at his sale; but I am not sure who the purchaser was, through Messrs Payne and Foss.

Margaret Wallace, wife of Mr Robert Charteris, Printer in Edinburgh, having died during his life, on the 1st of February 1603, an Inventory was taken of his stock, on behalf of their children. In this list we find,

Item, 600 (copies of) Dauid Lyndesayis buikis at vij s. the pece, *Summa* ij^c x li.
Item, 500 Dauid Lyndesayis Playis at iiij s. the pece. *Summa* j^c li.
(Bannatyne Miscellany, vol. ii., p. 236.

1604.

ANE SATYRE OF THE THRIE ESTAITS, &c. Edinburgh, Robert Charteris, 1604. 4to. Mr Chalmers refers to such an edition, and it is quite possible that copies of the 1602 edition might have had a new title, but I have shewn in the Notes, vol. ii., pages 288-292 that the two described by Chalmers, as distinct editions, are one and the same, notwithstanding slight variations that may have been made in the course of printing. Having 500 copies unsold in 1603, it is most unlikely he would have required to reprint it within twelve months.

One of these copies, in place of the proper title, has the title-page to an unknown edition of the Poems, dated 1604. It apparently however was nothing more than a new title to insert in the unsold copies of the edition of 1597 for the London market. This volume is now at Britwell. The title reads,

THE WORKES of the famous and Worthy Knight Sir David Lindsaie of the Mont, alias Lyoun King of Armes. Newly corrected and vindicate from the former errors, wherewith they were before corrupted, and augmented with sindrie workes never before imprinted. (*The Royal arms.*) Imprented at Edinburgh by Robert Charteris, Printer to the Kinges most excellent Majestie, and are to be solde *in London, by* Nathaniell Butter *at his shoppe, neare S. Austens Church in the old Change.* 1604.

There is no list of Contents on the back of this title.

1605.

"Sir David Lindsay's Works. Edinburgh, 1605," 4to. A copy of this unknown edition occurs in the "Catalogus Librorum A. C. D. A.—*Glasguæ*, 1758," 4to. This collection belonged to Archibald Campbell, Duke of Argyll; and I find it stated, in a MS. note, that "The Earl of Bute bought the whole library after the death of the Duke, 1790."

1610.

THE WORKS of the famous and worthy Knight Sir David Lindsay, &c. Newly corrected according to the Originall.

EDINBURGH

Printed by THOMAS FINLASON. 1610.

With the K. M. Licence.

In 4to, black letter, A to G in fours, and H to BB in eights, ending on p. 375.

A full page has 33 lines. The head lines,

The secund buke // of the Monarchie.

At the Roxburghe Sale in 1811, the fine copy of this 1610 edition containing The Squyer Meldrum was bought by Mr Heber, and, on the dispersion of his Library, it came into Mr Miller's possession, and is now at Britwell.

1610.

THE HISTORIE of a noble and valiant Squyer William Meldrum, umquhile Laird of Cleish and Binnes. Compyled be Sir David Lindesay of the Mount, alias, Lyoun King of Armes. The Testament of the said William Meldrum, Squyer. Compyled alswa be Sir David Lindesay, &c.

EDINBVRGH

Printed for RICHARD LAWSON, 1610.

with Licence.

In 4to, A to G in fours, 28 leaves not numbered: at the foot of the last page, is a woodcut with Finlason's monogram T. F.—The head line of each page is, *The Squyer of the Binnes.* With 35 lines on a page.

This edition is bound with the copy at Britwell, as above mentioned, of Finlason's edition of the Poems 1610, from the Roxburghe Library. I have a separate copy of this edition of Squyer Meldrum bound by itself.

1614.

THE WORKES OF the famous and worthie Knight Sir David Lyndesay, &c. Edinburgh Printed by Andro Hart, Anno Dom. 1614, small 8vo., bl. l. (See facsimile at p. 245.)

Sign. A, Bl. 4 in eights, not paged, but it has sign. R reprinted in place of P and R, the larger initial.

The woodcut on the title is repeated at the end of the Prologue, and of the 1st, E. 4, and 4th Books of the Monarchie. The head-lines are,

The third Booke // of the Monarchie.

A full page has 29 lines. It is in the British Museum.

1617.

THE WORKES OF THE FAMOVS and worthy Knight, Sr. David Lindesay of the Movnt, &c. . . . Newly corrected, &c.

EDINBV(R)GH,
Printed by Andro Hart, 1617

In small 8vo., black letter, pp. 376, title four leaves, A to Z in eights. The head-lines in small capitals, usually 30 lines in a page. The initial letters are a kind of interlaced form.

On the back of the title The Contents of the Booke, the next leaf The Printer to the Reader, and two leaves The Epistle Nuncupatorie. In the Advocates Library.

1628.

THE WORKES OF the famous, and worthie Knight, Sir David Lindesay of the Movnt, alias Lion, King of Armes. Truelie corrected and vindicated from the former Errours and now justly printed according to the Author's true Copie: with sundrie thinges adjoyned here-vnto agayne, which absurdlie were omitted in the Impressions printed here-to-fore.

ABERDENE,
¶ Imprinted by EDWARD RABAN, for
DAVID MELVILL. 1628.

In small 8vo, black letter, 31 lines on a page; sign. A to X eights, not paged. It has no preliminary matter, and the Table of Contents is on the reverse of the title. This edition is a reprint of one of Hart's. Henry Huth, Esq., London, a copy from a late London sale.

1630.

THE WORKES OF the famous and worthy knight, Sir Dauid Lindesay. . . . Newlie corrected, &c.

Printed at Edinburgh, by the Heires of Andro Hart: Anno Dom. 1630.

In small 8vo, black letter, title, and leaf The Printer to the Reader, sign. A to Y 6 in eights, the running titles in small roman letter, 32 lines on the page, the Contents the same as in Hart's earlier editions, except the omission of the Epistle Nuncupatorie.

The copy in the Advocates Library formerly belonged to Major Pearson.

1634.

THE WORKES OF the famous and worthy Knight Sir David Lindesay, &c. Edinburgh printed by [the Heirs of] Andrew Hart. 1634.

In small 8vo., bl. l., sign. A to Y in eights, a full page has 31 or 32 lines. A facsimile of the title is given at p. 247. By a strange blunder the words enclosed with brackets are omitted in the original. Andrew Hart (who always used the name Andro), died, as already stated, in December 1621.

Copies of this edition are in the British Museum, and at Britwell, (from the Roxburghe and Heber collections.) Another was recently sold at the Corser sale.

The edition is chiefly remarkable for the woodcut on the title page, which professes to be a likeness of the Poet, but no other portrait unfortunately has been discovered to test its authenticity.

Open initial letters, but no larger cuts.

The third Booke // Of the Monarchie.

1645. (?)

THE WORKS OF Sir David Lindesay, &c. An edition was probably printed by Gideon Lithgow, for Robert Bryson, about 1645, in small 8vo. Bryson died in that year, and in the inventory of his stock confirmed 16th March 1646, we find 1150 copies of "David Lyndsayes, estimat all to £220." (Bannatyne Miscellany, vol. ii. p. 264.)

I have a copy (wanting the title and a few leaves) apparently of this edition. It was reprinted page for page, in a coarser style, with occasional slight variations in the orthography, in 1648. Each page has 36 lines. The head lines of each are in small Roman letter.

1648.

THE WORKES OF the Famous and worthie Knight Sr. David Lindsay of the Mount, &c. Newly corrected, &c.

EDINBURGH,
Printed by GEDEON LITHGOVV,
Anno Dom. 1648.

In small 8vo, black letter, A to V 2 in eights. In the British Museum, at Britwell, and in the Earl of Minto's Library. Not paged, 36 lines on a page, the initial letters large coarse letters, not ornamental.

1665.

THE WORKS OF the famous and worthy Knight Sir David Lindesay, &c. Newly corrected, &c.

GLASGOW,
Printed by *Robert Sanders,* Printer to the Town,
and are to be Sold at his Shop, Anno 1665.

In 12mo, black letter, pp. 302 (including 3 pages at the end of the Contents) sign. A to L in 12s., M, N and O in eights. 35 lines on a page, the running title or head lines in small roman letter.

On the back of the title "The Printer to the Reader." It is the same as in Hart's editions slightly altered. I have a copy of this scarce edition.

1670.

THE VVORKS OF the famous and worthy Knight Sir David Lindesay of the Mount, &c. Newly corrected, &c.

Edinburgh, Printed by *Andrew Anderson,* and are to be sold at his House, on the north-side of the Cross, *Anno* Dom. 1670.

A to M 8 in twelves, pp. 279, black letter, 40 lines in a full page. Oblong 12mo. In the British Museum, Advocates Library, and in other collections.

This and the following impressions of the works are by no means rare.

1672.

THE WORKES OF . . . Sir David Lindesay, &c. Newly corrected.

Glasgow: By Robert Sanders, Printer to the City, and University, and are to be sold in his Shope, 1672.
In 12mo, black letter, pp. 252, or A to L 6 in twelves, 44 lines on a full page. In the Advocates Library.

1683.

THE WORKS of . . . Sir David Lindsay of the Mount, &c. Newly corrected, &c.

Glasgow, printed by Robert Sanders, One of his *Majesties* Printers. 1683.

In 18mo, black letter, small type, A to L 8 in twelves, Pp. 256 including the title-page. 43 lines on a full page.

In the British Museum, the University Library, Edinburgh, and in other collections.

1683.

THE HISTORY of the noble and valiant Squyer William Meldrum, umwhile Laird of Cleish and Bins. As also the Testament of the said William Meldrum. Compyleit by Sir David Lindsay of the Mount, alias, Lyon King of Arms.

Edinburgh, printed by the Heir of Andrew Anderson, Printer to the King's Most Sacred Majesty, and are to be sold at his shop. 1683. In 12mo, 24 leaves.

On the back of the title is a woodcut whole length figure (of the Squyer) smoking a pipe.

The copy in the sales of Heber and Utterson came into the possession of the Rev. Thomas Corsar. In the Catalogue of George Paton's books, sold at Edinburgh in 1809, (where Mr Heber obtained it,) the date, by the printer's mistake, was given as 1603. No such edition exists.

1690. (?)

A SUPPLICATION directed by Sir David Lindsay of the Mount with King's Grace in contemplation of Side Tailes and Muzzled Faces.

A single leaf broadside of two pages in double columns, without date, but printed at Edinburgh, about the year 1690. In the Advocates Library. I have it also.

1696.

THE WORKS of the famous and Worthy Knight Sir David Lindsay of the Mount, alias Lyon King of Armes. Newly corrected and vindicate from the former errors wherewith they were corrupted, &c.

Glasgow, printed by Robert Sanders, one of his Majesties Printers. 1696. 12o., bl. l., A to M 3 in twelves, or pp. 267. 40 and 41 lines to a full page.

This edition is not uncommon. Of two copies in the British Museum, one is on fine paper.

The date on the title of this edition is usually very indistinct, and in some Catalogues it passes for Glasgow 1636, or 1656, but no such editions exist. It was beyond all doubt printed by Robert Sanders, the younger. Printing in Glasgow was first introduced by George Anderson in 1638. Robert Sanders, the father, commenced printing in 1661, and died July 12, 1694. He was succeeded by his son Robert, who survived till January 1730.

1696.

THE HISTORY of a noble and valiant Squire William Meldrum, umquhile Laird of Cleish and Binns. Compiled by Sir David Lindesay of the Mount, alias Lyon King of Armes. With the Testament of the said Squire. Compiled also by Sir David Lindesay.

Glasgow, printed by Robert Sanders, one of His Majesties Printers, &c. 1696. 18mo.

1709.

THE WORKS of Sir David Lindsay of the Mount. Newly corrected, &c.

Edinburgh, printed by the Heirs and Successors of Andrew Anderson, Printer to the Queen's most excellent Majesty. Anno Dom. 1709. 12mo, pp. 264.

1711.

THE HISTORY of the noble and valiant Sqyer William Meldrum umwhile Laird of Cleish and Bins; as also, The Testament of the said William Meldrum. Compyled by Sir Dauid Lindsay of the Mount, alias, Lyon King of Arms. Printed by James Nicol at Aberdeen in the year 1711. 12mo, A to C in 12s, pp. 58.

On a blank leaf at the end there is a woodcut of 'Meldrum and Talbert' on horseback charging one another with their lances.

The copy in Mr Douce's possession, with the rest of his remarkable collection, is now in the Bodleian Library, Oxford. In the same volume are two other books, (one, The History of Bevis of Hampton), from the press of James Nicol, Printer to the Town and University of Aberdeen.

1712.

THE WORKS of Sir David Lyndsay, Newly corrected, &c.

Glasgow, printed by Robert Saunders, in the year 1712, pp. 296, 12o.

In the Advocates Library, and the University Library, Edinburgh.

1714.

THE WORKS of Sir Dauid Lindsay, &c. Newly corrected.

Belfast, Printed by James Blow, and are to be sold at his Shop. 1714. 18mo, in twelves and sixes alternately, A to O, and P in eight. A full page has 40 lines.

In the British Museum.

1716.

THE WORKS of Sir David Lindsay, &c. . . . Newly corrected, &c.

Edinburgh, printed by the Heirs and Successors of Andrew Anderson, Anno Dom. 1716. 12mo.

1720.

THE WORKS of Sir David Lindsay, &c. Newly corrected.

Edinburgh, printed by the Successors of Andrew Anderson, Printers to his M. Anno Dom. 1720, 12mo, pp. 264. In the Advocates Library.

1754.

THE WORKS of Sir David Lindsay of the Mount, &c. Newly corrected, &c.

Glasgow, printed by John Hall, near the middle of the Salt Market. M.DCC.LIV.

18mo, roman letter, pp. 287. One of the common impressions of no value, A to M in twelves.

1776.

THE WORKS of the famous and worthy Knight Sir David Lindsay of the Mount. Carefully corrected, &c.

Edinburgh, printed and sold by Peter Williamson, and

C. Elliott, Parliament Square, 1776, 12mo, pp. 151. This contains the Four Books of the Monarchy.

The Additional Poems of Sir David Lindsay of the Mount, alias Lion King of Arms. Taken from his own original Manuscripts, found in the Cabinets of the curious, consisting of many different entertaining subjects. Volume II. Edinburgh, printed (as above) 1777. 12mo, pp. 84. Notwithstanding this flourish on the title, it is a worthless edition, and in place of enlarging, it omits, for instance, the Answer to the King's Flyting, as well as Squyer Meldrum.

1792.

SCOTISH POEMS, Reprinted from Scarce Editions, &c. Collected by John Pinkerton, in Three volumes. London, printed by and for John Nichols. 1792, 3 vol., post 8vo.

Vol. I. includes The Historie of ane nobil and wailyeand squyer William Meldrum, &c., Reprinted from the edition of 1594.

Vol. II. has Eight Interludes, with additional passages selected from the printed Play, Ane Satyre of the Thrie Estaits, &c., 1602.

1802.

ANE PLEASANT SATYRE of the Thrie Estaitis, in commendation of Vertue, and vituperation of Vice; a Play, maid by Sir David Lindesay. Edinburgh: 1802 8vo, pp. xii., 143. The Preliminary Interlude occupies the first 12 pages.

This edition of Lyndsay's Satyre was edited by James Sibbald, bookseller in Edinburgh; and only fifty copies were printed, it is said, for private circulation. It is in fact a portion of his Chronicle of Scottish Poetry, (4 vols, Edinburgh 1802, 8vo.) with some additions, not suited for that work. It is a very unsatisfactory edition, altered to suit the editor's notions, and containing the

Interludes from Bannatyne's MS., with passages interpolated from the printed text of 1602.

1806.

THE POETICAL WORKS of Sir David Lyndsay of the Mount, Lion King at Arms, under James V. A new Edition, corrected and enlarged, with a Life of the Author; Prefatory Dissertations; and an appropriate Glossary. By George Chalmers, F.R.S., S.A. In Three Volumes.

London, printed for Longman, Hurst, Rees, and Orme, Paternoster Row; and A. Constable and Co., Edinburgh. 1806, 3 vols., post 8vo.

1867.

THE DIALOG and other Poems of Sir David Lyndsay. London, 1867-1869, 8vo.

Of this edition, edited by Fitzherbert Hall, Esq., four parts have appeared, but the work is not yet completed. It forms part of the series of publications of the Early English Text Society.

1870.

THE WORKS of Sir David Lyndsay, 2 vols. 12mo. The text of this edition is reprinted from the present volumes, with a selection of the Notes, for general circulation.

LIST OF EARLY MANUSCRIPTS.

No portions of Sir David Lyndsay's Poems in his own hand-writing or of his age have been discovered. If we had been restricted to the manuscript collections of George Bannatyne and of Sir Richard Maitland (which have preserved so much of our old vernacular poetry), the very existence of Lyndsay as a poet might have remained almost unknown. The numerous early editions, which show his great popularity, may perhaps account for their non-existence in the form of manuscript copies. A short notice, however, of such as have reached our times, although comparatively of little value, may be subjoined.

I.—THE LAMBETH MANUSCRIPT, 1556.

This volume is described as follows by Archdeacon Todd in his Catalogue of the Lambeth Manuscripts.

No. 332. *Codex chartaceus, in 4to., Sec.* 16 *folio* 132. "Heir begynnis ane litill Dialog betuix experience and ane courteoure of the miserabill estait of the warld compilit be Schir David Lindesay, of the mont, knicht, Lioun King of armis Quhilk is dividit in foure partis as efter followis. Begun on Thursday the 11 of Junij 1556." (Catalogue of the Archiepiscopal Manuscripts in the Library at Lambeth Palace. London 1812, folio.)

Many years have elapsed since I examined this MS., and concluded that Mr Chalmers was right in not thinking it worth collating, being evidently a mere transcript of the first printed edition of the Dialog by John Scot.

II.—THE EDINBURGH MANUSCRIPT, 1566.

The title is :—" Ane dialog betuix experience and ane courtiour of ye miserabill estait of ye varld : Compilit be Syr Dauid Lyndesay of ye Mont, kny^t. alias lyone kyng of armes. And is diuidit in four partis : As eftir follovis—

1.5.6.6."

In folio, 144 leaves, the contents are :—

The Dialog in four parts, including The Epistill to the Redar, and the Prolog. The Dialog followed by Ane Exhortatioun extends from .	fol. 1- 99
The Dreme, ...	99-117
The Complaynt, . . .	118-124

It breaks off, leaving three blank pages to contain the last 86 lines. See vol. i., p. 247.

The Deploratioun of the deyth of Quene Magdalene, . .	125-128
The Testament and Complaynt of our Souerane Lordis Papyngo, &c., .	128-144

This MS. of Lyndsay is bound along with an early MS. of "The Buikis of Eneados," translated by Gawin Douglas, with the name at the foot of the first page W. Hay, 1527, and this notice on the fly leaf :—

" This buik partinis to Dauid Andersone burges of Abirdene, be gift of Mr Wm. Hay, person of Turreff, 1563." It contains 367 folios, in a neat small hand, with rubrics, and the name apparently of the transcriber, M. Joannes Elphynstoun. Lyndsay's Dialog, as the above title states, was transcribed in the year 1566. Like the Lambeth MS., the portion of Lyndsay's Poems is a transcript of a printed copy, probably that issued with the name of Jascuy, in 1558 ; and of no critical value, having in addition some other poems by Lindsay, containing The Epistill to the Redar of the Monarché.

The volume itself, in old wooden boards, was presented to the University Library, Edinburgh, by John Aikman (styled "generosus juvenis") son of Mr William Aikman, of Cairnie. Anno 1692.

III.—GEORGE BANNATYNE'S MANUSCRIPT, 1568.

With the exception of Lyndsay's Satyre of the Three Estaits, (divided into what Chalmers calls "a thousand Interludes,") his other Poems are entirely overlooked. The text of the play, as written by Bannatyne, is already minutely described, with collations, in vol. ii., pp. 341-363. Allan Ramsay copied, in his usual careless manner, these Interludes, for a continuation of his Evergreen, which never appeared. His transcript is still preserved. [The Bannatyne MS. is now printed for the Hunterian Club, and the 4th part contains Lyndsay's Play.]

IV.—THE DRUMMOND MANUSCRIPT, before 1626.

In the printed Catalogue or List of Books presented by Drummond of Hawthornden, to his *Alma Mater* in 1626, there is entered "Sir David Lyndesay, A Satyre of the Three Estates, MS." See vol. ii., p. 341. Whether it was an old MS., or transcribed by Drummond himself, must be left to conjecture, as the MS. itself, unfortunately, is not known to exist; and no trace of it appears in the old MS. catalogues of the University Library of Edinburgh.

V.—THE GLASGOW MANUSCRIPT, 1636.

This little volume, containing Squyer Meldrum, written at Glasgow by James Clark, 1631, is already noticed as copied from one of the printed editions, in vol. i., p. 332.

Page 272.—Delete the words "The copy I have," &c. near the foot of the page: and add this sentence: The copy of the First edition of the Dialog, mentioned at the foot of page 264 as in private hands, used by the English Text Society, like the volume in the University Library, Edinburgh, also contains the Minor poems printed by Scot in 1559. The copy I have of the Second edition by John Scot, of the Dialog, is imperfect, wanting sign. C. and has not the minor Poems.

ERRATA.

VOL. I.

Page 41, Line 1084, for *Goddes* read *Goddis*.
" 61, " 6, for *everlike* read *everilke*.
" 87, " 698, for *chehnis* read *cheknis*.
" 89, " 771, for *pirmityvis* read *primityvis*.
" 173, " 443, for *nobilmen* read *nobil men*.
" 215, " 1727, for *ble* read *blew*.

VOL. II.

Page 39, Line 695, for *pray yow* read *I pray yow*.
" 106, " 2053, for *aad* read *and*.
" 152, " 3028, for *Sard* read *Fard*,
" 170, " 3434, for *luikit* read *luik it*.
" 199, " 4120, for *is* read *hes*.
" 202, " 4191, for *cartelcinis* read *canteleinis*.
" 282, " 1568, for *as* read *ar*.

VOL. III.

Page 58, Line 3186, for *krake* read *brake*.
" 119. " 4914, for *savis* read *sayis*.

GLOSSARY.

GLOSSARY.

ABBREVIATIONS.

A. N.—Anglo-Norman. *A. S.*—Anglo-Saxon. *Dan.*—Danish. *Dut.*—Dutch. *E.*—Old English. *Fr.*—French. *Gael.* Gaelic. *Germ.*—German. *Icel.*—Icelandic. *Moes. G.*—Moeso-Gothic. *O. Fr.*—Old French. *O. N.*—Old Norse. *Su. G.*—Suio-Gothic. *Adj.*, adjective; *adv.*, adverb; *comp.*, comparative; *conj.*, conjunction; *interj.*, interjection; *imp.*, imperative mood; *num.*, numeral; *prep.*, preposition; *pr. p.*, present participle; *p. p.*, past participle; *pr. s.* and *pr. pl.*, present and past tense, singular or plural; *sb.*, substantive; *v.*, verb.

Abak, ii. 79. *l.* 1482, *adv.* back, behind. *E. abacke.*

Abesie, ii. 66. *l.* 1218. *sb.* an *abbacy.*

Abill, i. 188. *l.* 894, *adj.* proficient. *A. S. abel.*

Abilzementis, i. 120. *l.* 86. **Abuilzement**. ii. 77. *l.* 1421, *sb.* habiliment, dress. *Fr. habillement.*

Abone, ii. 75. *l.* 1384, *prep.* above.

Abufe, i. 14. *l.* 351, *prep.* above.

Abusioun, iii. 26. *l.* 2250, *sb.* abuse.

Accowterit, i. 199. *l.* 1231, *p.p.* accoutred.

Addres, i. 193. *l.* 1071, *v.* to prepare. *Fr. adresser.*

Adjutory, iii. 167. *l.* 6265, *sb.* a helper.

Ado, ii. 250. *l.* 663, *v.* to do.

Afeir, i. 71. *l.* 266, *v.* to fear.

Affamysit, iii. 140. *l.* 5490, *p.p.* famished. *Fr. affamer.*

Affeard, ii. 31. *l.* 488, *p.p.* afraid.

Afferand, iii. 5. *l.* 1662, belonging to, proportioned to. **Afferis**, i. 20. *l.* 507, *pr. s.* belongs.

Affore, iii. 80. *l.* 3805. **Afore**, i. 36. *l.* 942. **Afforow**, ii. 264. *l.* 1053, *adv.* before.

Affrayd, iii. 58. *l.* 3160, *sb.* fear.

Agane, i. 53. *l.* 284. **Aganis**, i. 23. *l.* 605, *prep.* against.

Agast, ii. 78. *l.* 1449, *adj.* frightened. *Moes. G. usgaisjan*, to terrify.

Agit, i. 208, *l.* 1519. *adj.* aged.

Agment, iii. 52. *l.* 2998, *v.* to augment, increase.

Aige, i. 51. *l.* 209, *sb.* age.

Aile, i. 186. *l.* 837. **Aill**, i. 85. *l.* 646. **Ayle**, ii. 98. *l.* 1921. *sb.* ale. *A.S. eala.*

Air, ii. 276. *l.* 1376, *sb.* an oar. *A.S. are.*

Air, i. 190. *l.* 972, *sb.* an heir.

AIR, ii. 86, *l.* 1650, *adv.* early. *A.S. aer.*

AIRIS, ii. 134. *l.* 2652, *sb.* assizes, circuit courts. *See* Notes, ii. p. 315.

AIRIS, iii. 6. *l.* 1713, *sb.* of the air, atmosphere.

AIRLIE, i. 182. *l.* 713, *adv.* early.

AIRTIS, iii. 144. *l.* 5595, *sb.* quarters of the heavens, districts.

AITH, i. 194. *l.* 1095, *sb.*, an oath ; *pl.* AITHIS, i. 131. *l.* 107.

ALEWIN, iii. 90. *l.* 4081, *num.* eleven.

ALKIN, i. 53. *l.* 300. ALLKIN, ii. 219. *l.* 4562, of every kind. *A.S. ael cyn.*

ALLACE, i. 4. *l.* 92, *interj.* alas !

ALLANERLIE, iii. 35. *l.* 2516, *adv.* only, solely.

ALLHALLOW, ii. 56. *l.* 1000, All Saints, *be all hallows,* a common oath in Lyndsay's time,

ALMANE, ii. 52. *l.* 907, Germany.

ALMIS, ii. 30. *l.* 464, *adj.* charitable, kind. ALMIS, ii. 99. *l.* 4, *sb.* charity, alms.

ALRICH, ii. 82. *l.* 1544, *adj.* terrible, ghastly, elvish, applied to preternatural persons.

ALS, ii, 73. *l.* 1354, *adv.* also.

ALSWA, iii. 230. *l.* 6, *adv.* also.

ALTHOCHT, ii. 13. *l.* 60, *adv.* although.

ALUTTERLYE, i. 60. *l.* 497, *adv.* entirely, wholly,

ALYKE, ii. 257. *l.* 848, *adv.* alike.

ALYKEWYIS, iii. 109. *l.* 4620, *adv.* likewise.

ALYTE, i. 89. *l.* 766. *sb.* a little. *A.S. lytel.*

AMANGIS, i. 52. *l.* 254, *prep.* amongst.

AMESIT, i. 45. *l.* 42. *pt. s.* satisfied.

AMLAND, ii. 167. *l.* 3380, *pr. part.* ambling.

AND, ii. 86. *l.* 1654, *conj.* if.

ANEUCH, ii. 55. *l.* 981, enough.

ANENT, i. 39. *l.* 1021, opposite to.

ANIS, ii. 25. *l.* 349, *adv.* once.

ANKER, ii. 275. *l.* 1376, *sb.* an anchor.

ANNET, ii. 162. *l.* 3256, *sb.* the river Annat or Cambus, near Doune. *See* Notes, ii. p. 316.

ANSENZE, i. 14. *l.* 326, *sb.* mark, sign. *Fr. enseigne. See* Notes, i. p. 230.

A PER SE, ii. 52. *l.* 914, *sb.* an incomparable person, like *a* by itself, which has the first place in every alphabet.

APPARDOUN, ii. 40. *l.* 873, *v.* to pardon.

APPEISIT, i. 66. *l.* 133, *p.p.* appeased.

APPLEISIT, i. 175. *l.* 494, *p.p.* satisfied, pleased.

APPLYABLE, ii. 123. *l.* 2414, *adj.* docile.

APPOVENTABYLL, ii. 277. *l.* 1416, *adj.* terrible. *Fr. epouvantable.*

AQUAVITE, i. 187. *l.* 886, *sb.* spirits.

AREIR, ii. 69. *l.* 1286. AREIR, i. 48. *l.* 122, *adv.* backwards ; *rin areir,* to retire. *Fr. arriere.*

Arkis, i. 119. *l.* 73, *sb.* arches.

Armeit, iii. 40. *l.* 2667, *sb.* a hermit.

Armoneis, iii. 169. *l.* 6308, *sb.* harmonies.

Armyne, i. 99. *l.* 1047, *sb.* ermine fur.

Array, ii. 37. *l.* 630, *sb.* dress.

Art, iii. 129. *l.* 5177, *sb.* kind, nature. *Germ. art.*

Art, ii. 282. *l.* 1567, *sb.* quarter of the heavens, district.

Artailye, i. 95. *l.* 947, *sb.* artillery. **Artalyeit**, i. 95, *l.* 929; **Artailzeit**, i. 106. *l.* 31, *p.p.* equipped, armed. *Fr. artillé.*

Arthetica, iii. 119. *l.* 4918. *sb.* the gout.

Ascens, i. 74. *l.* 351, *sb.* ascent. *Lat. ascensus.*

Askar, ii. 76. *l.* 1401, *adv.* at a distance, away from.

Ass, i. 148. *l.* 240, *sb.* ashes. *A.S. asce.*

Assaill, i. 162. *l.* 89, *v.* to prove, try.

Assaye, iii. 58. *l.* 3159, *sb.* attack, onset.

Asseisit, i. 66, *l.* 130, settled, fixed.

Ather, i. 122. *l.* 139, each.

Atonis, iii. 9. *l.* 1781, at once.

Attentike, i. 201. *l.* 747, *adj.* authentic.

Attour, iii. 162. *l.* 6162, *adv.* besides. *more attour*, moreover.

Aucht, i. 15. *l.* 392, *num.* eight.

Auchtsum, i. 198. *l.* 1225, *sb.* eightsome, consisting of eight. *A.S. ahtasum.*

Auctour, i. 24. *l.* 639, *sb.* author.

Aughtest, ii. 225. *l.* 2, *pr. s.* oughtest.

Auld, i. 5. *l.* 103. *adj.* old.

Aulter, iii. 25. *l.* 2222, *sb.* an altar.

Aureait, i. 62. *l.* 16, *adj.* golden, polished. *Lat. auratus.*

Aurient, ii. 230. *l.* 136. Orient. *See* Notes, iii. p. 181.

Aurorall, ii. 231. *l.* 148, *adj.* morning.

Avance, i. 27. *l.* 707, *v.* to advance, to bring forward, to enumerate.

Awalk, ii. 21. *l.* 73, *v.* to awake.

Awe, ii. 234. *l.* 233, *pr. s.* owe.

Awin, i. 9. *l.* 208, own.

Austerne, i. 157. *l.* 21, *adj.* austere.

Ay, i. 183. *l.* 735, *adv.* always. **Ay**, i. 164. *l.* 156, even.

B.

Barris, i. 14. *l.* 353, *sb.* children, babes.

Babil Beirers, ii. 133 *l.* 2609, *sb.* tale bearers.

Babland, iii. 28. *l.* 2319, *pr. part.* babbling.

Bacheleris, i. 143. *l.* 116, *sb.* bachelors.

Bad, i. 174. *l.* 479, *p.p.* offered. *A.S. baed.*

Baill, i. 85. *l.* 645, *adj.* bad, wretched; **Baill**, ii. 35. *l.*

585, harm; BAILLIS, ii. 4. *l.* 585, *sb.* sorrows. BAILFULL, i. 13. *l.* 332, *adj.*, sorrowful, baleful. *A.S. bealu.*

BAIR, i. 3. *l.* 60, *adj.* bare.

BAIR, i. 176. *l.* 535, *pt.s.* did bore, pierced.

BAIRD, ii. 31. *l.* 490, *sb.* the beard.

BAIRD, i. 45. *l.* 491, *sb.* a bard, a poet.

BAIRDIT i. 171. *l.* 385, *p.p.* caparisoned, adorned with trappings.

BAIS, ii. 23 *l.* 316, *sb.* a bass part.

BAIT, i. 172. *l.* 407, *pt.s.* did beat.

BAITH, i. 4. *l.* 76. both.

BAITTAND, ii. 103. *l.* 1990, *pr. p.* pasturing.

BAK, iii. 169. *l.* 6310, *sb.* the bat.

BAKKIS, i. 183. *l.* 737, *sb.* backs.

BALDAR, ii. 332. *l.* 90, *comp.* more bold.

BALERIEBUM, ii. 212. *l.* 4410, an interjection.

BALINGAR, iii. 56. *l.* 3101, *sb.* a small sloop or barge.

BALLOKS, ii. 208. *l.* 4335, *sb.* the testicles.

BALME, iii. 164. *l.* 6180, *sb.* a drink flavoured with the juice of that shrub.

BAN, ii. 160. *l.* 3194, *v.* to excommunicate, curse.

BAND, ii. 29. *l.* 445, *sb.* a bond, vow, obligation.

BANEIST. i. 56. *l.* 392, *pt.s.* banished; BANESIS, i. 18. *l.* 462, *pr.s.* banishes.

BANIS, i. 156. *l.* 20, *sb.* bones.

BANKET, i. 209, *l.* 1558, *sb.* a banquet. BANKETTYNG, i. 120. *l.* 881. banqueting.

BANRENT, i. 121. *l.* 124, *sb.* a banneret, a knight made in the field.

BAR, i. 371. *l.* 980, *v.* to debar, shut out.

BARBOUR, i. 70. *l.* 246, *adj.* barbarous.

BARBULZEIT, iii. 240. *l.* 11, *p.p.* garbled.

BARDYNG, ii. 99. *l.* 1051, *sb.* ornamental trappings.

BARFIT, ii. 200. *l.* 4141, *adj.* barefooted.

BARMIE-AILL, ii. 200. *l.* 4146. ale well barmed or fermented.

BARNE, i. 169. *l.* 307, *sb.* a child; BARNES, i. 76. *l.* 95; BARNIS, i. 11. *l.* 256, *sb.* children, persons.

BARRAT, i. 33. *l.* 851, *sb.* misery.

BARRES, i. 125. *l.* 3, *sb.* barriers.

BASNET, i. 194. *l.* 1077, *sb.* a helmet. *Fr. bassinet.*

BASTAILYEIS, iii. 69. *l.* 3456, *sb.* strongholds; *Bastile* was originally a wooden tower used in warfare. *See* Notes, iii. p. 200.

BATYE TOUT, ii. 33. *l.* 541, *sb.* an invigorating drink, from *Dut. batig*, beneficial, and *togt*, *teug*, a draught. *O. N. tott*, a suck.

BAULD, i. 166. *l.* 215, *adj.* bold.

BAWBURD, ii. 39. *l.* 691, *sb.* a whore; BAWBURDIE, ii. 111. *l.* 2214, *sb.* whoredom. *Fr. bas* and *E. bird*, a mistress.

BAXSTER, i. 152. *l.* 352, *sb.* a baker; *pl.* BAXTERS, ii. 201. *l.* 4168.

BE, ii. 36. *l.* 605. for *abee*, alone. *E. abys.*

Be, i. 41. *l.* 1080. for, if they be.
Beand, ii. 217. *l.* 4539, *p.p.* being.
Beckis, i. 50. *l.* 181, *sb.* bows.
Become, i. 70, *l.* 3495 *pt.s.* happened.
Beforne i. 171. *l.* 376. *pre.p.* before.
Bedirtin, ii. 194. *l.* 3990. dirtied.
Beft, i. 183, *l.* 737, *sb.* a blow.
Begarie, i. 129. *l.* 35, *v.* to besmear; **Begairit**, i. 130. *l.* 83, besmeared; **Begaird**, iii. 152, *l.* 5863; **Begaryit**, i. 163. *l.* 126, *p.p.* ornamented, adorned.
Begouth, i. 189. *pr.s.* began.
Begyll, ii. 45, *l.* 804, *v.* to beguile.
Beiche, i. 114. *l.* 183, *sb.* a bitch.
Beid, i. 87. *l.* 706, *sb.* a prayer.
Beik, i. 101. *l.* 1099, *sb.* a beak, bill.
Beild, ii. 265. *l.* 1087, *sb.* refuge.
Beild, ii. 273. *l.* 1312, *v.* to build; *pl.* **Beildaris**, ii. 248. *l.* 590, *sb.* builders.
Beir, i. 7. *l.* 156, *v.* to bear; *pr. p.* **Beirand**, ii. 61. *l.* 1100 bearing.
Beir, i. 176, *l.* 518, *sb.* a bear, *pl.* **Beiris**, i. 201. *l.* 1301.
Beir, ii. 139. *l.* 2752, *sb.* barley.
Beir, i. 457. *l.* 49, *v.* to bawl; i. 45. *l.* 49. to vaunt.
Beiris, ii. 206. *l.* 4291, *sb.* noise.
Beiris, ii. 12. *l.* 26, *sb.* funeral biers. *A.S. bere.*
Beirnes, i. 78. *l.* 451, *sb.* children.
Beis, i. 53, *l.* 278. *sb.* bees.
Beird, ii. 54. *l.* 966, *sb.* the beard.
Beisy, i. 53 *l.* 278, *adj.* busy.
Beit, i. 164. *l.* 152. *pt.s.* struck, beat.
Bek, i. 47. *l.* 90, *sb.* a nod.
Beleve, ii. 260. *l.* 931, *sb.* belief.
Bellicall, i. 213. *l.* 1665, *adj.* warlike.
Bellie Blind, ii. 149. *l.* 2952. a person blindfolded for the purpose of playing at blind man's buff.
Bellis, i. 106. *l.* 39, *sb.* fights, battles.
Beltit, ii. 73. *l.* 1355. *p.p.* beaten with a strap or belt.
Belyve, i. 25. 649. *adj.* quickly, immediately. *O. Eng. bi life*, with life, quickly.
Ben, i. 114. *l.* 170, *adj.* within, along.
Bend, i. 176. *l.* 519, *sb.* a bound, a spring. *See* Notes. i. p. 248.
Bene, i. 45. *l.* 401, *v.* am, is, are, be.
Benefeits, ii. 203. *l.* 4223. *sb.* benefices.
Benesoun, i. 42. *l.* 1096; **Benisoun**, i. 122. *l.* 154, *sb.* a blessing, benediction, benison. *O. Fr. benisson.*
Bening, ii. 68, *l.* 1254, *sb.* favour, benignity.
Bent, i. 35. *l.* 919, *sb.* the open field. *Germ. Binse*, bent grass.
Benyng, i. 7. *l.* 149. *adj.* benign.
Berand, i. 56, *l.* 390, *p.p.* bearing.
Beriall, ii. 16. *l.* 132, *sb.*

a beryl, ii. 231. *l.* 142. *adj.* sparkling like beryl. *See* Notes, ii. p. 301.

BERNE, i. 35. *l.* 919, *sb.* a person, fellow. *See* Notes, i. p. 240.

BESEIK, i. 3. *l.* 50, *v.* to beseech; *pr.p.* BESEIKAND, i. 31. 809.

BESOUTH, i. 94. *l.* 918. to the south of.

BESTIALL, i. 31. 818, *sb.* beasts, cattle. *O.Fr. bestial.*

BESYNES, ii. 230. *l.* 121. *sb.* business.

BETRAIS, i. 198. *l.* 1210, *v.* to betray.

BEWIS, ii. 232. *l.* 183, *sb.* boughs.

BEWGRYE, ii. 264. *l.* 1043, *sb.* sodomy.

BIDDIN, iii. 40. *l.* 2660. *p.p.* remained.

BIGGYNG, iii. 5. *l.* 1684, *sb.* a building; *pl.* BIGGYNGIS, ii. 27. *l.* 1414.

BIKKER, i. 195. *l.* 1122, *sb.* a skirmish, fight. *Welsh bicre.*

BIRN, i. 101. *l.* 1109. *v.* to burn.

BIRNEIST, i. 200. *l.* 1279. *adj.* burnished, bright.

BIRNYNG, i. 30. *l.* 779, *pr.p.* burning.

BIRST, i, 130. *l.* 140, *v.* to burst.

BISMAIR, ii. 204. *l.* 4245, *sb.* a scold.

BISSY, ii. 338. *l.* 222. *adj.*, busy.

BLAID, ii. 107. *l.* 2091. *see Chafts.*

BLAITLIE BUM, ii. 140. *l.* 2774, *sb.* an ill-favoured simpleton; *blaitlie A. S. bleath,* and *bum,* a drone.

BLUDE, i. 200. *l.* 1264, *sb.* blood.

BLAK BYBILL, i. 86. *l.* 672. a funeral prayer for the remission of the sins of the dead.

BLASPHEMATIONIS, i. 13. *l.* 328. *sb.* blasphemies.

BLAW, ii. 199. *l.* 4124, *v.* to blow up. *p.p.* BLAWIN, i. 1. *l.* 5, blown.

BLE, i. 215. *l.* 1727, *adj.* for *blew,* blue.

BLEDDER, ii. 174. *l.* 3537, *sb.* bladder.

BLEDRAND, ii. 64. *l.* 1181, *pr.* babbling.

BLEIR, ii. 199. *l.* 4115, *v.* to obscure, blurr.

BLEIRIT, ii. 17. *l.* 173. *pt. s.* blurred, bedewed with tears.

BLENKIS, i. 16, *l.* 407, *sb.* glimpses, glances. *Dut. blincken.*

BLEW, i. 65, *l.* 111, *adj.* blue.

BLOKE, iii. 27. *l.* 2302, *sb.* a block of wood.

BLOMES, ii. 232. *l.* 183, *sb.* bloom.

BLUBERT, ii. 210. *l.* 4267. *pt. s.* blubbered, wept.

BLUDE, i. 200. *l.* 1264, *sb.* blood.

BLUNT, ii. 335. *l.* 168, *adj.* stupid.

BLYNDIT, i. 38. 1987, *p.p.* blinded.

BOCHT, ii. 11. *l.* 4. *pt. s.* bought.

BOCKET, ii. 210. *l.* 4367. *pt.s.* retched, vomited; BOCKING, ii. 209. *l.* 4358, *pr. p.* retching.

BODUM, ii. 276. *l.* 1382, *sb.* the bottom.

BOGILL, ii. 54. *l.* 950, *sb.* an apparition, hobgoblin.

BOIRD, iii. 27. *l.* 2302, *p.p.* bored, cut.

BOISIS, iii. 37. *l.* 2579, *sb.* casks. *O. Fr. bosse.* *See* Notes, iii. p. 194.

BOIST, i. 167. *l.* 266, *sb.* a boast, a menace.

BOISTEOUS, i. 106. *l.* 147, *adj.* boisterous, furious,

BOIT, i. 166, *l.* 211, *sb.* a boat; *pl.* BOITTIS, iii. 54. *l.* 3039.

BO-KEIK, ii. 86. *l.* 1640, *sb.* bo-peep. *See* Notes, ii. p. 308.

BOLDIN, iii. 88. *l.* 4049, *p.p.* swelled, overcharged.

BOLT, i. 164. *l.* 146, *sb.* a mace, a battle-axe.

BONE, i. 73. *l.* 337, *sb.* a bean. *See* Notes, i. p. 265.

BONNOKKIS, i. 157. *l.* 28, *sb.* cakes.

BONY, ii. 78. *l.* 1451, *adj.* beautiful.

BORDALL, i. 52. *l.* 250; BORDELL, ii. 39. *l* 690. *sb.* a brothel; *O. Fr. bordel.*

BORDOURIT, i. 5. *l.* 100, *p.p.* bordered.

BOROH, i. 87. *l.* 701, *v.* to become security.

BORROW, i. 38. *l.* 996, *sb.* a security, surety

BORROWSTOUNIS, i. 131. *l.* 89, *sb.* borough towns.

BOST, i. 17. *l.* 445, *sb.* a boast; BOSTIT, i. 93. *l.* 881, *pt. s.* boasted.

BOSTOUS, ii. 57. *l.* 1023, *adj.* rough, terrible.

BOT, i. 202. *l.* 1326, *conj.* but.

BOTE, iii. 56. *l.* 3101, *sb.* a boat.

BOUCHOUR, i. 110. *l.* 70, *sb.* a butcher; *pl.* BOUCHEOURIS. i. 203. *l.* 1360. *Fr. boucher.*

BOUMBARD, i. 95. *l.* 938, *sb.* a cannon. *Fr. bombard.*

BOUNDIS, i. 200. *l.* 1289, *sb.* bounds, reach.

BOUNDIN, i. 8. *l.* 173, *p.p.* bound together.

BOURD, ii. 137. *l.* 2722, *sb.* a jest; *pl.* BOURDIS, iii. 53. *l.* 3083.

BOUSTEOUS, i. 35. *l.* 919, *adj.* rude, rough, boisterous; BOUSTUOUSLIE, ii. 66. *l.* 1207, *adv.* rudely.

BOW, ii. 134. *l.* 2656, *sb.* a fold of cattle.

BOWCHOURIS, iii. 150. *l.* 580, *sb.* butchers.

BOWDERIT, i. 163. *l* 126, *p.p.* embroidered.

BOWIS, ii. 17. *l* 161. the streets called the Nether Bow and the West Bow of Edinburgh.

BOWIS, i. 51. *l.* 223, *sb.* papal bulls (a colloquial expression).

BOWNIS, iii. 169. *l.* 6037. *pr. pl.* repair, go.

BOWTIT, i. 176. *l.* 519. *p.p.* bolted, sprung; BOWTIT, iii. 25. *l.* 2225, bolted, sifted.

BRAGGAR, i. 98. *l.* 1015. *sb.* a braggart.

BRAID, i. 30. *l.* 791, *adj.* broad, wide, large.

BRAIKAND, ii. 36. *l.* 624, *pr.p.* breaking, breaking wind; BRAIKIT, ii. 210. *l.* 4167. *pt.s.*

BRAN, i. 187. *l.* 887, *sb.* brawn, the flesh of a boar.

BRAND, i. 200. *l.* 1279, *sb.* a sword.

BRANK, ii. 30. *l.* 468. *pr.s.* prance; BRANKRAND, i. 157. *l.* 38, *pr. pt.* swaggering, capering.

BRAIST, i. 177. *l.* 578; BRAISIT, i. 190. *l.* 954. *pt.s.* embraced, pressed.

BRAULL, ii. 147 *l.* 2915, *v.* to bluster.

BRAUNIS, i. 126. *l* 33, *sb.* the calves of the legs.

BRAWLL, ii. 222. *l.* 4647. *sb.* a quick dance.

BRAYE, i. 4. *l.* 76, *sb* an acclivity.

BREAK, ii 57. *l.* 1026. *v.* to break into, to rob.

BREID, i. 126. *l.* 31. *sb.* bread

BREID, iii. 43. *l.* 2729, *sb.* breadth.

BREID, ii. 53. *l.* 943, *sb.* a table; GODDIS BREID, the altar. *A.S. bred.*

BREIK, ii. 28. *l.* 434, *sb.* the breech.

BREIKKIS, i. 131, *l.* 89, *sb.* breeches.

BREIR, ii. 265. *l.* 1086, *sb.* a briar.

BREIS, i. 200. *l.* 1293, *sb.* brows.

BRESSE, ii. 37. *l.* 642, *v.* to press, to fold.

BRETHER, i. 74. *l.* 346, *sb.* a brother.

BREVE, i. 69. *l.* 225, *v.* to write; *pr. s.* BREVIS, i. 62. *l.* 38. *A.S. breve.* *See* Notes, i. p. 264.

BREVE, i. 140. *l.* 3, *adj.* brief.

BRIBOUR, i. 119. *l.* 66. *See Brybour.*

BRIG, i. 207. *l.* 1496, *sb.* a bridge.

BRIM, i. 201. *l.* 1301, *adj.* fierce.

BRIST, i. 176. *l.* 530. *pt.s.* burst.

BRITTILL BRATTILL, ii. 36. *l.* 621, *sb.* a hurried motion causing a clattering noise.

BROK, ii. 36. *l.* 624, *sb.* a badger; *pl.* BROKS, ii. 128. *l.* 2493.

BROTEKINS, ii. 158. *l.* 3145. *sb.* buskins.

BROUSTERS, ii. 200. *l.* 4147, *sb.* brewers. BROWSTER, i. 152. 352, *sb.* a brewer. *A.S. bredvan.*

BRUCH, ii. 93. *l.* 1802; BRUGH, ii. 214. *l.* 4457, *sb.* a borough.

BRUKE, i. 152. *l.* 353, *v.* to enjoy; BRUIKIT, i. 196. *l.* 1179, *p.p.* enjoyed.

BRUME, ii. 94. *l.* 1818, *sb.* the plant broom.

BRUNT, ii. 100. *l.* 1149, *p. p.* burnt.

BRUYLE, iii. 234. *l.* 22, *v.* to broil.

BRYBOUR, i. 118. *l.* 32, *sb.* a greedy rascal, a thief. *Fr. bribeur.*

BRYCHT, i. 3. *l.* 70, *adj.* bright; BRYCHTAR, ii. 231. *l.* 152, *comp.* brighter.

BRYDLIT, ii. 30. *l.* 468, *p.p.* bridled.

BRYG, iii. 49. *l.* 2906, *sb.* a bridge; *pl.* BRYGGIS, iii. 49. *l.* 2903.

BRYM, i. 176, *l.* 518, *adj.* violent. *A.S. bremman.*

BRYSTE, i. 56. *l.* 368, *v.* to burst.

BUCKLER, i. 107. *l.* 69, *sb.* *See* Notes, i. p. 275.

BUD, ii. 85. *l.* 1623, *sb.* a gift, a bribe.

BUIKS, ii. 60. *l.* 1088, *sb.* books.

BUIR, i. 205. *l.* 1434, *pt. pl.* bore, carried.

BUIRD, ii. 117. *l.* 2295, *sb.* a board.

BUIRDEN, ii. 144. *l.* 2868, *sb.* a burden.

BUIT, ii. 60. *l.* 1090, *sb.* advantage, boot.

BUITHIS, ii. 57. *l.* 1026, *sb.* shops, booths.

BUITTIS, ii. 158. *l.* 3545, *sb.* boots.

BULLER, i. 65. *l.* 95, *v.* to bellow. BULLERAND, i. 151. *l.* 338, *pr. p.* roaring; BULRYNG, ii. 281. *l.* 1553, *pr. p.* raging, boiling.

BUMMILL-BATY, ii. 21. *l.* 268, *sb.* a booby, a simpleton, from *bum*, a drone, and *batie* or *bawtie*, the name of a good-natured dog.

BUN, i. 130, *l.* 56, *sb.* the backside.

BURALL, iii. 164. *l.* 6198, *sb.* beryl.

BURD, i. 9. *l.* 210, *sb.* a board.

BURDOUNIS, i. 173, *l.* 445, *sb.* a staff with a pike, a spear.

BURE, i. 1. *l.* 8, *pr. s.* bore.

BUREIT, i. 155. *l.* 427, *pt. pl.* buried.

BURSIN, iii. 88. 4049, *p.p.* burst.

BUS, i. 3. *l.* 62; BUSK, ii. 262. *l.* 991, *sb.* a bush. *See* Notes, i. p. 255.

BUSKIT, ii. 41. *l.* 729, *pt. s.* dressed.

BUT, *conj.* without.

BUTTOCK MAILL, ii. 167. *l.* 3370, *sb.* the fine in place of penance for fornication imposed in the ecclesiastical courts.

BY, ii. 164. *l.* 3305, *adv.* besides, in addition to; iii. 67. *l.* 3395, beyond; ii. 83. *l.* 1566, aside.

BY, ii. 216. *l.* 4510, *v.* to buy.

BYDE, ii. 113. *l.* 2216, *v.* to remain. BYDAND, i. 106. *l.* 38, *pr. p.* abiding, lasting, but in a secondary sense exhausting.

BYGAINE, ii. 137, *l.* 2710, *adv.* past, bygone.

BYIK, iii. 150. *l.* 5798, *sb.* a beehive, nest, swarm. *See* Notes, p. 213.

BYILL, iii. 27. *l.* 2298, *sb.* an ulcer or boil.

BYNGIS, i. 8. *l.* 173, *sb.* heaps. *Dan. bing.*

BYRN, iii. 34. *l.* 2488, *v.* to burn.

BYSTOUR, ii. 151. *l.* 2992, *sb.* a violent or bitter railer. *O. N. byrstr, bystr. Dan. bister.*

BYTE, ii. 208. *l.* 4335, *v.* to bite.

C

CACE, i. 13. *l.* 335, a case, chance. *Fr. cas.*

CADYE, iii. 40. *l.* 2657, *adj.* cheerful, merry, wanton.

CAICHE, ii. 169. *l.* 3428, *sb.* catch, a game at hand-ball.

CAIFF, ii. 174. *l.* 3543, *sb.* chaff, refuse of corn.

CAILE, i. 152. *l.* 357, *sb.* broth of vegetables, colewort.

CAIR, i. 11. *l.* 268, *sb.* woe, care,

CAIRFULL, i. 7. *l.* 167, *adj.* sorrowful, full of care.

CAIRLS, i. 74. *l.* 1376, *sb.* churls, fellows.

Cairt, i. 17. *l.* 437, *sb.* a chariot.
Caissis, i. 213. *l.* 1651, *sb.* cases.
Caist, i. 107. *l.* 53, *pt. s.* did cast.
Calde, ii. 256. *l.* 815, *sb.* cold.
Calsay, i. 153. *l.* 378, *sb.* a causeway; Calsay-Paikeris, street walkers.
Campionis, i. 125. *l.* 2, *sb.* champions.
Can, i. 4. *l.* 92, for *gan*, began.
Cankart, ii. 74. *l.* 1367, *adj.* cross, ill-conditioned.
Canker, ii. 126. *l.* 2448, *adj.* eaten with the canker or rust, ill-conditioned.
Cap, ii. 211. *l.* 4392, *sb.* a wooden cup or bowl. Cap-out, ii. 33. *l.* 540, or *cop-out*, to drink freely.
Capis, i. 9. *l.* 216, *sb.* caps, head-dresses.
Careis, iii. 54. *l.* 3039, *pr. s.* carries.
Carlbaldis, i. 107. *l.* 51, *sb.* censorious fellows.
Cariage, iii. 147. *l.* 5705, *sb.* service due by tenants in men and horses to their landlords.
Cariounis, i. 12. *l.* 296, *sb.* carcases. *Fr. charoyne.*
Carling, ii. 74. *l.* 1367; Carlingis, i. 125. *l.* 16, *sb.* an old woman, a hag,
Carpe, i. 63. *l.* 46, *v.* to censure, cavil.
Carteleinis, ii. 202. *l.* 4191, *sb.* wiles, probably should be *canteleinis.* *O. Eng. cantilene.*
Cartis, i. 169. *l.* 3431, *sb.* cards. See Notes, i. p. 295.
Carvour, i. 2. *l.* 21, *sb.* a carver.
Cassin, i. 165. *l.* 181, *p.p.* cast, fallen.
Cast, ii. 37. *l.* 634, *sb.* a contrivance.
Caterve, iii. 120. *l.* 4923, *sb.* a catarrh.
Cat-harrow, i. 54. *l.* 308, *to draw at the cat-harrow*, to help or benefit one another.
Cattarve, iii. 127. *l.* 5112, *sb*, a catarrh.
Cautelis, i. 13. *l.* 311, *sb.* cautions, tricks. *Fr. cautelle.*
Cavell, ii. 144. *l.* 2865, *sb.* a sorry fellow. *O.Fr. caval*, a sorry horse.
Cawsa, ii. 206. *l.* 4301, *sb.* the causeway. Cawsay-Paker, ii. 3. *l.* 2206, a street-walker.
Cawteill, iii. 149. *l.* 5766, *sb.* caution, bail. *See* Cautelis.
Cederis, i. 78. *l.* 467, *sb.* cedars.
Cedull, i. 70. 234, *sb.* a schedule, writing. *Fr. cedule.*
Celsitude, i. 1. *l.* 3, *sb.* highness. *See* Notes, i. p. 264.
Chafts, ii. 140. *l.* 2772. *sb.* chops; Chaft-Blaid, ii. 107. *l.* 2091, *sb.* the jawbone. *See* Notes, ii. p. 311.
Chaifery, ii. 214. *l.* 4469, *sb.* wares, merchandise.
Chaip, i. 73. *l.* 331, *v.* to escape. Chaipit, i. 200. *l.* 1290, *pt. s.* escaped. *Fr. echaper.*
Chaiplate, i. 128. *l.* 12, *sb.* a chaplet.

Chaist, ii. 16. *l.* 135, *p.p.* chased.

Chalmer, i. 2. *l.* 24, *sb.* a chamber.

Chamber-Glew, ii. 110. *l.* 2163, *sb.* chamber enjoyment.

Channonnis, i, 8. *l.* 179, *sb.* canons.

Chapit, i. 145. *l.* 151, *pt. s.* escaped. *See* Chaip.

Charbunckle, i. 62. *l.* 26, *sb.* the carbuncle.

Chartereris, i. 8. *l.* 179, Carthusian friars.

Chease, ii. 156. *v.* to choose.

Cheikkis, i. 131. *l.* 90, *sb.* cheeks.

Cheip, i. 87. *l.* 698, *v.* to chirp, squeak.

Cheir, i. 18. *l.* 475, *sb.* aspect.

Cheir, i. 17. *l.* 427, *sb.* a chair.

Cheis, i. 171. *l.* 362; Cheiss, ii. 329. *l.* 42, *v.* to choose.

Chene, i. 99. *l.* 1053, *sb.* a chain.

Cherisit, i. 36. *l.* 942, *p.p.* nourished, cherished. *Fr. cherir.*

Ches and Tabill, i. 188. *l.* 893, chess and backgammon. *See* Notes, i. p. 318.

Chesit, i. 117. *l.* 10, *pt. s.* chose.

Chest, ii. 329. *l.* 56, *adj.* chaist; Chestely, ii. 329. *l.* 55, chastely.

Childerles, iii. 14. *l.* 1209, without children.

Chiragra, iii. 119. *l.* 4919, *sb.* gout in the hand. *Lat. chiragra.*

Chirurgience, i. 209. *l.* 1545, *sb.* surgery.

Christelling, iii. 159. *l.* crystalline.

Churle, i. 8. *l.* 179, *adj.* churlish.

Cincq, i. 136. *l.* 84, *num.* five, a term in dice play.

Circuleir, i. 24. *l.* 641, *adj.* circular.

Circuit, i. 232. *l.* 173, *pt. s.* made the circuit of.

Claff, ii. 48. *l.* 840, *sb.* a cant term. *Dut. kloof*, a slit.

Claggit, iii. 40. *l.* 2067, *p.p.* besmeared. *Dan. klag*, sticky.

Claggokis, i. 130. *l.* 62, *sb.* draggle-tailed wenches.

Clais, ii. 53. *l.* 930, *sb.* clothes.

Claith, ii. 213. *l.* 4432, *sb.* a cloth, a screen.

Clam, iii. 101. *l.* 4396, *pt. pl.* did climb.

Clatteraris, i. 75. *l.* 390, *sb.* tell-tales, tattlers. *See* Notes, i. p. 265.

Clattryng, ii. 281. *l.* 1529, *pr. p.* producing a rattling sound, resounding.

Claucht, i. 103. *l.* 1169, *pt. s.* clutched.

Clayis, ii. 103. *l.* 200, *sb.* clothes.

Cleik, i. 164. *l.* 158, *v.* to catch. Cleikand, i. 99. *l.* 1046, *pr. p.* catching, snatching.

Clekit, ii. 38. *l.* 669, *p.p.* hatched, born.

Clenelie, i. 9. *l.* *adj.* fully.

Clenge, i. 133. *l.* 163, *v.* to clean, *p.p.* Clengit, i. 133. *l.* 165.

Clethit, i. 3. 68, *pt. s.* clothed.

Clethyng, i. 13. *l.* 324, *sb.* clothing.

Clippis, i. 183. *l.* 744, *sb.* grappling irons, hooks.
Clippit - Hede, iii. 152. *l.* 5861, the tonsure of monks.
Clips, i. 48. *l.* 120, *sb.* an eclipse. *See* Notes, i. p. 250.
Clitter-Clatter, ii. 195. *l.* 4023, *sb.* tattle.
Cloiffis, i. 130. *l.* 80, *sb.* clefts.
Clois, ii. 53. *l.* 947, *adj.* close, secret.
Clois, i. 95. *l.* 939, *sb.* a narrow street, alley, court.
Cloke, i. 4. *l.* 71, *sb.* a cloak.
Clout, ii. 83. *l.* 1574, *sb.* a blow, a cuff.
Clout, ii. 117. *l.* 2292, *sb.* a rag, patch.
Cluke, i. 103. *l.* 1169, *sb.* a claw, talon. *Germ. klauwe.*
Clyppit, iii. 107. *l.* 4563, *p.p.* clipped, shorn. Clyppit crounis, tonsures.
Coactit, i. 49. *l.* 163, *p.p.* restrained, subjected.
Coattis, ii. 167. *l.* 3370, *sb.* for *quotts*, or the sum paid for the confirmation of the testament of a deceased person. *See* Notes, ii. p. 317.
Coffe, i. 156. *l.* 17, *sb.* a merchant. *See* Notes, i. p. 300.
Coft, ii. 68. *l.* 1258, *p.p.* bought.
Coill, ii. 102. *l.* 1982, *sb.* coal.
Coistis, i. 212, *l.* 1619, *sb.* cost, expenses.
Coit, i. 104. *l.* 1183, *sb.* a coat.
Cokis-passioun, ii. 25. 349, *sb.* an oath common in ancient times. Cok and Cokis, for *God* and *God's.* *See* Notes, ii. pp. 299, 302.
Cok's toes, ii. 54. *l.* 949, an oath of the period.
Collatioun, ii. 98. *l.* 1933, *sb.* a collation, repast.
Collatioun, i. 188. *l.* 890, *sb.* interview, conference; i. 3. *l.* 100, induction to a benefice.
Colleris, i. 137. l. 87, *sb.* collars.
Colpots, ii. 94. *l.* 1817, *sb.* coalpits. *See* Notes, ii. p. 309.
Colyearis, ii. 246. *l.* 549, *sb.* colliers.
Come, iii. 5. *l.* 1656, *pt. s.* became.
Commend, i. 158. *l.* 63, *sb.* a benefice.
Commoditeis, i. 31. 816, *sb.* advantages.
Commoun, ii. 13. *l.* 69, *v.* to communicate, to converse. Commonyng, i. 85. *l.* 3, conversation.
Commounweill, i. 85. *sb.* commonwealth.
Compare, i. 142. *l.* 67, *sb.* equal.
Companarie, ii. 43. *l.* 764, *sb.* companionship.
Compeir, ii. 12. *l.* 20, *v.* to appear.
Compleis, iii. 26, *l.* 2265, *v.* to please. *Fr. complaire.*
Complene, i. 37. *l.* 977, *v.* to complain.
Complexionate, i. 18. *l.* 460. *adj.* of a similar character.
Compositouris, ii. 135. *l.* 2664, *sb.* arbiters.
Compt, i. 37. *l.* 985, *sb.* account. Compt, i. 12. *l.* 301, *v.* to count. Comptit,

i. 9. *l.* 214, *pr. s.* accounted, valued.

COMPTES, i. 11. *l.* 268, a countess.

CON, iii. 40. *l.* 2657, *sb.* a squirrel.

CONDAMPNIT, i. 10. *l.* 248, *p.p.* condemned.

CONDING, ii. 171. *l.* 3466, *adj.* condign.

CONDUCT, i. 167. *l.* 268, *sb*, leadership.

CONDUCTS, ii. 279. *l.* 1474, *sb.* conduits.

CONFEITTIS, i. 187. *l.* 887, *sb.* comfits, sweetmeats.

CONFORTE, i. 41. *l.* 1061, *v.* to comfort.

CONJUNIT, i. 66. *l.* 125, *p.p.* conjoined.

CONQUEIS, ii. 52. *l.* 905, *v.* to conquer, acquire.

CONQUESSING, i. 212. *l.* 1633, *p.p.* acquiring; iii. 15. *l.* 1954, *pr. p.* conquering.

CONSAIT, iii. 56. *l.* 3119, *sb.* thought, idea.

CONSOCIABILL, ii. 92. *l.* 1781, *adj.* friendly.

CONSTRY, iii. 149. *l.* 5757, the Consistory, an ecclesiastical court. *See* Notes, iii. p. 213.

CONSUETUDE, ii. 105. *l.* 2032, *sb.* custom, common use.

CONTEINIS, i. 26. *l.* 666, *pr. s.* contains.

CONTEMPTIOUN, i. 128. *l.* 3, *sb.* contempt.

CONTRAFAIT, iii. 56. *l.* 3120, *v.* to counterfeit.

CONTRAMAND, i. 120. *l.* 92, *v.* to countermand. *Fr. contremander.*

CONVENABYLL, i. 32. 822, *adj.* suitable, convenient.

CONVOY, ii. 84. *l.* 1582, *v.* to visit, inspect; iii. 243. *l.* 14, *sb.* meaning.

COPPARE, i. 2. *l.* 21, *sb.* a cupbearer.

CORBIE, ii. 279. *l.* 1478, *sb.* a raven.

CORCE, i. 199. *l.* 1259; CORS, ii. 132. *l.* 2582, *sb.* the body.

CORDYNAR, i. 152. *l.* 353, *sb.* a cordwainer, shoemaker.

CORINOCH, i. 107. *l.* 51, *sb.* the coronach, or funeral cry of the Scoto-Irish women; also a war cry. *See* Notes, i. p. 275.

CORNIS, i. 31. 819, *sb.* corn, grain.

CORRAGE, i. 91. *l.* 818, *sb.* courage.

CORRYNOGH, i. 87. *l.* 702, *sb.* a coronach. *See* CORINOCH.

CORSIS, i. 50. *l.* 177, *sb.* persons.

CORS PRESENTIS, iii. 104. *l.* 4476, *sb.* a mortuary or funeral present given to the parson or vicar on the death of a parishioner, usually a cow, or the upmost clothing of the deceased. *See* Notes, ii. p. 319.

COT, ii. 138. *l.* 2736; COIT, i. 218. *l.* 1786; *sb.* a coat.

COULL, ii. 43. *l.* 761, *sb.* a cap, a cowl.

COUNTRAFAIT, i. 62. *l.* 15, *v.* to counterfeit. COUNTRAFAITIT, i. 64. *l.* 90, *pr. s.*

COUNTRYNG, iii. 110. *l.* 4672, *sb.* muttering, speaking. *Fr. couter.*

COUNNYNG, i. 152. *l.* 353, *adj.* skilful.

COUNSALABILL, ii. 87. *l.* 1673, *adj.* amenable to counsel.

Coup, ii. 124. *l.* 2434, *sb.* a capsize.

Courlyke, i. 190. *l.* 953, *adj.* short. *See* Notes, i. p. 297.

Courteslie, i. 163. *l.* 133, *adj.* courteously.

Courticiane, i. 208. *l.* 1535, *sb.* a courtier. Courticience, i. 98. *l.* 1006. Courtissianis, iii. 98. *l.* 4307.

Course, ii. 213. *l.* 441, *sb.* the body.

Covatyce, i. 8. *l.* 186, *sb.* coveteousness.

Cove, i. 6. *l.* 127, *sb.* a cave.

Cowclink, ii. 180. *l.* 3667, *sb.* a whore. See Notes, ii. p. 316.

Cowhubeis, i. 153. *l.* 381, *sb.* cowherds, persons in rustic attire.

Coy, ii. 11. *l.* 14; Coye, i. 66. *l.* 135, *adj.* quiet, still. *Fr. coy.*

Crabyng, i. 45. *l.* 32, *pr. p.* fretting, displeasing.

Crack, ii. 100. *l.* 1946, *v.* to converse; i. 127. *l.* 55, to boast.

Craft, i. 72. *l.* 288, *sb.* business; Craftie, iii. 20. *l.* 2096, *adj.* skilful, ingenious. Craftynes, i. 66. *l.* 128, *sb.* skill.

Craif, ii. 57. *l.* 1017, *v.* to crave. Craifis, ii. 115. *l.* 2264, *pr. s.* craves, seeks. Craifit, i. 209. *l.* 1555, *pr. s.* craved.

Craig, i. 6. *l.* 138, *sb.* a rock, crag. *Gael. creag.*

Craig, ii. 83. *l.* 1574, *sb.* the throat; *pl.* Craiggis, ii. 336. *l.* 189.

Crak, i. 51. *l.* 235, *v.* to chat, converse. *See* Notes, i. p. 243. Crak, i. 217. *l.* 1776, *sb.* the report of a cannon. Crakkis, i. 168. *l.* 294, talking, boasting. Crakkar, ii. 337. *l.* 200, a boaster.

Crammosie, i. 99. *l.* 1646, *sb.* crimson coloured silk or cloth. *Fr. cramoisi.*

Craw, ii. 204. *l.* 4254, *sb.* a crow.

Creillis, i. 125. *l.* 20, *sb.* wicker baskets, panniers.

Creipand, ii. 263. *l.* 1012, *pr. p.* creeping.

Creische, i. 137. *l.* 89, *sb.* fat; Creishie, ii. 16. *l.* 140, *adj.* greasy.

Croce, i. 173. *l.* 424, *sb.* a cross.

Crofte, iii. 169. *l.* 6309, *sb.* cultivated land.

Crok, i. 34. *l.* 893, *sb.* an old ewe.

Crowat, iii. 164. *l.* 6178, *sb.* a small vessel, a phial, a cruet.

Cruciate, i. 10. *l.* 241, *pt. p.* excruciated, tortured.

Cruckit, ii. 101. *l.* 1964, *adj.* crooked, lame.

Crysme, i. 219. *l.* 1839, *sb.* the anointing oil used in sacred ceremonies.

Cubiculare, i. 2. *l.* 24, *sb.* groom of the bed chamber. *Fr. cubiculaire.*

Cude, i. 146. *l.* 189, *sb.* a white linen cloth in which a child was wrapped at its baptism, a face-cloth. *See* Notes, i. p. 297.

Cuir, ii. 071. *l.* 1535, *v.* to care for.

Cuist, ii. 86. *l.* 1646. *pt. s.* cast.

CUITCHOURS, ii. 133. *l.* 2607, *sb.* gamblers. *Fr. coucheur.*
CUITTIS, ii. 158. *l.* 3546, *sb.* ancles.
CUKE, i. 104. *l.* 1184, *sb.* a cook.
CULLOURS, ii. 126. *l.* 2448, *sb.* colours.
CULUM, ii. 107. *l.* 2102, *sb.* the fundament, tail.
CUMIT, i. 51. *l.* 223. CUMDE, ii. 165. *l.* 3332, *p. p.* came.
CUMMER, ii. 71. *l.* 1324, *sb.* a female gossip.
CUMMER, i. 8. *l.* 178, *sb.* trouble, embarrassment.
CUMMERLES, ii. 134. *l.* 2640, *adj.* unencumbered.
CUNNING, i. 177. *l.* 556, *sb.* a covenant.
CUNNING, i. 13. *l.* 311, *adj.* skilful.
CUNZIE, ii. 27. *l.* 405, *sb.* money, coin.
CUPPILL, ii. 110. *l.* 2169, *sb.* a couple.
CURE, ii. 90. *l.* 1736, *pr. s.* I care; CURIT, iii. 26. *l.* 2266, *pt.s.* cared for.
CURE, i. 1. *l.* 14, *sb.* care. *pl.* CURIS, i. 9. *l.* 208; CURES, ii. 32. *l.* 513, charges, employment.
CURLOREOUS, i. 158. *l.* 49, *adj.* miserly.
CURNIS, i. 137. *l.* 90, *sb.* small quantities, grains. *Welsh, cwrn.*
CURRAS, i. 176. *l.* 537, *sb.* a cuirace.
CURSOUR, i. 215. *l.* 1711, *sb.* a charger.
CURSTER, ii. 164. *l.* 3301, *comp.* more cursed.
CURTILL, ii. 200. *l.* 4156, *adj.* sluttish. *O. E. curtail*, a drab.
CURTLIE, ii. 68. *l.* 1033, *adj.* courtly.
CUSTROUN, i. 157. *l.* 39; *sb.* a shallow pretender; *pl.* CUSTRONIS, i. 75. *l.* 390; *Fr. cuistre*, a pedant. *See* Notes, i. p. 265.
CUTE, i. 168. *l.* 294, *sb.* a small piece of straw.
CUTTIT, iii. 152. *l.* 5861, *p.p.* cut.
CYNAMOME, i. 213. *l.* 1650, *sb.* cinnamon.
CYPER, i. 213. *l.* 1648, *sb.* cypress.

D

DA, i. 32. 823, *sb.* a doe. *A.S. da.*
DADIE, ii. 71. *l.* 1310, *sb.* a father.
DAFFING, ii. 117. *l.* 2294, *sb.* sport, playing the fool.
DAFT, ii. 81. *l.* 1536, *adj.* mad.
DAINE, i. 134. *l.* 6, *adj.* gentle, modest. *Fr. daigne.*
DAIT, i. 101. *l.* 1113, *sb.* stipulated time, duration.
DAMAIS, i. 189. *l.* 943, *sb.* damask.
DAMPSTER, ii. 122. *l.* 2393, *sb.* the law officer who reads the judgment of the court. *See* Notes, ii. p. 313.
DANDIE, i. 136. *l.* 78. *See* HANDIE.
DANSKIN, ii. 52. *l.* 907, Dantzig.
DANTIT, i. 34. *l.* 902, *p.p.* trained, broken in.
DANTYNG, iii. 92. *l.* 4149, *pr.p.* subduing. *O. Fr. danter.*

DARFLYE, iii. 63. *l.* 3316, *adv.* vigorously.

DARTH, iii. 14. *l.* 1933, *sb.* want, dearth.

DASYIS, i. 5. *l.* 100, *sb.* daisies.

DAYIS-DERLING, i. 52. *l.* 248, *sb.* a dear one.

DE, iii. 128. *l.* 5131, *v.* to die. DEAND, i. 185. *l.* 814, *pr. p.* dying.

DEALL, ii. 68. *l.* 1262, *sb.* dealing, concern.

DEBAIT, i. 37. *l.* 974, *sb.* contest, complaint.

DEBELL, iii. 233. *l.* 31, *v.* to conquer.

DECERNE, ii. 143. *l.* 2829, *v.* to decree, or give judgment.

DECORE, i. 178 *l.* 603, *v.* to shew, display. DECORE, iii. 43. *l.* 2720, *v.* to decorate. DECORIT, i. 163. *l.* 123, *p.p.* decorated. *Fr. decorer.*

DECREITIS, i. 72. *l.* 299, *sb.* decrees.

DECRYIT, ii. 79. *l.* 1468, *p.p.* decreed.

DEDE, i. 13. *l.* 322, *adj.* dead.

DEDIS, i. 32. *l.* 835, *sb.* deeds, actions.

DEE, i. 61. *s.* 4, *v.* to die.

DEFAME, ii. 97. *l.* 1897, *sb.* infamy, disgrace. DEFAMIT, iii. 117. *l.* 4838, *p.p.* disgraced.

DEFENDIT, i. 14. *l.* 362, *p.p.* forbidden. *Fr. défendre.*

DEFICILL, i. 33. *l.* 862, *adj.* difficult.

DEFLORIT, iii. 13. *l.* 1905, *p.p.* ravished, deflowered.

DEGEIST, i. 134. *l.* 6, *adj.* grave. *Lat. digestus.*

DEGRESS, iii. 155. *l.* 5925, *sb.* a digression.

DEID, i. 18. *l.* 476, *sb.* dead.

DEID, ii. 176. *l.* 3577, *sb.* a deed, action, procedure.

DEIR, ii. 102. *l.* 1971, *adj.* dear.

DEIR, i. 90. *l.* 782, *sb.* hurt, injury.

DEIR, i. 109. *l.* 34, *sb.* deer.

DEJECTED, ii. 80. *l.* 1504, *p.p.* ejected, thrown out.

DELATIOUN, i. 42. *l.* 1088, *sb.* delay.

DELATOURIS, iii. 149. *l.* 5761, *sb.* accusers. *Lat. delator.*

DELIVERLIE, i. 176. *l.* 544, *adv.* nimbly, freely.

DENCE, ii. 247. *l.* 568, Danish.

DENNER, i. 112. *l.* 116; DENNEIR, ii. 93. *l.* 1806, *sb.* dinner.

DENERIS, i. 37. *l.* 985; DENEIRIS, i. 8. *l.* 196, *sb.* pence, money; *Fr. denier. See* Notes, i. p. 228.

DENZE, iii. 243. *l.* 23, *v.* to deign.

DEPART, i. 197. *l.* 1194, *v.* to separate, divide; i. 103. *l.* 1151, to share; DEPARTYNG, *l.* 1159, *p.p.* sharing.

DEPAYNT, ii. 232. *l.* 181, *p.p.* painted.

DEPLORATIOUN, i. 117, *sb.* a lament.

DEPOSSIT, i. 139. *l.* 7, *p. p.* deposed.

DEPRYSIT, 61. *l.* 1111, *p. p.* disgraced, literally disprized.

DEPURIT, i. 101. *l.* 1095, *p. p.* purified. *Fr. depurer.*

DERFLIE, i. 163. *l.* 143, *adv.* strongly.

DERIGEIS, iii. 114. *l.* 4777, *sb.* dirges.

Descryve, i. 2. *l.* 33, *v.* to describe.

Despite, i. 195. *l.* 1114, *sb.* contempt.

Desydit, ii. 281. *l.* 1543, *p. p* resolved on, decided.

Detfull, ii. 13. *l.* 49, *adj.* dutiful.

Devore, i. 77. *l.* 440, *v.* to devour; Devorit, i. 76. *l.* 415, *p. p.* destroyed.

Devyce, ii. 254. *l.* 752, *sb.* pleasure.

Devyse, i. 88. *l.* 730, *sb.* testament, will.

Devoyd, ii. 54. *l.* 961, *v.* to go out of, to void.

Dewitie, iii. 112. *l.* 4727, *sb.* duty, payment.

Deyand, i. 13. *l.* 322, *p. p.* dying.

Dicht, i. 191. *l.* 996, *pt. s.* wiped.

Diffame, iii. 105. *l.* 4509, *sb.* disgrace, insult.

Dificill, iii. 118. *l.* 4871, *adj.* difficult.

Digne, i. 119. *l.* 74, *adj.* worthy. *Fr. digne.*

Dilatioun, ii. 90. *l.* 1727, *sb.* delay, remand; Dillatoris, iii. 149. *l.* 5766, *sb.* delays, a law term.

Din, ii. 102. *l.* 1973, *adj.* dun, dark coloured.

Ding, i. 142. *l.* 87, *adj.* worthy. *Fr. digne.*

Dinnis, ii. 236. *l. pt. s.* resounds.

Dirk, iii. 9. *l.* 1791, *adj.* dark.

Dirkywit. ii. 277. *l.* 1411, *p. p.* darkened.

Disdaine, ii. 13. *l.* 59, *sb.* contempt.

Disesperance, i. 118. *l.* 48, *sb.* despair, without hope.

Disfigurate, i. 2. *l.* 17, *p. p.* disfigured.

Disherisit, i. 36. *l.* 940, *p. p.* disinherited. *Fr. desheriter.*

Disjune, ii. 211. *l.* 4388, *sb.* breakfast.

Disluge, i. 37. *l.* 969, *v.* to remove, dislodge.

Displesouris, ii. 281. *l.* 1531, *sb.* griefs, annoyances.

Dispaird, i. 46. *l.* 67, *p. p.* left without hope.

Dispone, i. 9. *l.* 206, *v.* to convey, dispose of. *See* Notes, i. p. 263.

Dispyte, i. 13. *l.* 318, *sb.* spite, revenge.

Dissagysit, i. 81. l. 560 *pt. s.* disguised. *Fr. desguiser.*

Distening, iii. 33. *l.* 2448, *pr. p.* staining.

Do, i. 58. *l.* 424, *v.* to make; Doand, ii. 46. *l.* 821, *pr. p.* doing.

Dochter, ii. 70. *l.* 1309, *sb.* a daughter.

Doitit, iii. 26. *l.* 2264, *pt. s.* did dote, became incoherent. *Dut. doten.*

Dok, ii. 36.. *l.* 626, *sb.* the backside.

Dolent, i. 76. *l.* 418, *adj.* sorrowful. *Fr. dolent.*

Dome, i. 93. *l.* 890, *sb.* judgment.

Donke, ii. 231. *l.* 146, *adj.* moist; Donkis, iii. 168. *l.* 6304, *pr. s.* moistens.

Dornik, i. 187. *l.* 884, *sb.* napery, stuff made at Dornick in Flanders.

Dortour, ii. 68. *l.* 1269, *sb.* a dormitory or sleeping room of the friars.

Dotit, ii. 253. *l.* 725, *p. p.* endowed.

DOUCHTY, i. 82. *l.* 584, *adj.* valiant, strong, worthy; DOUCHTINES, i. 160. *l.* 30, *sb.* valour. *A. S. dohtig.*

DOUNG, i. 148. *l.* 240, *p.p.* struck. DOUNGIN, iii. 64. *l.* 3350, *p.p.* cast down.

DOUNTHRYNG, i. 34. *l.* 896, *v.* to throw down. *Scand. träng-a*, to press, force.

DOUR, i. 79. *l.* 496, *adj.* severe, hard. DOURLIE, ii. 84. *l.* 1583, *adv.* severely, hardly. *Lat. durus*, heavy.

DOUTE, i. 15. *l.* 373, *sb.* doubt; i. 49. *l.* 170, fear; DOUTYNG, i. 79. *l.* 496, *p.p.* fearing.

Dow, ii. 200. *l.* 4127, *v.* to avail. DOWE, i. 63. *l.* 69, *pr. s.* avails. *A.S. dugan.* *See* Notes, i. p. 261.

DOWBYLL, i. 4. *l.* 72, *adj.* double. DOWBLING, i. 106. *l.* 39, *pr. p.*

DOWRIE, i. 191. *l.* 1003, *sb.* a gift, token.

DOWTANCE, i. 44. *l.* 5, doubt, uncertainty. *Fr. doutance.*

DOYTIT, i. 153. *l.* 384, *p.p.* confused, stupid.

DRAF, i. 107. *l.* 55. DRAIFF, ii. 174. *l.* 3541, *sb.* refuse of malted grain.

DRAME, i. 73. *l.* 321; DREME, i. 1, *sb.* a dream.

DRE, i. 111. *l.* 96, *v.* to suffer.

DRES, ii. 92. *l.* 1789, *v.* to redress.

DRESS, i. 40, *l.* 1043, *imp.* apply, prepare.

DROGS, ii. 210. *l.* 4371, *sb.* dregs, fæces.

DROUN, ii. 75. *l.* 1390, *v.* to drown; *p.p.* DROUND, ii. 107. *l.* 2101.

DROUTH, ii. 94. *l.* 1821, *sb.* drought, thirst.

DROWKIT, i. 107. *l.* 60, *p.p.* drenched.

DRYTE, ii. 72. *l.* 1341, *v.* to evacuate the fæces. *Dut. dryt.*

DUBBIS, i. 128. *l.* 14, *sb.* pools of water, puddles.

DUCHEREIS, i. 28. *l.* 726, duchies; DUCHES, i. 11. *l.* 268, *sb.* duchesses.

DUDROUN, ii. 72. *l.* 1346; DUDDROUN, i. 132, *l.* 120, *sb.* a slut, drab, lazy woman.

DUIKS, ii. 216. *l.* 4493, *sb.* dukes.

DUILE, i. 215, *l.* 1721, *sb.* mourning; DUILFULL, ii. 78. *l.* 1443, *adj.* miserable.

DUKE, i. 87. *l.* 714, *sb.* a duck.

DULCE, i. 4. *l.* 79. *adj.* sweet. *Lat. dulcis.*

DULCORE, i. 22. *l.* 5014, *sb.* sweetness. *Ital. dulciore.*

DULE, i. 4. *l.* 78. *sb.* sorrow. *Fr. deuil.* *Dule weid*, mourning dress.

DULFULLIE, i. 139, *l.* 7, *adv.* sorrowfully. DULLIT, i. 69, 224, *pt. s.* made dull, or sorrowful. DULLY, i. 13. *l.* 320, doleful, sad, miserable.

DUM, i. 150. *l.* 291, *adj.* dumb.

DUMISDAY, ii. 179. *l.* 3650, *sb.* doomsday.

DUNGEOUN, iii. 4. *l.* 1632, *sb.* a strong tower. *Fr. donjon.* *See* Notes, iii. p. 188.

DUNTIBOURIS, i. 133. *l.* 177, *sb.* harlots.

DUNTIS, i. 163. *l.* 143, *sb.* strokes.

DUPLICANDUM, iii. 149. *l.* 5767, a duply, a legal term.

DURLIE, ii. 156. *l.* 3119, *adv.* rudely.

DUSCHEIT, iii. 57. *l.* 3152, *pr. pl.* dashed down.

DYCHT, iii. 48. *l.* 2875, *p.p.* prepared, equipped.

DYGN, i. 70. 230, *adj.* worthy. *Fr. digne.*

DYK, ii. 332. *l.* 111, *sb.* a wall.

DYKE-LOWPARIS, i. 97. *l.* 992, *sb.* wall-leapers, thieves, interlopers. See Notes, i. p. 273.

DYNG, iii. 92. *l.* 4152, *v.* to strike.

DYNIT, i. 39. *l.* 1030, *pt. s.* dined.

DYNT, i. 74. *l.* 355, *sb.* a stroke, a blow. DYNTIS, *pl.* i. 79. *l.* 496, blows. *A.S. dynt.*

DYOSIE, ii. 32. *l.* 506, *sb.* a diocese.

DYSE, ii. 169. *l.* 3431, *sb.* dice.

DYTE, ii. 236. *l.* 289, *v.* to indite, compose.

DYTING, i. 63. *l.* 66, *sb.* composition, writing.

DYVOUR, i. 157. *l.* 41, bankrupt. See Notes, i. p. 302.

E

E, iii. 155. *l.* 5926; EE, i. 7. *l.* 161, *sb.* the eye.

EADGE, ii. 27. *l.* 404, *sb.* an edge.

EBURE, i. 101. *l.* 1107, *sb.* ivory.

EDIFICATE, i. 65. *l.* 110, *p.p.* laid out, provided with. *Lat. aedifico.*

EFFECTUOUSLIE, i. 31. *l.* 803, *adv.* ardently. *Fr. affectueusement*

EFFEIRIT, i. 169. *l.* 303, *p.p.* afraid.

EFFRAYIT, i. 199. *l.* 1236, *p.p.* afraid, terrified. EFFRAYITLIE, i. 180. *l.* 668, *adv.* with terror.

EFTER, i. 3. *l.* 64, *pr. p.* after.

EGGIS, i. 156. *l.* 14, *sb.* eggs.

EIK, iii. 38. *l.* 2601, *v.* to add.

EILD, i. 48. *l.* 115, *sb.* age. *A.S. ylde.*

EINE, i. 23. *l.* 594, *sb.* eyes.

EIR, ii. 30. *l.* 464, *sb.* the ear. *pl.* EIRIS.

EIRAR, i. 50. 193, *adv.* rather.

EIRD, i. 7. *l.* 162, *sb.* the earth.

EIS, iii. 162, *l.* 6136, *sb.* eyes.

EIT, i. 103. *l.* 1150, *v.* to eat. *pr. s.* EITIS, i. 158. *l.* 55. EITAND, i. 14, *l.* 362, *pr. p.* eating.

ELDARIS, i. 60. *l.* 507, *sb.* ancestors.

ELF, i. 38. *l.* 998, *sb.* a goblin.

ELIPHAND, i. 106. *l.* 25, *sb.* an elephant.

ELLIS, i. 182. *l.* 717, *adv.* else.

ELWAND, ii. 198. *l.* 4072, *sb.* an ell-measure.

ELWANDS, ii. 195. *l.* 4017, a proper name.

EMPRIOURIS, i. 8. *l.* 169, *sb.* emperors.

EMMOTIS, iii. 6. *l.* 1707, *sb.* ants.

ENAMELYNE, i. 163. *l.* 123, *sb.* enamel.

ENSEW, i. 42. *l.* 1112. *v.* to pursue, to follow.

ENTEIR, i. 83. *l.* 602, *adj.* entire, whole.

ENTRES, i. 93. *l.* 884, *sb.* entrance.

EOLE, i. 65. *l.* 114, Eolus, the God of the winds.

EPISTIL, i. 1. *sb* a letter.
ERAND, i. 189. *l.* 939, *sb*, errand, business.
ERRAND, ii. 231. *l.* 167, *pr. p.* erring, wandering.
ESCHAIP, i. 15. *l.* 366, *v.* to escape.
ESCHAMIT, i. 44. *l.* 17, *p.p.* ashamed.
ESPERANCE, ii. 60. *l.* 1082, *sb.* hope.
ESPOVENTABYLL, iii. 68. *l.* 3446, *adj.* dreadful, frightful, terrible. *Fr. épouvantable.*
ETAND, ii. 242. 444, *pr. p.* eating.
ETIN, i. 3. *l.* 35, *sb.* the name of a giant.
EUISDALE, i. 79. *l.* 495, the vale of the river Ewis in Dumfriesshire.
EURWINGS, ii. 195. *l.* 4017, Irvings.
EVIL-DEIDIE, ii. 196. *l.* 4039. *adj.* given to evil deeds.
EVIN, ii. 220. *l.* 4602, *adv.* equally.
EVERILK, i. 15. *l.* 370, *adj.* every.
EVIN, iii. 139. *l.* 5460, exactly, straight.
EVYR, iii. 22. *l.* 2141, *sb.* ivory.
EXAME, ii. 151. *l.* 2990, *v.* to examine.
EXCERCE, i. 71. *l.* 264, *v.* to exercise. EXCERST, i. 1. *l.* 7, *p.p.* exercised, employed
EXEMIT, i. 123. *l.* 181, *pr. p.* exempted.
EXERCITIOUN, ii. 166. *l.* 3339. *sb.* exercise, diligence.
EXPARTE, i. 16. *l.* 396, *adj.* expert.
EXEMPNE, i. 134. *l.* 7, *v.* to examine.
EXPONAND, ii. 156. *l.* 19, *pr.p.* expounding, explaining.
EXPREME, i. 10. *l.* 242, *v.* to express; i. 47. *l.* 100, *v.* to show, prove. *Fr. exprimer.*

F

FA, i. 200. *l.* 1280, *sb.* a foe.
FACOND, i. 49. *l.* 160, *adj.* having graceful utterance. FACUNDE, i. 87. *l.* 710, pleasing, graceful. *Lat. facundus.*
FAIK, i. 158. *l.* 53, *sb.* a clutch, a handful. *Pl. D. facken*, to grasp. *A.S. feccan*, to take away.
FAILL, iii. 19. *l.* 2056, *sb.* failure. BUT FAILL, without doubt.
FAILYE, i. 67. *l.* 158, *v.* to fail. FAILYEIT, i. 54. *l.* 311, *p.p.* failed. FAILYEIS, iii. 149. *l.* 5755, *sb.* failings. *Fr. faillir.*
FAIR, ii. 251. *l.* 684, *v.* to go.
FAIRDE, ii. 125. *l.* 2438, behaved. *Dan. faerd, adfaerd*, behaviour.
FAIT, i. 78. *l.* 472, *sb.* fate.
FALDOME, iii. 7. *l.* 1726, *sb.* a fathom. *A. S. faedem.*
FALL, i. 16. *l.* 420, *sb.* fail, failing.
FALL, ii. 47. *l.* 638, *v.* to befall.
FALS, i. 6. *l.* 129, *adj.* false.
FALSET, i. 37. *l.* 965, *sb.* falsehood.
FALTOUR, iii. 37. *l.* 2572, *sb.* a defaulter; *pl.* FALTOURIS, iii. 132. *l.* 5256, sinners.
FAMEILL, i. 45. *l.* 36, *sb.* a family.
FAMES, ii. 140. *l.* 2785, *pr. s.* foams.

Fane, i. 298. *l.* 1526, *adj.* glad.

Fang, i. 110. *l.* 69, *v.* to catch, seize. Fangit, ii. 112. *l.* 2224, *pr. s.* caught.

Fare, i. 84. *l.* 619, *sb.* state, condition.

Farik, ii. 18. *l.* 192, *sb.* ado, bustle.

Farie Folk, ii. 41. *l.* 732, the fairies.

Farrest, ii. 28. *l.* 420, *adv.* farthest.

Farsis, i. 1. *l.* 13, *sb,* farces, antics.

Fassinnyng, i. 74. *l.* 354, *pr. p.* fastening.

Fassioun, ii. 11. *l.* 2, *sb.* fashion.

Fat, i. 107. *l.* 52, *sb.* a vat.

Fatigate, i. 78. *l.* 474, *p. p.* fatigued.

Faucht, i. 160. *l.* 50, *pr. s.* fought.

Fauldit, i. 6. *l.* 135, *pr. s.* folded.

Fay, ii, 88. *l.* 1681, *sb.* a foe.

Fayned, iii. 24. *l.* 2209, *adj.* feigned, assumed.

Fead, ii. 59. *l.* 1053, *sb.* enmity.

Feard, ii. 57. *l.* 1024, *p. p.* afraid.

Fechtyng, i. 143. *l.* 115, *sb.* fighting.

Fedderis, i. 78. *l.* 466, *sb.* feathers.

Fedderem, i. 69. 206, *sb.* wings, feathers. *A.S. fether-homa,* a covering of feathers.

Fede, i. 84. *l.* 622; Feid, i. 77. *l.* 442, *sb.* enmity.

Feildit, i. 55. *l.* 355, *pt. pl.* fought in the field. *See* Notes, i. p. 254.

Feill, i. 36. *l.* 930, *sb.* knowledge. Feillyng, i. 13. *l.* 329, perception, sensation.

Feind, i. 1. *l.* 15, *sb.* a devil.

Feinyeit, i. 2. *l.* 40: *pr. s.* feigned.

Feinze, ii. 45. *l.* 806, *v.* to feign. Feinzeing, ii. 34. *l.* 569, *pr. p.* feigning.

Feir, i. 17. *l.* 447, *sb.* aspect, appearance. Feir of weir, i. 199. *l.* 1231, array of war.

Feir, ii. 38. *l.* 661, *sb.* apprehension, fear.

Feiralie, i. 1. *l.* 12, *adv.* nimbly.

Feirie, i. 161. *l.* 80, *adj.* active, strong.

Feistis, i. 212. *l.* 1610, *sb.* feasts.

Feit, iii. 34. *l.* 2487, *sb.* feet.

Feit, i. 45. *l.* 39, *pt. s.* feed, hired. *A. S. feh.*

Fell, ii. 106. *l.* 2072, *v.* to knock or cut down.

Fell, i. 7. *l.* 166, *adj.* cruel terrible.

Fell, i. 38. *l.* 1013, *sb.* a mountain; *pl.* Fellis, ii. 195. *l.* 4012. *See* Notes, i. p. 242.

Felloun, ii. 39. *l.* 687; Fellown, i. 39. *l.* 1022, *adj.* terrible, cruel. *Fr. felon.*

Feminine, i. 1219. *l.* 1813, *sb.* womankind.

Fence the Court, ii. 122. *l.* 2394, to proclaim the sitting of the court. *See* Notes, ii. p. 313.

Fend, ii. 132. *l.* 2585, *v.* to defend.

Fenyeit, i. 8. *l.* 193, *p. p.* feigned.

Ferd, iii. 73. *num.* the fourth.

FERIS, i. 68. 197, *sb.* companions. *A.S. fera.*

FERLYE, i. 151. *l.* 313, *v.* to wonder. FERLEIS, iii. 139. *l.* 5474, *sb.* wonders, strange things. *A.S. fearlic.*

FERME, ii. 243. *l.* 473, *adv.* firmly.

FERME, ii. 131. *l.* 2577, *sb.* rent farm.

FERY FARY, i. 53. 292, great ado, confusion. *Fery* or *Feirie*, strong, active. *Fary*, bustle. *Fr. faire.*

FESTNIT, i. 1201. *l.* 1302, *pt. s.* fastned.

FEW, ii. 131. *l.* 2576, *sb.* a lease.

FEY, ii. 337. *l.* 216, *adj.* fated to die.

FIDDER, ii. 18. *l.* 185, *sb.* a throng, a company.

FIE, ii. 30. *l.* 480, *sb.* fee, reward.

FIGOUR, ii. 194. *l.* 4, *sb.* a figure.

FILL, ii. 138. *l.* 2723, *adj.* full.

FILLOKIS, iii. 40. *l.* 2654, *sb.* young mares, wanton girls.

FINNANCE, ii. 144. *l.* 5853, *sb.* money.

FIRTH, i. 38. *l.* 1013, *sb.* a forest. *See* Notes, i. p. 242.

FISTAND, ii. 109. *l.* 2141, *pr.p.* cuffing, fisting.

FITHER, ii. 39. *l.* 673, *sb.* a load.

FLAG, ii. 109. *l.* 2141, *sb.* a jade,

FLAGARTIE FUFFE, ii. 109. *l.* 2141, a flouncing whiff.

FLAM, i. 209. *l.* 1562, *sb.* a flawn, or custard. *Fr. flan.*

FLAMMIS, i. 9. *l.* 223, *sb.* flames; FLAMMAND, iii. 11. *l.* 1828, *pr. p.* flaming.

FLATLYNGIS, i. 68. 184, *adv.* flat, flatwise.

FLAW, i. 173. *l.* 457, *p.p*: flew.

FLE, i. 133, *l.* 173, *sb.* a fly; *pl.* FLEIS, i. 98. *l.* 1008, flies.

FLE, i. 182. *l.* 718, *v.* to flee, to run.

FLE, ii. 334. *l.* 141, *v.* to frighten.

FLECHE, i. 45. *l.* 30; FLEICH, ii. 42. *l.* 742, *v.* to cajole, to flatter. FLEICHEING, i. 8. *l.* 193, *pr. p.* flattering. *Fr. flechir.*

FLEID, i. 157. *l.* 39, *pt. p.* cowardly, easily frightened.

FLEIT, i. 192. *l.* 1023, *v.* to float, flow, abound; i. 29. *l.* 759, *p. p.* floated, abounded: FLEITTAND, ii. 278. *l.* 1459; FLEITING, i. 9. 223, *pr. p.*, flowing, abounding. *A.S. fleotan.*

FLEME, i. 41. *l.* 1071, *imp.* banish. FLEMIT, i. 3. *l.* 62. *pt. s.* banished.

FLEND, ii. 213. *l.* 4426, *v.* to flee.

FLEWER, i. 131. *l.* 113; FLEWRE, iii. 69. *l.* 3480, *sb.* flavour.

FLEYD, ii. 36. *l.* 620; FLEYIT, ii. 16. *l.* 137, *p.p.* frightened.

FLICHT, ii. 27. *l.* 413, *sb.* flight.

FLICHTERAND, i. 12. *l.* 303, *pr. p.* fluttering.

FLINGING, ii. 29. *l.* 450, *pr. p.* tossing about.

FLINGIS, ii. 109, *l.* 2145, *pr. s.* upbraids.

FLOBBAGE, ii. 211. *l.* 4389, *sb.* phlegm, slime.

FLOCHT, ii. 220. *l.* 4589, *sb.* flutter, panic.

FLOKKIS, i. 4. *l.* 85, *sb.* flocks.
FLOT, ii. 210. *l.* 4372, on flot, afloat.
FLOUR, i. 107. *l.* 71, *sb.* a flower. FLOURIS, ii. 12. *l.* 38, *sb.* youth.
FLUDE, iii. 43. *l.* 2723, *sb.* a flood.
FLURE, i. 1. *l.* 13, *sb.* floor.
FLURIS, iii. 6. *l.* 1698, *v.* to flourish. FLURISTE, i. 32. 825, *p.p.* flourished.
FLYCHTER, i. 67. 172, *v.* to flutter.
FLYNGAND, iii. 40. *l.* 2662, *pr. p.* dancing.
FLYPIT, i. 131. *l.* 97, *pt. p.* turned inside out.
FLYTE, i. 13. *l.* 335, *v.* to scold. *A. S. flitan.*
FLYTS, ii. 109. *l.* 2145, *pr. s.* scolds.
FO, i. 197. *l.* 1188, *sb.* a foe.
FOILL, ii. 102. *l.* 1983, *sb.* a foall.
FOIR'D, ii. 127. *l.* 2490, for it.
FOIRFATHER, ii. 171. *l.* 3474, *sb.* ancestor.
FOLIE HATS, ii. 211. *l.* 4394, *sb.* fool's caps.
FOLLYSCHE, iii. 31. *l.* 2409, *adj.* foolish.
FON, iii. 40. *l.* 2654, *v.* to play, to fondle.
FOND, ii. 215. *l.* 4479, *adj.* foolish.
FONDE, iii. 37. *l.* 2566, *pr. p.* founded.
FONE, i. 79. *l.* 498, *sb.* foes.
FORCIE, i. 201. *l.* 1304, *adj.* valiant.
FOR'D, ii. 66. *l.* 1220; FORDE, ii. 88. *l.* 1684, for it.
FORDE, ii. 195. *l.* 4004, *adv.* forth; MAK YOW FORDE, make you forth, get you gone. *A.S. ford*, away.
FORDWARD, i. 5. *l.* 114, *adv.* forward.
FORE-GRANDSCHIR, iii. 26. *l.* 2254, *sb.* forefather.
FORELAND, i. 49. *l.* 145, *sb.* the sea shore.
FORFAIR, ii. 35. *l.* 669, *v.* to lose, perish, fail. FORFAIR, ii. 63. *l.* 1162, *v.* to wear. FORFAIRNE, ii. 209. *l.* 4350, *pr. p.* wasted, worn out.
FORFALT, ii. 261. *l.* 971, *sb.* a fault; i. 82. *l.* 586, *p.p.* forfeited. FORFALTIT, i. 77. *l.* 429, *pt. p.* forfeited. FORFALTOUR, iii. 21. *l.* 2106, *sb.* forfeiture.
FORTHERIT, i. 66. *l.* 128, induced.
FORGANE, ii. 282. *l.* 1568, opposite to, overagainst.
FORMOSE, i. 65. *l.* 104, *adj.* beautiful.
FORNAMIT, i. 63. *l.* 60, *pt. p.* before named.
FORNENT, i. 182. *l.* 733, opposite, overagainst.
FORTHINK, ii. 73. *l.* 1356, *v.* to think with regret, to repent; i. 88. *l.* 733, to be troubled at or grieved.
FORTUNIT, i. 187. *l.* 870, *pt. s.* chanced, happened.
FORYET, i. 92. *l.* 857; FORZET, ii. 197. *l.* 4069, *v.* to forget.
FOSTERIT, i. 152. *l.* 358. *pt. s.* bred up.
FOUND, i. 111. *l.* 88, *v.* to go. *A.S. fundian.*
FOUNDERIT, i. 164. *l.* 161, *pt. s.* fell.
FOUTHER, i. 103. *l.* 1154, *sb.* a company, group, literally a load. *A.S. fother.*
FOW, ii. 16. *l.* 139, *adj.* full, drunk.

Fowll, ii. 47. *l.* 838, *sb.* filthiness, foulness.

Fra, i. 35. *l.* 926, *pr.* from. **Fra hand**, ii. 156. *l.* 3118, offhand.

Fragilitie, ii. 171. *l.* 3464, *sb.* fragility.

Fraid, ii. 280. *l.* 1508, *p.p.* freed.

Fray, ii. 39. *l.* 687, *sb.* fear, a fright. **Fray**, ii. 22. *l.* 304, *v.* to fear. **Frayit**, i. 83. *l.* 609, *p.p.* frightened.

Fray, ii. 91. *l.* 1762. *pr.* from.

Fre, i. 188. *l.* 908, *adj.* free. **Fred**, i. 105, *l.* 3, *pt. s.* freed.

Freik, i. 114. *l.* 175, *sb.* an impertinent fellow. *Icel. frekr.*

Frelie, ii. 37. *l.* 644, *adj.* free, hearty. *A.S. freolic.* **Frelie Fude**, a hearty fellow. *See* Notes ii. p. 304.

Fremit, i. 157. *l.* 43. *adj.* foreign.

Frenyeis, i. 99. *l.* 1050, *sb.* fringes. *Fr. frange.*

Freris, i. 8 *l.* 177, *sb.* friars.

Frist, i. 157. *l.* 43, time for payment, credit. *O.N fristr.*

Fructuall, i. 31, *l.* 818, *adj.* fruitful. *See* Notes i. p. 238.

Frugge, ii. 138. *l.* 2731, *sb.* a rug, coverlid.

Fruschit, iii. 57. *l.* 3154, *pt. p.* crushed.

Frutage, i. 209. *l.* 1562, *sb.* fruit.

Fryand, i. 11. *l.* 266, *pr. p.* frying, burning.

Frynasie, iii. 127. *l.* 5103, *sb.* a frenzy, madness.

Fude, ii. 37. *l.* 644, *sb.* a person, a fellow. *A.S. fude, fade.* *See* Notes ii. p. 304.

Fude, i. 86. *l.* 674, *sb.* food.

Fuffe, ii. 109. *l.* 2141, *sb.* a whiff.

Fuffilling, i. 107. *l.* 54, *pr. p.* flapping.

Fuill, i. 170. *l.* 334, *sb.* a fool.

Fuilyeit, i. 162. *l.* 100, *p.p.* defiled, soiled.

Fuir, i. 187. *l.* 888, *pt. s.* fared.

Fule, i. 47. *l.* 98, *sb.* a fool, *pl.* **Fuilis**. **Fuliche**, iii. 7. l. 1721, *adj.* foolish.

Fulfillit, i. 1029. *l.* 921, *p.p.* filled.

Fulyeit, iii. 14. *l.* 1908, *p.p.* defiled, trampled in the mud.

Fure, i. 4. *l.* 74, *pt. s.* went, fared.

Furneis, i. 13. *l.* 320, *sb.* a furnace.

Furth, i. 4. *l.* 74, *adv.* forth.

Fute, i. 35 *l.* 920, *sb.* a foot.

Futtit, i. 157. *l.* 39, *adj.* footed.

Fut Before, i. 64. *l.* 88, a popular air for dancing. *Ow'r Fute* is a dance mentioned in *Cowkelbie's Sow.* *See* Notes i. p. 263.

Futher, i. 52. *l.* 242, *sb.* a large quantity, a great number, literally a load. *A.S. fother.*

Fyfe, i. 202. *l.* 1330. *num.* five.

Fyld, ii. 254. *l.* 765, *pt. s.* filled.

Fyll, i. 54. *l.* 306, *v.* to defile. **Fyles**, ii. 109. *l.* 2140, *pr. s.* defiles.

Fyne, i. 10. *l.* 237, *sb.* end, object. *Fr. fin.*

FIREFLAUCHT, iii. 75. *l.* 3660, *sb.* lightning, *pl.* FYRE-FLAUCHTIS, ii. 277. *l.* 1417.

FYSCHEARIS, iii. 113. *l.* 20745, *sb.* fishermen. FYSCHIS, i. 31. 817, *sb.* fish.

G

GA, ii. 123. *l.* 421, *v.* to go.

GADDIS, iii. 18. *l.* 2040, *sb.* goads, rods. *A.S. gad.*

GAID, ii. 210. *l.* 4264, *pt. s.* went.

GAIFF, iii. 40. *l.* 2659, *pt. s.* gave.

GAILL, i. 65. *l.* 96, *v.* to call or cry. *A.S. galan.*

GAILZEOWNIS, i. 57. *l.* 406, *sb.* galleys.

GAINING, ii. 43. 767, *sb.* gain, requirement.

GAIRD, i. 58. *l.* 449, *sb.* a guard; *pl.* GAIRDIS, i. 178, *l.* 591. *Fr. garde.*

GAIRTH, i. 29. *l.* 759, *sb.* a garden. *A.S. geard.*

GAIS, ii. 116. *l.* 2267, *pr.s.* goes.

GAIST, ii. 16. *l.* 137, *sb.* a ghost.

GAIT, iii. 145. *l.* 5624, *sb.* a goat.

GAIT, ii. 123. *l.* 2421, *sb.* a way; *pl.* GAITTIS, i. 9. *l.* 206, *sb.* ways, manners. *Icel. gaba*, a street.

GALAYIS, ii. 228. *l.* 95, *sb.* Chalmers glossed this word as "a kind of great gun," *O. Fr. galez*, but Jamieson expresses his opinion tha it simply means galleys *O.Fr. galion*, a ship of war

GALBARTE, i. 101. 1094, *sb* a mantle. *Fr. gabart.*

GALYEARDLYE, iii. 53. *l.* 3033, *adv.* gallantly. *Fr. gaillard.*

GALYEOUN, i. 182. *l.* 732, *sb.* galley, galleon.

GALMOUNDIS, i. 50. *l.* 181, *sb.* capers, gambols.

GALZARDLIE, i. 193. *l.* 1046; GALZEARTLIE, i. 121, *l.* 116, *adj.* gallantly.

GAM, i. 123. *l.* 174; GAME, i. 216. *l.* 1755, *sb.* sport.

GAMBIS, ii. 117. *l.* 2289; GAMMIS, i. 112. *l.* 103, *sb.* gums. *A.S. gauma.*

GAMOND, ii. 29. *l.* 452, *sb.* a caper, gambol.

GANER, ii. 104. *l.* 2027, *sb.* a gander.

GANESTAND, i. 77. *l.* 422, *v.* to withstand.

GANG, i. 1. *l.* 9, *v.* to go, to walk.

GANT, i. 188. *l.* 905, *sb.* a yawn.

GAR, ii. 274. *l.* 1339, *v.* to cause. GARRIS, i. 8. *l.* 187, *pr. s.* causes. GART, i. 25. *l.* 661, *pt. s.* caused. *Icel. göra.*

GARDING, i. 162. *l.* 105, *sb.* a garden.

GARMOUN, ii. 41. *l.* 735, *sb.* a garment. GARMOUNDIS, i. 53. *l.* 284, *pl.* dresses.

GARNISOUN, i. 51. *l.* 233, *sb.* a party, company, garrison. *Fr. garnison.*

GARTH, i. 63. *l.* 57, *sb.* a garden, enclosure. *A.S. geard.*

GAT, ii. 47. *l.* 822, *pt. s.* got, begot.

GEAPING, ii. 23. *l.* 324, *pr. p.* jaiping, jesting, copulating.

GEARKING, ii. 136. *l.* 2689, *adj.* vain, showy. *A.S. gearcian.*

GEASLYNGIS, i. 87. *l.* 698, *sb.* goslings.

GEILL, i. 47. *l.* 107, St Giles.

GEILL, i. 209. *l.* 1563, *sb.* jelly.

GEIR, i. 12. *l.* 308, *sb.* property, goods, chattels. *A.S. geara.*

GEIS, i. 87. *l.* 699, *sb.* geese.

GENNERS, ii. 205. *l.* 4272, *pr. s.* engenders, begets.

GENT, i. 187. *l.* 871, *adj.* gentle. *O. Fr. gent.*

GES, ii. 170. *l.* 3458, *v.* to guess.

GEVE, i. 34. *l.* 900, *conj.* if. *A.S. gif.*

GHAIST, i. 136. *l.* 64, *sb.* a ghost.

GIGLOTTIS, i. 131. *l.* 85, *sb.* playful wanton wenches. *See* Notes i. p. 288.

GIRNYING, i. 9. *l.* 224, *sb.* distorting the countenance with anger.

GLADER, i. 17. *l.* 423, *sb.* gladdener. *See* Notes i. p. 231.

GLAID, ii. 130. *l.* 2537, *v.* to gladden.

GLAIKIT, i. 131. *l.* 85, *adj.* foolish.

GLAIKS, ii. 96. *l.* 1878, *sb.* tricks, deception; ii. 211. *l.* 4399, here applied to a foolish girl. *See* Notes ii. p. 321.

GLASSE, iii. 94. *l.* 4195, *sb.* a sand-glass.

GLED, i. 64. *l.* 93, *sb.* the kite or hawk. *A.S. glide.*

GLENNIS, ii. 281. *l.* 1528, *sb.* valleys.

GLEW, i. 192. *l.* 1040, *sb.* joy.

GLORE, i. 46. *l.* 69, *sb.* glory, renown.

GLOWRIS, ii. 16. *l.* 136, *pr. s.* stares.

GLUIF, i. 194. *l.* 1076, *sb.* a glove, *pl.* GLUIFIS, i. 176. *l.* 537.

GOIK, i. 65. *l.* 96, *sb.* the cuckoo. *A.S. gaek.*

GOLDSPINK, ii. 232. *l.* 192, *sb.* the goldfinch.

GOR, iii. 127. *l.* 5108, for GRANDGORE, *q.v.*

GORMAN, i. 118. *l.* 26, *sb.* a glutton, gourmand. GORMONDLIKE, i. 103. *l.* 1149, like a gourmand.

GOULD, ii. 128. *l.* 2500, *sb.* gold.

GOUN, ii. 127. *l.* 2485, *sb.* a gown.

GOUNNIS, ii. 228. *l.* 95, *sb.* guns.

GOVERNALL, i. 142. *l.* 71, *sb.* Government. *Fr. gouvernail.*

GOWLES, i. 101. *l.* 1112, *adj.* red. *Fr. gules.*

GOWLAND, i. 14, *l.* 340, *pr. p.* howling.

GRAGIT, ii. 183. *l.* 3729, *pt. p.* excommunicated. *See* Notes ii. p. 317.

GRAIP, ii. 106. *l.* 2053, *v.* to feel, grope.

GRAITH, i. 172. *l.* 414, *sb.* harness, accoutrements; iii. 113. *l.* 4746, *sb.* goods, articles; ii. 213. *l.* 4433, *sb.* tools, appendages.

GRANDGORE, i. 53 *l.* 286, *sb.* the venereal disease.

GRANDMERCIE, i. 188. *l.* 892, or *gramercye*, for *grandem mercedem det tibi deus*, I thank you.

GRANDSCHYRE, i. 30. *l.* 781, *sb.* a grandsir.

Grane, i. 188. *l.* 905, *sb.* a groan, *pl.* Granis, i. 157, *l.* 23.

Grane, i. 121. *l.* 118, a cloth died red with cochineal. *See* Notes i. p. 282.

Graniter, ii. 128. *l.* 2499, *sb.* bailiff, granary-keeper. *See* Gryntaris.

Grave, ii. 235. *l.* 278, *v.* to pierce. *See* Notes iii. p. 183. Gravit, iii. 33. *l.* 2471, *p.p.* engraven, carved.

Gre, i. 83. *l.* 594, *sb.* degree, step. *Gre by Gre*, step by step. *Fr. gré.*

Greabill, ii. 32. *l.* 507, *adj.* agreeable.

Greath, ii. 181. *l.* 3692, *v.* to prepare.

Greislie, i. 1, *l.* 16, *adj.* grisly.

Greit, i. 65. *l.* 96, *v.* to cry, to weep. Greitand, i. 14. *l.* 340. Greityng, i. 9. 224, *pr.p.* weeping. *A.S. gretan.*

Grene, i. 5. *l.* 101, *adj.* green.

Grew, ii. 247. *l.* 563, *adj.* Greek.

Grice, i. 99. *l.* 1047, *sb.* a fur, probably so called from its greyish colour.

Grim, ii. 215, *l.* 4482, *sb.* probably for Grume, a man. Chalmers glosses it as an ugly or terrific countenance.

Grippit, ii. 16. *l.* 152, *p.p.* grasped, gripped.

Grittar, ii. 222. *l.* 4641, *comp.* greater.

Grote, i. 59. *l.* 482, *sb.* a groat, a coin of the value of fourpence.

Ground, i. 211. *l.* 1575, *sb.* foundation.

Grume, ii. 73. *l.* 1539, *sb.* a fellow, a person.

Grundin, i. 175. *l.* 493, *adj.* ground, sharpened.

Grunschyng, iii. 84. *l.* 3907, *pr. p.* grumbling, groaning.

Gruntill, ii. 107. *l.* 2903, *sb.* the snout.

Grunzie, ii. 126. *l.* 2466, *sb.* the mouth. *O. N. grön*, the lip.

Gryce, i. 150. *l.* 300. *sb.* a pig. Gryse, ii. 104. *l.* 2027, *sb.* a pig.

Grym, iii. 143. *l.* 5571, *adj.* cruel.

Gryntaris, iii. 98. *l.* 4306, *sb.* stewards, bailiffs. *Lat. granitarius*, or master of the victual. *See* Notes, iii. p. 204.

Gryppit, i. 102. *l.* 1138, *p.p.* clutched, grasped.

Gubernatioun, i. 34. *l.* 886, *sb.* government. *Lat. gubernatio.*

Guckit, ii. 216. *l.* 4494, *sb.* foolish, from *gowk*, to play the fool.

Gude, ii. 217. *l.* 4528, *sb.* good, goodness; i. 63. *l.* 67, *sb.* worth.

Gude-Man, i. 47. *l.* 104, *sb.* husband.

Gude-Chaip, ii. 197. *l.* 4066, *adj.* cheap.

Gudlie, i. 1. *l.* 7, *adj.* goodly.

Gudlingis, ii. 201. *l.* 4181, *sb.* alloys, or base metal.

Guerdonyng, i. 98. *l.* 1006, *sb.* rewarding. *Fr. guerdon.*

Gumis, ii. 33. *l.* 544, men. *A.S. guma*, a man.

Guoman, ii. 335. *l.* 158, *sb.* a man. *A.S. gumman.*

Guse, ii. 104. *l.* 2007, *sb.* a goose.

Gustyng, ii. 256. *l.* 825, *sb.* tasting. *Lat. gusto.*

Gut, i. 107. *l.* 63, *sb.* the gout.

Guydit, i. 179. *l.* 622; Gydit, i. 38. *l.* 1004, *ps. s.* guided.

Gyand, iii. 4. *l.* 1653, *sb.* a giant.

Gyder, i. 183. *l.* 743, *sb.* the steersman.

Gyle-Fat, ii. 201. *l.* 4158, *sb.* the mashing-vat.

Gylt, iii. 21. *l.* 2122, *sb.* guilt.

Gyn, ii. 31. *l.* 485, *sb.* art, contrivance.

Gynkartoun, i. 47. *l.* 96, *sb.* the name of a piece of musik.

Gyir Carlyng, i. 3. *l.* 1, *sb.* a witch of gigantic size and frightful appearance, of whom several stories were current in Scotland. *Carling*, an old woman.

Gyrsome, iii. 147. *l.* 5703, *sb.* the premium given for the lease of a farm.

Gyse, i. 151. *l.* 333, *sb.* a mask; ii. 40. *l.* 718, *sb.* fashion. *Fr. guise.*

H

Habbiegoun, ii. 178. *l.* 3636, *sb.* habergeon, a breast-plate, coat of mail.

Habitakle, i. 96. 954, *sb.* habitation.

Haboundance, i. 31. 817, *sb.* abundance.

Habyll, i. 2. *l.* 27, *adj.* able.

Hackit, i. 202. *l.* 1347, *pt. pl.* chopped, hacked.

Hackat, ii. 58. *l.* 1032, *see* Hurly.

Hag, ii. 214. *l.* 4452, *sb.* a notch, a hack. *See* Notes, ii. p. 322.

Hagbutteris, i. 214. *l.* 1692, *sb.* musketeers.

Haid, iii. 20. *l.* 2072, *sb.* head.

Haiffand, i. 10. *l.* 238, Haifing, i. 14. *l.* 81, *pr. p.* having.

Haiknay, ii. 161. *l.* 3238, *sb.* horse.

Haill, ii. 30. *l.* 474, *adj.* sound whole. Hailit, iii. 83. *l.* 3877, *pt. s.* healed.

Haill, i. 60. *l.* 489, *adv.* wholly.

Haill, ii. 36. *l.* 617, *v.* to haul, pull. *Fr. haler.*

Haillilie, i. 204. *l.* 1385, *adv.* wholly.

Hailschot, i. 182. *l.* 722, *sb.* a hail storm.

Hailsum, i. 29. *l.* 764, *adj.* wholesome.

Hais, ii. 23. *l.* 315, *sb. adj.* hoarse.

Haisted, i. 15. *l.* 367, *pt. pl.* hastened.

Hait, i. 41. *l.* 1070, *imp.* hate, detest.

Hait, ii. 117. *l.* 2287, *sb.* a heat.

Hakbut, i. 181, *l.* 702, *sb.* a short musket.

Hakkit, iii. 74. *l.* 3628, *pr. s.* hacked, cut.

Hakkat, i. 50. *l.* 176, *see* Hurly.

Hald, i. 36. *l.* 949, *v.* to hold.

Hald, i. 193. *l.* 1070, *sb.* a stronghold.

Halflingis, ii. 233. *l.* 198, *adv.* partly. *O.N. halving.*

HALKING, i. 192. *l.* 1043, *sb.* hawking.

HALS, i. 11. *l.* 258, *sb.* the neck.

HALY, i. 8. *l.* 182, *adj.* holy.

HANCLETHIS, i. 132. *l.* 123, *sb.* ancles. *A.S. ancleow.*

HAND, i. 51. *l.* 217, *sb.* a bargain, action, agency.

HANDIE, i. 136. *l.* 78, *handie-dandie,* or *bandie,* a cant expression.

HAPE, i. 47. *l.* 102, *sb.* good portion, luck. *See* Notes, i. p. 249.

HAPNIT, i. 3. *l.* 56, *pr. s.* happened.

HAPPIT, i. 1. *l.* 10, *pr. s.* wrapped.

HARD, i. 168. *l.* 284, *pt. s.* heard.

HARBREIT, ii. 207. *l.* 4313, *pt. p.* lodged.

HARBRIELES, ii. 65. *l.* 1203, without shelter, habourless.

HARBRY, ii. 68. *l.* 1249, *v.* to shelter.

HARD, i. 134. *l.* 21, *imp.* heard.

HARDINES, i. 174. *l.* 3549, *sb.* defiance.

HARDLIE, i. 218. *l.* 4559, *adv.* boldly.

HARD ON, i. 6. *l.* 1694, near or close to.

HARLD, i. 50. *l.* 176, *pt. pl.* dragged, hauled.

HARLIT, ii. 131. *l.* 2578, *pt. p.* hurled, turned out.

HARLOT, ii. 63. *l.* 1152, *sb.* a worthless person of either sex. *See* Notes i. p. 322.

HARMES, i. 190. *l.* 959, *sb.* sufferings, injuries.

HARMISAY, iii. 156. *l.* 5968, *sb.* supplication to be saved from harm, suffering.

HARNES, i. 174. *l.* 462, *sb.* harness, accoutrements, armour.

HARNIS, ii. 201. *l.* 4160, *sb.* brains. *Germ. hirn.*

HARNE PAN, ii. 73. *l.* 1363, *sb.* the scull.

HARNS-OUT, ii. 206. *l.* 4154, a name given to a strong kind of ale, from its effect on the brains, or *harns.*

HART, i. 3. *l.* 54, *sb.* the heart.

HASARDRIE, i. 76. *l.* 398. HASARTRIE, i. 150. *l.* 306, *sb.* gaming.

HASARTURE, i. 98. *l.* 1016, *sb.* a gamester.

HAT, i. 166. *l.* 147, *pt. s.*; i. 183. *l.* 735, *pt. pl.* hit, struck.

HATRENT, iii. 232. *l.* 6. *sb.* hatred. *Icel. hatr.*

HAULD, ii. 79. *l.* 1482 *v.* to hold, keep. HAULD, ii. 12. *l.* 31, *sb.* a hold, habitation, place. *A.S. hald.*

HAYIF, ii. 44. *l.* 781, *v.* to name, probably a corruption of *hait.* *A.S. haetan.*

HEAD, ii. 161. *l.* 3221, *v.* to behead.

HECHT, i. 55. *l.* 346, *v.* to promise; i. 1. *l.* 7, *p.p.* promised.

HEDE, i. 6. *l.* 134, *sb.* head

HEGE SKRAPER, i. 158. *l.* 49, *sb.* a niggard.

HEICH, ii. 12. *l.* 33, *adj.* high.

HEICHLY, i. 105. *l.* 1111, *adv.* haughtily.

HEICHTIS, ii. 131. *l.* 2573, *pr. s.* heightens, raises.

HEID, i. 53. *l.* 298, *sb.* the head; *pl.* HEIDIS, i. 182. *l.* 728, *sb.*

HEID, ii. 193. *l.* 3974, *v.* to behead.

HEIDLANGS, ii. 78. *l.* 1463, headlong.

HEILD, i. 171. *l.* 378, *v.* to preserve, hold.

HEILLIS, i. 125. *l.* 19, *sb.* heels.

HEIPIT, iii. 93. *l.* 4185, *p.p.* heaped up.

HEIR-CUMMING, ii. 88. *l. sb.* hither-coming.

HEIRFOIR, ii. 141. *l.* 2805, *adv.* therefore.

HEIRSCHIPPS, i. 143. *l.* 108; iii. 137. *l.* 5411, *sb.* plundering expeditions, depredations. *A.S. herescipe.*

HEISIT, ii. 204. *l.* 4253, *pt. p.* hoisted.

HEIT, i. 6. *l.* 137, *sb.* heat.

HEKLIT, i. 215. *l.* 1722, *pt. p.* pulled.

HELAND, i. 56. *l.* 384, *sb.* the Highlands.

HELIE, i. 157. *l.* 37, *adj.* haughty.

HELTER, i. 112. *l.* 121, *sb.* a halter.

HENT, i. 175. *l.* 490, *pt. s.* caught, seized. *A.S.hentan.*

HERAND, ii. 260. *l.* 937, *pr. p.* hearing.

HEREIS, i. 73. *l.* 38, *sb.* barons, lords. *A.S. hearra.*

HERETOURIS, i. 11. *l.* 275, *sb.* heirs, inheritors. *Fr. heritier.*

HERIELD, iii. 112. *l.* 4729, *sb.* a tribute paid on the death of a tenant to the landlord. *Eng. heriot*; *A.S. heragild.*

HERRYIT, ii. 46. *l.* 809; HERYIT, i. 163. *l.* 116, *pt. s.* harried, ravaged, wasted. *A.S. herian.*

HERYWALTER, iii. 113. *l.* 4756, *sb.* a net; *lit.* rob water.

HEVINNIS, i. 5. *l.* 110, of heaven.

HEWIS, i. 4. *l.* 81, *sb.* hues, colours.

HEYCH, i. 56. *l.* 386, *adj.* high; *sup.* HEYCHAST, ii. 282. *l.* 1573, highest.

HEYND, i. 205. *l.* 1426. *adj.* kind, courteous. *Swed. handig.*

HICHTIT, ii. 131. *l.* 2571, *p.p.* heightened; raised.

HIDDIE-GIDDIE, ii. 201. *l.* 4162, round about.

HIE, i. 22. *l.* 575, *adj.* high. HIEAR, i. 113. *l.* 140, *comp.* higher. HIEST, *sup.* highest. *A.S. hih.*

HINT, i. 190. *l.* 960, *pt. s.* caught.

HIPPIT, ii. 16. *l.* 151, *pt. p.* having hips.

HIRD, i. 34. *l.* 890, *sb.* shepherd.

HISTORICIANE, iii. 17. *l.* 1993, a historian; *pl.* HISTORICIENCE, ii. 271. *l.* 1253.

HO, ii. 109. *l.* 2143, *sb.* a stop, ceasing.

HOAW, ii. 23. *l.* 313, *interj.* ho!

HOBBELD, i. 157. *l.* 27, *adj.* mended, cobbled.

HOBILS, ii. 222. *l.* 4648, *pr. s.* dances.

HOBLAND, i. 125. *l.* 20. *pr. p.* hobbling. HOBLING, ii. 213. *l.* 4434.

HOCH, ii. 39. *l.* 693, *sb.* the leg; *pl.* HOCHIS, i. 202. *l.* 1347, houghs, legs.

HOG, i. 109. *l.* 26, *sb.* a sheep in the second year; *pl.* HOGGIS, i. 34. *l.* 903,

HOILL, ii. 57. *l.* 1028, *sb.* a hole.

HOILSUM, i. 4. *l.* 96, *adj.* wholesome.

HOIP, i. 220. *l.* 1842, *sb.* hope.

HOIR, ii. 102. *l.* 1978, *adj.* hoary.

HOIS, i. 189. *l.* 949, *sb.* stockings, hose.

HOIS-NETT, iii. 114. *l.* 4757, *sb.* a hose-net.

HOLE, i. 6. *l.* 132, *adj.* whole. HOLELYE, ii. 256. *l.* 812, wholly.

HOLESUM, i. 29. *l.* 761, *adj.* wholesome.

HOLKIT, ii. 281. *l.* 1528, *pt. p.* dug out, excavated.

HOLLYING, ii. 237. *l.* 308, *sb.* a holly.

HOLTIS, i. 102. *l.* 1135, rough ground, wooded heights. *A.S. holt.*

HORE, i. 102. *l.* 1135, *adj.* hoary. *A.S. har*, white.

HORN, ii. 113. *l.* 2231, at the *horn*, proclaimed an outlaw. *See* Notes, ii. p. 313.

HORSON, ii. 73. *l.* 1356, *sb.* whoreson.

HOULET, i. 161. *l.* 56, *sb.* an owl.

HOUNDIT, i. 34. *l.* 902, *p.p.* hunted, driven away.

HOUNTARIS, i. 57. *l.* 398, *sb.* hunters.

HOURIS, i. 67. *l.* 152, *sb.* morning prayers. *Fr. heures.*

HOWE, iii. 140. *l.* 5486, *adj.* hollow.

HOWIS, i. 130. *l.* 68, ii. 39. *l.* 693, *sb.* legs, houghs. *A.S. hoh.*

HOWLAT, iii. 169. *l.* 6310, *sb.* the owl.

HOYIT, i. 113. *l.* 145. *sb.* *p.p.* hooted.

HUDE, ii. 41. *l.* 728. *sb.* a hood.

HUIK, iii. 113. *l.* 4747, *sb.* a hook.

HUMLOIK, iii. 243. *l.* 32, *sb.* hemlock.

HUMMILL BUMMILL, i. 135. *l.* 44, a muttering repetition.

HUMYL, i. 7. *l.* 151, *adj.* humble; HUMILIE, i. 3. *l.* 50, humbly.

HURDARIS, i. 13, *l.* 310, *sb.* hoarders. *A.S. hordere.*

HURDIES, ii. 210. *l.* 4373, *sb.* buttocks.

HURIS, i. 9. *l.* 207, *sb.* whores.

HURLAND, ii. 39. *l.* 693, *pr. p.* driving. *Su. G. hwerfla.*

HURLIE-HACKAT, ii. 58. *l.* 1032; i. 50. *l.* 176, *sb.* a game which consisted in sliding down a steep incline. *See* Notes, i. p. 251.

HURSONE, ii. 55. *l.* 980, *sb.* whoreson.

HY, i. 198. *l.* 1229, HYE, i. 17. *l.* 442, *sb.* haste.

HYCHT, i. 64. *l.* 73, *sb.* height.

HYDDUOUS, iii. 8. *l.* 1751, *adj.* hideous.

HYDROPESIE, iii. 127. *l.* 5104, *sb.* the dropsy.

HYND, ii. 67. *l.* 1234, HYNE, iii. 45. *l.* 2800, *adv.* hence.

HYNDE, iii. 27. *l.* 2288, *sb.* a hind.

HYRALD, ii. 191. *l.* 3915. HYREILD, ii. 103. *l.* 1991, *sb.* heriot, or the fine paid to the landlord on the death of his tenant. *See* Notes, ii. pp. 310, 319. *See* HERIELD.

HYRE, iii. 148. *l.* 5738, *sb.* reward.

I

IDILTETH, iii. 234. *l.* 18, *sb.* laziness.

ILKE, i. 41. *l.* 1071, *sb.* each, every.

ILL-FAIRDE, ii. 140. *l.* 2774, *adj.* ill-looking.

ILLUDE, i. 57. *l.* 419, *v.* to delude.

IMMANENT, ii. 171. *l.* 3475, remaining.

IMMUNDICITIE, i. 69. *l.* 212, *sb.* corruption, uncleanness. *Lat. immunditia.*

IMPERIALL, i. 210. *l.* 1588, *adj.* empyreal.

IMPURPURIT, ii. 231. *l.* 146, *adj.* purple.

IMPIT, i. 124. *l.* 198, *p.p.* grafted.

IMPONE, ii. 253. *l.* 733, *v.* to impose. *Lat. impono.*

IMPORTABYLL, i. 10. *l.* 244, *adj.* unsupportable, intolerable. *Fr. importable. See* Notes, i. p. 229.

IMPUDICITIE, i. 11. *l.* 279, *sb.* shamelessness.

IMPUNG, i. 61. *l.* 13, *v.* to impugn.

IMPYRE, iii. 161, *l.* 6121, *sb.* empire.

IMPYRAND, iii. 96. *l.* 4259, *pr. p.* ruling, domineering.

INAMITIE, ii. 263. *l.* 1013, *sb.* enmity.

INARMIT, iii. 22. *l.* 2150, *p.p.* armed.

INCONTINENT, ii. 38. *l.* 651, *adv.* without delay. *Lat. incontinens.*

INCOUNSOLABLE, iii. 36. *l.* 2538, *adv.* not to be counselled, unreasonable.

INDEFICIENT, ii. 257. *l.* 847, not deficient, in plenty.

INDURING, ii. 228. *l.* 89, *prep.* during.

INDYTE, i. 29. *l.* 756, *v.* to describe.

INEURE, ii. 222. *l.* 4641. *v.* to happen, to come into effect, or intervene.

INFETCHING, ii. 134. *l.* 2652, *sb.* introduction.

INFFEANE, ii. 337. *l.* 218, the Bannatyne MS., as printed for the Hunterian Club, reads *ane jufflane jok*, a shuffling or fumbling Jock.

INFORTUNE, i. 44. *l.* 4, *sb.* misfortune.

INGENT, ii. 171. *l.* 3473, *adj.* huge.

INGINE, iii. 6. *l.* 1686, *sb.* an engine.

INGLIS, i. 134. *l.* 21, *adj.* English.

INGYNE, i. 32. *l.* 834, *sb.* genius, intellect. *Lat. ingenium.*

INNARRABYLL, iii. 162. *l.* 6126, inexpressible.

INNIS, i. 156. *l.* 13, *sb.* house, lodging.

INOBEDIENCE, i. 10. *l.* 226, *sb.* disobedience.

INOBEDIENTIS, i. 81. *l.* 537, *sb.* rebels.

INSIGNE, i. 216. *l.* 1732, *sb.* ensign, sign.

INTELLEBILL, i. 119. *l.* 60, untellable.

INTENDIT, i. 15. 372, *pr. s.* proceeded. *Lat. intendo.*

INTENDIMENT, i. 30. *l.* 799, *sb.* judgment. *Fr. entendement.*

INTOXICATE, ii. 59. *l.* 1066, *adj.* poisoned.

INTRUSIT, i. 97. *l.* 1001, *p.p.* intruded.

IPOCRAS, i. 209. *l.* 1564, *sb.* a drink composed of white or red wine and spices, strained through a bag called by the apothecaries *Hippocrates' sleeve.*

IPOCRASIE, iii. 35. *l.* 2523, *sb.* hypocrisy.

IRK, i. 129. *l.* 32, *sb.* uneasiness, vexation.

IRNE, iii. 18. *l.* 2040, *sb.* iron.

ISE, ii. 73. *l.* 1359, abbreviation for I shall.

J

JAIP, i. 161. *l.* 62, *v.* to play with.

JANEWAYIS, i. 27. *l.* 717, Genoese. *See* Notes, i. p. 238.

JOIS, ii. 53. *l.* 946, *sb.* beloved persons; *My jo,* my joy, or my beloved one.

JONET, i. 215. *l.* 1711, *sb.* a Spanish horse. *Fr. genette.*

JOURNELLY, ii. 239. *l.* 372, *adv.* day by day.

JUGGIS, i. 107. *l.* 55, *sb.* dregs.

JUNE, iii. 18. *l.* 2018. *v.* to join. JUNIT, ii. 275. *l.* 1371, *p. p.* joined.

JURDEN, ii. 127. *l.* 2478, *sb.* a chamberpot.

JUSTING, ii. 33. *l.* 546, *pr. p.* tilting, jousting, sporting.

K

KA, i. 65. *l.* 94, *sb.* a jackdaw. *A.S. ceo.*

KAILL, ii. 131. *l.* 2572, *sb.* broth made of vegetables, calewort.

KAISTE, iii. 6. *l.* 1700, *pt. pl.* did throw, dug.

KE, ii. 204. *l.* 4254, *sb.* a jackdaw.

KEIS, iii. 116. *l.* 4815, *sb.* keys.

KEIP, ii. 266. *l.* 1111, *v.* to take care; *pt. s.* KEIPIT, ii. 208. *l.* 4338.

KEITCHING, i. 113. *l.* 155, *sb.* a kitchen.

KEKELL, i. 65. *l.* 94, *v.* to cackle.

KEN, i. 158. *l.* 70, *v.* to direct; i. 127. *l.* 59, to know; i. 140. *l.* 35, *p. p.* known. KEND, ii. 49. *l.* 862, *pt. s.* knew.

KENDYLL, iii. 135. 5352, *v.* to kindle.

KENE, i. 185. *l.* 819, *adj.* daring, sharp.

KEST, i. 94. *l.* 911, *pt. pl.* threw open; iii. 12. *l.* 1872, cast.

KEPITH, i. 64. *l.* 72, *pr. pl.* keeps, tends. KEPPIT, i. 78. *l.* 469, *pt. pl.* kept, caught.

KEWIS, ii. 31. *l.* 493, *sb.* customs, ways, for *thewis.*

KEYTH, i. 66. *l.* 128, *v.* to make known.

KILT, ii. 75. *l.* 1388, *v.* to tuck up.

KIST, i. 189. *l.* 936, *sb.* a chest.

KIST, i. 134. *l.* 4, *p.p.* kissed.

KITCHING, ii. 215. *l.* 4476, *sb.* a kitchen.

KNAG, ii. 197. *l.* 4044, *sb.* a knob, a peg.

KNAIF, i. 114. *l.* 169, *sb.* a knave; i. 113. *l.* 155, *sb.* a boy, varlet.

KNAIFATICA, i. 157. *l.* 33, *sb.* a pedlar of mean servile origin. *See* Notes, i. p. 302.

KNAW, i. 51. *l.* 238, *v.* to know. KNAWIN, i. 1. *l.* 2, *p.p.* known.

KNAWLEGING, iii. 74. *l.* 3610. *sb.* acknowledgment.

KNOKKIS, i. 203. *l.* 1359; KNOK, ii. 83. *l.* *sb.* 1568, blows, knocks.

KOKS BONS, ii. 38. *l.* 660, an oath or exclamation common in anct. authors, God's bones. *See* Notes, ii. p. 304.

KOULL. ii. 43. *l.* 768, *sb.* a cowl.

KOW, i. 142. *l.* 2819, *sb.* custom, tax, often a cow.

KOW, i. 57. *l.* 408, *sb.* a cow, *the rysche bus kepis the kow*, the rush bush keeps the cow. It was a saying of James V., from his executing justice on rogues so steadily, "that he made the rush bush keep the cow."

KOW CLINK, ii. 71. *l.* 1323, *sb.* a harlot.

KUIK, ii. 17. *l.* 171, *sb.* a cook.

KY, ii. 102. *l.* 1984; KYE, i. 64. *l.* 72, *sb.* cows.

KYITH, i. 72. *l.* 288, *imp.* make to appear; i. 40. *l.* 1050, *pt. s.* shown.

KYN, i. 211. *l.* 1607, *sb.* kindred.

KYND, i. 67. 162. *sb.* nature. *A.S. cyn.*

KYNRENT, i. 212. *l.* 1631, *sb.* kindred, relations.

KYNRIK, i. 40. *l.* 1057, *sb.* kingdom.

KYRTYLL, i. 130. *l.* 70, *sb.* a gown.

KYTE, i. 138. *l.* 140, *sb.* the belly. *A.S. citte.*

L

LABORDE, ii. 72. *l.* 1332, *pt. s.* laboured; LABORAGE, ii. 272. *l.* 1278, *sb.* labour; LABORAND, ii. 133. *l.* 2621, *pr. p.* labouring.

LACK, i. 19. *l.* 484, *v.* to find fault. LACKIT, ii. 246. *l.* 551. *p.p.*

LADDIS, i. 75, *l.* 391, *sb.* lads, servants.

LADRONIS, i. 107. *l.* 50, *sb.* base females. *Fr. laidron.*

LAID, ii. 127. *l.* 2486, *sb.* a lad, a common person.

LAIDLIE, ii. 57. *l.* 1025, *adj.* loathsome, detestable.

LAIF, i. 19. *l.* 499, *sb.* the rest, remainder. *A.S. laf.*

LAIK, i. 152. *l.* 351, *v.* to want; i. 32. 826, *sb.* lack, want.

LAIR, ii. 25. *l.* 347, *sb.* learning.

LAIT, ii. 86. *l.* 1650, *adv.* late.

LAITH, i. 175. *l.* 507, *adj.* loath, unwilling.

LAITHLIE, i. 131. *l.* *adj.* loathsome.

LAIRD, ii. 127. *l.* 2486, *sb.* a proprietor, a lord.

LAKE, iii. 105. *l.* 4512, *sb.* disgrace; same as LACK.

LAME, i. 166. *l.* 234, a lamb.

LAMBER, ii. 33. *l.* 532; LAMMER, i. 191. *l.* 1608, *sb.* amber, used in making images for Roman Catholic worship; *l'amber.*

LANCE, ii. 162. *l.* 3243, *v.* to bound.

LANG, i. 3. *l.* 64, *adj.* long.

LANGITH, iii. 71. *l.* 3530; LANGIS, ii. 283. *l.* 1594, *pr.s.* belongeth. *See* Notes, iii. p. 187.

LANGSUM, i. 55. *l.* 359, *adj.* tedious. *A.S.* *langsum.*

LANSING, i. 4. *l.* 74, *pr. pt.* skipping running. *Fr.* *lancer.*

LAP, i. 171. *l.* 365; LAPPE, iii. 65. *l.* 3362, *pt. s.* did leap.

LAPPIT, iii, 86. *l.* 3971. *pt.pl.* enveloped, surrounded.

LAREIT, ii. 205. *l.* 4281, Loretto. *See* Notes, ii. p. 320.

LASER, i. 217. *l.* 1761, *sb.* leisure.

LAT, ii. 90. *l.* 1731, *pr. s.* let, permit. LAT BE, i. 21, *l.* 544. let alone.

LAT, i. 107. *l.* 50, *v.* to stop, cease.

LAUBORIT, i. 51. *l.* 215, *pt. s.* laboured.

LAUCH, i. 65. *l.* 97, *v.* to laugh.

LAUREAT, i. 38, 990, *p. p.* crowned, approved.

LAUTE, i. 36. *l.* 951, *sb.* loyalty, fidelity. *Fr.* *loyauté.*

LAVE, i. 163. *l.* 130, *sb.* the rest.

LAW, i. 4. *l.* 84, *adj.* low; i. 144. *l.* 140, *v.* to make low, to humble.

LAWAR, ii. 231. *l.* 154, lower.

LAWID, ii. 250. *l.* 644; LAWIT, ii. 17. *l.* 169, *adj.* unlearned, ignorant. *A.S.* *leod.*

LAWLYE, ii. 226. *l.* 30, *adv.* lowly,

LAWRER, i. 216. *l.* 1732, *sb.* a laurel. *Fr.* *laurier.*

LAWTIE, i. 2. *l.* 25, *sb.* loyalty. *Fr.* *loyauté.*

LAY, ii. 131. *l.* 2577, *v.* to lay down, to give up.

LAYID, i. 60. *l.* 495, common people.

LAYIK, ii. 106. *l.* 2057, *adj.* lay.

LAYSER, i. 67. *l.* 177, *sb.* leisure. *Fr.* *loiser.*

LEAR, ii. 242. *l.* 451, *sb.* a liar.

LEDDER, ii. 72, *l.* 1333, *sb.* a ladder, gallows: *pl.* LEDDERIS, i. 195. *l.* 1126, *sb.* ladders.

LEDDER, ii. 72. *l.* 1332, *sb.* leather.

LEDE, iii. 115. 4788, *sb.* lead.

LEICHE, i. 185. *l.* 807, *sb.* a surgeon.

LEID, i. 56. *l.* 388, *v.* to lead.

LEID, i. 18. *l.* 475, *sb.* lead. LEIDIS, iii. 127. *l.* 5098, *sb.* lead; *soddin into leidis,* boiled in molten lead.

LEID, ii. 140. *l.* 2778, *pt. s.* lied.

LEID, ii. 246. *l.* 553, *sb.* language.

LEIF, i. 194. *l.* 1075, *sb.* leave, departure. LEIF, ii. 31. *l.* 492, *v.* to leave.

LEIF, i. 10. *l.* 250, *v.* to live. LEIFIS, ii. 15. *l.* 106, *pr. s.* lives. LEIFIT, ii. 134. *l.* 2635, *pt. s.* lived. *A.S.* *lifan.*

LEIFSUM, iii. 107. *l.* 4574, *adj.* lawful. *A.S.* *leafsum.*

LEIFULL, i. 71. *l.* 274, *adj.* lawful.

LEIK, ii. 34. *l.* 565, *sb.* a leek.

LEILL, i. 36. *l.* 956, *adj.* true, faithful.

LEIR, i. 104. *l.* 1190, *v.* to learn. LEIRAND, ii. 47. *l.* 822, *p.p.* learning. LEIRIS,

ii. 12. *l.* 28, *pr. s.* learns. LEIRIT, ii. 17. *l.* 169, *adj.* learned.

LEIS, i. 89. *l.* 755, *sb.* falsehoods, lies.

LEISING, ii. 146. *l.* 2907, *sb.* lying.

LEIT, i. 10. *l.* 250, *p.p.* let, allowed.

LEIT, ii. 133. *l.* 2603, *for* LEID, language.

LEMAND, ii. 20. *l.* 238, *pr. p.* shining, gleaming. LEMANT, i. 219. *l.* 1819, *adj.* shining, flaming.

LEMIS, i. 3. 69, *sb.* beams. *A.S. leoma.*

LEMMAN, i. 161. *l.* 59, *sb.* a lover. *A.S. leof.*

LEN, ii. 39. *l.* 675. *v.* to lend.

LENTH, i. 1. *l.* 4, *sb.* length, LENTH, iii. 47. *l.* 2839, *v.* to lengthen.

LESTAND, i. 206. *l.* 1464, *pr.p.* lasting.

LEVEAND, ii. 269. *l.* 1188, *adj.* living.

LEVER, ii. 26. *l.* 394, *adv.* rather.

LEVIT, ii. 282. *l.* 158, *pr. s.* lived.

LEWTENNAND, iii. 97. *l.* 4268, *sb.* a lieutenant.

LEYNE, i. 35. *l.* 922, *adj.* lean,

LEYSOUR, ii. 187. *l.* 3799, *sb.* leisure.

LIBELLIS, i. 62. *l.* 20, *sb.* writings, poems. *Lat. libellus.*

LICENTS, ii. 165. *l.* 3327, *sb.* licentiates.

LICHTIT, i. 205. *l.* 1419, alighted.

LICHTLIE, i. 172. *l.* 420, *adv.* lightly, nimbly.

LICHTLYIT, ii. 35. *l.* 583, *pt. pl.* despised.

LICHTIT, i. 182. *l.* 731, *pt. pl.* alighted.

LICKINGS, ii. 211. *l.* 4392, refuse, what may be licked up.

LIDDER, i. 46. *l.* 75, *adj.* lazy. *A.S. lyther.*

LIFT, ii. 47. *l.* 826, *sb.* the sky.

LIG, i. 25. *l.* 644, *sb.* a league. *pl.* LIGGIS, i. 25. *l.* 642.

LIMMER, ii. 37. l. 649, *adj.* knavish, roguish.

LINNING, i. 137. *l.* 91, *sb.* linen cloth.

LIPPER, iii. 83. *l.* 3876, *sb.* a leper, leprosy.

LOCHIS, i. 31. 820, *sb.* lakes.

LODE STERNE, i. 79. *l.* 492, *sb.* the pole-star, or north star.

LOFT, ii. 276. *l.* 1375, *sb.* a gallery.

LOK, i. 34. *l.* 894, *sb.* a lock.

LORE, i. 209. *l.* 1544, *sb.* learning.

LOREIT, ii. 40. *l.* 2664, *sb.* the chapel of Loretto, near Musselburgh. *See* Notes, iii. p. 194.

LORIMERS, ii. 201. *l.* 4174, *sb.* saddlers, bridlemakers.

LOUCHE, iii. 51. *l.* 2959, *sb.* a lake.

LOUN, ii. 15. *l.* 126, *sb.* a fellow, a rogue, a knave.

LOUP, ii. 100. *l.* 1954; LOUPE, i. 52. *l.* 251, *v.* to leap. LOUPIS, i. 75. *l.* 391, *pr. s.* leaps. *A.S. hleopan.*

LOUSIS, iii. 99. *l.* 4352, *pr. s.* looses, frees.

LOVIS, ii. 79. *l.* 1471, *pr. s.* praises.

LOVYNG, i. 2. *l.* 26, *sb.* praise; i. 127. *l.* 68, *pr. p.* praising. *A.S. lofning.*

LOWNG, i. 102. *l.* 1024, *sb.* the lung.

LOWN, ii. 179. *l.* 3642, *sb.* a loon; *pl.* LOWNIS, i. 57. *l.* 405, fellows, rogues. *Dut. loen.*

LOWRANCE, i. 34. *l.* 895, *sb.* a fox, generally called *Lawrie* in Scotland.

LOWSE, ii. 86. *l.* 1632, *v.* to loose.

LOX, ii. 82. *l.* 1551, *sb.* locks.

LUCKY, ii. 330. *l.* 62, a familiar term used in addressing a woman.

LUDGE, ii. 61. *l.* 1102, *v.* to lodge. LUDGIT, i. 188. *l.* 917, *pt. s.* lodged, slept.

LUFE, ii. 52. *l.* 917, *sb.* the palm of the hand.

LUFE, i. 41. *l.* 1070, *v.* to love.

LUFERAY, i. 196. *l.* 1166, *sb.* livery.

LUFESUM, i. 30. *l.* 785, lovesome, lovely. *A.S. lufesum.*

LUFETENENTIS, i. 81. *l.* 536, *sb.* lieutenants.

LUFFARIS, i. 4. *l.* 82, *sb.* lovers.

LUFFER, i. 102. *l.* 1124, *sb.* the liver. *A.S. lifer.*

LUFFIT, i. 107, *l.* 57, *pt. s.* loved.

LUGEING, ii. 13. *l.* 67, *sb.* a lodging.

LUGGIS, ii. 219. *l.* 4572; LUGS, ii. 99. *l.* 1945, *sb.* ears.

LUIF, ii. 61. *l.* 1104, *sb.* love. LUFFIS, i. 16. *l.* 406, of love. LUIF, ii. 58. *l.* 1037, *v.* to love. LUIFIT, i. 181. *l.* 695, *p. pl.* loved.

LUIFFILLIS, i. 137. *l.* 90, *sb.* handfuls. *See* LUFE.

LUIKIT, ii. 83. *l.* 1566, *pt. s.* looked; ii. 170. *l.* 3435, *for* LUIK IT, inspect it.

LUIR, ii. 32. *l.* 525, *sb.* the lure.

LUKE, i. 18. *l.* 449, *sb.* look. LUKIS, i. 105. *l.* 8, *pr. s.* reads; LUKE, iii. 75. *l.* 3652, see, behold. *See* Notes, i. p. 274. *A.S. locian.*

LUMIS, ii. 33. *l.* 546, *sb.* tools, implements.

LUNZIE, ii. 27. *l.* 407, *sb.* the loin.

LUPIS, i. 34. *l.* 895, *for* LUPUS, *sb.* a wolf. *See* Notes, i. p. 239.

LURDANERIE, iii. 244. *l.* 13, *sb.* stupidity. *Fr. lourd.*

LURDEN, ii. 127. *l.* 2477; LURDOUN, ii. 45. *l.* 799, *adj.* dull, stupid.

LURIS, i. 11. *l.* 278, *sb.* lures, tempters.

LUSTELIE, i. 16. *l.* 404, *adv.* pleasantly.

LUSTIE, i. 187. *l.* 864; LUSTY, i. 17. *l.* 422, *adj.* pleasant, lovely.

LUSUM, ii. 21. *l.* 28, *for* LUFESUM, lovesome, lovely.

LYAND, i. 178. *l.* 600, *pr. p.* lying.

LYART, ii. 54. *l.* 966, *adj.* grey, hoary.

LYCHORYE, i. 11. *l.* 273, *sb.* lechery.

LYCHT, i. 3. *l.* 69. *adj.* light, bright.

LYCHTIT, i. 4. *l.* 87, *pt. pl.* alighted.

LYCHTLEIT, iii. 114. *l.* 4781, *pt. p.* slighted. LYCHTLYAND, i. 169. *l.* 329, *pt. p.* despising.

LYFFIS, ii. 11. *l.* 276, *sb.* lives.
LYMBE, i. 14. *l.* 360, *sb.* limbo, a place of torment.
LYNE, i. 3. *l.* 65, *p.p.* lain,
LYNG, i. 34. *l.* 895, *sb.* a line. *Fr. ligne.*
LYONIS, i. 11. *l.* 265, *sb.* lions.
LYPPER, i. 90. *l.* 793, *sb.* a leper.
LYNING, i. 131. *l.* 97, *sb.* linen.
LYRE, ii. 24. *l.* 341, *sb.* flesh.
LYSTE, i. 39. *l.* 1030, *sb.* pleasure, will. LYSTE, i. 149. *l.* 265, *pt. s.* liked, willed, chose. *A.S. listan.*
LYTTILL, i. 5. *l.* 117, *adj.* little.
LYVE, i. 47. *l. sb.* life; ON-LYVE, alive.

M

MA, i. 27. *l.* 712, *adv.* more.
MACULATE, i. 128. *l.* 11, *adj.* dirty.
MAHOWN, ii. 207. *l.* 4313, *sb.* Mahomet.
MAID, i. 2. *l.* 27, *p.p.* made.
MAIGLIT, i. 153. *l.* 385, *p.p.* mangled.
MAILL, ii. 276. *l.* 1402, *sb.* males.
MAILL, i. 201. *l.* 4170, *sb.* meal.
MAILL, iii. 147. *l.* 5703, *sb.* tribute, rent. *A.S. mal.*
MAINE, ii. 103. *l.* 1987, *sb.* moaning, complaining.
MAIR, i. 28. *l.* 728, *adv.* more.
MAIRATTOUR, ii. 235. *l.* 267, *adv.* moreover.
MAISTER, i. 2. *l.* 22, *sb.* a master.
MAITS, ii. 214. *l.* 4467, *sb.* companions.
MAKAND, i. 4. *l.* 86, *pr. s.* making.
MAKDOME, i. 309. *l.* 10, *sb.* appearance, dress.
MAKKAR, iii. 139. *l.* 2637, *sb.* maker.
MALANCOLIOUS, i. 19. *l.* 482, *adj.* melancholy.
MALESOUN, ii. 143. *l.* 2848, *sb.* malediction.
MALING, ii. 90. *l.* 1722, *v.* to malign.
MALKINNIS, i. 131. *l.* 90, *sb.* the pubes mulieris.
MALMONTRYE, ii. 234. *l.* 235, *sb.* for mammontry, idolatry. *See* Notes, iii. p. 182.
MALYNG, ii. 187. *l.* 393, *sb.* spite, malignity.
MALYSOUN, i. 145. *l.* 166, *sb.* malediction, curse.
MAN, i. 21. *l.* 544, *pr. s.* must.
MANASSYNG, iii. 9. *l.* 1785; MANESYNG, ii. 267. *l.* 1133, *pr. p.* threatening.
MANGIT, i. 81. *l.* 1518, *p. p.* confounded, marred. *A.S. mengan.*
MANKIT, iii. 240. *l.* 26, *p. p.* maimed. *Lat. mancus.*
MANSWEIT, ii. 235. *l.* 262, *adj.* meek.
MANSWEIR, i. 104. *l.* 1189, *v.* to perjure. MANSWORNE, i. 13. *l.* 309, *adj.* forsworn. *A.S. manswaerian.*
MAPAMOUND, i. 32. 834, *sb.* map. of the world. *Lat. mappa mundi.*
MARCHAND, i. 48. *l.* 144, *sb.* merchandise.
MARDE, ii. 233. *l.* 220, useless, destroyed. *A.S. mar.*
MAREGUILDIS, iii. 168. *l.* 6305, *sb.* marigolds.

MARIE, ii. 180. *l.* 3681, *v.* to marry. MARIAND, iii. 141. *l.* 5526, *pr.p.* marrying.

MARINALL, i. 48. *l.* 144, *sb.* a mariner.

MARK, ii. 189. *l.* 3858, *sb.* a Scottish silver coin equal to 13⅓d. sterling. *See* Notes, i. p. 288.

MARKIT, i. 93. *l.* 877, *pt. s.* travelled, *Fr. marcher.*

MARROW, i. 54. *l.* 307, *sb.* a mate, equal, companion. *Fr. mari*, a husband; or perhaps *A.S. mearu*, tender.

MARTRIK, i. 99. *l.* 104, *sb.* fur of the martin cat.

MARVILL, i. 213. *l.* 1655, *sb.* marble.

MARY, ii. 38. *l.* 663, By Mary! a common oath in Lyndsay's time.

MASERIS, i. 122. *l.* 139, *sb.* macers, ushers.

MASKING-FAT, i. 107. *l.* 52, the mashing-tub.

MATEIR, i. 14. *l.* 81, *sb.* matter, substance.

MATENIS, i. 153. *l.* 285, *sb.* matins.

MATUTYNE, ii. 231. *l.* 147, *adj.* morning.

MAVES, ii, 232. *l.* 189, *sb.* mavis, or thrush.

MAWKINE, ii. 98. *l.* 1926, *sb.* malking, the *pubes mulieris.*

MEAR, ii. 154. *l.* 3068, *sb.* a mare.

MEDECINAIR, ii. 28. *l.* 432, *sb.* a physician.

MEDIS, i. 32. 825; MEIDIS, ii. 280. *l.* 1523, *sb.* meadows.

MEINE, ii. 77. *l.* 1428, *v.* to mean, indicate.

MEINYE, ii. 272. *l.* 1305, *sb.* a family. MEINZIE, ii. 102. *l.* 1973, *sb.* a company.

MEIR, i. 81. *l.* 541, *sb.* a mare. *A.S. maere.*

MEISIT, iii. 92. *l.* 4156, *p. p.* assuaged.

MEIT, i. 12. *l.* 295, *sb.* meat.

MEITER, ii. 128. *l.* 2492, *comp.* more suitable.

MEITTING, ii. 37. *l.* 641, *sb.* meeting.

MEKILL, i. 181. *l.* 672, *adv.* much.

MELL, i. 54. *l.* 326, *v.* to meddle with. *Fr. mêler.*

MENCE, ii. 72. *l.* 1333, *v.* to grace. MENCE ANE LEDDER, to grace the gallows.

MENDIS, i. 33. *l.* 877, *sb.* amends, satisfaction. MENDIT, i. 12. *l.* 290, *pr. s.* amended. *Fr. amende.*

MENE, i. 37. *l.* 975, *v.* to make known, explain.

MENEVER, i. 99. *l.* 1047, *sb.* the white fur of the meniver.

MENIS, i. 207. *l.* 1507, *pr. s.* diminishes, or is unfortunate.

MENIS, i. 94. *l.* 918, means.

MENIS, i. 156. *l.* 18, *sb.* means, ends.

MENSTRALSIE, i. 197. *l.* 1174, *sb.* minstrelsy.

MENYE, i. 14. *l.* 357, *sb.* group, company, family. *Fr. maignee.*

MERCHETIS, iii. 147. *l.* 5706, *sb.* a fine paid on the marriage of a young woman to the superior for redeeming her virginity. *See* Notes, iii. p. 213.

MERCIALL, i. 59. *l.* 457, *adj.* martial.

MERY, i. 5. *l.* 123, *adj.* merry.

MES, i. 192. *l.* 1031, *sb.* the mass.

MESOURE, i. 7. *l.* 157, *sb.* moderation, measure. *Fr. mesure.*

MESSANE, i. 114. *l.* 185, *sb.* a lap dog. *Fr. mastin,* a cur, or from Messina in Sicily, from whence they were first brought to Scotland; or possibly from *Fr. maison.*

MEYNER, iii. 243. *l.* 18, *comp.* meaner.

MICHT, i. 183. *l.* 763, *sb.* might, power.

MIDDING, ii. 111. *l.* 2189, *sb.* a midden.

MINT, ii. 73. *l.* 1352, *sb.* an attempt.

MIRK, ii. 78. *l.* 1463, *sb.* darkness.

MISCARYIT, ii. 69. *l.* 1287, *pt. p.* hurt, miscarried.

MISCHEAND, ii. 234. *l.* 235, *adj.* wicked.

MISERICORDE, i. 228. *l.* 81, *sb.* pity.

MISERITIE, iii. 47. *l.* 2850, *sb.* misery.

MISCHEVING, iii. 244. *l.* 24, *pr. p.* injuring.

MISCUIKIT, i. 197. *l.* 1180, *p.p.* miscooked, spoiled.

MISDOARS, ii. 35. *l.* 598, *sb.* evil doers.

MISGYDIT, i. 9. *l.* 213, misguided.

MISKEN, i. 59. *l.* 459, *v.* to misknow, to affect not to know one.

MISORDOUR, ii. 158. *l.* 3150, *sb.* confusion.

MISOURIS, iii. 164. *l.* 6184, *sb.* measures for fluids.

MISREULL, ii. 12. *l.* 25, *sb.* misgovernment.

MISSE, ii. 65. *l.* 1198, *sb.* a fault.

MISTER, ii. 174. *l.* 3532, *sb.* need.

MISTOINIT, ii. 13. *l.* 75, *p. p.* mistuned. *A.S. mis-tonian.*

MITTANIS, i. 6. *l.* 137, *sb.* woollen gloves. *See* MYTTANIS.

MO, i. 11. *l.* 255, more. *A.S. ma.*

MOIT, i. 24. *l.* 625, *sb.* a mote.

MOLEST, ii. 79. *l.* 1472, *p. p.* injured.

MOLLET, i. 55. *l.* 333, *pt. s.* of MOLL, to amble, to ride: same as MOWIT. *See* MOW. *See* Notes, i. p. 254.

MON, i. 36. *l.* 941, *pr. s.* must.

MONE, i. 14. *l.* 353, *sb.* a moan, wailing.

MONE, ii. 27. *l.* 416, *sb.* the moon.

MONETHIS, i. 16. *l.* 429. *sb.* months.

MONIE, i. 192. *l.* 1038; MONY, i. 2. *l.* 40, *adv.* many.

MONYEOUN, ii. 21. *l.* 264, *sb.* a minion.

MONYFAULD, ii. 197. *l.* 4063, manyfold; MONYFAULD, ii. 210. *l.* 4374, *sb.* the intestines.

MONYSTE, iii. 68. *l.* 3441, *pt. s.* admonished.

MORT, i. 158. *l.* 56, *v.* to die.

MOST, iii. 16. *l.* 1959, *pr. s.* must.

MOSTOURIS, iii. 53. *l.* 3021, *sb.* musters, parades.

MOT, ii. 54. *l.* 968, may.

MOUTH-THANKLES, i. 106. *l.* 33, the *vulva.* Chalmers

remarks that it is the *belle chose*, which the Wife of Bath describes as "a thing that no man will his thankes helde." A poem called "The Auld Man's invective against mouth-thankles," will be found in the Bannatyne MS., No. 250.

MOW, i. 52. *l.* 247, *v.* to jest. MOWIS, ii. 17. *l.* 165. *sb.* jests, jokes.

MOWE, i. 87. *l.* 713, *sb.* the mouth.

MOWIT, i. 134. *l.* 16, *v.* had copulation, *pt. s.* of the verb *moll* to amble, to ride, pronounced Mow.

MOYLIE, i. 55. *l.* 333, *adj.* softly. *Fr. mol.*

MUCK, ii. 306, *l.* 4293, *sb.* ordure.

MUFE, i. 31. *l.* 811, *v.* to move, cause. MUIFING, ii. 220. *l.* 4583, *pr. p.* moving.

MUILL, ii. 167. *l.* 3380, *sb.* a mule.

MUK, i. 131. *l.* 98, *sb.* muck, ordure, dirt. *A.S. meox.*

MUMMILL, i. 153. *l.* 385, *v.* to mumble.

MUNZEON, i. 166. *l.* 233, *sb.* a minion.

MURDREISARIS, i. 56. *l.* 363, *sb.* murderers.

MURMELL, ii. 129. *l.* 2523, *sb.* a murmur.

MURNE, i. 181. *l.* 691, *v.* to mourn. MURNIT, i. 188. *l.* 903, *p.p.* MURNYNG, i. 13. *l.* 330, *sb.* mourning.

MUTE, i. 47. *l.* 91, *v.* to speak. *A.S. motian.*

MYCHT, i. 3. *l.* 66, *pr. s.* I might. MYCHTIS, i. 22. *l.* 570, *sb.* powers.

MYDDIS, i. 7. *l.* 161, *sb.* the midst.

MYLYEOUN, i. 239. *l.* 353, *num.* a million.

MYN, iii. 43. *l.* 2732, less.

MYNE ALLONE, i. 5. *l.* 116, by myself.

MYNNIE, ii. 70. *l.* 1308, *sb.* mother.

MYREAST, ii. 328. *l.* 20, *adj.* merriest.

MYRKE, i. 13. *l.* 325, *adj.* dark. *A.S. mirc.*

MYRTHLES, i. 14. *l.* 357, *adj.* sad, melancholy.

MYS, i. 85. *l.* 653, *sb.* faults.

MYSCHEANT, iii. 65. *l.* 3374, *adj.* wicked, bad. *Fr. mechant.*

MYSCHEVIT, iii. 32. *l.* 2425, hurt.

MYSKEN, iii. 154. *l.* 5896, *v.* to ignore. MYSKEND, iii. 83. *l.* 3866, *pt. pl.* misknew.

MYST, iii. 144. *l.* 5621, *p.p.* missed, overlooked.

MYTOUR, ii. 167. *l.* 3391, *sb.* a mitre.

MYTTANIS, i. 4. *l.* 72, *sb.* mittens, woollen gloves. *Fr. mitaine.*

N

NA, i. 13. *l.* 331, no; ii. 335. *l.* 164, now.

NAIKIT, ii. 173. *l.* 3522, *sb.* the naked.

NAMELYE, i. 46. *l.* 64, *adv.* principally.

NAR, ii. 95, *l.* 1859, *adv.* near.

NEDIS, i. 32. 826, *pr. s.* needs, requires.

Neif, iii. 116. *l.* 4817, *sb.* the fist.

Neir, i. 1. *l.* 5, *adv.* nearly, almost.

Neirs, ii. 152. *l.* 3028, *sb.* the kidneys, reins. *Germ. niere.*

Neis, i. 130. *l.* 77, *sb.* the nose.

Neist, ii. 210. *l.* 430, *sb.* the next.

Nether, i. 27. *l.* 708, *adj.* lower. *A.S. neother.*

Nippit, ii. 16. *l.* 150, *p.p.* pinched, curtailed.

Nobillis, i. 184. *l.* 790, *sb.* nobles.

Nocht, i. 1. *l.* 4, *adv.* not.

Noder, i. 80. *l.* 527, *conj.* neither. *A.S. nouther.*

Nois, i. 131. *l.* 102, *sb.* dirt. filth, noisomeness.

Nolt, ii. 132. *l.* 2581, *sb.* cattle,

Nommer, iii. 7. *l.* 1743, *sb.* number.

Non, i. 46. *l.* 65. no.

None, i. 192, *l.* 1015, *sb.* noon.

Nonis, iii. 22. *l.* 2139, *sb.* the nonce, occasion.

Nor, ii. 184. *l.* 3738, than; ii. 53, *l.* 935, used in the sense of *though.*

Noryce, i. 146. *l.* 189, *sb.* a nurse.

Not, i. 61. *l.* 3; Nott, ii. 226. *l.* 19, *pr. s.* know not.

Noter, i. 143. *l.* 2834, *sb*, a notary.

Nother, i. 50. *l.* 180, *conj.* neither.

Nouchtie, iii. 243. *l.* 26, *adj.* trifling, worthless.

Novellis, i. 167, *l.* 256, *sb.* news. *Fr. nouvelle.*

Nowmer, i. 62. *l.* 32, *sb.* number.

Nowreis, i. 47. *l.* 83, *sb.* a nurse.

Noy, ii. 66. *l.* 1209, *v.* to annoy; ii. 264. *l.* 1056, *sb.* annoyance.

Noye, ii. 269. *l.* 1190, Noah.

Noyis, ii. 232. *l.* 187, *sb.* noise.

Nuickit, ii. 170. *l.* 3434, *pr.p.* cornered.

Nummer, i. 13. *l.* 314, *sb.* number. Numerand, ii. 232. *l.* 191, *pr. p.* numbering.

Nycht, i. 3. *l.* 64, *sb.* night.

Nyll, i. 80. *l.* 509, *pr.s.* will not. *See* Notes, i. p. 267.

Nynt, i. 19. *l.* 498, *num.* the ninth.

O

Obleist, ii. 67, *l.* 1239, *p.p.* Oblyssit, i. 151. *l.* 328, obliged. *Fr. obliger.*

Occiane, i. 28. *l.* 732, *sb.* the ocean.

Ocht, i. 46. *l.* 71, *sb.* aught, anything.

Ociositie, i. 5, *l.* 121, *sb.* idleness. *Lat. ociositas.*

Ocker, ii. 197. *l.* 4069, *sb.* usury. Ockararis, iii. 148. *l.* 5723, *sb.* usurers.

Offensioun, ii. 227. *l.* 60, *sb.* offence, crime.

Oist, i. 38. *l.* 992, *sb.* a host, army. *Fr. ost.*

Oliphantis, iii. 52. *l.* 2995, *sb.* elephants.

On, i. 101. *l.* 1093. during.

Onis, i. 39. *l.* 1023, once.

Or, i. 14. *l.* 343, *adv.* before, ere. *A.S. aer.*

Oratour, iii. 22. *l.* 2156 ;

ORATORE, i. 39. *l.* 1031; ORITORE, iii. 169. *l.* 6326, *sb.* a private chamber, a study. *Fr. oratoire.*

ORDINANCE, i. 21. *l.* 533, *sb.* order of place; i. 167. *l.* 262, array; i. 181. *l.* 679, settlement.

ORDINANCE. i. 80. *l.* 506, *sb.* cannon. *See* Notes, i. p. 267.

OSTER-SCHELLIS, ii. 107. *l.* 286, oyster shells.

OUCHT, i. 41. *l.* 1076, *sb.* aught, anything. *A.S. oht.*

OUER, i. 1. *l.* 5, over.

OUERDRYVE, i. 2. *l.* 32, *v.* to pass, spend.

OUERMEN, i. 10. *l.* 228, *sb.* superiors.

OUERSENE. i 31. *l.* 806, *p.p.* overseen, viewed, iii. 107. *l.* 4581, overlooked, excused.

OUERSYLE, ii. 85. *l.* 1623, *v.* to cover over, to obscure. OUERSYLIT, i. 5. *l.* 106, *p.p.* covered over. *A.S. ofer-sylian.*

OUIR, i. 182. *l.* 730, *prep.* over.

OUIRMAN, i. 100. *l.* 1082, *sb.* oversman, arbitrator.

OUIRSET, i. 161. *l.* 81, *p.p.* overcome.

OUIRTHORTE, i. 4. *l.* 74, *adv.* across, athwart. *A.S. ofer-thwaer.*

OUIRTUIK, i. 205. *l.* 1418, *pr. s.* overtook.

OULE, i. 19. *l.* 478, *sb.* an owl.

OULKIS, i. 25. *l.* 657, *sb.* weeks. *A.S. uca.*

OUTHER, i. 182. *l.* 718, *adj.* either.

OUTTERIT, i. 175. *l.* 507, *pt. s.* swerved, ran out. *A.S. utter.*

OUT-THOART, ii. 195. *l.* 4012, for OURTHOART, across, athwart.

OVERSEYLL, i. 19. *l.* 229, *v.* to deceive.

OYL-DOLIE, ii. 197. *l.* 4068, *sb.* olive oil. *Fr. huile d'olive.*

OYSTE, i. 145. *l.* 163, *sb.* a host. *Fr. ost.*

P

PACOKE, i. 69. 207, *sb.* a peacock.

PADOKS, ii. 75, *l.* 1389, *sb.* frogs. *A.S. pada.*

PAICE, i. 112. *l.* 104, *sb.* Easter. *Sees* Notes, i. p. 279,

PAIKS, ii. 72. *l.* 1329, *sb.* strokes,chastisement. PAIKARIS, i. 153. *l.* 378, *sb.* stampers, beaters.

PAILYEOUN, i. 176. *l.* 569, *sb.* pavilion, tent.

PAIP, ii. 141. *l.* 2799, the Pope.

PAIRT, ii. 135. *l.* 2673, *pr. s.* depart.

PAIS, i. 25. *l.* 646, *sb.* a pace; *pl.* PASIS, iii. 7. *l.* 1733.

PAIST, ii. 75. *l.* 1386, *sb.* a repast. *O. Fr. paistre.*

PAK, i. 47. *l.* 87, *sb.* a pack or bale.

PAK, ii. 55. *l.* 974, *imp.* decamp.

PALLET, ii. 140. *l.* 2780, *sb.* the crown of the head. *Fr. pelote.* *See* Notes, p. 321.

PALYARD, iii. 41. *l.* 2692, *sb.* a cheat, an impostor.

PALZEOUN, ii. 75. *l.* 1396, *sb.* a tent or pavilion.

PANCE, i. 77. *l.* 444; PANS, i. 16. *l.* 397, *v.* to think, to meditate. *Fr. penser.*

PANDARIS, i. 75. *l.* 390, *sb.* panders. *See* Notes, i. p. 265.

PANE, i. 218. *l.* 1791, *sb.* pains, trouble.

PANTONIS, i. 189. *l.* 930. *sb.* slippers.

PAPE, i. 51. *l.* 214, the Pope.

PAPINGAY, ii. 248. *l.* 612; PAPYNGO, i. 61. *l.* 2, *sb.* a parrot. *Fr. papegay. See* Notes, i. p. 262.

PARDONERS, ii. 133. *l.* 2606, *sb.* sellers of indulgences.

PAREGALL, i. 141. *l.* 3, *sb.* an equal. *See* PEREGALL.

PARISCHOUN, i. 153. *l.* 367. PAROCHOUN, ii. 139. *l.* 2750, *sb.* a parish.

PART, ii. 220. *l.* 4602, *v.* to divide. PARTAND, i. 162. *l.* 112, *pr. p.* dividing.

PASCHE, ii. 164. *l.* 3296, *sb.* Easter. *See* Notes, i. p. 279.

PASSIONIS, i. 13. *l.* 329, *sb.* sufferings, agonies.

PASSIS, i. 52. *l.* 240, *pr. s.* surpasses, excells.

PASTANCE, ii. 58. *l.* 1030, *sb.* pastime. *Fr. passe-temps.*

PASTE, i. 142. *l.* 93, *pt. s.* did pass.

PAT, i. 135. *l.* 49, *pt. s.* put.

PATRONE, i. 84. *l.* 639, *sb.* pattern, example.

PATTRYNG, ii. 249. *l.* 635, *sb.* repeating or reciting quickly. *See* Notes, iii. p. 185.

PAUPIS, iii. 87. *l.* 4009, *sb.* paps, breasts.

PAVIN, ii. 180. *l.* 3663, *sb.* a dance, somewhat stately in character. *Fr. paon*, a peacock.

PAYNTOURIS, i. 16. *l.* 398, *sb.* paynters.

PEART, ii. 147. *l.* 2914, *adj.* pert.

PEDDER, i. 156. *l.* 3, *sb.* a pedlar, hawker.

PEGGRELL, ii. 134. *l.* 2655, *adj.* petty, beggarly.

PEICE, i. 178. *l.* 590, *sb.* peace, a truce.

PEIL'D, ii. 73. *l.* 1363, *adj.* bald.

PEIPAND, i. 157. *l.* 23, *pr. p.* piping, whining.

PEIR, ii. 14. *l.* 79, *sb.* an equal; *pl.* PEIRIS, i. 51. *l.* 216, equals. *Fr. pair.*

PEIRSIT, i. 11. *l.* 269, *pt. s.* peirced.

PEIRTE, i. 76. *l.* 400, *adj.* pert. PEIRTLYE, i. 49. *l.* 157, *adv.* pertly, impudently. *See* Notes, i. p. 250.

PEIS, i. 45. *l.* 24, *sb.* a piece, portion.

PEK, i. 134. *l.* 10, *sb.* a Scottish measure, the fourth part of a firlot.

PELLOUR, ii. 83. *l.* 1569, *sb.* a robber; *pl.* PELLOURS, ii. 127. *l.* 2473.

PENETRATYVE, i. *l.* 73, *adj.* penetrating.

PENNYBRAID, ii. 176. *l.* 3588, the breath of a penny.

PENSEIL, i. 214. *l.* 1689, *sb.* a pennon, a small flag.

PERDIE, ii. 67. *l.* 1232, *adv.* verily, truly, by God. *Fr. pardieu.*

PEREGALL, i. 82. *l.* 574, *sb.* an equal. *Fr. peregal.*

PEREMTOURIS, iii. 149. *l.* 5765, *sb.* peremptory orders; a law term.

PERFAY, ii. 48. *l.* 854, *adv.* truly, verily. *Fr. par foi.*

PERFORCE, iii. 4. *l.* 1654, by compulsion. *Fr. par-force.*

PERFURNEIS, iii. 92. *l.* 4148, *v.* to accomplish.

PERFYTE, i. 7. *l.* 148, *adj.* perfect.

PERLIS, i. 12. *l.* 297, *sb.* pearls.

PERQUEIR, i. 47. *l.* 93, by heart, perfectly. *Fr. par-coeur.*

PERRELL, i. 25. *l.* 653, *adj.* equal. *Fr. pareil;* BUT PERRELL, without equal.

PERROCHIOUN, iii. 111. *l.* 4687, *sb.* a parish.

PERS, iii. 79. *l.* 3780, Persia. PERSIENCE, iii. 79. *l.* 3776, Persians.

PERSONE, i. 154. *l.* 411, *sb.* a parson; *pl.* PERSONS, ii. 91. *l.* 1752.

PERTENAND, i. 76. *l.* 414, *pr.p.* succeeding.

PERTINAT, iii. 148. *l.* 5725, *adj.* pertinacious.

PERVERST, i. 8. *l.* 176. *adj.* perverse.

PERYSIT, i. 36. *l.* 943, *p.p.* perished.

PEW, i. 64. *l.* 93, *v.* to cry as a bird, *e.g.* a kite, young goose, &c.

PIETE, i. 47. *l.* 94, *sb.* goodness.

PIK, ii. 275. *l.* 1370, *sb.* pitch.

PILLOK, ii. 212. *l.* 4419, *sb.* the penis.

PIRMITYVIS, i. 89. *l.* 771, *for* primitives.

PLACEBO, ii. *l.* 17, a courtier, a sycophant. Knox speaks of *placeboes* and flatterers in his "Hist. of the Reformation."

PLACKIS, ii. 193. *l.* 3965, *sb.* Scots coins, each equal to the third of a penny.

PLAIGE, i. 88. *l.* 751, *sb.* a country. *Lat. plaga. See* Notes, i. p. 271.

PLAIGES, iii. 121. *l.* 4953, *sb.* plagues.

PLAINE, ii. 188. *l.* 3898, *adv.* plainly.

PLAINT, ii. 137. *l.* 2722, *v.* to complain.

PLAIT, i. 127. *l.* 58, *sb.* mail.

PLAK, i. 136. *l.* 75, *sb.* a Scots plack or coin equal to the third of an English penny.

PLASMATOUR, ii. 258. *l.* 865, a framer, moulder. *Fr. plasmateur. See* Notes, iii. p. 185.

PLAT, ii. 50. *l.* 866, *sb.* a plate.

PLAT, ii. 98. *l.* 1926, *v.* to place close or flat; iii. 84. *l.* 3904, flattened; PLATT, i. 48. *l.* 135, *pt. pl.* placed.

PLATFUTE, i. 64. *l.* 88, probably the name of a popular tune, also mentioned in "Christ's Kirk on the Green." *See* Notes, i. p. 263.

PLAYAND, i. 1. *l.* 13, *pr. p.* playing.

PLAYFEIR, ii. 17. 176, *sb.* a playfellow.

PLEAD, ii. 115. *l.* 2253; PLEID, ii. 90. *l.* 1726, *sb.* dispute.

PLEAGIS, i. 144. *l.* 145, *sb.* pledges.

PLEINZIE, ii. 183. *l.* 3730, *v.* to complain.

PLENE, i. 103. *l.* 1167, *v.* to complain.

PLENEIS, ii. 257. *l.* 842, *v.* to replenish, to stock. PLENISCHIT, i. 26. *l.* 682, *p.p.* furnished, stocked. *O. Fr. plenir.*

PLE•ANCE, i. 7. *l.* 152, *sb.* pleasure. *Fr. plaisance.*

PLESAND, i. 16. *l.* 410, *adj.* pleasant.

PLESOUR, i. 181. *l.* 681; PLESOURE, i. 2. *l.* 20, *sb.* pleasure.

PLETT, iii. 84. *l.* 3896, *pt. p.* plaited, did plait.

PLEUCH, ii. 121; *l.* 2558, *sb* the plough.

PLEY, i. 106. *l.* 22, *v.* to debate, plead; ii. 179. *l.* 3649, *sb.* debate, plea; *pl.* PLEYIS, ii. 145. *l.* 2883, pleadings. *Fr. plaidir.*

POAST, ii. 214. *l.* 4452, *sb.* a post or pole.

POILL, ii. 57. *l.* 1027, *sb.* a pole; i. 88. *l.* 751, *sb.* the North Pole. *See* Notes, iii. p. 182.

POLEIT, i. 63. *l.* 59; POLIT, ii. 152. *l.* 5865, *adj.* polite, polished.

POLESYE, iii. 10. *l.* 1804; POLLESYE, iii. 14. *l.* 1927, *sb.* pleasure grounds.

POLESYE, iii. 13. *l.* 1893; POLICIE, ii. 207. *l.* 4316; POLLICYE, iii. 73. *l.* 3599, *sb.* policy, government.

POPLESIE, iii. 127. *l.* 5112, *sb.* apoplexy.

POPULAIR, iii. 121. *l.* 4961, *sb.* people, populace.

PORT, iii. 115. *l.* 4810; PORTE, i. 95. *l.* 939, *sb.* a door, a gate.

PORTOUNS, ii. 43. *l.* 769, rather PORTOUS, *sb.* a mass-book, breviary.

PORTRATOUR, ii. 16. *l.* 133; PORTRATURE, i. 19. *l.* 479, *sb.* figure, appearance.

POSSEDIT, ii. 256. *l.* 820, *p.p.* possessed. *See* Notes, iii. p. 185.

POTESTATIS, ii. 34. *l.* 565, *sb.* powers. *Lat. potestas.*

POULDER, iii. 65. *l.* 3363, *sb.* powder; i. 39 *l.* 1025, *sb.* gunpowder. POULDERIT, iii. 106. *l.* 4545, *pt. p.* powdered, sprinkled.

POWN, i. 88. *l.* 728: POWNE, ii. 232. *l.* 188, *sb.* a peacock. *Fr. paon.*

PRACTYKE, i. 145. *l.* 176, *sb.* policy; PRACKTICK, ii, 700. *l.* 4126, *sb.* practice. PRACKTICKIT, ii. 65. *l.* 1185, *p.p.* practised.

PRACTICIANE, i. 208. *l.* 1536, *sb.* practitioner.

PRAIS, i. 195. *l.* 1135, *sb.* tumult, fight.

PRECELL, i. 210. *l.* 1576, *v.* to excell. PRECELLAND, i. 29. *l.* 755. PRECELLENT, i. 171. *l.* 430, *adj.* excellent. *Fr. preceller.*

PRECEID, iii. 52. 2989, *pt. s.* excelled, went before; other editions here read PRECELLAND.

PRECHE, i. 54. *l.* 323, *v.* to preach.

PRECLARE, i. 23. *l.* 591, *adj.* supereminent. *Lat. præclarus.*

PRECORDIALL, i. 74. *l.* 346. *adj.* most cordial. *Fr. precordial.*

PREDICATION, i. 97. *l.* 991, *sb.* preaching.

PREICHE, ii. 42. *l.* 741, *v.* to preach.

PREIF, i. 186, *l.* 836, *v.* to prove, try, taste.

PREINE, ii. 17. *l.* 155, *sb.* a pin ; *pl.* PRENIS, ii. 249. *l.* 635 ; PREINIS, ii. 201. *l.* 4180.

PREIS, i. 122. *l.* 140, *sb.* the press, crowd. PREIS, i. 71. *l.* 257, *imp.* endeavour ; *pt. s.* PREISIT, i 65. *l.* 117. PREISSIT, i. 173. *l.* 439, pressed.

PRENCIS, i. 35. *l.* 913, *sb.* princes.

PRENT, i. 40. *l.* 1040, *v.* to print ; i. 40. *l.* 1047, to mould, form.

PRENTEISCHIP, ii. 190. *l.* 3895, *sb.* apprenticeship.

PREORDINANCE, i. 40. *l.* 1037, *sb.* foreordination.

PREORDINAT, ii. 97. *l.* 1886, *adj.* preordained.

PREPARATYUIS, i. 120. *l.* 99, *sb.* preparations.

PREPLESANDE, i. 92. *l.* 846, *adj.* more pleasing.

PREPOTENT, i. 69. *l.* 227, *adj.* more potent.

PRESOUN, i. 13. *l.* 317, *sb.* a prison. PRESONING, iii. 46. *l.* 2835, *sb.* imprisonment.

PRETERIT, i. 74. *l.* 364, *adj.* past.

PRETTIKE, iii. 40. *l.* 2654, *sb.* practice. *Fr. pratique.*

PREVE, ii. 260. *l.* 932; PREIF, i. 175. *l.* 504, *v.* to prove.

PREVENE, i. 156. *l.* 6, *v.* to prevent. *Lat. praevenio.*

PRINCIPATE, ii. 59. *l.* 1068, *sb.* principal.

PROCURATURE, i. 40. *l.* 1049, *sb.* a proctor, advocacy.

PROFECT, i. 35. *l.* 919; PROFFECT, i. 142. *l.* 68, *sb.* profit.

PROFEST, i. 87. *l.* 708, *p.p.* declared friends; to *profess*, used by Spenser and Shakespeare to declare or profess friendship.

PROHEMIATE, iii. 229. *l.* 2, *v.* to preface. *Lat. proemium.*

PROMOVE, i. 98. *l.* 1031, *v.* to promote, advance. PROMOVIT, 1. 8. *l.* 193, *p.p.* promoted.

PRONUNCE, i. 86. *l.* 672, *v.* to pronounce, to recite.

PROPONE, i. 31. 808, *v.* to propose.

PROPYNIS, i. 55. 346, *sb.* presents, gifts. *Lat. propino.*

PROSTERNIT, iii. 11. *l.* 1833, *p.p.* prostrated.

PROUDELY, i. 9. *l.* 211, *adv.* lavishly.

PROVIANCE, i. 93. *l.* 872, *sb.* providence, foresight. *Fr. pourvoyance.*

PROVOCATOURIS, i. 76. *l.* 400, *sb.* inciters.

PRUIFIT, i. 167. *l.* 243, *pt. p.* proved.

PRUNYEAND, iii. 84. *l.* 3897. *pr. p.* trimming ; probably from *Fr. brunir*, to polish.

PRUNYEAND, iii. 84. *l.* 3897, pricking. *O.N. bryni*, *Dan. bryne*, sharpness.

PRYIS, i. 218. *l.* 1795; PRYSE. iii. 12. *l.* 1869, *sb.* praise, prize. *Fr. pris.*

PRYME, i. 139. *l.* 1, *sb.* the dawn, *the hour of pryme*, the first canonical hour, or six o'clock in the morning. *See* Notes, i. p. 294.

PUDDYNGIS, i. 103. *l.* 1157, *sb.* the intestines.

PUDLIT, ii. 207. *l.* 4307, *p.p.* puddled.

PUISSANCE, i. 117. *l.* 1, *sb.* power.

PULCHRITUDE, i. 22. *l.* 5010, *sb.* beauty.

PUNEIS, i. 33. *l.* 866, *v.* to punish. *Fr. punir.* PUNEISSIOUN, i. 71. *l.* 282. *sb.* punishment. *O. Fr. punission.*

PUNGITIVE, i. 103. i. 1147, *adj.* pungent.

PUNYST, i. 11. *l.* 261, *p.p.* punished. PUNYTIOUN, i. 8. *l.* 184, *sb.* punishment. *Fr. punition.*

PURCHAIS, ii. 17. *l.* 155, *sb.* a purchase. PURCHEIST, i. 142. *l.* 68, *pt. s.* purchased.

PURE, i. 206. *l.* 1451, *sb.* the poor; ii. 235. *l.* 251, *adj.* poor. PURIS, iii. 157. *l.* 5977; PURELLIS, iii. 81. *l.* 3818, *sb.* poor people.

PURPOISAND, i. 194. *l.* 1101, proposing.

PYE, i. 85. *l.* 647, *sb.* a magpie.

PYIKSTAFF, i. 35. *l.* 925, *sb.* a pointed staff.

PYK, iii. 6. *l.* 1715, *sb.* pitch.

PYKE, i. 86. *l.* 678, *v.* to pick out. PYKAND, ii. 134. *l.* 2659, *adj.* picking, peddling.

PYKTHANKIS, i. 75. *l.* 390, *sb.* officious persons, tell-tales. *See* Notes, i. p. 265.

PYNE, ii. 139. *l.* 2747, *sb.* labour; i. 10. *l.* 235, *sb.* pain, vexation. *A.S. pin.*

PYND, i. 188. *l.* 912; PYNIT. i. 11. *l.* 270, *p.p.* tormented, pained.

Q

QUAIF, i. 171. *l.* 378, *sb.* a coif, a band to keep the hair in place.

QUAIR, ii. 225. *l.* 1, *sb.* a book.

QUARTANE, ii. 112. *l.* 2193, *adj.* coming every fourth day, applied to fevers.

QUAW MYRE, ii. 47. *l.* 837, *sb.* a quagmire.

QUEINE, ii. 200. *l.* 4156, *sb.* a quean, or wench; ii. 203. *l.* 4242, a queen.

QUEIR, iii. 27. *l.* 2280, *sb.* a choir. *Fr. choeur.*

QUELLING, ii. 51. *l.* 898, *pr.p.* killing.

QUENT, ii. 232. *l.* 180, *adj.* nice, quaint.

QUERRELL, i. 160. *l.* 52, *sb.* a quarrel.

QUERRELL HOLLIS, ii. 154. *l.* 3061, quarryholes.

QUHALIS, ii. 278. *l.* 1449, *sb.* whales.

QUHAIR, ii. 23. *l.* 319; QUHARE, i. 18. *l.* 458, *adv.* where. *A.S. hwar.*

QUHAIRIN, i. 213. *l.* 1656, wherein.

QUHAIRFORE, i. 213. *l.* 1670, wherefore.

QUHAIRTHROW, i. 213. *l.* 1664, whereby.

QUHAIS, i. 217. *l.* 1780, *pron.* whose.

QUHAT, i. 6. *l.* 146, what.

QUHEILL, iii. 27. *l.* 2287, *sb.* a wheel; *pl.* QUHEILLIS, i. 129. *l.* 43, wheels.

QUHILES, ii. 26. *l.* 372, *adv.* at times.

QUHILK, QUHILKIS, i. 166. *l.* 227, *pron.* which.

QUHILL, i. 178. *l.* 590, *conj.* while, until.

QUHILLIE-LILLIE, ii. 210. *l.* 4382, *sb.* the penis. The word also occurs in Clerk's *Brash of Wooing.*

QUHIMPERAND, i. 107. *l.* 60, *pr. p.* whimpering. *Germ. wimmeren.*

QUHISCH, ii. 98. *l.* 1926, *sb.* a hissing noise.

QUHISSILL, i. 34. *l.* 899, *sb.* a whistle. QUHISTLAND, ii. 34. *l.* 553, *pr. p.* whistling. *A.S. hwistle.*

QUHO, i. 213. *l.* 1665, *pron.* who.

QUHRYNE, i. 107. *l.* 60, *sb.* a whine. *A.S. hrinan.*

QUHYLL, ii. 12. *l.* 38, *sb.* time, occasion.

QUHYLUMIS, i. 16. *l.* 410, *adv.* sometimes. *A.S. hwilum.*

QUHYTE, i. 189. *l.* 949, *adj.* white.

QUICK, ii. 109. *l.* 2139, *adj.* living.

QUIDDER, ii. 115. *l.* 2259, *conj.* whether.

QUIETIE, i. 12. *l.* 283, *sb.* quietness.

QUINTACENSOURS, ii. 133. *l.* 2608, *sb.* pretenders to alchemy, empirics.

QUINTESSENCE, ii. 51. *l.* 898, *sb.* alchemy.

QUOD, i. 24. *l.* 637, *pt. s.* said, quoth. *A.S. cwethan.*

QUYKE, i. 86. *l.* 670, *adj.* alive, living. *A.S. cwic.*

QUYTE, i. 183. *l.* 760, quit.

R

RA, i. 32. 823, *sb.* a roe. *A.S. ra.*

RACHIS, i. 114. *l.* 171, *sb.* dogs that follow their prey by the scent. *B. Lat. racha.*

RACK, ii. 82. *l.* 1548, *sb.* care, matter.

RACKAT, ii. 58. *l.* 1031, *sb.* the game of tennis. *See* RAIFFELL.

RACTIS, iii. 127. *l.* 5100, *sb.* racks.

RADIOUS, i. 82. *l.* 578, *adj.* radiant.

RAGMENT, i. 105. *l.* 1, *sb.* a rhapsody, speech, discourse.

RAID, i. 182. *l.* 706, *sb.* a road, anchorage.

RAID, i. 199. *l.* 1260, *adj.* afraid.

RAIF, i. 137. *l.* 93, *v.* to rave. RAIFFAND, iii. 128. *l.* 5132, *pr. p.* raving.

RAIFFELL, i. 49. *l.* 175, *v.* to play, revel. RAIFFELL AT THE RAKKAT, to play at tennis. *See* Notes, i. p. 251.

RAIK, i. 84. *l.* 643, *v.* to go; *raik on raw,* to march in order.

RAIPE, i. 103. *l.* 1165, *sb.* a rope; *pl.* RAIPIS, ii. 114. *l.* 2238.

RAIR, i. 14. *l.* 340, *sb.* a roar; iii. 139. *l.* 5464, to shout. *A.S. rarian.*

RAIS, i. 5. *l.* 112, *pt. pl.* arose.

RAIT, iii. 236. *l.* 16, *sb.* custom, rote.

RAK, ii. 33. *l.* 545, *sb.* care, matter. QUHAT RAK, what matter.

RAKARIS, i. 153. 377, *sb.* rangers, walkers.

RAKLES, ii. 140. *l.* 2776, *adj.* thoughtless. RAKLESNES, i. 85. *l.* 664, *sb.* carelessness.

RAKKAT, i. 49. *l.* 175, *sb.* a racket or tennis bat. *Fr. raquette. See* RAFFELL.

RAMPAND, iii. 32. *l.* 2426, *pr. p.* stamping, prancing.

RANG, i. 207. *l.* 1494, *pt. s.* reigned.

RANK, i. 184. *l.* 772, *adj.* strong, coarse.

RANSONING, ii. 172. *l.* 3489, *sb.* ransom. RANSONIT, ii. 11. *l.* 4, *pt. s.* ransomed.

RAPLOCH, i. 99. *l.* 1045, coarse woollen cloth.

RATTONE, iii. 86. *l.* 3982; *pl.* RATTONIS, iii. 34. *l.* 2495, *sb.* rats. *Fr. raton.*

RAUCHT, i. 126. *l.* 45, *p.p.* reached.

RAVEAND, ii. 234. *l.* 237, *pr. p.* raving.

RAW, i. 158. *l.* 69, *sb.* row, rank.

RAX, i. 51. *l.* 213, *pr. s.* stretch or hang. *A.S. racan.*

RAY, iii. 53. *l.* 3023, *sb.* array.

REAVERS, ii. 203. *l.* 4216, *sb.* robbers.

REBALDIS, i. 111. *l.* 75; REBAULDIS, i. 35. *l.* 914, *sb.* rogues, rascals.

RECANTIT, ii. 210. *l.* 4370, *pt. s.* decanted, discharged.

RECREATIOUN, i. 42. *l.* 1090, *sb.* revival.

RED, i. 127. *l.* 60, *v.* to separate, to part combatants.

RED, i. 103. *l.* 1, *pt. s.* read.

RED, ii. 60. *l.* 1091, *pr. s.* advise.

REDARIS, i. 62. *l.* 21, *sb.* readers.

REDDIE, i. 192. *l.* 1027, *adv.* ready.

REDDING, i. 200. *l.* 1263, *sb.* separating.

REDOLENT, ii. 63. *l.* 1158, *adj.* sweet smelling. *Lat. redolens.*

REDOUND, i. 217. *l.* 178, *v.* to resound.

REDOUTTIT, i. 74. *l.* 358, *adj.* dreadful, redoubted. *Fr. redoubté.*

REFT, ii. 43. *l.* 761, *pt. s.* took by force.

REFUGE, ii. 155. 3097, *sb.* protection, redress.

REGIMENT, ii. 218. *l.* 4546, *sb.* management, government.

REGRATOUR, i. 157. *l.* 46, *sb.* a retailer. REGRAITANDLY, i. 156. *l.* 15, retailing. *A.N. regrater.*

REHABILIT, ii. 192. *l.* 3949, *p.p.* reinstated, reestablished. *See* Notes, ii. p. 319.

REHEIRS, i. 187. *l.* 879, *v.* to rehearse.

REID, i. 199. *l.* 1240, *pr. s.* to advise.

REID, i. 3. *l.* 1, *adj.* red.

REIDIS, i. 60. *l.* 40, *pr. s.* reads.

REIDWOD, i. 156. *l.* 12, *adj.* furious.

REIF, i. 80. *l.* 529, *sb.* robbery, pillage. *A.S. reaf.*

REIF, i. 114. *l.* 185, *v.* to rob. REIFFIS, i. 50. *l.* 104, *pr. s. A.S. reafian,*

REIF, i. 81. *l.* 560, *sb.* or *Reeve,* a steward. The tale of John the Reif will be found in Percy's folio MS., vol. ii. p. 550.

REIFFARIS, i. 8. *l.* 172, *sb.* robbers.

REIK, i. 56. *l.* 367, *sb.* smoke. *A.S. rec.*

REIK, i. 103. *l.* 1152, *v.* to reach.

REILL, i. 14. *l.* 154, *v.* to roll or run about.

REIRD, i. 180. *l.* 653, *sb.* din, outcry.

REIST, i. 125. *l.* 32, a rest.

REJOSE, i. 62. *l.* 21, *v.* to rejoice. REJOSIT, i. 4. *l.* 94, *pt. s.* rejoiced.

RELENT, ii. 26. *l.* 391, *v.* to assuage.

RELICTS, ii. 114. *l.* 2235, *sb.* relics.

REMEDE, i. 13. *l.* 321; REMEID, i. 33. *l.* 876, *sb.* remedy.

REMORD, iii. 153. *l.* 5880, *v.* to recollect with remorse. *Fr. remordre.*

RENT, i. 181. *l.* 687, *sb.* income, revenue.

RENT, i. 73. *l.* 318, *p.p.* riven, torn.

RENZE, iii. 243. *l.* 21, *sb.* a rein.

REPAIR, ii. 32. *l.* 518, *sb.* a resort. *Fr. repaire.*

REPERCUSSION, ii. 233. *l.* 201, *sb.* reverberation. *Lat. repercutio.*

REPLEGEAND, ii. 11. *l.* 5, repledging, redeeming by a pledge.

REPLEIT, i. 22. *l.* 580. *adj.* full.

RESORT, ii. 55. *l.* 984, *v.* to come; ii. 20. *l.* 242, *sb.* a dwelling-place.

RESSAIF, ii. 76. *l.* 1417, *v.* to receive.

RESTRINGITYVE, i. 88. *l.* 737, *adj.* astringent.

RETRAITIT, iii. 149. *l.* 5771, *p.p.* retracted, reversed. *See* Notes, iii. p. 213.

REUIN, i. 9. *l.* 209, *p.p.* torn, rent.

REULIT, i. 216. *l.* 1742, *p.p.* ruled, arranged.

REUTH, i. 12. 285, *sb.* pity.

REUTHFULL, i. 11. *l.* 271, *adj.* pitiful. *A.S. hréow.*

REVER, i. 184. *l.* 772, *sb.* a robber. REVARIS, i. 13. *l.* 312, *sb.* robbers.

REVIN, i. 35. *l.* 921, *p. p.* torn.

REW, i. 218. *l.* 1804, *v.* to pity; ii. 115. *l.* 2258, *v.* to repent; i. 13. *l.* 321, *sb.* repentance.

REWARRIS, iii. 77. *l.* 3714, *sb.* spoilers.

REWIN, i. 36. *l.* 945, *p.p.* riven.

REWLL, ii. 27. *l.* 14, *v.* to govern. REWLIT, i. 9. *l.* 210, *p.p.* ruled. REWLIS, i. 130. *l.* 59, *sb.* rules.

REWME, iii. 119. *l.* 4914, *sb.* a humour, rheum.

REWYNE, i. 78. *l.* 475, *sb.* ruin.

RICKILL, ii. 210. *l.* 4266, *sb.* a heap, collection.

RIFTIT, ii. 210. *l.* 4363, *pt. s.* belched.

RIGGYNG, ii. 276. *l.* 1385, *sb.* top, ridge.

RINK-ROUME, i. 175. *l.* 505, room on the course.

RINNIS, ii. 47. *l.* 824 *pr. s.* runs.

RIPPIT, ii. 194. *l.* 3996, a scrape, dilemma, bad business.

ROCHE, i. 5. *l.* 119, *sb.* a rock; *pl.* ROCHIS, ii.

282. *l.* 1570, rocks. *Fr. roche.*

ROIPLOCH, i. 130. *l.* 62, *sb.* coarse woollen cloth.

ROIS, i. 184. *l.* 790, *sb.* the rose; ROIS-NOBILLIS, rose nobles, Scottish gold coins.

ROISTED, i. 107. *l.* 54, *adj.* rusty. ROISTED HOCH, crazy leg.

ROKATS, ii. 139. *l.* 2753. *sb.* surplices. *Fr. rochet.*

ROKKIS, i. 126. *l.* 28, *sb.* distaffs. *See* Notes, i. p. 286.

ROLLAND, ii. 32. 522, *pr. p.* rolling.

ROLPAND, i. 85. *l.* 661, *pr. p.* croaking. *Icel. hropa.*

ROME RAKARIS, i. 153. *l.* 377, rakers of Rome for pardons, relics, &c.

RONE, ii. 59. *l.* 1060, *sb.* a crustation, a sheet of ice. *E. roine. Icel. hraun.*

ROPLOCH, iii. 112. *l.* 4717, *sb.* coarse woollen cloth made in the natural colour of the wool.

ROSTE, i. 153. *l.* 372, *sb.* a disturbance, tumult. *Icel. rosta.*

ROUN, iii. 94. *l.* 4195, *p.p.* run out.

ROUND, ii. 182. *l.* 3716, *v.* to whisper. ROUNDAND, i. 50. *l.* 185, *pr. p.* whispering. *A.S. runian.*

ROUNG, iii. 45. *l.* 2797, *p.p.* reigned.

ROUSTYE, ii. 233. *l.* 213. *adj.* rusty.

ROUT, i. 126. *l.* 45, *sb.* a blow.

ROUT, iii. 139. *l.* 5464, *v.* to bellow, to roar. *A.S. hrutan.*

ROUTE, i. 6. *l.* 144, *sb.* a roar, a cry.

ROUT, ii. 26. *l.* 400, for ROUTH, *v.* to gather, to abound.

ROUTE, i. 180. *l.* 651, *sb.* a crowd, company.

ROWBOURRIS, iii. 25. *l.* 2224, *sb.* wine measures, probably oaken casks. *Lat. robur.* Jamieson derives the word from *Dan. rubbe*, a basket; *B. Lat. rubus*, a measure of grain, synonymous with *Fr. caque*, a cag, a barrel.

ROWKAND, i. 50. *l.* 185, *pr. p.* lying close, crouching. *E. rouke*, to squat.

ROWME, i. 175. *l.* 496, *sb.* room.

ROWPAND, i. 100. *l.* 1083, *pr. p.* croaking.

ROWST, iii. 116. *l.* 4816, *sb.* rust.

ROY, i. 105. *l.* 1; ROYE, i. 60. *l.* 498, *sb.* a king. *Fr. roi.*

ROYATOUSLIE, i. 107. *l.* 48, *adj.* riotously.

RUBEATOR, i. 107. *l.* 48; RUBIATOUR, ii. 204. *l.* 4265. *sb.* a robber, libertine. *Ital. rubatore.*

RUDE, i. 86. *l.* 675, *sb.* the cross. *A.S. rode.*

RUFE, ii. 276. *l.* 1384, *sb.* a roof.

RUFFEIS, i. 12. *l.* 285, *sb.* ruffians.

RUG, i. 103. *l.* 1148, *v.* to pull violently. RUGS, ii. 99. *l.* 1944, *pr. s.* draws.

RUGLAND, ii. 52. *l.* 911, Rutherglen.

RUIKS, ii. 154. *l.* 3076, *sb.* rooks.

RUISSE, ii. 149. *l.* 2961, *sb.* praise. *Icel. hrosa.*

RUMMEIS, iii. 149. *l.* 5464, *v.*

to make a noise, to roar. *A.S. rymian.*

RUSCHIT, i. 180. *l.* 653, *pt. pl.* rushed.

RUTE, i. 34. *l.* 880, *sb.* a root.

RUTHER, i. 49. *l.* 146, *sb.* a rudder.

RUTLANDE, i. 86. *l.* 668, *pr. p.* croaking. *Dut. rotelen.*

RUTTIT, ii. 92. *l.* 1767, *pt. s.* rooted.

RYBALDS, ii. 203. *l.* 4239, *sb.* rogues, rascals.

RYCHT, i. 1. *l.* 1, *adj.* right; i. 8. *l.* 172, *sb.* a just claim.

RYDAND, i. 203. *l.* 1382, *pr.p.* riding.

RY-MEILL, ii. 197. *l.* 4067, *sb.* rye-meal.

RYNDES, iii. 152. *l.* 5843, *sb.* the name of two promontories in Galloway. *Gaelic, rinn,* a point. *See* Notes, iii. p. 214.

RYNG, i. 23. *l.* 609, *v.* to reign; *pr. p.* RYNGAND, i. 44. *l.* 8.

RYNGIS, i. 8. *l.* 172, *sb.* kingdoms. *Fr. regne.*

RYPE, ii. 146. *l.* 2896, *adj.* ripe, mature.

RYPE, ii. 114. *l.* 2245, *v.* to search.

RYSCHE, i. 57. *l.* 408, *sb.* a rush; RYSCHE BUS, a rush bush. *A.S. risc. See* Notes, i. p. 255.

S

SABILL, i. 215. *l.* 1701, *adj.* black.

SAIF, i. 160. *l.* 43, *v.* to save.

SAIFFER, iii. 106. *l.* 4527, *sb.* the Saviour.

SAIKLES, iii. 3. *l.* 1620, *adj.* innocent.

SAILYE, i. 190. *l.* 952, *sb.* an assault.

SAINE, ii. 206. *l.* 4283, *v.* to bless, by making the sign of the cross; *pr. s.* SANIS, i. 156. *l.* 20.

SAIP, ii. 197. *l.* 4067, *sb.* soap.

SAIR, ii. 37. *l.* 636, *v.* to serve. *See* Notes, ii. p. 304.

SAIRIS, i. 208. *l.* 1542, *sb.* sores.

SAIT, i. 16. *l.* 405; SAITT, iii. 97. *l.* 4269, *sb.* a seat; *pl.* SAITS, ii. 189. *l.* 3847.

SALT, ii. 330. *l.* 70, *pt. s.* shalt.

SALTIT, i. 149. *l.* 266, *pt. pl.* salted, embalmed.

SALUS, i. 7. *l.* 149, *v.* to salute; SALUST, saluted. *Fr. saluer.*

SANE, i. 191. *l.* 999, *v.* to say.

SAPIENCE, i. 16. *l.* 396, *sb.* wisdom. SAPIENS, ii. 50, *l.* 866, a wise man.

SAPOUR, ii. 254. *l.* 761, *sb.* drowsiness.

SAPOURIS, iii. 163. *l.* 6153, *sb.* flavours. *Lat. sapor.*

SARKIS, ii. 110. *l.* 2169, *sb.* shirts.

SARD, ii. 152. *l.* 3029, error, for *fard,* went.

SARE, i. 48. *l.* 124, *adj.* sore.

SARVAND, ii. 76. *l.* 1417, *sb.* a servant.

SAUL, i. 217. *l.* 1775, *sb.* a soul; *pl.* SAULIS, i. 14. *l.* 343.

SAULD, i. 192. *l.* 1019, *pt. s.* sold.

SAVIS, iii. 119. *l.* 4914, *sb.* error for sayis.

SAW, iii. 244. *l.* 10, *sb.* a salve.

SAW, i. 148. *l.* 236, *sb.* a saying, proverb.

SAWIN, iii. 153. *l.* 5868, *p.p.* sown.

SAWRLES, ii. 247. *l.* 564, *adj.* savourless.

SAXTEIN, ii. 189. *l.* 3861, *num.* sixteen.

SAY, iii. 17. *l.* 1984, *pr. s.* tell.

SCABBIT, i. 34. *l.* 893, *adj.* covered with sores or scabs.

SCAPIT, ii. 37. *l.* 627, *p.p.* escaped.

SCHAIP, ii. 41. *l.* 738, *imp.* intend, propose; *pr. s.* SCHAIPS, ii. 91. *l.* 1317; SCHAIPPIS, ii. 220. *l.* 1582, intends. SCHAIPPING, ii. 109. *l.* 2136, *pr. p.* shaping.

SCHALME, iii. 35. *l.* 2505, a kind of hautboy. *Pl. Dut. schalmei.*

SCHANK, ii. 30. *sb.* the leg; *pl.* SCHANKIS, i. 189. *l.* 949.

SCHAVELINGIS, iii. 243, *l.* 20, a contemptuous term for Romish priests, from their shaven crowns.

SCHAW, i. 33. *l.* 857, *v.* to show.

SCHAWIN, ii. 51. *l.* 896, *p.p.* shewn. SCHAWAND, iii. 11. *l.* 1838, *pr. p.* shewing.

SCHED, ii. 39. *l.* 692, *p.p.* divided.

SCHEIF, ii. 139. *l.* 2752, *sb.* a sheaf.

SCHEIR, iii. 153. *l.* 5868, *adj.* to cut down, mow, shear.

SCHELL, i. 106. *l.* 45, *sb.* a shell; *pl.* SCHELLIS, i. 106. shells, used metaphorically for the pudendum muliebre.

SCHENE, i. 42. *l.* 1098, *adj.* bright, fair, shining. *A.S. scene.*

SCHENT, ii. 26. *l.* 389, *p.p.* destroyed, confounded. *A.S. scendan.*

SCHIFT, ii. 161. *l.* 3212, *sb.* a shift; ii. 81. *l.* 1534, a resource, expedient.

SCHIR, i. 1. *sb.* sir, generally given to priests, hence called Pope's knights. *See* Notes, iii. p. 208.

SCHO, i. 24. *l.* 631, *pron.* she.

SCHO-STREIT, i. 158. *l.* 70, the shoe-street, or Grassmarket of Edinburgh. *See* Notes, i. p. 303. SCHO-GAIT, ii. 206. *l.* 4295, *sb.* the Shoegate, a street in Cupar.

SCHONDER, i. 17. *l.* 446, asunder, sunder.

SCHONE, i. 192. *l.* 1016, *sb.* shoes.

SCHONE, ii. 26. *l.* 381, *adv.* soon.

SCHOO, iii. 127. *l.* 2300, *sb.* a shoe.

SCHORTE, i. 4. *l.* 75, *v.* to amuse, shorten the time.

SCHOURIS, i. 4. *l.* 91, *sb.* showers.

SCHOURIS, iii. 47. *l.* 2838, *sb.* sorrows. *A.S. scur.*

SCHREW, i. 103. *l.* 1156, *pr. s.* I curse. *A.S. screowa.*

SCHRYVE, i. 12. *l.* 282. *v.* to confess. *A.S. scrifan.*

SCHURE, i. 201. *l.* 1306, *pr. s.* cut.

SCHUTE, i. 217. *l.* 1777, *v.* to shoot. SCHUTAND, i. 106. *l.* 37; SCHUTTYNG, i. 77. *l.* 439, *pr. p.* shooting.

SCHYREF, i. 208. 1538, *sb.* a sheriff.

SCOLIS, ii. 247. *l.* 580, *sb.* schools.

SCOLLARIS, iii. 92. *l.* 4152, *sb.* scholars.

SCROG, i. 109. *l.* 29, *sb.* a stunted mass of shrubs.

SCROPPIT, i. 156. *l.* 10, *adj.* contemptible.

SCROW, iii. 244. *l.* 12, *sb.* a scroll.

SCULE, i. 47. *l.* 97, *sb.* a school; *pl.* SCUILIS, i. 48. *l.* 132.

SEAGE, i. 95. *l.* 946, *sb.* a siege; i. 94. *l.* 907, a seat. *Fr. siége.*

SEARS, i. 153. *l.* 363, *v.* to search.

SEE, i. 43. *l.* 1119, *sb.* an abode.

SEE, i. 26. *l.* 669, *sb.* the sea.

SEGE, i. 21. *l.* 548, *sb.* a seat.

SEID, i. 99. *l.* 1054, *sb.* seed.

SEIGIT, i. 193. *l.* 1052, *pt. s.* besieged.

SEIK, ii. 28. *l.* 433, *adj.* sick.

SEILIT, i. 59. *l.* 465. *p. p.* sealed.

SEINDALL, i. 53. *l.* 287, *adv.* seldom. *A.S. seldan.*

SEIME, ii. 199. *l.* 4125, *v.* to seem.

SEINZIE, ii. 102. *l.* 1972, *sb.* the consistory court. *See* Notes, ii. p. 310.

SEIR, i. 204. *l.* 1406, *adj.* several. *Icel. ser.*

SEIS, i. 80. *l.* 524, *sb.* seats. thrones. *p.p.* SEISIT, i. 196. *l.* 1143, settled. *Fr. saisir.*

SELL, ii. 44. *l.* 784, *pron.* self.

SELY, i. 34. *l.* 896; SELYE, iii. 111. *l.* 4707, *adj.* silly, simple, innocent. *Germ. selig.*

SEMPYLL, i. 3. *l.* 52, *adj.* simple.

SEN, i, 188. *l.* 911. *imp.* send, grant.

SEN, i. 202. *l.* 1338, *adv.* since.

SENE, ii. 232. *l.* 175, *v.* to see, *A.S. seon.*

SENOWNIS, iii. 119. *l.* 4918, *sb.* sinews.

SENSYNE, ii. 79. *l.* 1405, *adv.* since then.

SENYE, i. 87. *l.* 720, *sb.* the consistory or ecclesiastical court. *See* SEINZE.

SENYEORIE, i. 70. *l.* 249, *sb.* dominion. *Fr. seigneurie.*

SENYEOURIS, iii. 149. *l.* 5753, *sb.* lords of session.

SEPULTURE, i, 213. *l.* 1653, *sb.* a sepulchre; *pl.* SEPULTURIS, ii. 183. *l.* 3734.

SERS, i. 34. *l.* 892, *v.* to seek.

SERVE, ii. 135. *l.* 2665, *v.* to deserve.

SESSOUNE, i. 152, *l.* 357, *v.* to season.

SET, ii. 53. *l.* 930, *v.* to become.

SETT-ON, ii. 276. *l.* 1384, incumbent, a term applied to a roof. *A.S. on-sittan.*

SEWARE, i. 2. *l.* 21, *sb.* an officer who serves up a feast and arranges the dishes. *See* Notes, i. p, 226.

SEWCH, ii. 213. *l.* 4437, *sb.* a ditch, furrow. *A.S. sich.*

SEY, i. 28. *l.* 732, *sb.* the sea; *pl.* SEYIS, i. 6. *l.* 143.

SEYCHIS, ii. 233. *l.* 214, *sb.* sighs.

SHED, i. 191. *l.* 994, *pt. s.* separated.

SHENT, ii. 15. *l.* 122, *pt. p.* confounded, ruined. *A.S. scendan.*

SIATICA PASSIO, iii. 120. *l.* 4922, *sb.* sciatica.

SIC, i. 169. *l.* 308; SICK, iii. 8. *l.* 1766, *conj.* such; SICLYKE, i. 169. *l.* 323, the same.

SICHAND, i, 180. *l.* 905, *pr.p.* sighing.

SICHT, i. 161. *l.* 55, *sb.* the sight.

SICKER, i. 50. *l.* 197, *adj.* sure, firm. SICKERNES, ii. 14. *l.* 91, *sb.* surety, security.

SICLYKE, ii. 190. *l.* 3892, such.

SIE, ii. 12. *l.* 30, *v.* to see.

SIKKER, i. 195. *l.* 1121, *adj.* sure, firm.

SILLABIS, i. 47. *l.* 91, *sb.* syllables.

SINDRY, i. 31. 821, *adj.* sundry, various.

SINE, ii. 249. *l.* 634, *adv.* afterwards, then.

SING, ii. 284. *l.* 1613, *sb.* a sign.

SITTIL, ii. 201. *l.* 4179, *adj.* subtle.

SKAID, ii. 127. *l.* 2489, *adj.* scald, scabby.

SKAIR, ii. 211. *l.* 4391, *v.* to share. *A.S. scear.*

SKAITHLES, ii. 209. *l.* 4349, *sb.* harmless.

SKANT, ii. 42. *l.* 753, *adj.* scanty, scarce.

SKAP, ii. 127. *l.* 2489, *sb.* the scalp or skin.

SKAPELLARYE, iii. 152. *l.* 5853; SKAPLARIE, ii. 178. *l.* 3628, a scapulary or vestment worn by the friars. *See* Notes, ii, p. 317; iii. p. 215.

SKAR, ii. 86. *l.* 1640, *sb.* a fright, an object of terror. SKARD, ii. 56. *l.* 992, *p.p.* frightened.

SKEICH, iii. 244. *l.* 3, *adj.* skittish, shy.

SKER, i. 66. *l.* 126, *sb.* a fright. SKER, i. 112. *l.* 116, *v.* to scare, to frighten.

SKOWLAND. i. 6. *l.* 138, *adj.* overhanging, scowling.

SKYRE, ii. 127. *l.* 2489, *adv.* quite, sheer. *A.S. scir.*

SLAIF, i. 114. *l.* 158, *sb.* a slave.

SLAIK, i. 196. *l.* 1141, *v.* to quench, appease. SLAKE, i. 39. *l.* 1020, *pt. s.* slacken.

SLEIFE, ii. 219. *l.* 4560, *sb.* a sleeve.

SLEIPAND, ii. 61. *l.* 1104, *pr. p.* sleeping. SLEIPIT, ii. 193. *l.* 3971, *p.p.* slept.

SLEIT, i. 4. *l.* 95, *sb.* sleet.

SLEUTCHERS, ii. 133. *l.* 2615, *sb.* loungers.

SLEUTHFUL, i. 34. *l.* 890, *adj.* lazy.

SLIDDER, i. 74. *l.* 352; SLIDDRIE, ii. 59. *l.* 1060, *adj.* slippery; i. 183. *l.* 748, *sb.* slipperiness. *A.S. slidder.*

SLOP, i. 183. *l.* 736, *sb.* a slap, blow. SLOPPIT, i. 182. *l.* 723, *pt. p.* dashed.

SLOUG, i. 34. *l.* 890, *v.* to be idle, to lounge.

SLYCHT, i. 17. *l.* 439, *sb.* skill.

SLYDDER, iii. 77. *l.* 3708, *adj.* slippery.

SMAIK, i. 158. *l.* 55, *sb.* a mean fellow; *pl.* SMAIKS, ii. 71. *l.* 1328, *Icel. smeykr*, pusillanimous. *See* Notes, i. p. 302.

SMEDIE, i. 103. *l.* 1168, *sb.* a smithy.

SMOIRD, ii. 161. *l.* 3224, *p.p.* smothered.

SMUKE, i. 103. *l.* 1168, *sb.* smoke.

SMURE, i. 160. *l.* 45. *v.* to smother. SMURIT, i. 77. *l.* 427, *pt. s.* was smothered.

SOBERLIE, i. 5. *l.* 113; i. 91. *l.* 828, poorly, feebly.

SODDIN, iii. 127. *l.* 5098, *p.p.* steeped, boiled.

SOILLIS, i. 137. *l.* 87, *sb.* soles.

SOLACE, i. 13. *l.* 331, *sb.* comfort, diversion, sport.

SOLIST, ii. 84. *l.* 1592; SOLYST, iii. 167. *l.* 6271, *pt. p.* solicited.

SOMER, i. 4. *l.* 90, *sb.* summer.

SONE, i. 207. *l.* 1484, *adv.* soone

SOPIT, i. 38. *l.* 998, *p.p.* steeped, soaked.

SORIE, ii. 15. *l.* 107, *sb.* a sorry person.

SORNAND, i. 156. *l.* 11, *pr. p.* sorning, sojourning.

SORS, ii. 234. *l.* 167, *adj.* source.

SORT, i. 201. *l.* 1301, *sb.* a lot, a company.

SOUER, ii. 231. *l.* 167, *adj.* sure. SOUERTIE, iii. 112. *l.* 4726, *sb.* security.

SOUMAND, ii. 256. *l.* 811, *pr.p.* swimming.

SOUNE, i. 37. *l.* 969, *adv.* soon.

SOUP, i. 129. *l.* 30, *pr.s.* sweep. *A.S. sweopan.*

SOWNE, ii. 96. *l.* 1870, *sb.* a swoon. *A.S. swun.*

SOWTTAR, ii. 69. *sb.* a shoemaker, cobbler.

SPAIKS, ii. 63. *l.* 1147, *sb.* members, literally spokes.

SPEDALYE, i. 15. *l.* 366, *adv.* speedily.

SPEID, ii. 13. *l.* 53, *v.* to speed.

SPEIK, i. 67. *l.* 177, *v.* to speak.

SPEILE, i. 67. *l.* 154, *v.* to climb.

SPEIR, ii. 122. *l.* 2385, *v.* to inquire. SPERIS, ii. 272. *l.* 1307, *pr. s.* inquiries. SPEIRIT, i. 135. *l.* 37, *pt. s.* inquired.

SPEIRIS, i. 173. *l.* 451. *sb.* spears.

SPERIS, i. 15. *l.* 385, *sb.* spheres. *See* Notes, i. p. 230.

SPEW, ii. 72. *l.* 1337, *v.* to vomit.

SPILL, ii. 101. *l.* 1961, *v.* to spoil.

SPLENE, iii. 22. *l.* 2137, *sb.* the spleen, here used for the heart. *See* Notes, iii. p. 191.

SPOILYEIS, iii. 97. *l.* 4291 *pr. s.* spoils, plunders.

SPORTOUR, ii. 17. *l.* 176, *sb.* a sportsman.

SPREIT, ii. 283. *l.* 1589, *sb.* spirit; *pl.* SPREITIS, i. 5. *l.* 125.

SPRYNGIS, i. 47. *l.* 93, *sb.* tunes.

SPUILZE, ii. 180. *l.* 3664, *v.* to spoil. SPUILYEIT, i. 162, *l.* 109, *p.p.* spoiled, robbed.

SPUR-GAID, ii. 127. *l.* 2487, scratch-marked. *A.S. spor*, a trace or mark. *O. Fr. galler*, to scratch.

SPYIT, i. 5. *l.* 117, *pt.s.* spied.

STAGIS, iii. 7. *l.* 1741, *sb.* furlongs.
STAID, i. 199. *l.* 1249, *pt. s.* situated.
STAIKS, ii. 96. *l.* 1880, *sb.* stakes.
STAIT, i. 12. *l.* 304, *sb.* state.
STANCHIT, ii. 131. *l.* 2557, *pr. p.* abated, stopped.
STANG, i. 102. *l.* 1140, *sb.* a sting, a shooting pain.
STANIS, i. 217. *l.* 279, *sb.* stones.
STANKIS, iii. 124. *l.* 5018, *sb.* ponds.
STARCK, ii. 161. *l.* 3240; STARK, i. 69. 221, *adj.* strong, stout. STARK, i. 138. *l.* 132, *v.* to strengthen.
STAW, ii. 83, *l.* 1565, *pt. s.* did steal.
STEDIS, i. 17. *l.* 438, *sb.* steeds, horses.
STEID, ii. 131. *l.* 2577, *sb.* a place, station, farm; IN-STEID, i. 13. *l.* 323, in place of.
STEIDING, i. 114. *l.* 166, *sb.* a place, situation. *A. S. stede.*
STEIPILL, i. 126. *l.* 32, *sb.* a steeple.
STEIR, i. 48. *l.* 121, *sb.* a stir, bustle. *A.S. styra.*
STEIRBURD, ii. 36. *l.* 618. *sb.* starboard.
STEIRMAN, iii. 117. *l.* 4859, *sb.* a helmsman, steersman.
STENDS, ii. 210. *l.* 4363, *sb.* springs, leaps.
STENT, ii. 222. *l.* 4650, *pr. s.* stops, desists.
STEPBARNE, i. 103. *l.* 1155, *sb.* a stepchild.
STERIT, iii. 32. *l.* 2442, *p.p.* moved, stirred.
STERNE, i. 219. *l.* 1824, *sb.* a star. STERNIE, i. 217. *l.* 1783; STERRY, ii. 252. *l.* 687, *adj.* starry.
STERVE, iii. 120. *l.* 4924, *v.* to die. STERVIT, iii. 12. *l.* 1874, *pt.s.* perished, killed. *Germ. sterben. A.S. sterfian.*
STEW, i. 131. *l.* 116, *sb.* fume, bad smell. *Fr. estuve.*
STEWAT, ii. 127. *l.* 2490, *sb.* a stinker, a brothel haunter.
STIK, ii. 41. *l.* 730, *v.* to stick, stab.
STING, i. 167. *l.* 254, *sb.* a pole, a pike. *A.S. steng.*
STIRLING, ii. 248. *l.* 612, *sb.* a starling.
STOB, i. 67. 169, *sb.* a sharp stump of wood. *A.S. steb.*
STOLLIN, i. 153. *l.* 373, *p.p.* taken away.
STOPE, iii. 164. *l.* 6178, *sb.* a pitcher.
STOPPIT, i. 180. *l.* 657, *pt. s.* remained.
STOUITH, i, 80. *l.* 529, *sb.* theft, stealth. *A.S. staelth.*
STOUND, i. 102. *l.* 1140, *sb.* pain, sorrow.
STOUR, i. 180. *l.* 657, *sb.* battle.
STRAIK, i. 183. *l.* 743, *pt. s.* struck.
STRAIKIS, i. 207. *l.* 1507, *pr.s.* strikes; i. 126. *l.* 40, *sb.* strokes, blows.
STRAIS, ii. 90. *l.* 1736, *sb.* straws.
STRAIT, i. 185. *l.* 801, *adj.* strict.
STRANDS, ii. 59. *l.* 1066, *sb.* streams.
STRAUCHT, i. 171. *l.* 374, *pt.s.* stretched.

STRENTH, iii. 7. *l.* 1723, *sb.* a stronghold.

STRYDLINGIS, i. 47. *l.* 89, *adv.* astride.

STRYIFFIS, i. 130. *l.* 72; STRYVIS, iii. 151, *l.* 5830, *pr. s.* strives.

STRYPIS, i. 131. *l.* 102, *pr. s.* strips.

STUFFAT, i. 153. *l.* 373, a footman, a groom. *Fr. estafette.*

STUMP, ii. 200. *l.* 4133, *sb.* a remnant.

STURT, ii. 108. *l.* 2115, *sb.* vexation, trouble.

STYLL, i. 6. *l.* 107, *adj.* still, quiet.

STYLLIT, ii. 131. *l.* 2567, *pt. p.* styled, called.

SUBDITIS, i. 9. *l.* 213, *sb.* subjects. *Lat. subditus.*

SUDGEORNE, i. 14. *l.* 359, *sb.* delay, sojourn. SUDGEORNING, i. 18. *l.* 455, delaying, SUDJORNE, ii. 279. *l.* 1487, *v.* to delay.

SUGGURIT, ii. 233. *l.* 201, *adj.* sugared, sweet.

SUIR, ii. 89. *l.* 1702, *adj.* sure.

SUITH, i. 31. *l.* 801, *sb.* the truth. *A.S. soth.*

SUNE, ii. 24. *l.* 333, *adv.* soon.

SUNZIE, ii. 27. *l.* 406, *sb.* an excuse. *Fr. essoinze.*

SUPPLIE, iii. 89. *l.* 4054; SUPPLYE, i. 148. *l.* 255, *sb.* assistance.

SUPPONE, iii. 164. *l.* 6199, *v.* to suppose. *Lat. suppono.*

SUPPRISIT, i. 4. *l.* 80, *p. p.* surprised.

SUPPRISIT, iii. 80. *l.* 3783, *pt.s.* oppressed, kept under. *See* Notes, iii. p. 203.

SUTE, ii. 188. *l.* 3819, *sb.* staff, company.

SUTH, ii. 102. *l.* 1968, *sb.* the truth.

SUTHEROUN, i. 181. *l.* 678, *sb.* a native of the south.

SWAGIS, i. 16. *l.* 413, *pr. s.* assuages. *A.S. swaes.*

SWAP, i. 203, *l.* 1355, *v.* to fall down suddenly. SWAPPIT, i. 68. 184, *pt. s.* fell suddenly.

SWATTERIT, ii. 278. *l.* 1454, *p.p.* weltered, turned about quickly. *Su. G. sqwoetta.*

SWAY, ii. 197. *l.* 4056, *adv.* so.

SWEIR, ii. 24. *l.* 344, *v.* to swear.

SWEIR, i. 37. *l.* 962, *adj.* lazy, backward. SWEIRNES, ii. 173. *l.* 3520, laziness. *A.S. sweor.*

SWEIT, i. 4. *l.* 93, *adj.* sweet.

SWEITIE, i. 130. *l.* 82, *adj.* sweaty, covered with sweat.

SWESCHE, i. 217. *l.* 1778, *sb.* a drum. *See* Notes, i. p. 330.

SWETTERAND, i. 107. *l.* 58, *pr.p.* weltering.

SWINGEOUR, ii. 110. *l.* 2166; SWYNGEOUR, i. 156. *l.* 17, *sb.* a drone, a sluggard; *pl.* SWYNGEORIS, i. 37. *l.* 962. *A.S. sweng.*

SWOIR, i. 194. *l.* 1103, *pt. s.* swore.

SWOMAND, ii. 278. *l.* 1450, *pr. s.* swimming.

SWORILIS, i. 115. *l.* 203, *sb.* swivels.

SWYTH, i. 37. *l.* 971, *interj.* away!

SWYFE, ii. 23. *l.* 318; SWYVE, ii. 17. *l.* 162, *v.* to copulate.

SYCE, i. 136. *l.* 84, six, a term in dice play.

SYCHING, i. 13. *l.* 333, *pr. p.* sighing.

SYCHT, i. 5. *l.* 113, *sb.* sight.

SYDE, i. 128. *adj.* long, large. SYDEST, iii. 151. *l.* 5830, longest. *A.S. side.*

SYDLINGIS, iii. 43. *l.* 2730, sidewise.

SYIS, ii. 277. 1407, *sb.* times.

SYLE, i. 137. *l.* 103, *v.* to obscure, deceive. SYLIT, iii. 25. *l.* 2241, *pt. p.* deceived, abused. *A.S. sylian.*

SYLLIE, i. 4. *l.* 92, *adj.* simple, innocent.

SYMENT, iii. 6. *l.* 1715, *sb.* cement.

SYNDRIE, i. 121. *l.* 111, *adj.* separate.

SYNE, ii. 63. *l.* 1163, *adv.* afterwards, then. *A. S. sythan.*

SYNOPEIR, i. 101. *l.* 1112, *sb.* of a vermillion or carmine colour, like synopar or cinnabar.

SYPER, ii. 253. *l.* 712. cypress.

SYSE, i. 184. *l.* 788, *sb.* times.

SYSTERN, iii. 120. *l.* 4945, *sb.* a cistern.

SYTE, i. 13. *l.* 333, *sb.* sorrow, grief. *Icel. syta.*

T

TABILL, i. 188. *l.* 893, *sb.* a table, backgammon, or any game played with a table and dice; *pl.* TABLIS, ii. 169, *l.* 3431, tables.

TABRONE, i. 122. *l.* 136; TABURNE, i. 164. *l.* 173; TABROUN, i. 215. *l.* 170, *sb.* a tabor, a kind of drum.

TADIS, i. 13. *l.* 324, *sb.* toads. *A.S. tade.*

TAFTAIS, i. 163. *l.* 125, *sb.* taffeta. *See* Notes, i. p. 313.

TAILYEOUR, ii. 69. *sb.* a tailor.

TAINE, ii. 113. *l.* 2218, the one.

TAIRT, i. 209. *l.* 1562, *sb.* a tart.

TAIS, ii. 75. *l.* 1389, *sb.* toes.

TAK, i. 50. *l.* 196, *sb.* a lease.

TAK. i. 50, *l.* 193 *v.* to take. TAKKAND, i. 1. *l.* 14, *pr. s.* taking. *A.S. taecan.*

TAK AND SLAY, i. 180. *l.* 655, take and kill.

TAKING, i. 165. *l.* 195, *sb.* a token; *pl.* TAKINNIS, i. 168. *l.* 274.

TALBRONE, iii. 35. *l.* 2505; TALBURNIS, i. 217. *l.* 1778, *sb.* tabors.

TAPESSIT, i. 13. *l.* 325, *p.p.* hung with tapestry.

TARGIS, i. 118. *l.* 31, *sb.* shields.

TARIE, ii. 68. *l.* 1259, *sb.* delay.

TAULD, i. 167. *l.* 256, *pt. p.* told.

TAVERNAR, i. 183. *l.* 762, *sb.* a tavern keeper, here used as a term of reproach.

TCHEIR, ii. 101. *l.* 1959; TCHYRE, ii. 100. *l.* 4, *sb.* a chair.

TECHE, i. 54. *l.* 324, *v.* to teach.

TEDDER, ii. 101. *l.* 1957, *sb.* a halter; *pl.* TEDDERIS, i. 78. *l.* 469.

TEICHEOURIS, ii. 190. *l.* 3889, *sb.* teachers.

TEIND, ii. 103. *l.* 2007, *sb.* tithes.

TEINE, iii. 230. *l.* 22, *v.* to deceive.

TEILL, ii. 84. *l.* 1601, *v.* to till, to plough.

TEIRIS, iii. 81. *l.* 3836, *sb.* tears.

TELL, ii. 110. *l.* 2158, *imp.* say. TELL ON, speak out.

TELLYNG, i. 37. *l.* 985, *pr. p.* counting, reckoning.

TEMPERALL, i. 218. *l.* 1789, *sb.* temporality, temporal goods.

TENNENTIS, i. 194. *l.* 1093, *sb.* tenants.

TENT, ii. 31. *l.* 492, *v.* to tend, attend to; i. 106. *l.* 34, *sb.* care, heed.

TENT, iii. 74. *l.* 3620, *num.* the tenth.

TEUCH, i. 174. *l.* 463, *adj.* tough. *See* Notes, ii. p. 306.

TEYNEFULL, iii. 243. *l.* 463, *adj.* raging. *A.S. teona.*

THAI, i. 11. *l.* 261; THAY, ii. 71. *l.* 1328, these.

THAN, i. 8. *l.* 183, *adv.* then.

THARE, i. 8. *l.* 169, *adv.* there.

THEIFFES, i. 13. *l.* 312, *sb.* thieves.

THEIS, iii. 120. *l.* 4922, *sb.* thighs.

THESAURARE, i. 2. *l.* 22, *sb.* a treasurer. *See* Notes, i. p. 252.

THIR, i. 9, *l.* 188, *pron.* these.

THIRLAGE, ii. 171. *l.* 3476, *sb.* bondage.

THO, ii. 234. *l.* 224, *pron.* those.

THOCHT, i. 3. *l.* 51, although.

THOCHT, i. 167. *l.* 257, *pt. s.* thought.

THOILL, ii. 66. *l.* 1163; THOLE, i. 23. *l.* 628, *v.* to suffer.

THOLIS, i. 4. *l.* 97, *pr. s.* suffers, allows. THOLAND, i. 106. *l.* 45, *pr. p.*

THRALL, i. 14. *l.* 345, *sb.* a slave, bondage. *A.S. thrall.*

THRANG, i. 175. *l.* 491, *pt. s.* pressed, grasped.

THRAW, i. 204. *l.* 1392, *sb.* a throe, a struggle.

THRESAURAIR, i. 50. *l.* *sb.* a treasurer.

THRESOURE, i. 151. *l.* 321, *sb.* a treasure.

THRETTY-SUM, i. 157. *l.* 26, a party of thirty. *See* Notes, i. p. 301.

THRID, i. 9. *l.* 205, *num.* third. THRIDLIE, i. 214. *l.* thirdly.

THRIFT, ii. 160. *l.* 3210, *sb.* state of thriving, sustenance. *O.N. thrifa.*

THRING, i. 112. *l.* 118, *v.* to thrust.

THRIST, i. 191. *l.* 983, *v.* to press. THRISTIT, i. 184. *l.* 766, *pt. s.* thrust.

THRIST, i. 13. *l.* 323, *sb.* thirst.

THRISYLL, ii. 265, *l.* 1086, *sb.* a thistle.

THRONIT, iii. 20. *l.* 2098, *pt. s.* enthroned.

THROCH, ii. 21. *l.* 259; THROUCH, i. 15. *l.* 372, *adv.* through.

THRYNFOLD, ii. 227. *l.* 48, threefold.

THYE, iii. 27. *l.* 2298, *sb.* the thigh.

THYNE, iii. 9. *l.* 1770, *adv.* thence. *A.S. thaen.*

THRYNGAND, iii. 75. *l.* 3662, *pr. p.* throwing, thrusting.

THRYFES, ii. 81. *l.* 1531, *pr. s.* thrives.

TIMPANE, i. 216. *l.* 1751, *sb.* a drum. *Lat. tympanum.*

TINT, ii. 131. *l.* 2565, *pl. p.* lost.

TIPPIT, ii. 194. *l.* 3995, *sb.* a tippet, a collar.

TOCHER-GUDE, ii. 185. *l.* 3769, *sb.* a marriage-portion.

TODS, ii. 176. *l.* 3586, *sb.* foxes.

TOSTIT, ii. 36. *l.* 9, *p.p.* tossed.

TOUN, ii. 134. *l.* 2637, *sb.* a town.

TOUN, i. 60. *l.* 50. *l.* 508, *sb.* a tun, tub.

TOUNDER, i. 17. *l.* 443, *sb.* tinder. *See* Notes, i. p. 231.

TOWART, ii. 22. *l.* 289, *adj.* docile, toward. *A.S. toward.*

TOWKIT, i. 131. *l.* 94, *p.p.* tucked up.

TRAILLIS, i. 128. *l.* 14. *pr. p.* drags. TRAILLAND, i. 129. *l.* 26, dragging. *Fr. trailler.*

TRAINE, ii. 54. *l.* 950, *sb.* a company.

TRAISSIS, i. 189. *l.* 944, *sb.* tresses.

TRAISSIT, i. 191. *l.* 985, *pt. pl.* embraced.

TRAIST, ii. 29. *l.* 450, *pr. s.* I trust.

TRAIT, i. 73. *l.* 332, *v.* to treat. TRAITTIT, i. 185. *l.* 799, *pt. s.* treated.

TRAMALT NETT, iii. 114. *l.* 4766, *sb.* a trammel-net.

TRAMMIS, i. 126. *l.* 33, *sb.* shafts.

TRANSCEND, i. 33. *l.* 858, *v.* to descend, to come to.

TRANSCURRIS, i. 30. *l.* 777, *pr.s.* overruns. TRANSCURRIT, i. 88. *l.* 750, *pt. s.* overran. *Lat. transcurro. See* Notes, i. p. 271.

TRANSFIGURATE, i. 1. *l.* 15, *p.p.* transformed.

TRATTYLL, i. 86. *l.* 695: i. 52. *l.* 245, *v.* to prattle or tattle.

TRAVELL, i. 102. *l.* 1123, *sb.* labour; iii. 229. *l.* 3, *v.* to work.

TRAVERS, i. 76. *l.* 402, *sb.* crosses, vexation. *Fr. travers.*

TREDDINGIS, i. 115. *l.* 208, *sb.* tracks, courses.

TREIT, ii. 250. *l.* 656, *v.* to entreat, to fee. TREITIT, i. 186. *l.* 852, *p.p.* treated.

TRENCHEOUR, i. 176. *l.* 539, *sb.* the blade of the spear. *Fr. trencher.*

TRENTALLIS, i. 86. *l.* 695, *sb.* services of thirty masses each for the dead.

TREST, ii. 337. *l.* 201, *pr. s.* I trust. TRESTIS, i. 158. *l.* 60, *pr. s.* trusts.

TREUKOURIS, i. 97. *l.* 1001, *sb.* truckers, buyers and sellers of benefices. TREWKER, ii. 72. *l.* 1333, *sb.* a sorry fellow, a cheat. *Fr. troqueur.*

TREWLIE, ii. 33. *l.* 543, *sb.* truly.

TRIBILL, ii. 16. *l.* 147, the treble part.

TRIMBLIS, ii. 25. *l.* 371, *pr. s.* trembles. TRIMBLIT, i. 114. *l.* 177, *pt.pl.* trembled.

TRIPLICANDUM, iii. 149. *l.* 5767, a triply, a law term.

TRITTIL TRATTILL, ii. 210. *l.* 4376, an interjection. TRITTYL, i. 52. *l.* 245, *sb.* prattle.

TROCH, i. 107. *l.* 53, *sb.* a trough.

TROLYLOW, i. 52. *l.* 245, *interj.*

TROMPOURIS, ii. 12. *l.* 39, *sb.* deceivers. *Fr. trompeur.*

TROW, i. 129. *l.* 54, *v.* to believe. TROWS, ii. 81. *l.* 1536, *pr. s.* thinks. TROWIT, ii. 54. *l.* 953, I believed.

TRUCOUR, ii. 212. *l.* 4411, *sb.* trucker, rogue; *pl.* TRUCKERS, ii. 127. *l.* 2470.

TRYIST, ii. 328. *l.* 24, *sb.* an appointment, meeting.

TRYIT, ii. 127. *l.* 2470, *p.p.* experienced.

TRYNE, i. 115. *l.* 205, *sb.* a train. *Fr. traine.*

TRYPARTIT, i. 9. *l.* 202, *p.p.* divided into three.

TRYPES, i. 102. *l.* 1123, *sb.* the intestines. *Fr. tripe.*

TUICH, ii. 213. *l.* 4436, *adj.* tough.

TUIK, i. 185. *l.* 797, *pr. s.* took.

TULZEOUR, i. 109. *l.* 27, *sb.* a wrestler.

TUMBE, ii. 134. *l.* 2634, *sb.* a tomb.

TUMDE, ii. 101. *l.* 1959; TUMED, ii. 210. *l.* 4374, *p.p.* emptied.

TUME, ii. 26. *l.* 395, *adj.* empty.

TUMLYNG, ii. 230. *l.* 125, *pr.p.* tumbling.

TUN, ii. 180. *l.* 3682, *v.* to put into a tun or barrel.

TURCUMIS, i. 131. *l.* 105, *sb.* clots of dirt. *O.N. turrka,* to dry.

TURS, ii. 134. *l.* 2657; TURSSE, ii. 17. *l.* 157, *v.* to carry off.

TURTUR, i. 88. *l.* 725, *sb.* a turtle dove.

TWA, ii. 129. *l.* 2517; TWAY, ii. 13. *l.* 77, *num.* two.

TWISTIS, ii. 230. *l.* 136, *sb.* branches.

TWYCHE, ii. 254. *l.* 750, *v.* to touch. TWYCHEIT, i. 41. *l.* 1086. *pt. s.* touched. TWYCHEYNG, ii. 246. *l.* 2, relating to.

TWYSTIS, i. 66. *l.* 139, *sb.* twigs.

TYDAND, i. 182. *l.* 720, *sb.* tidings.

TYDIER, ii. 103. *l.* 1985, *adj.* neater.

TYISTING, i. 11. *l.* 273, *pr. p.* enticing. *A.S. tihtan.*

TYKE, i. 114. *l.* 166, *sb.* a dog.

TYLDE, iii. 6. *l.* 1702, *sb.* tiles.

TYNE, i. 45. *l.* 48, *v.* to lose. TYNT, iii. 26. *l.* 2276; TYNTE, i. 30. *l.* 783, *pt. s.* lost.

TYRIT, ii. 47. *l.* 829, *p. p.* tired, fatigued.

TYSDAY, ii. 340. *l.* 271, *sb.* Tuesday.

TYST, ii. 29. *l.* 456; TYSTE, i. 137. *l.* 107, *v.* to entice.

TYTHANDS, ii. 25. *l.* 370, *sb.* tidings.

U

UGLY, iii. 68. *l.* 3445, horrible. *A.S. oga.*

UMEST, ii. 103. *l.* 2000, uppermost. *See* Notes, ii. p. 319.

UMQUHILE, i. 4. *l.* 82; UMQUHYLE, i. 141. *l.* 1, formerly, late, deceased.

UNBLOMIT, i. 4. *l.* 76, *p.p.* without bloom.

UNCOUTH, ii. 68. *l.* 1250, *adj.* unknown, strange.

UNDERLY, ii. 188. *l.* 3839, *v.* to be subject to.

UNDREST, i. 207. *l.* 1492, *p.p.* unredressed.

UNDOCHT, ii. 148. *l.* 2941, *sb.* a silly fellow.

UNFEINZEITLIE, ii. 171, *l.* 3459, *adv.* unfeignedly. UNFENYEIT, i. 57. *l.* 415, *adj.* unfeigned.

UNHAP, i. 43. *l.* 1117, *sb.* misfortune.

UNHELTHSUM, ii. 201. *l.* 4167, *adj.* unwholesome.

UNLEIFSUMLIE, i. 10. *l.* 230, *adv.* unlawfully.

UNLEILL, i. 13. *l.* 313. *adj.* unfaithful, dishonest.

UNMERCIABLE, iii. 37. *l.* 2563, *adj.* unmerciful.

UNPISSILIT, iii. 111. *l.* 4702; UNPYSALT, ii. 139. *l.* 2767, *adj.* without restraint, unpizzled.

UNPROPONIT, ii. 145. *l.* 2891, unannounced.

UNPROVISIT, i. 150. *l.* 308, *p.p.* unprovided.

UNROCKIT, i. 96. *l.* 969, reckless. *O.N.* *uroekjia*, to be careless.

UNRYCHTIS, i. 11. *l.* 262, *sb.* wrongs. *A.S.* *unriht.*

UNSELL, ii. 106. *l.* 2055, *adj.* evil, wicked. UNSELL, ii. 38. *l.* 671, *sb.* a knave, a bad person. *A.S.* *unsel.* *See* Notes, ii. p. 305.

UNSAWEN, ii. 84. *l.* 1601, *adj.* unsown.

UNTHRALL, i. 95. *l.* 924, *adj.* not enslaved, free.

UNTHRIFT, i. 37. *l.* 965, *sb.* want of thrift.

UNTROWABYLL, iii. 44. *l.* 2760, *adj.* incredible.

UNWERLY, iii. 69. *l.* 3466, *adv.* unawares.

UPALAND, ii. 201. *l.* 4183; UPALANDS, ii. 197. *l.* 4052, *sb.* country, literally upon land. UPELAND, i. 57. *l.* 407; UPLANDS, ii. 200. *l.* 4132, *sb.* a country fellow. *Jhone Upeland*, the Jack Upland of Chaucer. *See* Notes, i. p. 255.

UPONLAND, i. 66. *l.* 132. See *Upaland.*

UPDRYIS, i. 66. *l.* 138, *pr. s.* dries up.

UPSETTING, i. 121. *l.* 108, *sb.* setting up.

UTTER, i. 95. *l.* 945, outer.

UTTERANCE, i. 175. *l.* 505, *sb.* extremity. *Fr.* *outrance.*

V

VACANDS, ii. 56. *l.* 998, *sb.* vacancies.

VAGERS, ii. 151. *l.* 3004, *sb.* vagabonds.

VAIK, i. 50, 188, *v.* to become vacant. VAKIT, i. 98. *l.* 1019, *pt. s.*

VAILE, i. 31. 819, *sb.* a valley.

VAILITH, i. 123. *l.* 180, *pr. s.* availeth. VAILS, ii. 25. *l.* 355, *pr. s.* avails. *Fr.* *valoir.*

VAILYE QUOD VAILYE, i. 67. *l.* 161, happen what may, at all events. *Fr.* *vaille que vaille.* *See* Notes, i. p. 263.

VAILZEAND. i. 106. *l.* 26, *adj.* valiant. *Fr.* *vaillant.*

VEIRS, iii. 67. *l.* 3393, *sb.* verse.

VELVOIT, i. 130. *l.* 73, *sb.* velvet.

VERAMENT, ii. 48. *l.* 844. VERRAYMENT, i. 31. 801, *sb.* truth, verity. *Fr. vraiement.*

VERRAY, i. 11. *l.* 278, *adv.* very.

VESCHAILL, i. 181. *l.* 700; VESCHELL, i. 11. *l.* 254, *sb.* a vessel, a ship. *Fr. vaisselle.*

VESIE, i. 167. *l.* 257; VISIE, ii. 32. *l.* 505, *v.* to view. to visit. VESIAND, ii. 279. *l.* 1466, *pr. p.* viewing. VESYIT, i. 15. *l.* 386, *pt. s.* visited. *Fr. visée.*

VESPERTYNE, ii. 231. *l.* 150, evening. *See* Notes, p. 181.

VILIPENDIT, ii. 190. *l.* 3887, *p.p.* vilified.

VILITIE, i. 75. *l.* 376, *sb.* vileness.

VINCUSTE, iii. 42. *l.* 2707, vanquished.

VITTAILLIT, i. 194. *l.* 1102, *pt. s.* supplied with provisions.

VOCE, i. 162. *l.* 106, *sb.* voice.

VOLT, i. 14. *l.* 358, *sb.* a vault. *Fr. vaulte.*

VYCIS, ii. 48. *l.* 848, vices. *See* Notes, ii. p. 305.

W

WA, i. 65. *l.* 96, *adj.* sorrowful. WA, ii. 35. *l.* 579, *sb.* woe. WAIS, ii. 35. *l.* 588, for woe is, WA SAIR, ii. 37. *l.* 636, woe serve. *See* Notes, ii. p. 304.

WAIFFIT, i. 125. *l.* 19, *pt. pl.* waved.

WAIK, ii. 103. *l.* 1986, *adj.* weak.

WAILLIS, i. 182. *l.* 724, *sb.* the wales or sides of the ship.

WAILLIT, i. 178. *l.* 606, *p.p.* chosen.

WAINE, ii. 213. *l.* 4426, *v.* to wish.

WAIRD, i. 196. *l.* 1143, *sb.* custody. WAIRDIT, i. 186. *l.* 844, *pt. s.* guarded, imprisoned. *A.S. waerd. See* Notes, i. p. 315.

WAIRDANIS, ii. 195. *l.* 3997, *sb.* wardens of the Borders.

WAIRDE, ii. 216. *l.* 4504, for WARE IT, to expend it.

WAIRIT, i. 200. *l.* 1286, *pt. s.* spent, used.

WAIRNE, ii. 123. *l.* 2417, *pr. s.* I warn.

WAIS ME, ii. 202. *l.* 4201, alas!

WAIST, i. 184. *l.* 773, *adj.* empty, waste. WAISTAND, i. 106. *l.* 46, wasting.

WAIT, i. 216. *l.* 1740, *pr. s.* I know.

WAK, i. 15. *l.* 388, *adj.* moist, cloudy. WAKNES, i. 18. *l.* 460, *sb.* moistness. *Dut. wak.*

WALKER, ii. 199. *l.* 4118, *sb.* a fuller or dyer.

WALKIN, ii. 88. *l.* 1693, *v.* to awaken. WALKING, i. 3. *l.* 65, *pr. p.* awake.

WALKRYFE, i. 34. *l.* 897, *adj.* wakeful, watchful.

WALLIE FALL, ii. 125. *l.* 2438, good befall. *A.S. waela*, and fall.

WALLIS, i. 6. *l.* 128, *sb.* waves. *Germ. welle*, a wave.

WALLOPE, i. 50. *l.* 179, *v.* to gallop. *Fr. galoper.*

WALLOWAY, ii. 63. *l.* 1153, *interj.* alas! *A.S. wa la! wa,* woe lo! woe.

WALTER, i. 15. *l.* 376, *sb.* water.

WAMBE, iii. 78. *l.* 3738, *sb.* the belly. WAME, i. 191. *l.* 985. *A.S. wamb.*

WAN, i. 178. *l.* 582, *pt. s.* got.

WANDE, ii. 89. *l.* 1710, *sb.* a rod.

WAN-FORTUNE, ii. 196. *l.* 4033, *sb.* misfortune.

WAR, i. 67. *l.* 157, *adj.* wary, cautious. *A.S. waer.*

WAR, i. 4. *l.* 82, *pt. pl.* were.

WAR, ii. 76. *l.* 1400, *comp.* worse; iii. 19. *l.* 2050, *sb.* the worse. *A.S. waerra.*

WARK, i. 163. *l.* 120, *sb.* work.

WARLD'S-SCHAME, ii. 45. *l.* 794, *sb.* a spectacle of shame.

WARYE, i. 79. *l.* 490, *v.* to curse. WARYAND, i. 7. *l.* 168, *pr. p.* cursing. WARYIT, i. 4. *l.* 91, cursed. *A.S. wyrian.*

WASSALL, i. 70. *l.* 256, *sb.* a vassal.

WAT, ii. 148. *l.* 2928; WATT, i. 63. *l.* 56; WATE, i. 50. *l.* 207, *pr. s.* knows, know. *A.S. witan.*

WATTAND, i. 98. *l.* 1008, *pr.p.* waiting.

WEDDER, i. 74. *l.* 355, *sb.* weather.

WEDDERIS, iii. 138. *l.* 5438, *sb.* of a sheep.

WEID, i. 78. *l.* 453, *sb.* a weed; *pl.* WEIDIS, i. 128. *l.* 11.

WEID, i. 87. *l.* 707, *sb.* dress, clothing. *A.S. waed.*

WEILL, i. 1. *l.* 2, *adj.* well. WEILL-FAIRDE, ii. 209. *l.* 4343, *adj.* well-favoured, handsome.

WEIN, ii. 59. *l.* 1063; WEINE, ii. 77. *l.* 1430, *pr. s.* I think, consider.

WEIR, i. 19. *l.* 485, *sb.* doubt; BUT WEIR, doubtless.

WEIR, i. 17. *l.* 448, *sb.* war.

WEIR, ii. 167. *l.* 3391, *v.* to wear.

WEIRD, i. 206. *l.* 1466. *sb.* lot, fate. *A.S. wyrd.*

WEIRLYKE, i. 175. *l.* 498, *adj.* warlike.

WEIT, i. 192. *l.* 1024, *adj.* wet.

WELTERLAND, i. 184. *l.* 770; WELTRYNG, ii. 282. *l.* 1575, *pr. p.* rolling, wallowing.

WEND, i. 75. *l.* 366, *pt. pl.* thought, imagined.

WEND, ii. 163. *l.* 3272, *v.* to go.

WERIE, i. 203. *l.* 1378, *adv.* very.

WERIOUR, i. 168. *l.* 281, *sb.* a warrior; *pl.* WERIOURIS, i. 173. *l.* 432, *sb.* warriors.

WERP, i. 137. *l.* 91, *sb.* a warp. *A.S. wearp.*

WES, i. 5. *l.* 115, *pt. s.* was.

WESCHE, i. 187. *l.* 872, *v.* to wash. WESCHE, ii. 127. *l.* 2478, *sb.* wash, urine.

WEYIS, iii. 27. *l.* 2286, *sb.* scales, weights; ii. 161, *l.* 3227, *pr. s.* weighs. WEYIT, i. 182. *l.* 708, *p.p.* weighed.

WICHT, i. 169. *l.* 300, *adj.* strong. WICHTLIE, i. 178. *l.* 582, *adv.* stoutly, actively.

WICHTIS, i. 181. *l.* 695, *sb.* persons. *A.S. wiht.*

WIDCOK, ii. 174. *l.* 3540, *sb.* a woodcock.

WIDDIE, i. 113. *l.* 152, *sb.* a halter made of pliant twigs.

WIDDIEFOW, ii. 111. *l.* 2185, a rascal, one fit for the gallows.

WILK, ii. 213. *l.* 4428, *sb.* a periwinkle.

WILL OF WANE, i. 115. *l.* 213, uncertain of a place of habitation.

WIN, ii. 173. *l.* 3519, *sb.* gain, profit.

WINNING, i. 13. *l.* 309, *sb.* gain, profit. *A.S. winn.*

WIRREAR, i. 109. *l.* 26, *sb.* a worrier. WIRREIT, i. 111. *l.* 74, *p.p.* worried.

WIRRYHEN, i. 157. *l.* 41, *sb.* a greedy person.

WIS, i. 219. *l.* 1829, *sb.* a wish.

WISCHE, ii. 99. *l.* 4, *v.* to direct, instruct.

WITTIN, i. 131. *l.* 111, *p.p.* known.

WITTIT, ii. 50. *l.* 867, *p.p.* possessed of mind.

WOBSTER, ii. 199. *l.* 4117. *sb.* a weaver.

WOD, ii. 46. *l*, 814, *v.* to pledge, wager.

WOD, i. 11. *l.* 265, *adj.* wild, mad, furious.

WODBIND, i. 191. *l.* 991, *sb.* the woodbine.

WODDER, i. 29. *l.* 774, *sb.* weather. WODDERCOK, i. 75. *l.* 368, *sb.* a weathercock.

WOFT, i. 137. *l.* 91, a woof.

WOID, ii. 197. *l.* 4043, *v.* to wager, to bet. *A.S. veddjan.*

WOLLIN, i. 137. *l.* 91, *sb.* woollen cloth.

WOLTERING, i. 6. *l.* 128, *pr. p.* rolling. *A.S. waltian.*

WOMENTYING, ii. 267. *l.* 1126, *sb.* lamentation.

WOO, iii. 67. *l.* 3417, *adj.* sorry.

WOUN, i. 60. *l.* 507, *p.p.* won, acquired.

WOUNDER, i. 174. *l.* 460, *adv.* wonderfully.

WOUNT, i. 9. *l.* 109, *p.p.* wont.

WOURDIS, ii. 47. *l.* 839, *sb.* words.

WOWER, ii. 110. *l.* 2156, *sb.* a wooer.

WRACHE, i. 41. *l.* 1076, *sb.* a wretch; *pl.* WRACHEIS, ii. 240. *l.* 407; WRACHEIT, i. 2. *l.* 27, *adj.* wretched.

WRAIK, i. 214. *l.* 1697, *v.* to wreak, to revenge.

WRAIT, i. 160. *l.* 24, *pt. s.* wrote.

WRAITH, ii. 213. *l.* 4431, *adj.* wroth. *A.S. wraeth.*

WRAKYNG, i. 80. *l.* 530, *pr. p.* wreaking.

WRANGUS, iii. 15. *l.* 1954, *adj.* wrongful, unjust.

WREIK, i. 105. *l.* 16, *v.* to revenge.

WRESTIT, ii. 30. *l.* 469. *p.p.* twisted.

WRINKS, ii. 106. *l.* 2060, *sb.* tricks.

WROCHT, ii. 68. *l.* 1257, *p.p.* made.

WROKIN, i. 126. *l.* 41, *p.p.* revenged.

WUISCHE, i. 203. *l.* 1371, *pt. s.* did wash.

WYSE, iii. 11. *l.* 1825, *adj.* wise.

WYCHT, i. 67. 163, *adj.* strong, active.

WYDDER, iii. 139. *l.* 5467. *v.* to wither.

WYIS, i. 218. *l.* 1792, *s.* manner.
WYIT, i. 10. *l.* 234, *v.* to blame. *A.S. wytan.*
WYLE, ii. 19. *l.* 278, *v.* to beguile.
WYLL, i. 34. *l.* 894, *adj.* astray. To GO WYLL, to go astray.
WYLLIS, ii. 197. *l.* 4063, *sb.* wiles.
WYRK, i. 95. *l.* 943, *pr. pl.* they work.
WYS, i. 45. *l.* 26, *pr. s.* I wish. *A.S. wiscan.*
WYSTE, i. 7. *l.* 163, *pt. s.* knew, became aware.
WYTE, ii. 78. *l.* 1458, *pr. s.* blame.

Y

YAIRNIS, i. 59. *l.* 1471; YARNIS, i. 45. *l.* 50; YEARNIS, ii. 53. *l.* 941, *pr. pl.* desire, long for; YARNING, ii. 239. *l.* 360, yearning, desiring.
YAMER, iii. 157. *l.* 5997, *v.* to cry out, to groan. *A.S. geomerian.*
YCE, ii. 59. *l.* 1060, *sb.* ice.
YDILL, ii. 272. *l.* 1266. *adj.* idle.
YE, ii. 27. *l.* 410, *adv.* yes, yea.
YEALOW, ii. 63. *l.* 1160, *adj.* yellow.
YEID, i. 25. *l.* 655, *pt. s.* went.
YEILD, ii. 210, *l.* 4264, *pt. s.* gave way.
YEIR, i. 110. *l.* 53. *sb.* a year.
YEIS, ii. 33. *l.* 537, *for* ye shall.
YERIS, i. 53. *l.* 296, *sb.* years.
YET, ii. 43. *l.* 778; YETT, iii. 156. *l.* 5959, *sb.* a gate, door; *pl.* YETIS, ii. 66. *l.* 1207.
YISTRENE, i. 188. *l.* 908, *sb.* yesterday.
YIT, i. 3. *l.* 53, yet.
YLE, i. 30. *l.* 789, *sb.* an island; *pl.* YLIS, i. 28. *l.* 731.
YNEUCH, i. 73. *l.* 336, *sb.* enough, sufficiency.
YON, ii. 53. *l.* 939, *sb.* the person yonder.
YOUTHAGE, ii. 32. *l.* 513, *sb.* youth.
YOWIS, i. 64. *l.* 72, *sb.* ewes. *A.S. eowe.*
YOWLING, i. 7. *l.* 165. *pr. p.* howling. *Icel. gaula.*
YOWTING, i. 7. *l.* 165, *pr. p.* crying, roaring.
YOWTIS, ii. 277. *l.* 1418, *sb.* cries, roars.
YPOCRITE, i. 37. *l.* 719, *sb.* a hypocrite.
YSCHARE, i. 2. *l.* 23, *sb.* an usher.
YUILL, ii. 36. *l.* 9, *sb.* Christmas.

Z

ZAID, i. 81. *l.* 560, *pt. s.* went.
ZALD, iii. 87. *l.* 3997, *pt. pl.* yielded.
ZIT, iii. 244. *l.* 25, yet.

FINIS.

TURNBULL AND SPEARS, PRINTERS, EDINBURGH.

www.ingramcontent.com/pod-product-compliance
Lightning Source LLC
Chambersburg PA
CBHW030858270326
41929CB00008B/478